BUT SERIOUSLY...

Also by Steve Allen

BUT SERIOUSLY...
STEVE ALLEN
SPEAKS HIS MIND

 **Prometheus Books**
59 John Glenn Drive
Amherst, NewYork 14228-2197

Published 1996 by Prometheus Books

00 99 98 97 96   5 4 3 2

Library of Congress Cataloging-in-Publication Data

Allen, Steve.
    But seriously— : Steve Allen speaks his mind / Steve Allen.
        p.   cm.
    ISBN 1–57392–090–8 (cloth : alk. paper)
    1. United States—Politics and government—1989–   2. Social problems—United
States. I. Title.
E839.5.A58   1996
818′.5409—dc20
                                                                                    96–24257
                                                                                        CIP

Printed in the United States of America on acid-free paper

Contents

5

Published Articles

Speeches

Miscellaneous Writings

Foreword

It was not long after World War II that a fellow student in philosophy class told me I had to listen to a guy on the radio named Steve Allen. "He is really funny," he said. So I tuned in one evening, and was hooked.

In the thirties I had hardly ever missed a broadcast of Fred Allen and Jack Benny, the two best known radio comedians of the period. But Steve Allen was different. His humor seemed more sophisticated. He was more a wit than a comic. He interviewed members of the studio audience, and the repartee was hilarious—always sharp, teasing, but never unkind. And of course, he played the piano, which is like saying Wynton Marsalis knows how to play the trumpet.

I recently noticed Steve Allen's name on an advisory board of a foundation. Not surprisingly, he was identified as a comedian. In light of what I now know about him, I feel that's like calling Leonardo da Vinci a military engineer and Tom Paine a farmer. It's all true of course, but it's hardly informative. Maybe Mr. Allen prefers it that way. In contemporary America, it's less threatening to present oneself as a comedian than what Allen really is: a thinker, a scholar, and an educator. People will listen to comedians, whereas they are likely to banish a Tom Paine and force a Socrates to drink Hemlock. They are too dangerous to the established order.

I have met Mr. Allen only once. It was in the early sixties when we were both involved in the peace movement. From then on I took him much more seriously. I think it was about that time that he put my name on his mailing list. To the people on this list Mr. Allen sends copies of articles he has read and thinks are important. I read a lot, but I have seldom previously seen the material I receive from him, which comes from a vast array of sources. Clearly he reflects on what he reads. These articles, speeches, and whatnot are always underlined, annotated, and sometimes marked up with what look like arcane, Leonardian symbols. If I were Shirley MacLaine I'd wonder about this. I've never been able to decipher the system, but I have always agreed that the material was significant.

But more important of course are the books and articles Mr. Allen has written himself. I confess I have not read them all, but I have read a lot of them. They make me wish I could start my teaching career all over again.

I taught international relations for thirty-five years in a large urban university which was at the epicenter of all the social turmoil of the 1960s and '70s. It had the longest academic strike in U.S. history; students thought they could help end racism and the war in Vietnam by trashing the university.

I felt then that we educators had failed in a very important way. We had not convinced our students of the true value of learning and the settings in which it takes place. Somehow universities had become merely training schools for the students and havens for pompous pedants. Those of us who thought universities should be temples of enlightenment and engines of civilization were hopelessly out of date.

In one sense the students were right. By the fifties the academy had lost sight of its idealistic origins, and had become big business. Students were preoccupied with career training while faculties were focussed on research grants, salaries, tenure, and parking. The 1960s' extreme reaction against all this was probably inevitable, but it did a lot of damage. The budget-cutting and privatism of the 1980s and '90s made matters worse. We haven't recovered; the trend is still downward.

If I were starting my teaching career today, I would campaign for the introduction of two courses to be required for all freshmen. The first would be entitled "The Role of the University in Society." It would not simply trace the history of learning, but would focus on all the bloodshed and sacrifice endured in order to achieve academic freedom. It would also explain how easily it can be swept away by dictators or the tyranny of the majority. Most important, such a course would examine the relationship between education and learning on the one hand, and religion and superstition on the other.

If I could teach such a course I would have students begin by reading Steve Allen's *Dumbth.** (I can already hear some of my more supercilious colleagues snickering. Either they haven't read it, or they don't understand freshmen.) This is a book about how to think, not what to think. It is wise, well-written, and interesting.

After *Dumbth,* mercifully subtitled *And 81 Ways to Make Americans Smarter,* the students would be ready for *Steve Allen on the Bible, Religion & Morality.*† This is the point at which they would come to grips with the difference between religion and superstition, and learn to distinguish ritual from true spirituality. In this book Mr. Allen describes his own religious background and how he progressed from dogma to spiritual maturity. It is an account of personal growth that can be a useful model for confused youth. I can't imagine young people who have pondered and understood Steve Allen's books burning Black churches, blowing up abortion clinics and government buildings, murdering their doctors, painting swastikas on synagogues, sending bombs through the mail, bashing gays, or marching to the muffled drums of incipient Christian fascism.

The other required course I would like to see taught would be on parliamentary procedure. We talk about democracy, but most Americans don't know how to democratically conduct an efficient, fair business meeting when there is controversy or a contest for power. We need to learn how to do this on a small scale so we can understand how to do it at the state and national level. *Robert's Rules of Order* ought to be a required text. Respect for democracy on a campus is essential to respecting it in the national arena.

---

*(Amherst, N.Y.: Prometheus Books, 1991).
†(Amherst, N.Y.: Prometheus Books, 1990).

As far as I know, Steve Allen hasn't written anything on this, but if I understand how his mind works, he will probably look into it as soon as he reads this. This is a man who is always interested in ideas that might make the world a better place for all of us.

You can see the breadth of Steve Allen's interests and the depth of his thinking in the present collection of his writings. You will find here some risk taking when he engages that skilled debater of the right, William F. Buckley, and later the brilliant leftist, screenwriter Dalton Trumbo. Buckley and Trumbo try too hard to be comics, while Allen insists on being more serious than one would expect of a professional comedian. In the end, everybody's blood is on the floor, and we learn how the anticommunism of the cold war diverted us all from what was really happening in the world.

Compare the Allen of the Buckley debate with the Allen of the "Eleventh Hour Speech." The growth is apparent. Here is a wiser voice, but one that has lost none of its passion: "You don't have to put up with rotten meat, with vegetables or fruits contaminated by pesticides, with devices or medicines that harm, maim, and kill. You do have the power in your capacity as the American people—to put a stop to that kind of outrage. But you must organize and study and participate in organized campaigns or the old evils will simply continue."

Somewhere the ghost of "Old Common Sense," Tom Paine, is smiling, and so is Joe Hill.

Is it any wonder that in an age of political attack ads and cynical electioneering, liberalism has become a dirty word among those who hold power? In such a climate, who but a comedian, a musician, a composer, actor, and television scriptwriter would dare to defend liberal values and the power of reason? A few, it is true. But not enough. This book will increase their numbers.

Marshall Windmiller
Professor Emeritus
San Francisco State University

Alameda, California
June 12, 1996

Tribute to Steve Allen
from Norman Cousins

Others would speak of Steve Allen's outstanding versatility and the magnetic attraction he exerts, no matter what he does. I would speak of just one attribute of Steve Allen. I refer to that wondrous and infallible instrument that he uses constantly and that, indeed, is the source of his abundant electrical energy. This instrument is built-in. I refer, of course, to his conscience.

This is a prodigious thing, the Allen conscience. It sends him rocketing from one place to another in defense of people who need defending in order to live. It causes him to risk his career—indeed, everything he has—in pursuit of a world at peace. It compels him to use all the communications means within his reach to proclaim against authorized murder whether the target is one man or the species of man.

The Allen conscience does not function in splendid isolation. It is nourished by hard study. Few men I know pursue knowledge more conscientiously. Few men I know are better informed in all matters related to the complex operation of our human society. His personal library and filing system are wonders to behold.

Reprinted by permission from *Sane* magazine, November 1962. Since publication of this tribute, *Sane* has changed its name to *Peace Action*.

In any inventory of the natural resources on this planet, the Allen conscience is high on the list.

Forewords

God and the H-Bomb

Though we often say, at present, that atomic and nuclear weapons are obviously too horrible to ever be used, the fact is that they have been used, twice, by the United States, with tremendous loss of life, and suffering that continues to the present day. Though the cruelty of Communism in action—as distinguished from scholarly Marxism as theory—has been well demonstrated, it nevertheless occurred to me, in the late 1950s, that attacking civilian populations with super-weapons could not possibly be accommodated within the context of any sort of Just War theory. This simple moral perception had not, as of 1960, become part of the national mind-set. I thought it might be helpful to demonstrate that American theologians, by and large, had properly and courageously addressed the moral dimensions of the problem and therefore I arranged for the publication of *God and the H-Bomb*.

That our nation is in the throes of a moral collapse of serious dimensions is, apparently, no longer a debatable conclusion. Liberal and conservative spokesmen vie to see who shall express the

From *God and the H-Bomb,* edited by Donald Keys (New York: Bellmeadows Press with Bernard Geis Associates, 1961).

15

conviction most vigorously. Churchmen and secularists, too, agree that we have fallen upon evil days. These various groups naturally differ as to the reasons for the situation, but that it exists no one seems prepared to deny.

The dreary litany of specifics is by now all too familiar:

> The corruption of labor;
>
> The corruption of big business;
>
> The ever-growing power of organized crime which, having taken its initial strength from the traffic in illegal alcohol, narcotics, gambling, and prostitution, now reaches into the garment industry, boxing, the restaurant and night-club field, transport, and a host of other legitimate business areas;
>
> The corruption that has long been characteristic of big-city politics;
>
> The recurring waves of scandals involving cheating in school examinations and "throwing" of athletic contests;
>
> The moral cancer implicit in racial segregation;
>
> The increase in crimes of violence;
>
> The recent television and radio scandals;
>
> And so on, God help us, ad infinitum.

Such examples come to mind readily. Others, no less harmful, are somewhat less obvious. A television program dramatically reveals the sorrowful plight of the nation's migrant farm workers, in itself a situation deplorable morally as well as economically. But the reaction of some Americans (insinuating that the program was "Communistic" rather than expressing the slightest charitable interest in the unfortunate condition of the thousands of citizens involved) was as depressing, judged morally, as was the callousness of the robber barons of an earlier generation.

One's daily newspaper is the source for more additional evidence than one can countenance without literally wincing:

> Two-thirds of the world goes hungry while we stockpile food till it decays.
>
> Five hundred thousand men, women, and children in the United States rot their lives away in mental hospitals, some of which would have been a disgrace in the nineteenth century.

Our prisons are full to overflowing, while our society continues to ignore the question as to what turns innocent children into criminals.

When it appears that a notorious offender might not be killed by the state, a governor receives thousands of letters of protest, most of them deeply shocking in their naked, savage cruelty.

Certain Indian tribes in our western states live in squalor and poverty that, while it may be casually dismissed from American minds, serves as handy fuel for the lighting of Communist fires in other parts of the world.

But above and beyond all of these, there is an example of our moral insensitivity that cries out for attention, the same sort of attention that the world all too belatedly gave to the Nazis' extermination of millions of Jews. The sin of which I speak is not, to be sure, the exclusive property of Americans. The Russian Communists are as guilty as we are—probably more so—though only God is qualified to judge. But their participation, *morally* speaking, is utterly irrelevant. Evil may sometimes be a social business but one is called to account for it individually nevertheless.

The Nazis are regarded as animals in human form because they gassed, shot, or burned perhaps as many as six million Jews. Today the people of the United States are quite prepared, if provoked, to actually burn alive *hundreds* of millions of innocent men and women, young and old. I deliberately put the matter in such blunt terms because it is long past time to do so and because there is apparently no other way to start people thinking of the moral questions raised by nuclear weapons.

To those of my readers who are usually described by the term "professional patriot" (true patriots will have no trouble understanding me) I wish at once to make clear that they will find between the covers of this book no apology for communism. I share their horror of its tyranny and would hope that each and every one of them shares my opinion of *Fascist* tyranny. Some of them say "better dead than Red." I say "better neither dead nor Red," nor have I the slightest interest in "appeasing" the Russians. This book is not intended as an argument for unilateral disarmament. Indeed it is not intended, properly speaking, as an argument for disarmament at all, although I happen to agree with Presidents Eisenhower and Kennedy that the nuclear arms race must somehow be stopped and our present direction reversed. But concerning disarmament, arms control, unilateral initiatives, and related questions, let other books be written. This one will restrict itself to questions such as the following: *Are there any moral restrictions whatsoever upon the use of H-Bombs? If so, what are they? Have the churches spoken of the issue? Did they speak loudly enough to be heard?*

C. Wright Mills, in his "Pagan Sermon to the Christian Clergy" (included in his illuminating book, *The Causes of World War III*), has clearly stated the challenge:

> The verbal Christian belief in the sanctity of human life has not been affected by the impersonal barbarism of twentieth-century war. But this belief does not itself enter decisively into the plans now being readied for World War III. . . . Total war ought indeed be difficult for the Christian conscience to confront, but the Christian way out makes it easy; war is defended morally and Christians easily fall into line—as they are led to justify it—in each nation in terms of Christian faith itself. . . . To ministers of God we must now say . . . If you do not alarm anyone morally, you will yourself remain morally asleep. If you do not embody controversy, what you say will inevitably be an acceptance of the drift to the coming human hell. . . . Yet who among you has come out clearly and unambiguously on the issues of internecine war and the real problems of peace? Who among you is considering what it means for Christians to kill men and women and children in ever more efficient and impersonal ways? . . . As pagans who are waiting for an answer, we merely say: You claim to be Christians. And we ask: What does that mean as a biographical and as a public fact?

"The task facing us," Father Theodore M. Hesburgh, C.S.C., president of the University of Notre Dame, has said,

> will not be done if our philosophers and theologians continue to live among, work with, and speak to people and problems long since dead and buried. . . . Here is an age crying for the light and guidance of Christian wisdom. What must future judges think of

us if we live in the most exciting age of science ever known to mankind and philosophize mainly about Aristotle's physics? We live today in the threatening shadow of cosmic thermonuclear destruction and often theologize about the morality of war as though the spear had not been superseded by the I.C.B.M.

Obviously, churchmen have expressed convictions in regard to this complex matter; they can scarcely be expected to give approval to the mass incineration of innocent civilian populations. Pope Pius XII has referred to the nuclear arms race as "homicidal, suicidal madness," although in so doing he was not speaking morally, merely indulging in common sense. But I have arranged for the publication of this book [*God and the H-Bomb,* edited by Donald Keys] because of the disquieting realization that theological commentary on the morality of nuclear war, for all practical purposes, *has made no impression whatsoever upon the national conscience!*

There has been only one similar instance of such widespread moral blindness in our century. The German people somehow never got around to really hearing the moral criticism of Nazism that was voiced here and there, now and then, by German clergymen. Professor Gordon Zahn of Chicago's Loyola University has explained that a fierce nationalistic spirit, a surge of patriotism of the most unthinking sort, simply encapsulated the German conscience so that any crime, no matter how horrible, came to be tolerated if not brazenly approved so long as it was in the supposed interest of the Fatherland.

If such a thing was wrong in Germany, it is wrong anywhere, though I am certainly suggesting no point-by-point analogy between the German situation and our own. I merely ask: Is it possible that America's conscience at the present moment of history is becoming similarly callous? Is it conceivable that our minds, so heated at contemplation of the infamy of communism, are prepared to throw overboard the moral heritage that, somewhat paradoxically, we are sworn to defend to the death? I suggest that at the present moment, perhaps, these questions cannot be conclusively answered. But I think they deserve the most solemn consideration.

Man has always, of course, had something to blame for his tendency to commit evil acts. We do not know what it was called a million years ago but in time it came to be called Original Sin, then the Devil, and eventually heredity and environment. And from time to time, in certain circumstances, it was considered that the Jew or the Catholic or the infidel literally *was* the Power of Darkness upon the earth. Today the figure of evil in our minds is the Communist. Right or wrong, this belief has contributed to our further moral breakdown. It has led, for example, to daily transgressions of the Commandment *Thou shalt not bear false witness against thy neighbor,* among others.

Right-wing elements of the French military have, in the heat of battle, developed a doctrine called "revolutionary warfare," the essential thesis of which is that in fighting Communists one must freely employ the sort of dirty tactics that are usually associated with Communists: secret organizations, torture, reprisals, and terror. The conscience of the West is revolted by this philosophy but is usually willing to admit that, war itself being a brutal and inhuman business, it is difficult to draw a line between "gentlemanly" and atrocious acts of violence.

Right-wing extremists around the world, however, have now come to apply the revolutionary warfare philosophy to *peacetime* anti-Communist activity and thereby hangs a fascinating and tangled moral tale. While only a handful of irresponsibles would go so far as to resort to physical violence in this context, one need only consider the program of action recommended by a recently exposed anti-Communist society to realize that the spirit of the "new anticommunism" is scarcely in accord with our moral tradition.

But all of this is counterpoint to the question with which this book deals, which is, of course, the ancient question about ends and means. May a bad means be employed to achieve a good result? We have always insisted that the answer to this question is no. To some this may seem to conclude immediately the debate about the use of H-Bombs. Burning millions of people alive, they say, is evil. Therefore such a means may not be employed to achieve a good end and is doubly forbidden when it is by no means clear that the end will be achieved even *if* such weapons are used.

But there are others who say that while burning innocent civilians in large numbers is admittedly profoundly evil, nuclear weapons will not *necessarily* be used for such a purpose. They might legitimately be used, for example, against a missile base or a fleet of ships at sea. Each group of disputants tends to concentrate on the hypothetical instance that supports its case. The situation, however, can be neatly summed up as follows:

Moralists agree that *nothing* could justify participating in the mass incineration of innocents, while most admit that the use of nuclear weapons against *military* targets is morally permissible. Now a nuclear war would almost certainly involve some acts that, though regrettable, are not necessarily immoral and certain other acts that would constitute the supreme atrocities of human history. The burden of the argument, therefore, is upon those who defend the use of nuclear weapons and are prepared to employ them in all-out war. As Father John C. Ford, S.J., professor of moral theology at Catholic University, says, "If I assert that it is wrong to kill a million schoolchildren, I do not have to prove my assertion. It is those who assert the contrary who have the burden of proof."

*   *   *

I am assuming that this late in the game there is no longer any respect for armaments that purposely ignore the basic question and instead concentrate on side issues. Such, for example, is the argument that nuclear weapons are really quite wonderful because our possession of them has blocked the Communists from accomplishing their aims. Since such armaments invariably come from those who in the next breath assert that communism has *not* been blocked but has relentlessly continued to exert its influence over the surface of our planet, one is, to say the least, confused by such a method of debate. But what we must do is return to the heart of the matter. "Quite right," we must say. "If nuclear weapons are truly never used and serve only to deter war, then they will have indeed achieved a worthy end. Granted. But *now let us take up the question as to their use.* Surely you are not suggesting that because we have tiptoed through history these past sixteen years without a nuclear outburst, it may therefore be assumed that we will continue to march forward decade after decade into a safe and fearless future."

Another absurd idea of which this book should at last dispose is that nuclear pacifists are motivated by the personal fear of death. Pamela Frankau, writing in the *Catholic Pax Bulletin,* explains ". . . we are concerned not with death but with dishonour. We do not fear death. But we cannot embrace sin."

It would indeed be tragic if the reader concluded from an examination of the contents of this book that the question with which it deals is, morally speaking, none of his business. To restate the obvious: the churchmen *are* speaking. It is my purpose to make people listen to them. The obligation to do so certainly exists.

"As a moral problem," Father John Courtney Murray says,

war is ultimately a problem of policy, and therefore a problem of social morality. Policy is made by society, especially in a democratic context, and society bears the moral responsibility for the policy made. As a problem in justice, the problem of war is put to the people, in whom, according to good medieval theory, the sense of justice resides, and from whom the moral judgment, direction, and correction of public policy must finally come. As a moral problem in the use of force, war is not simply, or even primarily, a problem for the generals, the state department, the technologists, the international lawyers. Here, if anywhere, "the people shall judge." This is their responsibility, to be discharged before the shooting starts, by an active concern with the moral direction of national policy. My impression is that this duty in social morality is being badly neglected in America at the moment.

But enough. Let the reader now refer to the following statements by leading Jewish, Catholic, and Protestant spokesmen. The silence has at last been broken. We no longer have the excuse of ignorance. Will our nation be guided in this dread hour by the moral code it professes to honor?

The Book of Ammon

Among the thousand-and-one concepts concerning which the great majority of Americans are poorly informed is that of pacifism. The most simplistic form of common error on the point is that pacifists are simply cowardly people who, being afraid to fight, clothe their reluctance in a philosophical rationale.

Needless to say this is not the case at all. Being an avowed pacifist in a society as violent as ours requires phenomenal courage. And there is good reason, needless to say, for pacifist courage given that in times of international conflict pacifists may literally be arrested, imprisoned, and subjected to great indignity as well. Consequently, although I am not spiritual enough to be a pacifist myself, I willingly provided a few observations when requested to do so by Ammon Hennacy.

If Jefferson was right that government is best which governs least, it would follow that the perfect government is that which does not govern at all. Some would conclude that the perfect government would be that which did not exist; such is the anarchist view. While

I am sensitive to its beauty I cannot accept its logic. I prefer that a policeman be available in my neighborhood, though I am perfectly prepared to concede that ideally he ought to do nothing official whatever.

Such issues, having remained unsettled for the hundreds of thousands of years of man's development, will presumably remain so for the predictable future, if not through all eternity. What one can hope is that in the meantime we will keep fresh enough our dedication to freedom—that ideal so elusive because it is a negative—that men will at least be left free to debate it. I am never sure whether our society presently permits Ammon Hennacy to roam the streets because we really want him to be free or merely because the laws prevent our terminating his freedom with our bare hands.

Ammon serves somewhat the same function in the American context that is served by Lenny Bruce, though on another level. Both men outrage us, both see social reality with the fresh eye of the poet or artist, and we make both pay dearly for their presumption.

So long as our Ammon Hennacys merely theorize about a utopian absence of legal restraint we are disposed to tolerate them. But it is when we are launched upon wars to defend everyman's freedom that we undertake to limit theirs. Of all the unfair charges we bring against them, the most absurd is that of cowardice. It requires enormous courage to live up to the pacifist philosophy. The man who refuses to bear arms is not trying to avoid being killed, he is hoping to avoid killing. It is no sin to be murdered; it is a sin to murder.

The treatment of pacifists in the United States during the First World War was frequently shameful and uncivilized. The nation obviously did not need the handful of individuals involved; their contribution to the war effort would have been negligible. What was at the heart of the vicious harassment meted out to the various anarchists, socialists, and Protestants who refused military service was nothing more edifying than the feeling: if *I* have to suffer well, then, by God, you're going to suffer right along with me. Misery not only *loves* company, it is quite prepared to demand it.

Now, of course, there are Catholic pacifists, too. For that matter there always were, here and there. There have even been nonviolent saints in the church and certainly there is no question but that in the first years of Christianity the ideal of meekness and submission, of the-turning-of-the-other-cheek, of loving one's enemy, was dominant to a degree that is clearly no longer the case. While all three would protest vigorously at being considered potential saints it is significant nevertheless that when one asks oneself just who in the United States now might one day achieve beatification, the names most likely to come to mind are those of the dedicated workers for peace Thomas Merton, Dorothy Day, and Ammon Hennacy. It might be argued that the three, though virtuous, are not saintly at all—the embarrassing debate is certainly best put immediately to rest—but all one can say is that if the objection is valid then the Church in the United States today, whatever other virtues it may boast, would not seem to number the development of a calendar of saints among them.

If Ammon has the storyteller's gift it is perhaps chiefly because he has participated in so many stories. How he ever condensed the many and varied events of his life into an account running to just 474 pages I do not know. He has lived in and through so much of our modern history, has suffered so many things, and met so many interesting people that he surely must have acquired more wisdom than most of us, even if his intelligence and sensitivity were no greater than average. His prison adventures alone would have provided some authors with material enough for a dozen books. Those Catholics who suppose that Ammon Hennacy is perhaps the only Catholic who refuses to register for the draft will in the pages of this book encounter men like John Dunn, a conscientious objector who was sentenced to a twenty-year prison term and who, after his release, studied for the priesthood and is now serving the Church in Portsmouth, Ohio.

Our prisons do not, of course, customarily produce priests. They usually teach a man far more about crime and cruelty than he knew when he was arrested and most American penitentiaries stand as tangible proof that we still have much ground to cover in our long march up out of barbarism. The typical American prison—due chiefly to the lust for revenge, insensitivity and ignorance that perpetuates it—is more a zoo for human animals than a place where children of God are rehabilitated. Ammon draws no such sweeping conclusions in his autobiography but by his unruffled, matter-of-

fact account of his prison experiences must surely lead all but the
most selfish reader to ponder the reality for which our selfishness
is responsible.

It is remarkable how many heroes of our cultural and moral tradition were committed to the revolutionary ideal of social development achieved by interior commitment rather than exterior coer-
cion. What an amusing paradox that today's new Conservatives—
who spend more time than most in insisting on their own
freedom—are more disposed than most to limit the freedom of
those who dare to suggest that the status quo cannot be wholly
sanctified. Ammon Hennacy acknowledges his debt not only to history's supreme Subversive—and hence most stable Conservative—
Christ, but also to Tolstoy, Emerson, Thoreau, Gandhi, Dostoevsky,
St. Theresa, St. Francis, Clarence Darrow, Peter Maurin, Dorothy
Day, and a host of other free and radical souls.

Although it may come as a surprise to him, Ammon is a superb
historian, if we correctly assume that the historian's function is to
interest us in what has gone before. Most of us, even those in public life, tend to find our rut, live out our experiences within its confines, and become aware of the significant events of our time
largely by reading or hearing about them. Ammon Hennacy has
somehow managed to fall in amongst the marchers on the road of
history. He has *experienced*—not just read about—atheism, socialism, anarchism, pacifism, Communism, anti-Communism, violence, poverty, civil disobedience, Christianity, Protestantism,
Catholicism, Mormonism, picket lines, freedom rides, imprisonment, hunger, manual labor, farming, vegetarianism, despair, faith,
hope, and love. Though the list is incomplete, it testifies to the open
zest for bare, natural principled life that seems so characteristic of
Ammon and so rare in the rest of us. Even if Ammon were mistaken
in every single one of his fundamental beliefs and assumptions—
which is true of no man—we could still learn something from him
because of his love for the world. Such men cannot be bored. If
they could teach us nothing more than how to feel a sense of commitment we should pay them much honor.

American Natives

We Americans often have very little understanding of how we are
perceived by others. A good antidote to such blindness is to read
what thoughtful observers from beyond our borders have to say
about us.

When my secretary first brought these drawings to my attention I
somehow drew the erroneous conclusion that I was being asked to
write an introduction to a book of humorous illustrations, if not outright cartoons. Imagine my puzzlement then when I examined these
striking moral X-rays that Erich Sokol has produced.

"Why, these drawings are not funny at all," I said to myself.
"They are tragic." At that point I sought clarification by reading the
letter from the publisher that had accompanied the sheaf of
sketches, a letter that fortunately quoted Mr. Sokol himself.

"It is the intention of these drawings," the artist explains, "to
show that normal people, in their normal environment, engaged in
the normal routine of their everyday lives, involuntarily are tragically ludicrous and ludicrously tragic. This truth is the simple 'gag'
in all my pictures."

From *American Natives*, by Erich Sokol (New York: Harper & Brothers, 1960).

27

Mr. Sokol has realized his intention and then some. Looking at his people (if one is an American) one has first of all a feeling of familiarity, recognition, and then a sudden rush of insight of the sort usually communicated by a lightning-bolt line of poetry or the wry observation of a deeply sophisticated philosopher. "My God," one thinks, frowning, "here is truth, and typicality, and a peculiar mixture of savagery and sympathy."

Ink, in Erich Sokol's hands, is an acid that dissolves sham. He has not, it seems to me, drawn an untrue line. Indeed, as I looked through his sketches, I was haunted by the fear that somewhere in the stack I might even come across myself. The feeling merged into relief as I put aside the last drawing knowing that I had escaped being trapped, caged, and labeled by Mr. Sokol.

Whether this particular omission or any omission in this context results from carelessness on the artist's part or a certain predominance of individuality over typicality in the subject it would be impossible to say, but no reader who fails to find himself between these covers will ever breathe entirely easy so long as Mr. Sokol is still at his drawing board, which (since he is only twenty-six years old) would seem to be a long time indeed.

Although these sketches are grouped under the title *American Natives,* it should be clear, I think, that Americans are targets for Mr. Sokol's pen through the simple accident of his residence here. Were he living in Australia his characters would have turned out to be "Australian Natives," for it is essential humanity that he reveals, and only secondarily national characteristics. "My book deals with people," he says in explanation of this point. "The fact that it deals with Americans in particular is incidental. I feel about people in this book just as I feel about myself. Usually I either like or hate myself; but often, against all reason, I do both at the same time. . . . I call this book an unobjective comment because I am prejudiced. I am pro-American and pro-people and against their idealization."

Again the artist has perfectly realized an intention. One reason his sketches shock us is that we are accustomed to seeing ourselves in idealized forms. Motion pictures, television, the theater, advertising, popular magazine illustration, all present us in semidivine likeness. Young men are handsome, young women beautiful, and the old are silver-haired repositories of sugar-coated wisdom. High-school girls imagine that they resemble Marilyn Monroe, teen-age boys squint into their mirrors, somehow contriving to see James Dean, or (if they are more ascetic) Tony Perkins, rural types feel a certain John Wayneish twinge as they saunter manfully into a country store, and—well, to get to the point, Erich Sokol awakens us rudely from our dreams of glory. But his ruthless methods, I think, serve an ultimately good purpose. Certainly anyone, finding himself displayed here like a dried butterfly, would be bound to feel, however faint, a surge of nonconformist rebellion. Breathes there a man with soul so dead that, coming upon a picture of himself as the bloated, oatmeal-brained, beer-out-of-the-can schlunk staring heavy-lidded at the TV screen (which has—significantly?—*nothing* on it), he would not at least once in the future flick off the set and, somewhat guiltily, pick up a book?

But I must make clear my feeling that Sokol's commentary is not entirely critical. He bitterly resents (if I understand his work) the dehumanization of man, the mechanization of man, the glorification of the body and its senses at the expense of the spirit, but he deeply sympathizes with the weak, the frightened, the insecure, the bored, the lost, and the lonely.

It would take a foreigner, I think, to see us so well. Familiarity may or may not breed contempt but it certainly breeds insensitivity. Burns's plea for a power to see ourselves as others see us is plainly answered in these pages.

As I leaf again through these sketches I am seized by the idea that this book should be made required reading in all creative *writing* courses, for what makes one writer better than another is not, at heart, a deftness with words, but the ability to look beneath the surface, to recognize essence and significance. Erich Sokol's drawings speak the proverbial volumes. To consider only one example, look long at the old pipe-smoker, blankly barbecuing hot dogs in his star-splashed California or Florida back yard, a man who feels alien in that subtropical retirement which the insurance-company ads always make look so inviting. He seems like a character dreamed up by Nathanael West or James Purdy or anyone, perhaps, except himself or a merciful God.

But enough of *my* analysis; the reader is no doubt anxious to begin his own. I promise him that once he meets Sokol's characters he will not easily forget them. He will go back to them again and again, in much the same way he goes back to pictures in a family album.

And probably for the same reasons.

Farm Labor Organizing 1905-1965: A Brief History

I have often been asked what public figures of the present age might rightly be chosen as guests on the "Meeting of Minds" television program if it were to be in production a hundred years or more into the future. If the next century is anything like all those of the past, it is probable that some public figures of recent decades will be perceived as very minor players in the drama of history and, moreover, that at least a few who are presently obscure will ultimately be better appreciated. To give an example from the past, the great poet Emily Dickinson was totally overlooked by her fellow Americans in her lifetime but now—thanks to the sensitivity of certain English critics—is recognized for her brilliance. Cesar Chavez, the heroic organizer of the United Farm Workers Union, was accorded only a tiny fraction of the public approbation accorded the average rock musician. Conservatives, in particular, publicly despised him, and of course he was not considered great in the eyes of the agribusiness executives who wished to employ farm workers at the lowest possible cost to themselves. But if the word "hero" any longer has true meaning

From *Farm Labor Organizing 1905–1965: A Brief History,* by the National Advisory Committee on Farm Labor (New York: National Advisory Committee on Farm Labor, 1967).

in our depraved society, it must certainly be applied to Cesar
Chavez.

The United States is the richest nation on earth, presently enjoying
the richest moment of its history. But for all our affluence and charitable impulses the ideal of social justice is far from completely
realized in our land. Countless millions live in abject poverty and
squalor. The cold-hearted often categorize these poor as worthless
people too lazy to work for a living. But in addition to the millions
on welfare (less than one percent of whom are actually employable,
according to a recent presidential study), there are millions, including most farm workers, who work hard yet cannot even afford the
basic necessities. The frustrations of these "working poor" should
be one of our country's gravest concerns.

Though big-city poverty attracts most public attention, the fact
is that 43 percent of the nation's poverty exists in rural areas. The
urban poor have become vocal and attention has at last been
attracted to their needs. But the poor of the countryside are for the
most part unorganized, isolated, powerless, invisible.

I do not see how this nation can continue to justify the treatment
to which our farm workers have long been subjected. These people
work at physically exhausting labor for very low pay. Most of them
live in disgracefully inadequate quarters and receive little or no
medical attention; their children are given a poor substitute for an
education.

It was not very many years ago that an American working man
could be fired without being given cause or notice, when his salary
could be reduced at an employer's whim, when he had to work ten
or twelve hours a day, when young children labored in dangerous
factories to earn pennies a day, when workers were beaten and
killed if they attempted to organize. Three things were required to
change the situation: public indignation, rights of collective bar-
gaining, and civilized legislation.

Americans are rightly proud today of the security now enjoyed
by the average working man, But looking back over our shoulders we
see that the farm laborer has been left behind in the forward march.

There can be legitimate differences of opinion among reasonable men as regards the best solution to the farm worker's problem.

But there can be no justification for those who are simply determined to keep the field hand in his place, to intimidate or even to ignore him. To become familiar with the information in this pamphlet is to automatically come under a moral obligation.

It is sometimes erroneously supposed that the farm labor problem is serious only in the deep South, or in the Southwest. But the problem is national. While an entire farm family in Texas may work a year and earn only about $1500, things are bad enough in Massachusetts. On a farm north of Boston men put in as many as fourteen hours a day, seven days a week, for ninety-five cents an hour. They live in shacks with cardboard on the floor. In Rochelle, Illinois, a migrant family of ten was recently "living" in one room with a cement floor and walls and one small window, all surrounded by a sea of mud.

As if their lives were not bad enough, farm laborers must also contend with dangerous hazards. Although they comprise about 7 percent of the U.S. work force they suffer over 22 percent of all fatalities from work accidents.

It would be unwise to view the farm labor predicament as a controversy pitting workers against growers and then, on the basis of one's social biases, choose to support one side or the other. Both forces must be supported. Even the wealthiest farmers are faced with a cost-price squeeze and they are certainly as entitled to a profit as employers in any other industry. But that same understanding should be accorded those decent men and women without whose labor the farm owner would be out of business overnight.

A generation ago certain shortsighted representatives of management predicted that economic disaster would follow recognition of the rights and privileges of the working man. Instead American industry today is more powerful and successful than ever. If, as Senator Robert Kennedy has observed, we can plan to put a man on the moon before the end of this decade, surely we can devise a solution to the farm labor problem.

One of the philosophical foundation stones upon which our civilization is proudly based is the belief that a man is more important than an object, that human rights, in other words, are more important than property rights. Since we proclaim this view to the world it does not seem to be too much to suggest that we start acting as if we believed it.

Doing Philosophy

Since, partly because I attended eighteen different schools, my formal education was not very effective, I knew close to nothing, by the age of thirty, about the monumental achievements of the major philosophers since the days of the ancient Greeks. It is horrifying to think that most Americans not only share my ignorance but far exceed it as regards not only the history of the discipline of philosophy but the basic philosophical questions themselves.

A fundamental axiom of the free-enterprise economy is: you can't sell the customer unless you first pull him into the store. Even as regards absolute necessities it is considered necessary to present what is required in the most favorable light possible.

On a more rational planet it should not prove necessary to sugar-coat any intellectual pills. On this one, however, countless factors of media inevitably affect the reception of message. Perhaps for a few years after Gutenberg's invention of the press the unadorned reality of type on paper was sufficient to transfix the literate. Except for a fortunate few, however, the fascination with the

From *Doing Philosophy,* by Thomas Ellis Katen (Englewood Cliffs, N.J.: Prentice Hall, 1973).

bare thing-in-itself did not historically persist. To keep readers interested publishers and educators resorted to various forms of printing type, to richly colored book-covers, to illustration, and other appeals to the senses.

At the present moment keeping young people acutely interested in the educative process is nothing less than a matter of the survival of our total culture. This seems now generally acknowledged as regards children of pre-school and primary-grade ages. The entire thrust of the new approach to basic education, in fact, involves approaching the student's mind through as many physical channels as possible so that the brain will be better enabled to retain important impressions. It is no longer considered enough, for example, to tell a child that one-third and one-third and one-third add up to a whole. We now reinforce the abstract message with three pie-slices of brightly colored wood which, when placed together, form a full circle.

Today the mind of man is assailed by an enormous amount of raw material, particularly in our large urban centers. People, objects, sounds, lights, colors, movement, dangers, pleasures, pressures of all kinds compete on the stage of our attention. Perhaps in a cloistered monastery concentration on dry and weighty texts might still be easily accomplished. And there are some, of a naturally scholarly bent, who apparently contrive to get a good education regardless of the physical environment. In the 1970s, however, particularly in the context of the experience of the American young, the distractions are of such an order that, if the vitally important message of philosophy is to really *reach* us, it must employ means specifically chosen because they are competitive in the present sensory context.

It has been said that war is far too important a matter to be left to the generals. Just so philosophy is far too important to be left to the philosophers, or even to those few students who are by nature inclined to a strong interest in such matters. For in the difficult world that now presses in upon all of us we greatly handicap ourselves if we face dangerous and puzzling questions unarmed by some degree of familiarity with thousands of years of philosophical speculation and debate.

This is not to say that to know what to do about problems of war and peace, nuclear disarmament, urban unrest, social injustice and race tensions we need only refer to Thomas Aquinas, John Locke, or Bertrand Russell. But it *is* to say that a reasoned and scholarly approach to the difficulties that perplex us is far preferable to the emotion-laden prescriptions of, say, either the Minutemen of the Right or the Weathermen of the Left. Most Americans rule out the appeal to naked violence that presently arises from the inflamed passions of both the Nazis and Fascists and the Revolutionary Marxists. But on what grounds, for precisely what reasons, do we regard such appeals as counterproductive? This question *can* be answered within the context of philosophy—those branches of it dealing with morals and politics.

Are all wars unjust? Was the Second World War justified but the Vietnamese War unjustified? Is capital punishment civilized? Thomas Aquinas thought it was perfectly proper to burn heretics alive. Today no philosopher would agree with him.

Are you frustrated by the "stubbornness" of those with whom you argue? Is there then a proper technique of argument? What is *logic*? Are men really more logical than women? These are only a few of the many thousands of timely, where-it's-at questions that philosophy deals with. The reality, then, is clear enough. But how do you get young people interested in it?

In far too many cases, you don't; the average citizen is a philosophical illiterate. But it need not be so and along comes Thomas Katen to dramatize the point and to offer an attractive solution.

That he unashamedly "popularizes" philosophy in this entertaining book is evident. The important thing is he carries the trick off successfully. His success, I would think, is rooted in his motivation, which is a simple *love* for the field to which he has devoted his life.

Philosophy itself is, of course, the love of wisdom, and love implies joy.

"Having experienced a lot of joy doing philosophy with my students and friends," Katen has explained, "and always having tried to bring philosophy out of the classroom and into life, I came to feel I would like to try to translate this approach which bad been so enriching to me and many of my students into the form of a book. . . . If something of this approach can come across in this book, those who read it may not only gain some information about the business of philosophy, but be moved a little by the spirit of it."

As a humorist, I found myself attracted by Katen's zest for his assignment.

"There is much humor in the lives of men such as Diogenes, Thomas Aquinas, Voltaire, Kant, and Bertrand Russell," and he says "there are many humorous possibilities in the development of philosophical ideas and problems. . . . Behind the fun in philosophy, however, there is a seriousness that mankind requires to understand and cope with its deepest problems."

What I believe Katen will achieve by his revolutionary approach to subject matter that too many young people regard as not only serious but dull is to demonstrate that the shape of today's world has been largely *determined* by philosophy. The systems of ideas with which all major philosophers have been concerned have had practical consequences that affect all of us. The awe-inspiring conflict between East and West on our planet is not merely a confrontation between large states in the historic sense; it is a conflict of philosophies. Not to understand both our own and that of our Marxist opponents is folly since it means playing a dangerous game without taking the trouble to learn the rules.

Once, hearing a teenager say that he did not like jazz music but did like rock 'n' roll, I explained to him that rock is merely a subdivision of jazz, that it grew out of jazz. The same young man might today say that he is interested in Marx but has no interest in philosophy. Since Marx was a political philosopher the assertion is senseless.

Man today wants to understand himself, his fellow-man, his earthly environment, the realm of outer space, the mysteries of time, matter, nature, God. There are no more important questions. Thomas Katen demonstrates in this lively, seemingly irreverent outline, that there are no more interesting questions either.

A Nuclear War Would Just
Ruin My Day

Comedy—if I may quote one of my favorite authorities on the subject: myself—is about tragedy. Consequently it should come as no surprise that considerable humor can be mined from such grim soil as the clear possibility of nuclear holocaust.

A French thinker once said that he would not care who wrote the laws of the nation if he were permitted to write its songs. This observation, of course, was merely a clever way of drawing attention to the fact that songs, as well as other forms of popular art, can have a powerful effect on the public consciousness.

In the present human predicament, characterized by a list of social problems far longer than that faced by any previous period of history, we must, first of all, use any and all means to capture the simple attention of Just Plain Folks and, secondly, suggest a variety of reasonable approaches to the dilemmas that perplex us.

Given the literally life-and-death nature of the nuclear weapons threat, nothing whatever is to be sneezed at in the campaign for not only nuclear sanity but social justice generally. Philosophers and other scholars are already engaged in the process of public education. So, happily, are legions of individuals active in the creative arts. The publication of the present work does not, needless to say, suggest that cartoonists are only now joining ranks with other peace activists. Newspaper and magazine artists have been concerned about the problem since the early 1950s and have frequently made their views known. But this book provides an important service in that for the first time it draws together, from a large number of distinguished political cartoonists, those contributions which specifically address the issue of nuclear madness.

In perusing this book, one of the first things that strikes the reader is how remarkably similar the stands of the cartoonists are towards this crucial issue. I would be very surprised to learn that there were a single pacifist among the artists whose works are reproduced here. If there is anything, in the philosophical sense, that unites them, it is probably nothing more than the general considerations which grow out of a combination of simple common sense, concern for the preservation of human life, and an equally admirable desire that the few concrete and abstract benefits of Western civilization be preserved rather than reduced to cinders.

The sort of laughter produced by an examination of the following cartoons is not, obviously, the same as that occasioned by a Mel Brooks film, a Richard Pryor monologue, or a Sid Caesar television sketch. The present laughter is wry, even rueful. But it is laughter, and as such makes its contribution to social sanity.

Given the fact that the question of avoiding the burning-alive of hundreds of millions of innocent civilian men, women, and children is more important than the harm done by former Interior Secretary James Watt, one should not expect, in reading *A Nuclear War Would Just Ruin My Day,* the same sense of hilarity reported by readers of the editors' earlier work: *100 Watts: The James Watt Memorial Cartoon Collection.*

The unfortunate Mr. Watt will almost certainly go to his grave thinking that he was routinely picked on simply because he was a conservative. Why it has not occurred to him to observe that cartoonists and journalists have not heaped similar ridicule on George Will, William F. Buckley, or Milton Friedman, God knows. And, despite Mr. Watt's apparent sense of having a special relationship with the deity, the relevant information would not appear to have been vouchsafed. Nature itself is cruel enough, and there is more than enough unfairness in the conduct of human affairs. It was certainly not Mr. Watt's intention to be tactless and charmless any more than it was his intention to be hairless. He just seemed to rub a good part of the human race the wrong way. It was for that reason—and, be it duly noted, for that reason only—that his personal friend Ronald Reagan got rid of him.

Cartoons on the subject of nuclear holocaust, then, will rarely make a reader laugh aloud as did a good many of the anti-Watt cartoons, but they are important nevertheless and eminently worthy of being gathered together for preservation in public and private libraries.

While there is, as mentioned earlier, no shortage of societal dilemmas, the problem posed by the massive stockpiling of nuclear weapons deserves a separate kind of attention. For one thing it gives rise to a bizarre form of moral insensitivity that itself cries out for attention, the same sort of attention that the world all too belatedly gave to the Nazis' extermination of millions of Jews.

The sin of which I speak is hardly attributable only to Americans. The Communists of the world are equally to blame. But their participation, morally speaking, is irrelevant when we examine our own consciences. Evil is often a social business, but one is called to account for it individually nevertheless. The Nazis are reviled because of the atrocities they committed against several million Jews. But today the American people, among others, seem quite prepared, if provoked, to actually incinerate a good part of the human race. How can it be that individuals who would find it difficult to personally inflict harm on one other person can nevertheless be complacent about the prospect of an atrocity of such vast proportions as to be almost unimaginable?

The question contains its own answer. Evil and suffering on that enormous a scale are unimaginable except by an effort of the most painful and long-sustained concentration. We are, after all, only individuals, and the millions of years of evolutionary history have prepared us, physically and psychologically, to respond to suffering—either our own or that of others—on a limited, personal basis. We are truly solicitous about individual injuries, accidents, and attacks—and especially shocked at individual killings. During or after the personal experience of such tragic events, it would be possible, I suppose, to scientifically measure the physical evidence of our sympathetic and sorrowful concern. The left eye might weep seventeen tears, the right twenty-two. We might be deeply depressed, calculably, for fourteen days, six hours, and twelve minutes. But at the contemplation—or even, God forbid, the witnessing—of hundreds of millions of burnings, maimings, and deaths, could we really cry any additional tears? Could we really feel any more depressed than in the context of localized, personal suffering? We probably could not, and therein lies part of the danger.

There is also something in us, partly self-protective and partly stupid, that finds it difficult to bring the reality of our own pain and death into clear focus. Intellectually we know that we will die and that we are likely to suffer in a number of instances between the present moment and our last. However, there is something about that reality that we are quite gifted at shunting aside, and there are more pleasant prospects and considerations which we prefer to rush to the forefront of our conscious attention. . . .

To the great credit of individual Christian leaders and theologians, scores of them have wrestled, publicly and painfully, with the moral dilemma posed by C. Wright Mills. In 1961 I wrote a foreword for, and published, a book titled *God and the H-Bomb,* which included courageous and morally sensible commentaries on the question at hand by Bishop Fulton J. Sheen, Martin Buber, Paul Tillich, Israel Goldstein, Pope Pius XII, the Central Conference of American Rabbis, and assorted other believers.

There is some hope, then, in the fact that not only theologians but political officeholders, scholars, scientists, journalists, dramatists, performing artists, and cartoonists have joined the growing ranks of those who realize that there is no profession—no person— exempt from responsibility to prevent nuclear suicide.

The Confessions of the Tortilla Priest

Even the casual student of social history eventually wonders how long the same story will have to be told, over how many centuries, in which a brave reformer, acting either alone or with a relatively small group, speaks out in opposition to segments of society that, for purely selfish reasons, subjugate the poor and powerless. On precisely such subject matter, hundreds of stories, books, essays, editorials, documentaries, films, and television dramas have been based. In some of these, the underdog finally triumphs, though never without a long, exhausting struggle. In other instances, the social critic goes to his or her own grave before the scales of justice are more reasonably balanced. And, in other instances, alas, history has not as yet seen a final resolution that would satisfy the saints. Such a reformer, to get to the point, is Father Victor Salandini.

In the context of the struggle for social justice for America's farm workers, Father Victor's name is not nearly as well known as that of the courageous leader of the United Farm Workers Union, Cesar Chavez, but it might be of some slight comfort to the priest

From *The Confessions of the Tortilla Priest,* by Victor Salandini (San Diego: The San Diego Review, Inc., 1992).

that he has not been subjected to nearly as much criticism as has fallen on Chavez.

Being personally the product of a lower middle-class Catholic background, I am perhaps something of a relic of a day when, at least in the Catholic community, the words and works of priests were accorded a certain degree of respect. This is not to argue that the clergy, of any faith, are or ought to be immune from criticism. Both their personal lives and their political and social views are as properly the object of critical analysis as those of any other citizens. But it initially came as a shock to me, nevertheless, to notice—as I first did in the 1960s—that the degree of contempt heaped upon the liberal clergy, almost invariably by their fellow Christians, was far more extreme than it had been thirty years earlier. This ugly reality first impressed itself not only on my own, but on the national consciousness in the context of such public dramas as civil rights marches in which, along with Protestant and Jewish clergymen, many nuns and priests took up their posts in picket lines and protest demonstrations, appealing for no politically radical solutions whatever but simply speaking up for that minimum of social justice that one might even expect for animals. But for making even such modest demands and—well, actually, for exposing the ugliness of the systems of exploitation, privilege, and cruelty that for centuries have kept the powerless subject to their masters—they were treated with the sort of both private and public scorn that might make an observer wince even if the victims were convicted criminals.

Civil rights marches through overwhelmingly Catholic neighborhoods in the 1960s, for example, led to the shouting of obscenities at Catholic nuns and priests, not excluding the casting of vile sexual aspersions and the shouting of suggestions that if a white nun and a black man happened to be marching side-by-side, it was to be assumed that they were sexual partners. It is hardly surprising that such "Christian" crowds also threw the proverbial sticks and stones. The hurling of weapons, some of them capable of causing death, was only the last visible outbreak of a viciousness of mind that was the far greater sin. As one nun sadly commented at the time, after a particularly vile attack at the hands of fellow Catholics, "It's sad to think how poorly we must have taught them."

I have known Father Victor since 1967, though I'd first heard of his help to farm workers two years earlier when he made the national news for supporting a tomato workers' strike in the border community of San Ysidro, California, near San Diego. I later made mention of this in my book *The Ground Is Our Table.* I had also read in Cesar Chavez's newspaper, *El Malcriado,* that Father Salandini was lobbying for Chavez's then fledgling new National Farm Workers Union.

Father Salandini brings a unique background of experience to the writing of this book, that of trying to implement the Catholic Church's teachings on social justice during his more than forty years as a priest. The purpose of his book is not to criticize the Church, but to explain his social gospel ministry in light of the mandates of the papal social encyclicals. One of the highlights of his ministry to the farm workers was the instance in which he was suspended (that is, his powers of the priesthood were taken from him by his bishop). At that time, the courageous Dolores Huerta, the first vice-president of the United Farm Workers, said, "No other priest has ever lost his priestly powers because he helped the farm workers." To this day no other priest except Father Victor has been suspended for helping the United Farm Workers.

The tragedy of this highlight in Father Victor's life is that his suspension from the priesthood, in July 1971, has only been rescinded in theory. It is true that it was removed after some two weeks, but, in reality, since 1971 Father Victor has never been given any responsibility in the Church. This is compounded by the fact that he has much to offer the Church, yet is placed on the back burner, so to speak, because he has had the courage to be a prophet in speaking out and trying to do something practical about farm worker problems in California.

At a time when vocations to the priesthood are dwindling, and few priests are prophetic, Father Victor's book can be an inspiration to America's youth, some of whom may see the priesthood not as a challenge but as just another job. Perhaps no other priest knows better what is going on in our public high schools. Since 1983 he has dealt with the problems of high school youths. Throughout the high schools of the San Diego area, Father Victor is known to thousands of young people. They are aware of his work with the farm workers, know that he went to jail with Cesar Chavez, and that he has been arrested several times. During the last eight years Father Victor has helped many students to find a purpose in life and to get off drugs and alcohol, having the same sort of influence with high schoolers as Mr. Escalante of Garfield High School in Los Angeles who received a great deal of publicity in the film *Stand and Deliver.*

All readers, whatever their bias, will be enlightened by Father Salandini's story. On the farms and fields of California, where for decades most of the back-breaking labor has been done by Mexicans and Mexican-Americans, those who suffered were an almost totally Catholic constituency, a fact which accounted for literally nothing whatever so far as their continuing abuse at the hands of usually Christian employers was concerned. When the showdown came, it turned out that the enemies of the farm laborers were motivated by the idol they truly worshiped, the dollar sign. They were not in the least civilized by the other symbol, the crucifix, to which, on Sunday mornings at least, a good many of them paid lip service.

Jelly Roll, Bix, and Hoagy

Popular music is sometimes viewed as a relatively inconsequential artifact of American culture, a view which has a very poor relationship with social reality. Actually, we can tell a great deal about a people from nothing more than a study of the music they produce. It is, consequently, one more sobering bit of evidence that we are in a serious period of decline if we compare the popular music of a true Golden Age—the 1920s, '30s, and '40s—with what passes for high achievement in the present marketplace. Rick Kennedy's study, although it deals with popular music, jazz, and the recording industry, tells us a great deal about twentieth-century America itself.

Most books based on historical research appeal only to those who already have an interest in the basic subject matter. Rick Kennedy's study of a now-obscure Indiana record company, by way of contrast, is so inherently fascinating that even those who have heretofore evidenced no particular interest in American cultural history,

Reprinted by permission from *Jelly Roll, Bix, and Hoagy,* by Rick Kennedy (Bloomington: Indiana University Press, 1994).

and even those with no special involvement with jazz, will be stimulated by the combination of the many cultural and social threads the book weaves together.

From his remarkable account one learns not only a great deal of the origins of the now gargantuan record industry, but about our national patterns of migration, about the roots of the modern American economy, and about the U.S. contribution to the Industrial Revolution itself.

As a traveling concert entertainer, I have noted how similar many Midwestern communities are. So many factories surrounded by farms, so many nineteenth-century self-made millionaires and their surviving descendants—who still tend to dominate their local scenes, sometimes distinguishing themselves for their philanthropic contributions and interest in the arts and education.

Given that jazz itself is the only art form ever created in America, *Jelly Roll, Bix, and Hoagy* must be considered required reading for anyone with an even casual interest in the history of American popular music. Many separate audiences will find Kennedy's study of particular interest. Those who care about the background of popular music will consider it a treasure, as will those who care only about jazz.

It's also highly recommended for African Americans concerned with their special cultural history. One of the sadder aspects of the current general national ignorance is that many of today's black teenagers are unfamiliar even with such giants as Count Basie, Duke Ellington, and Louis Armstrong. The number who have never even heard of Jelly Roll Morton, about whom Kennedy provides a great deal of information, is depressing enough.

Although the Gennett Company released now historically important material by Duke Ellington, Fletcher Henderson, Louis Armstrong, and other giants, Gennett was by no means a purely jazz label. Lawrence Welk and Guy Lombardo also recorded for them, as did many other nonjazz dance bands, and the company's importance in being the first to record many pioneer country-and-western artists is also impressive.

Even though my childhood was spent largely in Chicago, which meant I was familiar with country radio station WLS, I never knew until reading *Jelly Roll, Bix, and Hoagy* that that station was owned by Sears, Roebuck and Co., which consciously catered to its millions of rural catalog customers, even though its programs originated from Chicago's very cosmopolitan Sherman Hotel. The Gennett Company provided records, in massive amounts, to Sears catalog customers.

The word *treasure* must be used for any book that surprises the reader with so many previously unknown but fascinating faces. Despite my own love of Hoagy Carmichael's immortal "Stardust," from the first moment I heard it as an impressionable teenager, I didn't know until now that it was originally conceived, performed, and recorded as an up-tempo novelty rather than a ballad. Nor did I know that the original lyric was written not by Mitchell Parish but by Carmichael himself.

Considering that Carmichael and I were personal friends in his late years, I feel like a dunce for never having known, until reading Rick Kennedy's book, that the great composer had also been a cornet player and had recorded, as a vocalist, with the famous Paul Whiteman orchestra.

If Kennedy's account doesn't excite you, you have no serious interest in the history of American music.

Vows of Silence

If Diana Louise Michael were a purely fictional character, a professional editor would reject her story as inherently preposterous.

It occurs to most of us late in life, and to some of us probably not at all, that there would appear to be no justice whatever in the workings of the great natural universe. What precious little justice we do encounter is all imposed by humans. This is assuredly a sobering reflection, but since it conforms quite comfortably to the massive accumulation of sensory evidence, it must be faced, as must all truths.

But the great unfairness is even worse than that, for justice and good fortune are by no means apportioned evenly. Some are, from the very moment of their conception, granted numerous advantages. At the opposite end of the spectrum, however, there are those whose lives are characterized by a thousand-and-one painful slings and arrows.

And yet it is part of the great and no doubt eternal mystery of life that not all of those who are rich in advantage maintain their

---

From *Vows of Silence,* by Diana Louise Michael (Minneapolis: Trust Publishing, Sharp Sally's Press, Inc., 1993).

good fortune to the grave. There are also cases of those who begin the race of life far behind the starting line and yet somehow manage to improve their situation.

Such a person is Diana Louise Michael.

We know there is suffering in this world; we observe it every day and, because of the modern technology of communication, we are more aware of it than any previous generation. But we would still tend to doubt the reasonableness of Ms. Michael's story were it only the product of an author's imagination.

Her early life was unfortunate from the start. Diana's mother, a devout Catholic, suffered from uterine tumors after giving birth to three children, all boys, who, at the time of her diagnosis, were all under the age of seven.

Despite medical advice to have no more children, Diana's mother became pregnant again and when she was due to deliver, her doctors, who could hear no fetal heartbeat, informed her that she would have a stillbirth. To their surprise she delivered premature twins, the second of which, named Diana, weighed only four pounds.

Life is difficult enough for premature children even at present. In the late 1940s many did not survive. Improperly administered radiation treatments further damaged the mother's system. As a result, she became addicted to amphetamines and barbiturates.

It is difficult enough for even a normal healthy young woman to raise five children under the age of seven. For Diana's mother, giving such care was even more difficult.

Although religion brings comfort to many, Diana's mother had no such luck. She became a recluse, obsessed rather than comforted by her faith, and racked by excessive guilt—a guilt Diana did not understand until many years later when a shocking revelation provided the explanation.

Diana herself suffered from guilt on the groundless belief that she was personally responsible for her mother's suffering, believing her birth had caused it. As if the general chaos of her early years was not bad enough, she was, at age fourteen, the victim of an awful crime. Just as religion had failed her, so did the services of psychiatrists who misdiagnosed her case. After escaping from the hospital, she attempted suicide but *somehow* survived. It was at this point I first heard of Diana Louise Michael.

Having seen my television shows, she concluded—correctly as it turned out—that I might be sympathetic to her plight and wrote to me, confessing to her suicidal emotions. Something about the advice I was able to provide seemed to give Diana a reason for hope. Perhaps I should explain that many public figures receive a certain number of letters from deeply troubled people. It is not that difficult to write a letter of sound advice, but I have always been disappointed that it was not possible to do more for the various troubled souls with whom I have communicated over the years.

Separated as we were by so much space and time, I could have no direct effect on Diana's personal fate, which continued to be almost impossibly negative and destructive.

Diana, a relentless young woman indeed, has survived the remarkable blows that life has thrown at her. We can all learn from her story. All of us suffer disappointments, setbacks, even tragedies. Perhaps, from this young woman's history, we can learn something of the human capacity for survival and the ability of hope to bring us through even the darkest days.

Laurel and Hardy:
The Magic behind the Movies

It is by no means only the fact that I am a professional practitioner of the art of comedy that occasions my interest in the art form. It is more the case that the interest in those performers apparently genetically gifted with the ability to make others laugh started in my childhood and will apparently persist until the day of my death. There have been a number of comedy teams that made us laugh: George Burns and Gracie Allen, Jackie Gleason and Art Carney, Abbot and Costello. But none of these approached the sheer funniness of Stan Laurel and Oliver Hardy.

For whatever the point is worth—and I say this as a Chaplin fan—from early childhood I have considered Laurel and Hardy *funnier* than Chaplin. Perhaps the point will be clarified if I refer to the modern comedy of Lily Tomlin. Lily is unquestionably one of our *greatest* comediennes. She is, however, by no means always the *funniest*.

This essay appeared as the foreword to *Laurel and Hardy: The Magic behind the Movies,* by Randy Skretvedt (Beverly Hills, Calif.: Moonstone Press, 1992), but it was originally published in Steve Allen's book *More Funny People* (New York: Stein & Day, 1982).

Part of the explanation for the great superiority of Laurel and Hardy over other comedy teams—the Marx Brothers, for example—is that you cared about them as human beings. Jokes, as such, were of little importance to Stan and Oliver. Stan and Oliver simply *were* funny, just by showing up.

In the successful Laurel and Hardy formula Ollie was the aggressor. But the relationship is much different from that which prevailed between Abbott and Costello. Bud Abbott was always sharp, demanding, strongly manipulative. It was never thus with Oliver Hardy. He dominated in a gentle, if-you-will-permit-me way. From time to time Stanley's ineptitude would drive him to moments of fury. But the dominant element in his character was his strange, silly courtliness, his niceness and decency. Oliver Hardy played straight to Stan Laurel but was brilliantly, richly funny in his own right. As my wife, Jayne, has pointed out, in many filmed sequences Hardy is actually doing funnier things than Laurel, but is more subtle. His tie-twiddling, drumming of his fingers on air, and his ways of conveying exasperation are among these.

Garson Kanin in his *Together Again!,* a study of great Hollywood teams, makes the insightful observation that although on screen Oliver Hardy was dominant, the pattern was completely reversed in reality. Stanley was the writer, the creator, the director. Ollie, for the most part, did as he was instructed. To his credit, he repeatedly conceded that Laurel was the more creative member of the team and deferred to Stanley on practically every question where judgment was required.

In 1959 some of my writers and I visited Stan. All of us reminisced about particular favorite films, scenes, and comedy routines we remembered seeing Laurel do, and were thunderstruck when it became apparent that he was more interested in talking to us about our shows and sketches than recalling his old films. He was a gentle, soft-spoken man and could not have been more charming.

Because Stan in person seemed like his screen image—though much more intelligent—I was surprised when a painter who did some work at my home early in 1982 told me that when he had worked as part of the crew on a Laurel and Hardy film many years earlier, he had liked Oliver but not Stan.

"What was wrong with Stan Laurel, in your opinion?" I asked.

"Oh," replied the painter, "he just seemed stuck-up. He was too much of a perfectionist. He always wanted everything to be just right and if it wasn't, he could be kind of a son-of-a-bitch about it."

The same might be said, I suppose, of every talented perfectionist who ever lived.

Book Excerpts

Dialogues in Americanism

Steve Allen vs. William F. Buckley, Jr.
The Presidency
"Resolved: The foreign policy of
John F. Kennedy has been successful."

Back in the early sixties, although my political consciousness had itself been awakened for only a few years, I was invited by a conservative friend, Michael Gazzaniga, to debate William F. Buckley, Jr., at that time the nation's leading conservative spokesman, on the subject of foreign policy. The confrontation was interesting for a number of reasons. First of all, Mr. Buckley had no serious rivals as a debater, whereas I not only had never debated anyone but knew close to nothing whatever about the formal rules of the game. As a result of that ignorance, in fact, I showed up with several pages of my remarks.

If it were not for the fortunate fact that the proceedings were

audiotaped I would by now have little conscious memory as to
what either Mr. Buckley or I said on the evening of our meeting.
What remains clear, however, is the nature of the audience gathered at the Hollywood Palladium that night. It was quite unlike the
typical entertainment audience but remarkably similar to that associated with athletic competitions, particularly boxing-matches.
About 90 percent of those in attendance were politically conservative, probably because the proceedings had been organized by a
conservative group. It is at least conceivable that, given Mr. Buckley's preeminence as a debater, those who were generally unsympathetic to my own views had gathered in the hope of witnessing
my public humiliation.

William F. Buckley, Jr.: Opening Statement

Steve Allen told me last spring when we met to consider this invitation that he had never before in his entire life debated with anyone. That was of course a joke; probably the only poor one he has
ever made. The remark, needless to say, was intended sincerely.
The worst thing about Steve Allen is that he sincerely believes what
he says. He meant to make a gesture of respect for my allegedly
superior experience. But consider whence the compliment came:
from a master verbalist, a born showman, a fabulous extemporizer
who, almost every night, dating back to when I was a schoolboy
being trained to make the world safe for democracy, has faced vast
audiences, making them laugh or cry, feel happy or feel sad, by the
use of his great art. It is I who am destined to play the fool for my
cause, who have stepped in where angels fear to tread.

In remarking his innocence of the science of debate he meant, I
suppose, to disarm me. Heaven only knows how many weapons
this great showman has neatly hidden in that disarmingly unruffled
suit (which I learned from a recent advertisement in *Esquire* is "all
wool"), how many rabbits, pumpkins, balloons, lizards, dolls, saws,
incenses, stink bombs are neatly tucked away there. One by one he
will bring them out and hurl them against the impregnable virtue of
my position.

I say impregnable because in the end I doubt that the magician
lives who can make the case for the foreign policy of John F.
Kennedy before an American audience. It takes a different audience

to appreciate that case, from a different vantage point. Like a Russian audience.

Now, now, now, let me first of all make plain that I do not consider that Mr. Steve Allen is pro-Communist. Let me go further and say that I consider that any man who suspects him of being pro-Communist is evil or witless. Let me concede (for I know that the subject weighs heavily on Mr. Allen) that he has been treated outrageously by individual members of the so-called right. Let me concede that there are members of what goes by the name of "the right wing" who cherish a great ignorance of the realities. And let me say that some of these men and women, in pursuit of their fantasies, do damage to persons who are subjectively innocent of the offenses they are charged with. Such persons—some of them malicious, some of them misinformed—exist on the right; but so do they exist on the left.

It was a half century ago that [G. K.] Chesterton complained of the allure that so-called "progressive" movements have for (as he put it) "every fruit juice drinker, nudist, sandal wearer, sex maniac, Quaker, pacifist, and feminist in England." He could have retained the list intact to describe many of the current admirers of Mr. Allen's position. There is, as I say, a lot of loose talk going on and California is no doubt the world's principal exporter of it. I remember Mr. Stanley Mosk, California's Attorney General, saying a couple of years ago that the John Birch Society was a collection of "little old ladies in tennis shoes." And now Mr. Mosk has informed a convention of California Democrats that the Republican party is in danger of being taken over by the John Birch Society—raising the question whether he got hit on the head by a tennis shoe or whether he is just scared of little old ladies. But we are not here tonight to talk about eccentrics, we are here to talk about the foreign policy of Mr. Kennedy, and never mind why it appeals to eccentrics. We wish to know, what is worse still, why it appeals to noneccentrics.

In assessing the foreign policy of *any* administration, it is always possible to dwell on a single success or on a single failure and go on to construct an apology or an indictment on the basis of it. Much of what passes for objective evaluation is based on selectivity of this kind. In meditating on liberalism, its foreign policy, and the shambles thereof, I am reminded of the man who, having heard a direful sermon on the subject of the Ten Commandments, walked out of the church alongside his wife, with head bowed, looking neither to right nor to left. Suddenly, approaching his car, his eyes lit up. He turned to his wife jubilantly: "I just remembered—I've never made any graven images!" So a defender of Mr. Kennedy might say that after all, he has not yet turned Washington over to the Communists—at least not *all* of Washington. (Having read last week about the twentieth or so Communist spy caught within the past nine months, I recall morosely Bob Hope's statement on returning this summer from abroad, that "in England there is the best secret service in the world. The trouble is the Russians own it.")

Under the circumstances, in an attempt to avoid polemical selectivity, I shall permit an official spokesman for liberalism no less authoritative than Mr. Lyndon Johnson to select three areas for discussion. "During the campaign of 1964," Mr. Johnson said last October, "this administration will go to the people and defend its foreign policy on the basis of its record in Berlin, Laos, and Cuba."

1. Whence the triumph of Berlin? Because West Berliners are still free? But it does not prove success merely to prove that all is not yet lost. West Berliners are still relatively free, true; but Berlin is a sundered city because President Kennedy, who alone could have prevented it, permitted its division. He had no idea, he told the press early in 1962, that the Soviet Union had been preparing during the preceding July to build a wall through the city. I believe him. (Although as I remarked at the time, it is extraordinary that such large reserves of standby brick and mortar could have escaped the attention even of our CIA.) Even so, the deed was done. Subsequently, the West has stood firm in denying the balance of the city to Mr. Khrushchev, whose appetite for it has sharpened precisely because of the ease with which he had succeeded in planting down the wall.

But whose fortitude is today responsible for the maintenance of a free West Berlin? It is widely known that Mr. Kennedy and his aides sought to discuss with the Russians (under the pressure of the Soviet ultimatum) alternatives to the present arrangements more satisfactory to them. But it is known that Charles de Gaulle flatly refused, for so long as Berlin was being illegally threatened, to participate in any discussion whatsoever over its future. It is generally accepted, in other words, that it was the granitic de Gaulle who provided the stamina on which West Berlin survives. And indeed it is conjectured—and one has no alternative to conjecture when discussing an administration which has developed so effectively the science of news management—that one of the reasons why Mr. de Gaulle has shown an increasing reluctance to rely on American foreign policy is because American foreign policy is not reliable. One is never quite sure whether, at a critical moment in Western affairs, the chiefs-of-staff will make the operative decisions or Mr. Norman Cousins will. Others have leaned on American foreign policy over the years—Poles, Czechs, Chinese, and Tibetans; Cubans and Laotians; and Vietnamese. The crowning pity is that *Americans* have to rely on American foreign policy.

2. The claim that Mr. Johnson can point to *Cuba* as a victory for his foreign policy is a venture in utter audacity. It is as though Mr. Hoover had run for reelection in 1932 on the basis of the raging national prosperity. I have written a great deal about the Cuban disaster and tried to analyze it at some length; and I have spent my rhetoric on the subject. I do not have the stomach to restate the case, any more than some of you have the stomach to hear it. I can only reassert, in the simplest terms, my conviction that our failure to move decisively against Castro continues as the most conspicuous symptom of our degeneracy.

What will bring this administration to save Cuba? Nothing, presumably; unless Castro finds a few Buddhists to persecute. It appears to be safe to say that we *have* no policy as regards Cuba. Our policy toward Cuba is to behave toward it peevishly. We address her, from within our fastness, with the petulance of the prudent man who has been bested in an encounter, dares not risk another, but for vanity's sake needs to keep his tongue stuck out at his adversary. Mr. Kennedy's solemn retaliation against Cuba's importation of the thermonuclear intermediate range missiles was to forbid American tourists to visit Cuba. It was the Cuban admittance of the missiles that was apparently the unfriendly act—not the Russian-manufactured transportation and installation of same, we are to gather from the workings of Mr. Kennedy's foreign policy. After all, we *do* allow American tourists to go to the Soviet

Union (in fact, encourage them to go there); and we do allow our wheat to go to the Soviet Union; but not to Cuba—no sir, no señor, no Mr. Kennedy.

And then, to drive home the dead seriousness of our Cuba policy, Mr. Kennedy devoted a whole speech to the subject of the forthcoming liberation of Cuba before survivors of the Bay of Pigs invasion assembled at the Orange Bowl in Miami, one paragraph of which Mrs. Kennedy spoke in Spanish. Why he was not torn limb from limb by that company of soldiers betrayed, I'll never know. I finally understand the meaning of the *mañana* attitude.

Our policy as regards Cuba will, then, presumably bear fruit (like our so-called policy toward Hungary) on the day when we will have resumed diplomatic relations; as we have for all intents and purposes done under Mr. Kennedy with Hungary. Do not ask what American foreign policy has accomplished in Hungary, or what it is accomplishing in Cuba; to do so would be to disconcert nondebaters. In fact, Hungary yielded nothing. Not freedom for the students of Budapest. Not even freedom for the mortal remains of Imre Nagy,* whose bones the government refuses to return to his family. When Mr. Kennedy's present policy toward Cuba reaches its radiant fruition, i.e., when we agree to give Cuba not only our drugs but *also* our tourists and our wheat, Cuba will still be free to conspire against us, against our people, and against our truths everywhere in the hemisphere by the continued use of guile, subversion, treachery, blasphemy, torture. Ask not what Cuba can do for us, ask what we can do for Cuba.

3. In Laos we triumphed under Mr. Kennedy by refusing, to give aid to the anti-Communist forces who were resisting a coalition government with the neutralists and the pro-Communists.

Here is the background of *that* triumph! In Moscow, Mr. Khrushchev told Mr. Harriman† that if he would bring pressure to

---

*Premier of Hungary from 1953 to 1955, Imre Nagy was an ardent supporter of peasants' interests. A Communist, Nagy called for the neutralization of Hungary, including withdrawal from the Warsaw Pact. He protested the 1956 Soviet invasion of Hungary and was tried and executed by the invaders. [This and all footnotes, unless otherwise noted, have been added by the editors of *But Seriously. . . .*]

†Averell Harriman, an American statesman, was the leading U.S. diplomat in dealings with the USSR during the Cold War.

bear on President Kennedy to consent to the coalition government, he, Khrushchev, would promise to see to it that the Communist and pro-Communist members of the coalition behave; would see to it, presumably, that they cease to be Communists, since nothing short of that would cause them to behave. Intoxicated by that news, Mr. Harriman rushed back to Washington and in a matter of weeks the triumph was consummated.

So taken was the New Frontier by this new mode in diplomacy that in due course Mr. Harriman was bounced back to Moscow, where he got a still further promise from the Soviet government to behave in respect to nuclear testing, whence the derivative triumph of the Treaty of Moscow, the test-ban treaty. Just eight years ago, surveying the Spirit of Geneva proclaimed by President Eisenhower, Mr. Harriman had publicly proclaimed, "Unhappily, at the conference of the Summit, President Eisenhower was quoted as crediting the Russians with no less a desire for peace than that of the West. As a consequence, there occurred a psychological disarmament throughout the free world. It is a tragedy," he concluded, "that the president didn't do something *else*. He did mention, but he did not keep insisting, that Stalin should carry out his wartime agreements, to permit free elections in Poland and Eastern Europe."

But when psychological disarmament is administered by Mr. Harriman himself, in behalf of the Democratic party, it is something else, is it not? It is a triumph. Ask Lyndon Johnson. Ask Steve Allen. Ask a cuckoo clock.

We are living, ladies and gentlemen, in an age when direct communication becomes increasingly difficult. We need to rely increasingly, those of us in any case who care, on a kind of Aesopian prose which at the ordinary level says one thing, but if you listen very, very hard, and if you are truly disposed to hear, is saying something very different. We all know that a political party must defend its record, for such are the iron requirements of partisan politics. But the present administration seeks to defend its record by paying the conventional obeisances to traditional policy, at the same time suggesting, sometimes explicitly, more often subliminally, the necessity for "new approaches," the common factor of which is appeasement.

The policy suggested by George Kennan when he wrote in *For-*

eign Affairs on the necessity for containment we practiced inter-
mittently as for instance at Iran and South Korea under Mr. Truman; and under Mr. Eisenhower at Lebanon and Quemoy. But even
under the rubric of Kennan's policy Czechoslovakia fell; as did
China; as did Tibet and Cuba; as, for all intents and purposes, did
Indonesia and British Guiana. But the policy of containment
remained, nevertheless, as the official paradigm: the policy that
under no circumstances whatever will the Soviet Union be permitted to advance its imperialism over any area not already subjugated
in 1947.

The policy was never inherently sound for the reason that it was
dogmatically *defensive,* and failed to reckon with the advantages
that go to the side that monopolizes the initiative. The policy of
containment is based on repressing the enemy's salients rather than
striking our own. Trotsky told his generals, when on one occasion
they asked him how most profitably to pursue the war against the
capitalist world, that the Soviet high command must constantly
gyrate a finger around the perimeter of the enemy world. "And
where it probes a weakness, *there,*" said Trotsky, "is our salient."

And so the Communists over the years have been operating.
They have not looked alone for military weaknesses in contiguous
geographical areas, though they probed these too; they looked for
weaknesses of *every* kind: weaknesses in our economy; weaknesses
in our race relations; weakness in our system of alliances; weakness
in our internal security; weakness in our military technology; weakness, above all, in our soul. And it is these weaknesses, above all
others, that they have feasted upon; for at the moments of truth in
great battlefronts merely suggested by the place-names Warsaw,
Budapest, Berlin, Peking, it was not a lack of Western power that
proved decisive, but a lack of Western will. Our policy postulated
no salients of our own, even on ascertaining gaping weaknesses in
the enemy:

When she is militarily weak as after the last war, we stand by
and let her acquire nuclear weapons. When she is guilty of a fresh
act of aggression as at Berlin, we close ranks against Tshombe in
Katanga and censure South Africa. When she staggers from a mortal wound as after Budapest, we initiate cultural exchanges. Where
she desires a temporary cessation of certain types of nuclear testing,

we go to Moscow and sign the dotted line. When her agricultural program collapses, we send her wheat.

We permit ourselves only countersalient expressions of life: They fight us in Korea, we fight back in Korea. They fight us in Vietnam, we fight them in Vietnam. They threaten Lebanon, we land troops in Lebanon. They bomb Quemoy, we fortify Quemoy. But now, even that policy of containment seems to be requiring an effort beyond the will of the American government to generate. In the past three years, we tried, because of the forward inertia still left in the old idea, to generate the countersalient in Cuba; but we could not arouse ourselves off the beach. In Laos, instead of countering the offensive decisively, we retreated behind the skirts of neutralism. In Berlin, we did not tear down the wall, but learned instead to live under its humiliating shadow. Again in Cuba, we retreated on our demand to inspect the Russian missile bases.

But meanwhile, the *rhetoric* of defiance, even of liberation, continues as a basso sostenuto throughout our strategic variations. I could not myself, in my most abandoned moments of hope, compose a speech more inspiring to direct action against Castro than Mr. Kennedy's, delivered to the ransomed Cuban prisoners in Miami about three weeks before he cracked down on every Cuban who was subsequently engaged in trying to do something about the liberation of his homeland, i.e., every Cuban who at Miami took Mr. Kennedy at his word. Who would guess that the speech delivered at American University in Washington last June, calling for an end even to *philosophical* differences with the Soviet Union, and that given in August in Berlin calling for victory over the Soviet Union at any cost, had been delivered by the same man?

There is at work against us an assault on the meaning of words, those instruments of civilization by which we communicate with one another and correspond with our governors. Would that we could have a treaty suspending the abuse of rhetoric! The worst enemy of America is the debauchery of language, the loss of whose meaning would deprive us even of the power to express our fear of the abomination of desolation.

"I have sometimes thought," Albert J. Nock wrote in his last years, "that it would be interesting to write an essay on the subject of 'How One Can Tell One Is Living in a Dark Age.' " I have never doubted that George Orwell, writing ten years later, gave Nock the answer when he wrote his incandescent novel about the society whose tablets proclaim that War is Peace, Freedom is Slavery, Ignorance is Strength. The trouble with our foreign policy is less its intrinsic defects than that men of intelligence and good will actually rise to defend it.

Steve Allen: Opening Statement

Good evening conservatives, liberals, and little old ladies in tennis shoes or not. It was apparent to Mr. Buckley and myself as we stood backstage listening to the opening remarks, that this audience tonight was a very special one and that it was absolutely determined to derive enormous emotional satisfaction from whatever might occur on the stage here. I would by no means seek to deny any audience emotional satisfaction; I would simply suggest that we make the attempt to distinguish emotional satisfaction from wisdom, from the accumulation of necessary information. Perhaps I should next point out that I am not officially or unofficially representing the president. I represent only myself. I shall consider my time not wasted this evening (and I direct this remark to my fellow citizens in the conservative camp who are present) if even a few of my ideas succeed in penetrating the screen of your prejudices—the screen of your prejudices and your long-denied hunger for political representation. (Human nature being what it is, I don't object at all to a few cat-calls and boos when I use the word *prejudices,* but I would hope that you would at least grant that we all *have* prejudices.)

Mr. Buckley has just finished demonstrating his skill at polemics. Many of you, especially those in his own camp, are of course familiar with him. But some here are familiar with him only slightly perhaps, or in a general way, so I will take just a moment to tell you something about Mr. Buckley (since doing so may help you put what he tells us this evening in better perspective. And also since he has established, a few minutes ago, precedent for remarks of this kind by references to my tailoring and so forth).

Mr. Buckley, as you have seen, is not only a gifted speaker and writer, but he is also a very courageous man. Indeed he has been courageous enough to do battle in print with the late Pope John

XXIII concerning matters on which the pope was expert, and he was not. And that not once, but repeatedly (going so far on one occasion as to refer to the historically important papal encyclical *Mater et Magistra* as "a venture in triviality"). Now Mr. Buckley, as you have seen, is a wonderfully entertaining man; and we might be tempted to interpret such a statement as indicating nothing more than a "Groucho Marxish" desire to shock. But such is not the case. Mr. Buckley *does* indeed feel that, in the context of the fearful struggle between Western man and the forces of Communism, Pope John's admonitions concerning social justice *were* truly trivial. All of which has led me to compose two limerick paragraphs describing my distinguished opponent:

> There is a young man named Bill Buck-i-ly
> Who debates all the liberals quite pluckily
> When all's said and done,
> It must be just in fun,
> For few are persuaded—quite luckily.
> He selects foes with great impartiality
> Sans regards for race, creed, or nationality,
> But he makes some mistakes,
> And the worst of his breaks
> Was that "venture in—uh—triviality."

Mr. Buckley and I have fortunately nothing worth dueling about; we are not enemies, but friends. And had I any interest in somehow defeating him, as distinguished from merely rubbing our conflicting ideas together in the hope that the sparks might provide some intellectual light, I would certainly never have selected the weapon of formal debate (at which Mr. Buckley is apparently undisputed champion, not only because of his erudition, but because of his uncanny gift for sarcasm, for the creation of political poetry, and a dramatic delivery reminiscent of Lionel Barrymore's). And now to work!

In any debate on foreign policy today, between any conservative and any liberal, the conservative of course has one advantage; and that is that he has nothing practical to defend. Today's conservative has not put a team on the ball-field, whereas the liberals have; and therefore the conservative can point to the mistakes that the liberal team has made. What the liberals *can* do to counter is to say, "Well we see no reason to believe that had your team played the game, it would have played it any better. And there are those who believe it would have played it a good deal worse." But what's important to understand is that there is no way whatsoever to settle that issue. The only method by which the opposing arguments could be logically tested would be to turn back the clock of history and simply live again through the events of the last twenty-five or fifty years, depending on how far back one might want to go, to get a running head start on the difficult problems looming up. That, of course, is fantasy. As regards reality, the issue simply cannot be settled.

I ask you to consider next the very great improbability that any one program, be it conservative, liberal, or what-have-you, is a golden key which would magically open all doors and solve all difficult problems. Now Americans are a practical people—very few of us are philosophers, few of us are artists, few of us are scholars; but many of us are tinkerers and bookkeepers and businessmen. We tend, therefore, to desire solutions that are simple, sensible, and brass tacks. Our popular magazines are full of articles which favor the perpetuation of such attitudes: how to play the piano in ten easy lessons, five rules for personal happiness, seven ways to a successful marriage, and so forth. Quite aside from the fact that such solutions usually do not teach us to play the piano, improve our marriages and our personal lives, there is no question but that the simplistic approach to such a matter as foreign policy brings about little but frustration. The world is so incredibly complex today that it is perhaps a blessing for the average man that he is unable to appreciate the dimensions of its complexity. Perhaps if he really understood how difficult our problems are, he would not be able to sleep at night.

For example, we are currently doing business with 112 other nations, and about forty of them will be changing governments during the coming year—and not all peaceably. The tides of history are sweeping high and fast. We live, indeed, in a time of great danger, but also great challenge. It is no time to listen to voices of pessimism or defeat or empty bluster. Influential right-wing spokesmen, whom I am happy to say Mr. Buckley has personally disallowed, have apparently induced some Americans to believe that by

1972 the Communists plan to take over the United States. Is comment really necessary? Now a conservative gentleman wrote to me some time ago that the foreign policy of the U.S. is or should be "the defeat of Communism." But this is like saying that the Christian religion *is* the salvation of souls. No, the Christian faith is a *means* toward the salvation of souls. The two things, in other words, are distinct, though related.

As regards the ultimate defeat of the forces of Communism, that is the most appealing idea in the world, however interpreted. The foreign policy of the United States *may* or *may not* bring such an ideal to realization, but what is important for us to appreciate is that the two are distinct.

It will be helpful, in attempting to understand what a nation's foreign policy is, if you think of the word "policy" not as suggesting a single sentence stating a lofty aim, but rather in the sense in which it is used in the phrase "insurance policy." An insurance policy, as we know (sometimes to our chagrin!), is quite a lengthy document; and yet it covers particulars that, compared to the conduct of the nation's foreign relations, are simplicity itself. I say this because you are daily being led to believe that Communist advances are explained either chiefly or *solely* because of what American foreign policy is, for better or for worse. And I tell you this is nonsense.

Now I am sure you would agree that the average United States *senator* knows a great deal more about foreign policy than does the average *citizen*; and I imagine that most of you would be as willing to grant that in the Senate, the average member of the committee on Foreign Relations knows *somewhat* more about foreign policy than does the average senator *not* a member of that committee. I solicit your consent on these generalities by way of drawing attention to the following specifics:

In 1958, the Committee on Foreign Relations of the Senate, having realized that its members were experiencing difficulty in getting questions of foreign policy into sharp focus, established a special subcommittee consisting of Senators Green, Fulbright, Wiley, and Hickenlooper, and instructed it to explore the feasibility of an extensive study of our nation's foreign policy. Subsequently the subcommittee reported it was possible to undertake such a

study, which the subcommittee believed would lead to a better
national understanding of international problems. At this point the
members of the subcommittee turned to various private research
organizations by way of assuring that our nation's best minds
would concentrate their creative attentions to the problems at hand.
(The intellectuals employed by these distinguished research organizations are those terrible "eggheads"—commonly referred to so
derisively in the conservative press.)

On January 5, 1959, it was announced that the following studies were being undertaken:

(1) the nature of foreign policy and the role of the United States
in the world; (2) the operational aspects of U.S. foreign policy; (3)
the principal ideological conflicts and their present and potential
impact on foreign policy; (4) worldwide and domestic economic
problems and their impact on foreign policy; (5) foreign policy
implications for the United States of economic and social conditions in lesser-developed and uncommitted countries; (6) possible
developments in military technology, their influence on strategic
doctrine, and the impact of such developments on U.S. foreign policy; (7) possible nonmilitary, scientific developments and their
potential impact on foreign policy; (8) formulation and administration of U.S. foreign policy; (9) U.S. foreign policy in Western
Europe; (10) U.S. foreign policy in the USSR and Eastern Europe;
(11) U.S. foreign policy in the Near East; (12) U.S. foreign policy
in Southeast Asia; (13) U.S. foreign policy in Africa.

Now I suggest that if the members of the United States Senate
who are most conversant with foreign policy problems felt that they
absolutely required this sort of backing in helping them to understand
the difficult area which is *their professional specialty,* it would be
presumptuous for those of us who are less well informed to assume
that all there is to this business of foreign policy is asserting that we
are determined to "defeat the Communists" and then just rolling up
our sleeves and going out and doing it.

Now if there is anything that today's conservatives find annoying, it is the criticism that Senator Goldwater is forever suggesting
simplistic solutions for complex problems; but the conservative
camp had better get ready to feel good and annoyed for many
months to come, because the senator deserves precisely this sort of

criticism. Indeed, the only way he can put a stop to it is to throw overboard his past recommendations and replace them with some that have a lesser burden of belligerence and a greater part of wisdom and originality.

But I am here tonight to make a more important point, and it is that to a certain extent we are almost *all* guilty of Senator Goldwater's sin. The United States has been a long time developing its present sense of international maturity and responsibility. Traditionally we were suspicious and uneasy, as some of us still are, about what we call "foreign entanglements." We had the Atlantic and Pacific to protect us and weak neighbors to the north and south, so we felt secure in our isolation. Isolationism, of course, is not solely indigenous to the American continent. In fact, the very word is a euphemism for one that is more familiar: selfishness. We are then ignorant and selfish, not because we are Americans, but because we are human. It was an Englishman, Neville Chamberlain, speaking on December 26, 1938, who said the British people ought not to be expected to involve themselves in the approaching war because of "a quarrel in a far away country between people of whom we know nothing." That far away country, as you know, was Czechoslovakia.

I wonder if man has now learned the lesson that *there are no longer any far away countries.* Morally, there never were. Morally, we were always supposed to know that we are our brothers' keepers. Morally, those of us who preach the Fatherhood of God should always have known that the brotherhood of man follows logically. But now, what irony! Now, for the most selfish of reasons, we can no longer afford to be selfish.

One of our foreign policy triumphs was the Marshall Plan. The Marshall Plan restored the economic strength of Western Europe after World War II, and this, my friends, was *real* anti-Communism. The kind that not only helped the West, but *hurt actual Communists.* But it was resisted by congressional isolationists, and to this very day Senator Goldwater says that "the foreign aid program has had dire consequences. The foreign aid program is unconstitutional, and is not only ill-considered, but ill-conceived. It has not made the free world stronger," the Senator continued, "it has made America weaker."

After isolationism, I would list *ignorance* as an important cause contributing to our present dilemma. We have belatedly begun to do our international homework but, if I had time this evening, I could tell you some hair-raising stories of American ignorance, in high places and low, concerning the rest of the world and its peoples. Just for a moment, test your own geographical knowledge (and none of us, of course, could score a hundred points on this kind of a test): Could you point to Indonesia on the map? Are you aware that it has a population of 100 million people, the fifth largest in the world? Are you aware that potentially it is the fourth richest nation in the world? If you are . . . good for you.

Next on our list of complicating factors, I would include *the delusion of omnipotence*. This is a very important point: even if we made all the right decisions, the fact remains that we do not run the world. Not only can we not dictate to our enemies or to the neutrals, we cannot even dictate to our allies. The Communist powers *are* loosely united, at least, in working toward their large goal. The free world, on the other hand, is merely a group of rival, individualistic states that even today compete for advantage or prestige just as they did during the long centuries of European history. Now let those who are surprised that the West cannot completely unite to fight Communism remember that even when the nations of Europe were all securely under the banner of Christendom, or indeed even when they all professed allegiance to the one Catholic Church, they were still regularly at each other's throats. This is political reality, and we forget it at our peril.

And now a word in defense of our critics on the right. It is sometimes said that conservatives don't really believe the scare talk they broadcast, to the effect that the Communists are steadily winning the Cold War while we are constantly retreating, failing, and so forth. It is claimed that critics of the administration deliberately distort reality to this extent because they know that if they can alarm enough voters, a change in administrations might take place. But I believe that the critics on the right are completely sincere in their criticism. Sincere, and frequently as wrong as Hell. The way they tell it, the Communists are winning the game all the way, and nothing short of putting in a new coach could save the day. Nonsense. *Certainly* there have been Communist victories, and they are enough to cause us the gravest concern. But there have been hopeful developments too, and we must look at the total picture, not just that part of it that satisfies either our emotional predispositions or our political ambitions. Consider the following:

(1) In Berlin, though the wall is still up (I will be talking later about the suggestion that we break it down), the Russians now know that we cannot be either bluffed or forced out of the city. And the wall, despite its ugliness, is a tremendous propaganda plus for our side. The Communists are no more proud of it than they were of putting down the Hungarian uprising [of 1956]. (2) In the Congo, we stuck with the United Nations, contrary to Senator Goldwater's advice. Order has been restored and Russian desires frustrated. (3) In the Middle East, the Communists have suffered major setbacks during the past year, particularly in Iraq. In Egypt, though the Russians have poured in millions of dollars in aid, they have not reaped a corresponding political influence.* (4) Since the attack on India by Red China, relations between India and the United States are considerably improved. Nehru learned his lesson the hard way, and the result is a gain for our side. (5) In Algeria, which conservatives had told us was lost to the Communists, a government that is socialist, but neutral, has emerged. And our timely foreign aid has helped us win a significant degree of Algerian friendship. (6) In Cuba, Soviet missiles have been withdrawn and so have thousands of Soviet personnel, if not enough. Though Castro is still in power, it costs the Soviet Union a million dollars a day to keep him propped up. He is no longer as popular throughout Latin America as he was a year or two ago, and there are signs that another invasion by Cubans and sympathetic forces may be in the planning stage. (7) Since Hiroshima, the world's spiritual shepherds, philosophers, scientists, and political leaders have pointed out the dangers of approaching nuclear war. Pope Pius XII, for example, called the nuclear arms race "homicidal, suicidal madness." Now, at last, a test-ban treaty has been signed. It is, as President Kennedy has said, only the small first step on a thousand-mile journey to peace; and we don't even know if another step ever will be taken. But the overwhelming majority of the world's peoples rejoice that it has been taken. (8) Mr. Buckley has referred to the Truman Doctrine con-

*This statement was true in late 1963 but Khrushchev's recent visit to Egypt makes it necessary to review the situation in that nation—S. A., June 1964.

tainment policy. I say that though it deals only with the matter of *military* encroachment, it has on the whole accomplished its objective: to convince the Soviets that they would not be permitted to conquer additional territory. We made this clear in Greece and Turkey, and we showed our determination concerning Korea, Formosa, and the offshore islands.

(9) NATO [the North Atlantic Treaty Organization] exists and represents a Western success. In the early postwar years, the Communist parties of Western Europe were very strong and very threatening. Today, they are no more dangerous than they were then.

[*Following a rash of cat-calls and boos from the audience, Mr. Allen made this statement—Ed.*]:

I'm going to interrupt my formal remarks to give you a suggestion. I accepted this debate because, as I pointed out, Bill and I are friends of quite a long time standing, and because I have attempted on a number of occasions to make public the distinction between the respectable conservatives in this country, a number of whom besides Bill are among my personal friends, and the irresponsibles. I think responsible conservative voices are utterly necessary in the present difficult moment, and Mr. Buckley's magazine has done a great deal to distinguish between the intelligent conservatives, and the people (to use Mr. Nixon's phrase) who are described as "the nuts and the kooks." Now any time you get several thousand people in one room, it's inevitable, no matter what they are—they can all be liberals, all be anything—you will inevitably have a few nuts and kooks. But I ask the nuts and kooks here this evening to shut up, not because it is the easiest way in the world to deal with them (since I am by twenty years of professional training equipped to handle hecklers), but because it represents a foolish digression from our central purposes. These debates, the series of debates, are being staged by an organization that I respect and admire, a responsible conservative organization. And their loud-mouth representatives here are doing them no credit. So for your own sake, if you want these next two debates to occur, please conduct yourselves like ladies and gentlemen—those of you who are not.

(10) The transition out of the long period of colonialism, an era which, never let us forget, involved actual slavery, has been made rather more peaceably than the historians may have anticipated.

The angry debate is substantially over, and the new nations now know that our face is not set against them. I shudder to think how the United States would have dealt with the anticolonialist upsurge had a conservative administration been in power.

Now these observations obviously do not give the whole picture, but they are sufficient to establish my point. So, it may be arguable as to how good a senator Mr. Goldwater has been; but it is undeniable that he is a successful businessman. When I lived in Phoenix, Arizona, in the early forties, he was even then successfully running the department store his father had left him. He therefore must know a great deal about bookkeeping; but what sort of foreign policy bookkeeping is it to list *only debts and losses* and pay no attention whatsoever to profits? It may eventually appear this evening that I am debating Senator Goldwater, rather than Mr. Buckley. I plead guilty to that charge; Bill Buckley is a more formidable opponent than the senator. Bill is an intellectual and a skillful debater. Mr. Goldwater, who is a fine man in many respects, is neither. Now let us take up his foreign policy views.

It is the senator who is the leader of the present conservative movement, and one is certainly entitled to take up the question as to what might result in the event he became our president. *National Review* magazine once editorialized as follows: "What Mr. Kennedy has discovered during his first 100 days is that being president and facing up to the Communists is far more difficult than subjugating the Democratic party or impressing the American people." This, of course, is what every modern president has learned and will learn. So Mr. Goldwater would discover first that he faces the same dilemmas faced by Messrs. Truman, Eisenhower, and Kennedy. He would find that it is the easiest thing in the world to criticize from outside the palace gates, but that when one is on the inside, problems that may have appeared simple loom in sharp focus and terrifying complexity.

Because the senator is a completely honest man, I therefore conclude that being president of the United States would be an enormously frustrating and humiliating experience for him, and I'll explain that. Consider the following evidence: he has now for several years, as James Reston of the *New York Times* has observed, entertained the illogical belief that our nation can on the one hand significantly decrease the power of the federal government and greatly reduce the budget, while on the other it can be harder on the Communists all over the world. The senator has been arguing that we should do more with our military power to oppose the expansion of Communist influence. He has recommended blockading Cuba indefinitely, which naturally would mean stopping Russian and perhaps other ships going into Havana. But he has not made clear what he would recommend if the Russians appeared determined to run the blockade, or what he would do if, in retaliation, they began to stop our ships carrying arms to Turkey or some other nation.

Now it's of enormous importance in this connection that the editors of *National Review* have long been calling for, not merely air cover for invasions of Cuba by natives of that island, but outright war and invasion by the United States. The reason this is important is that it is these gentlemen and their colleagues who tell Mr. Goldwater much of what he thinks, since he is himself neither a political philosopher nor a man accustomed to wielding power. There is yet additional inconsistency in his attitude toward the nuclear weapons dilemma: he asserts he does not want to see the uncontrolled spread of nuclear weapons, but on the other hand, he is against the administration's disarmament, arms control, and nuclear testing recommendations.

Next item: he approves of any actions that would tend to introduce wedges into the Communist bloc, any ventures that would tend to pit one Communist nation against the other—as for example, Russia against China. But on the other hand, he has said "we should withdraw diplomatic recognition from all Communist governments, including that of the Soviet Union." And these are not merely isolated instances. The senator is opposed to Communist expansion into the newly emerging nations, but he voted *against* the Mutual Security Act in 1960 and is, as you have seen, hostile to almost all forms of foreign aid. It's no wonder then that the senator's overall political program has been termed by Mr. Reston "a fantastic catalogue of contradictions."

Senator Goldwater is forever calling for, to use his own words, "total victory over Communism." But he has not made clear precisely what he *means* by "total victory," nor how he would achieve it if he did know exactly what it meant. The idea, however defined, is, as I say, unassailable. Certainly no American in his right mind would say he is opposed to total victory over Communism. But concentration on victory in these terms can mislead us into supposing that the day such victory was achieved would usher in a new millennium of prosperity and happiness. Unfortunately, if Communism were to disappear from the face of the earth this evening, tomorrow would still bring us an intricate array of problems. After all, the last two world wars ended in total victory, but they did not bring worldwide peace, prosperity, or social justice. Now does the senator contemplate achieving his total victory by a nuclear attack on the Soviet Union? If the answer is yes (and I don't believe for a moment that it is), then I say whosoever does recommend such a course of action is a madman. If the answer is no, then I am sure we would all appreciate it if the senator would say as much aloud, as soon as possible. Does the senator contemplate achieving total victory over Communism by conventional war? I rather doubt this, too; but here again I wish he would answer yes or no soon to the simple proposition.

There are millions who look forward with happy anticipation to the day when Senator Goldwater might be our commander in chief. And all of us have a right to know if on the day he is sworn into office, he plans to involve this nation in war, nuclear or conventional, with the Communist third of the world. If the senator has no such intentions, which would seem to be the case, then we return to the question, What on earth does he mean by the phrase "total victory over Communism"? Now if I may offer the senator a helpful suggestion, I would recommend that he consider that the word "victory" has more than one meaning, and that there is one interpretation of it which is in accord with the dictates of our national security, common sense, and morality. I refer to the two relevant definitions as the prize-fighting and the horse-racing definitions. Victory can be achieved in a horse race and it can be achieved in the boxing ring. If the senator believes it is possible, given the present military realities, to defeat the forces of Communism the way one prize fighter defeats another, by slugging him to the floor, then he has a great deal of explaining to do. But if he simply means that in the race between two rival ideologies we will win that race by finishing well ahead of the Communists, then he is being rational. (Unfortunately, he is not being very original since such victory is exactly what our present leadership is already striving to accomplish.)

Now conservatives assert that we must adopt an *offensive* strategy that is, as Mr. Bozell has written, "every bit as serious about liberating Communist territory as the Communists are about enslaving ours." Well, *where is* this offensive strategy? What are its particulars? It's occurred to me that one reason right-wing alternatives so often deal with wishful generalities rather than specifics is that on the rare occasions when practical suggestions are vouchsafed, they are so often seen as hollow bombast. Mr. Buckley has already told us (and *National Review* has been specific on this point) about the Berlin Wall. The solution: *break down the wall!* All right, let's think about that. This, of course, would be accomplished by an invasion of the Soviet sector of Berlin, since the wall is on that side of the boundary, you understand. Now are the Russians going to stand idly by and permit our tanks to roll in? Obviously not; they are going to shoot back. Reinforcements will be rushed up by both sides. Indeed, they will have already been moved up since our side would have had to prepare for the attack, while the Russian and German Communists will have observed our own build up (Berlin you understand being an *island inside Communist territory*) and will have matched or bettered it. Now has *National Review* magazine consulted the Berliners and Germans to see if *they* want war, at best tragic and at worst nuclear? Perhaps Mr. Goldwater's advisors have not thought matters through quite that far.

It may interest conservatives, in this connection, to know that I sometimes indulge in the creation of dramas in which I imagine myself in my opponent's shoes. Were I to picture myself in the position of Mr. Buckley, I might recommend for example the following—just to run it up the flagpole as they say: that the United States do everything in its power to eliminate nuclear weapons from the armories of the world, since all authorities agree that a full-scale nuclear war would simply result in mutual suicide for the engaged nations. And that on the very day the last A-bombs and H-bombs are dismantled, we initiate war with the Soviet Union and Communist China with *conventional* weapons. I think that to do so would be only slightly lesser folly than to become engaged in a nuclear war, but in any event there would be a certain consistency to such a policy and the acts flowing from it. Now to suppose that we could march across the vast face of the Asiatic mainland, mowing the enormous Chinese and Russian armies before us like wheat, is to suppose a great deal indeed. But at least we would be able to tell ourselves that we were engaging in this peculiar enterprise in an attempt to *liberate* Communist territory. Whereas when we recommend nuclear war—on China, on the Soviet Union—what we are talking about in terms of reality is not the *liberation* of the long-suffering Russian and Chinese peoples, but their *incineration.* And when dealing with words like incineration, of course, one thinks of the tragic gap between the word—it comes easily out of the mouth—and the reality it is intended to convey.

I am no more afraid of death than is Mr. Buckley; it comes to us all, as he pointed out to us recently in an editorial. But I should not want to commit either murder or suicide.

William F. Buckley, Jr.: Rebuttal

Mr. Allen presumably thought, at the beginning of his remarks, to rob me of the possibility of any authority in what I have to say by saying, that after all, so rash am I that I oppose *the pope himself!* Having read the autobiography of Mr. Allen, I was not aware that he respected the pope's opinion on theological matters, let alone political matters. I suppose it deserves to get said, for the record (which record Mr. Allen did not see fit to introduce into the context of his remarks) that *National Review* is not a Catholic magazine. It is a magazine whose leadership I share with Protestants and with Jews and in point of fact with atheists. And it was our collective judgment, *not* that the pope needs not to be taken seriously in the course of evaluating his encyclicals, but that in point of fact an encyclical issued to a waiting world in 1961 which sought to address itself to the major aspirations of the world and did not once *mention* the subject of Communism, would in the future, as we put it, *by some* be considered to be a venture in triviality. We were, of course, correct.

Obviously, for instance, it would be considered a venture in triviality by Cubans (who were much less interested in whether or not there should be agricultural subsidies than they were in the question whether or not Mass could be celebrated in Havana). And under the circumstances, I think it a pity that Mr. Allen sought to invoke the majesty of the pope, for purposes highly tendentious, in an effort to show that the position adopted by myself and my colleagues is essentially irresponsible. This happens, have you noticed, to be the essence of his general charge. He manages, with wonderful geniality (which I so much admire and which I would like sometime to emulate), simultaneously to get inside the "democratic vibrations" between himself and the crowd, and also to condescend.

In effect, his argument tonight is based on experts. He is here, in effect, to say to us that, as a result of all of his reading, of all of his meditation on the subject, he understands our primitive impulses! But that the subject of foreign policy is of such an elusive complexity that we cannot begin to hope to understand it, that after all it is fit only for study by whomever is undertaking to do thirteen reports for a subcommittee of the Foreign Relations Committee of the United States Senate. We cannot cope with these problems, Mr. Allen says, simply by focusing our mere minds on the problems and coining such empty phrases as, "We want victory over Communism," coining such phrases presumably as, "Give me liberty, or give me death," coining such phrases as, for instance, that "We take these truths to be self-evident," which in fact tended to represent the moving force of American idealism at every critical juncture of American history . . . if Mr. Allen's point is as simple as this, and I *shudder* to think that it is, if it is as simple as to say that we cannot by a *mere act of will* cause the Soviet Union to go away, then let us instantly concede that point.

But if he wishes us, in effect, to say that as a result of the fact that we have not sat in on the deliberations between Senators Green and Fulbright and Wayne Morse on the Senate Foreign Relations Committee, we are not therefore equipped to understand the fact that Cuban freedom cannot be restored; that it was *absolutely* necessary for us to back Sukarno* against those people in West Irian

---

*An Indonesian politician, Sukarno obtained independence from the Netherlands for his country in 1949. Although he achieved gains in health and education, his regime (which he called "Guided Democracy") was marked by corruption and extravagance.

who wanted freedom; that it was *absolutely* necessary for us to send wheat to the Soviet Union when they asked for it; *absolutely* necessary for us to go right *to* the Bay of Pigs and then withdraw from it, then let me tell him something which will entitle him to think the worst of me. In all frankness, *I* would sooner (judging from the performances of the senators in question) have our foreign policy written by the Marx Brothers.

What *especially* struck me about the performance of Mr. Steve Allen was that he attempted, with his customary finesse, to lay tablet upon tablet in order to create the overarching structure on which he will repose his argument and his final conclusions. But the only thing that he said *effectively* tonight was "Shut up!" And when he did, he cut through, in my judgment quite properly, to something that needed to be said; because Mr. Steve Allen is here as a gentleman to share his platform with me, to do his best—as I am here to do my best—to present a competing point of view. And he was entitled to demand courtesy as a minor reciprocity for his kindness in coming. But all of a sudden, he took direct action. He didn't suggest to the moderator that this be referred to a committee in order to consider the psychological complexities involved.

I hasten to say that my own admiration of the penetrative power of the will and tenacity of Mr. Steve Allen is extraordinary. I sat as his guest two or three days ago at his studio and saw him with the most extraordinary equanimity, simultaneously in the course of one hour and a half without being ruffled in the least, preside over a show at which one woman wanted to show that she was the greatest bubble gum blower in the world, another three girls wanted to demonstrate that they had developed a new Twist in Chicago, Mr. Oleg Cassini wanted (within the bounds of what is permitted by the FCC) to demonstrate new foundation garments, and Mr. Steve Allen undertook to fly like a batman on roller skates while pushed by a wind machine. A man who can schedule shows of *that* character four nights a week is hardly a man to be stayed by complexity (unless for some reason it has to do with foreign relations).

Let me repeat: the *besetting sin* of modern intellectuals, of which Mr. Allen is an unfortunate example, is ambiguity. What has happened in effect in our time, is that the nation has become convulsed as a result of its collision with certain philosophical trends which rob us of a sense of identity, and rob us of a sense of purpose, and rob us of *any idea that we are actually engaged in something that is worth doing for its own sake.* One has only to read the autobiography of Mr. Steve Allen to see how tormented he is by the groaning paradoxes of our time. And there is no question at all but that the kind of ambiguity that is represented in the deliberations of men like George Kennan, and men like Adlai Stevenson, and men like Professor Barghoorn (who has just returned from Soviet Russia) reflect this failure in America to come to grips with the essential question: namely, *Is this society worth defending at whatever is the necessary cost?*

It is perfectly easy to go to the library at Harvard University and look under "China, why it fell," and see two hundred volumes why it was "absolutely necessary" that it should go. By the same token, there will be apologies written for the "necessity" of the fall of South Vietnam when that happens, of Laos when that happens, and the rest of it. And what has recently come (which causes Mr. Allen—who is primarily, philosophically ambiguous—great concern) is what he calls the "oversimplicity" of Mr. Goldwater; because Mr. Goldwater says that he wants victory over the Soviet Union. How, says he—incidentally rhetorically—is he going to accomplish this? Well, it is very carefully spelled out in 370 pages in a book by Mr. Goldwater that apparently Mr. Steve Allen would rather ridicule than read. But to the extent that he is alarmed by the prospect of a person who seeks the presidency and who has no "program" for achieving victory over the Soviet Union, I recommend that book to him.

Now, actually, I think that the formulation "victory over the Soviet Union" is the improper one; it should rather be to "neutralize the Soviet threat"—because Mr. Allen is quite correct in suggesting that it is going to be impossible to have "victory over Communism" for so long as, hypothetically, a single person wishes to become a Communist. He is right in suggesting that such is the complexity of human nature and such the venality of so many human beings, that it is impossible to go out and wage the kind of mission that was attempted by, for instance, Woodrow Wilson (a great philosophical mentor of Mr. Allen) when he set out to make the world safe for democracy. No, we want, pending the successful completion of the objectives of the "Committee to Abolish Original

Sin," not to convert all people from Communism, but to make it impossible for them to shatter our peace, to shatter our freedom. And it is the crowning responsibility—for which they shall have (I hope) to answer to a divine tribunal—it is the crowning blame of the liberal leadership of the past twelve or fifteen years that they may have made it possible for the enemy to have accumulated the power to "end (as Mr. Steve Allen puts it) life on this continent." No, the "complexity" is not the problem.

Mr. Allen, for instance, hasn't said what kind of "complexity" it was that caused Mr. Kennedy suddenly to draw back at the Bay of Pigs. Was it because he had read only twelve out of the thirteen projected studies of the Senate committee, and under the circumstances felt that he was not equipped to proceed with the operation? No, it was rather that fatal ambiguity which unfortunately is fed by people like Mr. Allen and his friends who are constantly talking about the apocalyptic horrors of nuclear war without understanding the essential realism of American foreign policy: which is, that it *rests* on the necessity for strength and the necessity for purpose. And that in the absence of the union of those two imperative qualities in our foreign policy, we will continue to lose our Cubas; we will continue to be humiliated in Berlin; we will continue to be surprised in India; we will continue to fail in Southeast Asia; we will continue to succumb to the drab, pusillanimous servilities of the Committee for a Sane Nuclear Policy.

And at *that,* simple though it is by contrast with the way Mr. Allen describes it, it is more complex than sometimes he assumes. Do you, he says rhetorically, know where Indonesia is? And you answer "Yes." He is transparently bowled over, and might in fact be bowled over by your answer to the questions:

Is there any rational reason for a Cuban to have any faith in American foreign policy?

Is there any rational reason for an Eastern European to have any faith in American foreign policy?

Or is there any rational reason for a Southeast Asian to have any faith in American foreign policy?

And, in fact, is there any rational reason to believe that in his entire eloquent but meandering statement Mr. Steve Allen made any kind of defense of our miserable policy of the last three years?

Steve Allen: Rebuttal

Mr. Buckley has seen fit to imply that one who is not a Catholic
cannot respect the social and moral commentaries of the pope. In
doing so he has offended first against logic, since the simple fact of
the matter is that I do. And he has offended secondly against charity. I would like to think that this is uncharacteristic of him. I was
moderately dismayed that Mr. Buckley would introduce a note of
that sort into the exchange, but more so by his apparent willingness
to appropriate to himself (and to his political counterparts) the Constitution of the United States, the American flag, and Almighty
God. I had been under the impression until that moment that we all
held these in common. My blood races at the same rate as Mr.
Buckley's at phrases such as "We take these truths to be self-evident," such phrases as "Give me liberty, or give me death." And I
stand shoulder to shoulder with him in absolutely insisting that this
society and our way of life is worth defending at all costs. And
therefore I am entitled to resent his inferences to the contrary.

   Now as I have suggested, there are two ways, generally speaking, of looking at the subject matter of this evening's discussion.
One question, which we've already taken up, is: how good is what
might loosely be described (since this thing does go back, you
know) as the Truman-Eisenhower-Kennedy foreign policy—how
good has it been? The other question is: how good is the foreign
policy with which today's conservatives would replace our present
policies? We must, I'm sure Mr. Buckley would agree, deal with
both these questions. For if you do nothing more than criticize our
present foreign policy, you're going only half way, if that. The most
effective political criticism, unfortunately, is almost always vague.
If the voters respond favorably to your emotional tone, if you tell
them often enough to throw the rascals out, they may well usher
you into office (even if they do not clearly know the nature of the
beast that you recommend they mount).

   I told you earlier that conservatives are invariably annoyed, if
not infuriated, by references to Goldwater's simplistic approach to
complex problems. And if the point is not particularly important
coming from me, perhaps you will not mind my quoting Mr. John
Foster Dulles, who wrote this: "Those who are most positive about

political problems are able to be positive only because they do not know all the relevant facts. There are no longer any simple problems," Mr. Dulles said, "nor any easy solutions." But I do not mean to suggest that either Mr. Goldwater or Mr. Buckley have failed to give us *any* specific alternatives. They indeed have, which Mr. Buckley has brought to your attention. Let's take up, therefore, some of these particulars.

Contrary to what some of their more hot-headed followers suppose, many responsible conservatives share with liberals the opinion that one of the primary objectives of American foreign policy must be the *prevention* of nuclear war. Neither conservatives nor liberal leaders, however, have maintained that nuclear war must be avoided at all costs. Now let's get this very straight! If the Soviet Union this evening were to present us with the strictly limited choice between nuclear war and surrender, the response, as everyone knows perfectly well, would be to decide in favor of war—which is why the Soviet Union will present us with no such choice. Therefore, many conservatives and liberals conclude, we must develop techniques necessary to counter Communist aggression within the context of the present nuclear stalemate. Now you might suppose that a favorite right-wing alternative would be the one recommended by General Maxwell Taylor (among others), that we prepare for limited or nonnuclear war. But surprisingly enough, this is not acceptable to the right, according to M. Stanton Evans, writing in *National Review,* January 29, 1963: "Confronted by our atomic arsenal," he says, "the Soviets are not likely to send their armies marching across borders. In the assumed condition of nuclear deadlock, the more probable form of aggression is 'sublimated'—guerrilla action, the capture of nationalist movements, subversion." And, no doubt feeling under pressure to be specific, Mr. Evans spelled out the required counter measures: the helicopter airlift of troops and strategic village tactics employed in South Vietnam. Well now, it is immediately apparent Mr. Evans has led us down the garden path which has curved full circle, for these are precisely the tactics already being employed by armed forces operating under a commander in chief who is a member of the hated liberal establishment.

Do not suppose, by the way, that spokesmen of the right feel the least bit comfortable in the arena of mutual nuclear deterrents. For this situation, Mr. Evans and his colleagues tell us, does not deter the Communists; it deters only us. "We are prevented," he says, "from bombing north of the Yalu River or helping Hungarian freedom fighters because such action might 'touch off a nuclear holocaust.' The Communists," he continues, "are not prevented from subverting Laos or the Congo or Cuba." Now, Mr. Evans is confusing us, possibly because he is confused himself. Let's see if I can make this clear to you. He opposes an entity identified as "we" on the one hand, to an entity identified as "the Communists" on the other. So let us try to identify the "we," and try to identify "the Communists." By "we" he means the armed forces of the United States. But it's not so easy to determine what he means when he says "the Communists." He cannot possibly mean the armed forces of the Soviet Union, since Russian troops have *not* been responsible for subverting Laos, or Cuba, or the Congo, or Vietnam. No, unfortunately the Communists we are talking about (damn the complexity of it all!) are a combination of native Communists and foreign revolutionaries. It's therefore nonsense to pretend that there is some sort of balanced choice between the activities of the United States Army on the one hand, and, for example, the peasant supporters of Fidel Castro on the other. Now when we speak in large generalizations about those we call (a) the Communists, and (b) the armed forces of the Soviet Union, we must get it through our heads that the two, though obviously related, are distinct entities.

To give but one example of the ways in which failure to make this basic distinction confuses us, consider the right-wing argument one sometimes hears to the effect that though a nuclear war would be an ultimate horror (which no one denies), at least by wiping the Soviet Union off the map—or at the very least destroying the bulk of its armed forces—we would thereby put an end to Communism. Would that it were so. But the claim is absurd. To begin with, Communism is essentially an *idea*—perhaps the most evil idea the mind of man has ever conceived. It exists, unfortunately, in the minds of millions of people who are not Russian at all. So what would actually happen, in the full-scale nuclear war that some critics of the administration are able calmly to contemplate, is not the destruction of Communism but (a) the destruction of the Soviet Union (with, remember, its largely innocent and non-Communist populations), and (b) the destruction of the United States (after which isolated Communist infection spots all over the world would be able to breed and flourish anew, feeding on the chaos of war and having no longer to worry about the retaliatory power—military, economic, or moral—of the United States). And such belligerent nonsense, if you please, is invariably considered by those who are forever demanding an *offensive* strategy.

Such particulars of strategy are indeed offensive: offensive to common sense, offensive to the Judaeo-Christian moral tradition, offensive to human dignity, and offensive to our national security.

It's been brought to your attention this evening that I am affiliated with the National Committee for a Sane Nuclear Policy, an organization which has devoted its efforts chiefly to informing the American people of the realities and implications of the nuclear arms race. For some reason, our conservative brethren seem to be infuriated when we point out that full-scale nuclear war is immoral; and that it would result in widespread death and suffering today, and untold genetic tragedy for the unhappy generations to come. Now this is important: these assertions are never denied, they are *never* denied; it's just that they make the warhawks squirm uncomfortably. Very well, gentlemen, if you will not listen to SANE, will you listen to General David M. Shoup, Commandant of the United States Marines, who has predicted time and again that a full-scale nuclear war will cause 700 to 800 million deaths? He correctly points out, by the way (and this is a fascinating point to be considered by, first of all, every man—with special interest to our southern conservatives), that the great majority of these deaths would be suffered by members of the white race, and therefore concludes that for all practical purposes, the white race would be finished on this planet by a nuclear war of such a magnitude. So, when it comes to planning with such matters, we may not really be dealing so much with "policy" as with lunacy and absurdity.

Or again, gentlemen, if you will not listen to SANE, will you listen to Pope John XXIII, who has said the following:

> It is with deep sorrow that we note the enormous stocks of armaments that have been and still are being made in more economi-

cally developed countries, with a vast outlay of intellectual and economic resources. And so it happens that while the people of these countries are loaded with heavy burdens, other countries as a result are deprived of the collaboration they need in order to make economic and social progress. The production of arms is allegedly justified on the grounds that in present day conditions, peace cannot be preserved without an equal balance of armaments. And so, if one country increases its armaments, others feel the need to do the same. And if one country is equipped with nuclear weapons, other countries must produce their own, equally destructive. People live in constant fear, lest the storm that every moment threatens should break upon them with dreadful violence; and with good reason, for the arms of war are ready at hand. It cannot be denied that the conflagration may be set off by some uncontrollable and unexpected chance. It is to be feared that the mere continuance of nuclear tests, undertaken with war in mind, will have fatal consequences for life on earth. Justice then, right reason and humanity urgently demand that the arms race should cease, that the stockpiles which exist in various countries should be reduced equally and simultaneously by the parties concerned, that *nuclear weapons should be banned,* and that a general agreement should eventually be reached, about progressive disarmament and an effective method of control. In the words of Pius XII, our predecessor of happy memory, "The calamity of a world war, with the economic and social ruin and the moral excesses and dissolution that accompany it, must not be permitted to envelop the human race for a third time."

That's the end of the pope's statement.

Another point which I wish to make very clear is that the National Committee for a Sane Nuclear Policy does *not* recommend unilateral nuclear disarmament. It supports the longstanding, *American* principle of phased mutual disarmament controlled by inspection. I personally see very little likelihood of greater progress being made at the present time. (And this, of course, is an enormously complicated area, fraught with—as Mr. Buckley has pointed out—ambiguities and dangers. But the general outlines of a sound policy are distinguishable.)

Lastly, if you will not listen to SANE, will you listen to General of the Army, Douglas MacArthur, who has written:

The tremendous evolution of nuclear and other potentials of destruction has suddenly taken the problem of war away from its primary consideration as a moral and spiritual question and brought it abreast of scientific realism. It is no longer an ethical question to be pondered solely by learned philosophers and ecclesiastics, but a hard core one, for the decision of the masses whose survival is the issue. Many will tell you, with mockery and ridicule, that the abolition of war can only be a dream, that it is but the vague imagining of a visionary. But we must go on toward the goal of peace or we will go under.

Now, just quickly, a few words on *Cuba*. Conservatives tell us daily that the administration (and it was Republican, remember) and the State Department were remiss, to say the least, in not recognizing Fidel Castro for the Marxist that he eventually proved to be. Concerning this, a number of things need to be said.

First, the mistake about Castro was made by practically our entire people. Mr. Buckley might blame the *New York Times,* but all of us have to share some of that blame, I believe.

Second, the CIA (which until this evening I was not aware was a liberal organization) must have been party to the error.

Third, there was available, evidently, information about Castro's Marxist background in his college days, but this could have proved nothing about his present sympathies (for the reason that many a man who was a college Communist leaves the party when he becomes better informed and more mature). Some of Mr. Buckley's best friends, as the saying goes, are former Communists. There were, it seems reasonable to assume, a few who raised their voices from the very first to call Castro a Communist. Unfortunately, some of these voices had cried "wolf" too long to be taken seriously. Those who later told us that Dwight and Milton Eisenhower and John Foster Dulles and Charles de Gaulle, among others, were Communists can scarcely suppose that such credentials establish their rating as reliable political prophets.

Fourth, the most important point of all, the crime of those Americans who were taken in by Castro assumes somewhat smaller proportions when we consider that many of the Cuban freedom fighters, who now live in Florida, were once Castro's staunchest supporters and right-hand men. They were with him all the way, in the mountains, in the villages; and their suspicions were not aroused. Now, it seems to me that there is definite evidence of hypocrisy in the conservative criticism of Fidel Castro on the grounds that he turned out to be a Marxist. For such criticism implies that if he had not been a Marxist, but only a liberal agrarian reformer, then conservatives would have joined the American majority in welcoming him. Nothing could be further from the truth! Conservatives were against him, *whatever* he was, simply because he proposed to do something about the disgraceful economic injustice under which the Cuban people had suffered for so many years. His right-wing critics were actually *overjoyed* when it became possible to accurately describe him as a Communist.

Now, criticism of the fact that we did not provide air cover for the Bay of Pigs invasion force labors under the invalid assumption that the invasion would have been a certain success if air cover had been provided. I know of no evidence to substantiate this. While I would be every bit as gratified as Mr. Buckley would if Fidel Castro would suddenly disappear in a puff of smoke, I am nevertheless forced to take into consideration that a great many Cubans, unhappily, still support Fidel Castro. And even more supported him two years ago when the invasion attempt occurred. It was comparatively easy to overthrow Batista because he was a widely despised tyrant and murderer, corrupt in both his personal and political capacity. His power came from the machine guns of his army and from the cordial support of the United States. But Fidel Castro came to power on a wave of the most enthusiastic popular support. That his revolution has in many respects gone sour is apparent to the proverbial six-year-old child. We don't need any conservative advice to tell us that! But, evidently many Cubans still consider themselves better off than they were formerly and so are content to go along with the present regime. It may well be, therefore, that those who hope for a popular anti-Castro uprising in Cuba are deluding themselves. I very much hope not, but it would be presumptuous of me to assert that my hopes necessarily reflect the political realities.

All the real experts on Latin America agree that Castro is merely a symptom of the dread economic disease that afflicts Latin American nations. It can scarcely be maintained by any fair-minded man that a system whereby the overwhelming majority of the people are poverty-stricken and a tiny minority are incredibly wealthy is just one. But as far as Senator Goldwater can see, the answer to Fidel Castro is not American support for a profound democratic social revolution, but rather the mere rolling up of sleeves and the landing of American troops in Cuba.

Steve Allen: Conclusion

Conservatives are entirely correct in pointing out that liberals have made mistakes, but the reason is not that they are liberals but that they are human beings. Conservatives over the years have made their share of mistakes, and if fewer have been observable it's simply because they have less frequently held positions of power. One example: in the issue of *National Review,* December 3, 1960, the editors complimented themselves on the fact that in November of that year, the magazine had published a special supplement, edited by James Burnham, in which eight of the world's leading geopoliticians detailed why no split between Russia and Red China was likely, though liberal commentators had long pointed to the possibility. Now if eight of the world's leading geopoliticians were wrong about this (as they obviously were), then it is small wonder that we lesser mortals are from time to time mistaken.

Those who would light the torch of war now are not only closing their own minds to future possibilities: they would take it upon themselves to deny the rest of us the right to live out the human adventure in all its constructive potential. Asserting our right to the simple continuing projection of human history would seem to involve making the barest minimum demand, but there are a few among us who seem to question even that right. Now our conservative advisers frequently tell us that we ought not to give military or economic assistance to nations that are not fervently committed to the side of freedom, as Mr. Nixon has put it. At first glance there might seem to be some merit to this idea, but when it's applied to actual cases, one realizes again the danger of naive approaches to complicated, sophisticated problems.

A basic question here, of course, is exactly what countries are meant when we refer to nations that are not "firmly committed to the side of freedom" (and do we really mean freedom or only anti-Communism?). Now, if we're talking about, say, Yugoslavia or Poland, the issue may be at least relatively unambiguous. But if we are referring to the uncommitted nations, then the advice of our conservative brethren may be dangerous because it could mean cutting off aid to neutral countries from whom we could eventually work some advantage.

And what of the Western nations of today's world that are firmly committed to one degree of socialization or another? Conservatives tell us that socialism is slavery, that it is flatly opposed to freedom. Therefore, according to conservative logic, the Scandinavian nations, for example, are not firmly committed to the side of freedom. Would Mr. Goldwater perhaps eventually go so far as to refuse to engage in political dialogue with them too?

Or let us be dramatic and suppose that the argument between China and the Soviet Union eventually leads to an outbreak of hostilities between the two powers—there's no immediate prospect of that happening but we don't know what the future will bring (at the end of this century half the people on this planet will be Chinese). Now would we then be willing to give military aid to one side or another? We damn well might, for it might serve our own interests. After all, during the Second World War we gave an enormous amount of military equipment to the Soviet Union, despite the deep mutual distrust between the two nations, simply because we knew that the business at hand was the defeat of the Nazi and Fascist powers.

Now our conservative critics have every right to be dismayed, as is every intelligent human being, by the threat that Communism poses to the world. But they have no right to suppose or insinuate that our leaders are secretly sympathetic to Communism, or that they are totally uninformed about the realities of the situation, or that they lack courage.

I must say, in conclusion, that I see something enormously comic—as well as tragic—about a man with Mr. Goldwater's intellectual credentials in effect telling Walter Lippmann* or President

---

*A Pulitzer Prize-winning American journalist, Walter Lippmann served as assistant to the secretary of war and took part in the Paris Peace Conference of 1918–1919.

Kennedy or Dean Rusk or Senator Fulbright that they just don't understand the business of conducting foreign relations. Now when right-wing foreign policy alternatives are distilled to their essence, we find that they consist of exactly two substances: one involves our committing acts of war, and the other involves simply quitting (childishly walking off the field, ending foreign aid, abandoning the United Nations, withdrawing our representatives from any nation that displeases us and sulking in the corner while the march of history sweeps past us). Both alternatives—and I use the word with the utmost precision—are *un-American.* The United States has always been a peaceful nation, though its people are mighty when attacked. And the American people have never been quitters; nor, I am confident, will they be now.

William F. Buckley, Jr.: Conclusion

For the record, I want to get this pope stuff straight. I did *not* imply that someone who is not a Catholic should not respect a statement of the pope, unless "respecting a statement of the pope"—which is something Catholics do because they feel the distinct possibility that a statement from the pope may under certain circumstances have God as its provenance—means simply discovering in it a similarity to one's own, pre-established political views. For instance, when the socialist *Manchester Guardian* proclaimed the arrival of a new socialist pope on earth at the moment when *Mater et Magistra* was promulgated, it seemed to me anomalous that the editors of the *Manchester Guardian* were showing such deep reverence for the wisdom of a man who is after all the chief figure in a religion which said editors believe, most of them, to be merely the dregs of religious superstition. I don't mind at all Mr. Steve Allen quoting popes when he wants to. But I do wish he would quote more representative statements of them. The popes are, of course, and have proved themselves consistently to be, the most implacable enemies of Communism that exist on this earth. It was Pope Pius XII, whom Mr. Allen refers to as of "blessed memory," who said that anyone who cooperated with the Communists in any enterprise whatsoever was excommunicated from the Catholic Church.

Now having got through *that,* let me just say that Mr. Allen's confusion is not unique. That is to say, that although he is here (as he has told us twice) representing himself only, his confusion is a shared confusion. And under the circumstances he does belong intimately to the fraternity of foreign policy makers which we are here to examine tonight.

I do not know how it is possible to correct or to try to amplify to a man whose idea of Cuba is as is Mr. Allen's idea of Cuba; who, for instance, will tell you that the reason why Communism exists in Cuba is as a sort of reaction to the days of Batista, when in point of fact, despicable though Batista was, he in fact did preside over a country in which there was dissent, in which there was freedom of opposition in the press, in which occasionally there were elections, in which in fact the economic standard of life was high. And there is no doubt in my mind that 98 percent of the Cuban people today, if given the horrible choice between Castro and Batista, would instantly choose Batista. Cuba was, under Batista, the second richest country per capita in Latin America and this included the people and not merely the gamblers, "most of whom were American exploiters," and the rest of it. Let's not turn this into a question of "Ought we all to despise Batista?" My credentials go back rather earlier than those of the left wing, whose hero he was, you may remember, for many years before they decided that he had betrayed them in 1957.

Now, how can one discuss these matters with a man so confused? A man who says of Algeria that Algeria is merely a "kind of socialist state"—and more or less implies that Suzanne Labin (a socialist) and Sidney Hook (a socialist) would not find very much to quarrel with contemporary Algeria about. (Suzanne Labin and Sidney Hook endorse most fervently the anti-Communist foreign policy described over the years in *National Review,* I am proud to say.) How can one edge forward to an understanding of what is going on when Mr. Steve Allen simply refuses to acknowledge that something of great dramatic moment happened at the Bay of Pigs, when a liberation movement that had been planned was suddenly withdrawn. He insists that, after all, everybody, or more or less everybody, in the Sane Nuclear Policy Committee is absolutely agreed on the proposition that if necessary we will use a nuclear force in order to prevent the takeover of the world by the Soviet

Union. But he is absolutely and flatly wrong. One third, for instance, of the student body of Harvard University has said in a recent poll (*one-third*) that they would sooner surrender to the Soviet Union than fight a nuclear war; and a substantial portion of that third belongs to the Committee for a Sane Nuclear Policy. I was there at Hunter College when I saw young girls embracing each other, expecting not to see themselves again the next day, because Mr. Kennedy had just gone on the air giving an ultimatum to the Soviet Union to withdraw its missiles from Cuba.

Such is the kind of emotional confusion that it represents, in my judgment, a syndrome. The reason why the Committee for a Sane Nuclear Policy (though it may not in some of its crystallizations be shown to be ambiguous on the point of "Give me liberty or give me death") is a mischievous force in American affairs—the kind of force that is always there, incapacitating and paralyzing the executive department of this country—is because it is obsessed with the idea of the bomb. I once debated with Mr. Norman Cousins on foreign policy and he spent the first fifteen minutes describing graphically, as Mr. Steve Allen has done in fewer minutes, the terrible ravages of the bomb if one fell here, how far would it spread over, how many people would it kill, and so on. . . . I remember that my mind tended to wander after absolutely establishing that the hottest blast, if it fell on the Battery, would reach to the *New York Times* building. But the kind of obsessiveness with the bomb, the kind of willingness to believe that it was the "economic misery of Cuba that caused Castro," the kind of willingness to believe that the United Nations is a *deus ex machina, that* is what in fact incapacitates not only Mr. Allen but the president of the United States from wooing effective policy.

Says he, how dare we, in effect (referring to his original theme), criticize men like Rusk, men like Lippmann, men like Fulbright? Mr. Lippmann was back there applauding Mussolini thirty years ago, in the early stages of his punditry, and telling us we had nothing whatever to fear from Hitler. Rusk was telling us in 1951 that the time had probably come to recognize that we couldn't hang on to the offshore islands. Mr. Fulbright has compiled an obstinate record of derelictions which are very hard even, I should think, for *Mrs.* Fulbright to defend, let alone Mr. Allen.

So what we do have is a syndrome, and I conclude by simply stating one simple thing: if we cannot yet recognize a foreign policy, which over a period of fifteen years has resulted in the Soviet Union's accumulating the strength to destroy us, all at the will of a single individual, then we have not begun to learn the necessity for reexamining our premises and doing something before it is too late.

What Are We Laughing At?

The following essay was written at the request of the editors of the 1970 *Compton Yearbook.*

We are by now accustomed to the idea that in the fields of science and technology more has been learned in the past 50 years than in all the previous ages of human history and that, of all the scientists who have ever lived, over 80% are active today. Because each new discovery makes others possible, not only is knowledge accumulating in greater supply than ever before, but—what is more startling—the very pace of progress is also constantly accelerating. Predictions of future achievements therefore are risky and will probably prove to have been wide of the mark, most likely far below it.

To a degree the same evolutionary process is discernible in the arts, including humor. Certainly it is true that the sheer volume of humor produced in the last half century—essays, light verse, jokes, cartoons, comedy presented in films, radio, and television—far outweighs everything created during earlier periods of man's history.

And, of all the professional humorists and comedians, those alive at the present moment must far outnumber the always thin ranks of funnymen of ages past.

It does not automatically follow in the arts as in the sciences, however, that quantitative progress will also entail qualitative improvement. There are many more painters today than in earlier times, but few if any who put Rembrandt van Rijn, Leonardo da Vinci, or Michelangelo to shame. As to whether today's best comedians surpass the wits of former years it is difficult to say. Comparing Jules Feiffer to Mark Twain, or Bill Cosby to Will Rogers, may be as impossible of resolution as are the endless arguments as to whether John L. Sullivan could have defeated Joe Louis or whether Jack Dempsey was a better fighter than Cassius Clay.

The Phenomenon of Humor

To understand the humor of the 1970's—or, for that matter, the humor of the 16th century—one must, of course, first grasp the phenomenon itself. This is no easy task.

There are simple dictionary definitions of words such as "humor" and "comedy," but they are not truly instructive. Most are incomplete; others are rewordings of things we already sense intuitively. The philosopher Aristotle defined the ridiculous as that which is incongruous but does not represent actual pain or danger. Had there been many vulgar wits in the Athens, Greece, of his day, presumably one would have told Aristotle that incongruity not related to danger is by no means *always* amusing. An all-embracing definition of humor has been attempted by many philosophers but no entirely satisfactory formula has yet been devised. Aristotle's definition is consistent with the theory that much humor is based on a frustrated expectation, but he reported another concept, derived from Plato, which states that the pleasure of laughter grows out of a sense of the misfortune of others and a sudden awareness of self-superiority in that we ourselves are not in the predicament observed. The two theories are obviously mutually exclusive. Laughter, being essentially an emotional response, appears in too many varieties to be adequately encompassed by any one definition.

Another common theory claims that laughter originated in the vindictive shout of triumph to which early man gave vent at the moment of victory over an enemy. In our daily experience we are all familiar with laughter that has an essentially sadistic undercurrent. One of today's most popular comedians, Don Rickles, employs almost no other form of humor; his popularity may, in fact, reveal something about the present mood in the United States. The fact that Rickles offstage is a decent and cordial fellow is, of course, irrelevant to an understanding of his professional style—his barbed humor draws a consistently favorable response from audiences.

Then, there is another laughter, the innocent laughter of young children. It is the sheer, gleeful, silly, having-a-good-time laughter, to which even sober adults will occasionally succumb.

There is also a familiar theory—which I believe does go far to throw light upon, if not actually explain, the origins of humor—that holds that the funniest individuals, and the most amusing social groups, are those which have known a tragic history. It is difficult to determine how much weight to attribute to the hypothesis since there is apparently no ethnic or tribal group that has not known its share of tragedy. But presumably there is a connection between the tragic theme of Jewish history and the fact that most of our leading humorists, comedians, gag writers, and wits are Jewish. (The list includes Jack Benny, Groucho Marx, Sid Caesar, Milton Berle, Jack Carter, Victor Borge, Jan Murray, Red Buttons, Jack E. Leonard, Jackie Mason, Phil Silvers, Joey Bishop, Lou Holtz, Sam Levenson, Woody Allen, Jerry Lewis, Henry Morgan, Paul Winchell, Phil Foster, Myron Cohen, Ben Blue, Abe Burrows, Irwin Corey, Buddy Hackett, Shecky Green, Alan King, George Burns, Charlie Chaplin, Mel Brooks, Danny Kaye, Jerry Lester, Larry Storch, Bill Dana, Louis Nye, Sid Gould, Dayton Allen, Henny Youngman, Shelley Berman, Mort Sahl, and David Steinberg.)

Another factor explaining Jewish wit and humor is that the Jews have historically been a literate, scholarly people with a respect for the subtleties of language and sophistication of thought. But if these elements explain Jewish humor, how does one account for the recent emergence in the American culture of a vigorous Negro comedy? Tragedy is no stranger to North American blacks, but they have not enjoyed—either in their original African home-land or in their U.S. environment—the benefits of that education which the Jews developed for themselves over the centuries. The apparent paradox evaporates when we consider the differences between Jewish and Negro humor. There is still little highly literate black humor in the United States; rather the vigorous comedy of today's black wits rises up out of the streets and ghettos, at best from the emerging Negro middle class.

The humor of the American Negro is not a new phenomenon, of course; it has merely been hidden underground heretofore, along with black emotional states generally. Largely because of the lack of civilization among whites, Negro comedians of past years were limited to playing Uncle Tom-ish, lazy, smiling, shuffling menials. The humor with which Negroes amused each other had elements of satire, bitterness, sarcasm, and even self-deprecation that were rarely if ever revealed to the white man. But in either form, humor for the American black was an important emotional outlet—as, for that matter, it is for all men. To look purposely for the element of humor in an uncomfortable situation is to make use of an important procedure in emotional control, in the maintenance of one's own mental health. The commonplace observation that we laugh because we are too embarrassed to cry may be amended to include the truth that we sometimes joke and laugh because we do not wish to fight.

Until recently American Negroes had not been permitted to advance to the point of social evolution from which the develop-ment of literate, outspoken comedians could be expected of their culture. Restless, reluctant submission to dominant authorities, combined with the inevitable yearning for freedom, can be a pow-erful mainspring supplying energy to those who have the mysteri-ous comic gift. It is only to be expected, therefore, that so many young Negro comedians are presently emerging in the entertain-ment world of the United States.

The Demand for More Freedom

To understand the current revolutionary aspect of American com-edy we must consider it in relation to the increased demands—on the part of the young, the alienated, the black, and the rebellious—for more "freedom." It is not difficult to see that when the American Negro, in 1970, demands freedom, he has specifics in mind: the freedom to send his children to certain schools, the freedom to move into certain neighborhoods, the freedom to compete for certain jobs, the freedom to vote for candidates truly of his choice. But it is less clear what the word "freedom" means in the mouths of some young radical whites.

As for the youthful Marxists, the puzzle is particularly acute in that, if they had their way, they would lead us into a societal form that even they concede would be much less free than the one we presently enjoy. Of the non-Marxist young, some may wish to be free to smoke marihuana, to be free of the military draft, to be free to grow long hair. One can take time here to observe only that their freedom in these areas is increasingly less restricted. It is against this cultural background that more freedom is being granted to comedians who appeal primarily to the young, and inferentially to American comedians and humorists generally.

As the decade of the 1960's moved to a close, the two television programs best dramatizing the new freedom were The Smothers Brothers Comedy Hour and Rowan and Martin's Laugh-In. Both programs, though well produced and successful, may have been substitutes for those forms of comic entertainment the rebellious young might have devised had they been fully able to dictate their wishes to the television network. As regards Dan Rowan and Dick Martin of Laugh-In, they must have been surprised by their sudden appeal to a youthful audience after many years of success in nightclubs. They had appealed primarily to the Las Vegas (Nev.) habitués who enjoy Danny Thomas, Sammy Davis, Jr., Dean Martin, Frank Sinatra, Buddy Hackett, Milton Berle, and other entertainers whose popularity lies almost entirely with the over-35 crowd. Only within the framework of Laugh-In did Rowan and Martin become attractive to the chronologically or psychologically young and even here it is possible that the most youthful members of that enjoyable program's viewing audience attached their personal loyalties more to the program's supporting players than to its stars.

As regards the Smothers Brothers, it is odd that they became known as specialists in social satire. Tom and Dick were members of my television show family in 1962, by which time it was apparent that essentially they were not political or social satirists. It would be more nearly correct to say that political and social satire were eventually presented on their series for the Columbia Broadcasting System (CBS). Their personal specialty is the marvelously winning routine they present standing alone on the stage developing humor out of a musical context, with Tom singing his dumb songs and Dick trying to talk some sense into him. Both brothers nevertheless deserve credit for their strong social conscience, a sense that it is proper to employ the power of television to affect society in the ways that their progressive orientation suggests to them that it ought to be affected, and a willingness to use their program as a platform from which to advance modern ideas and attitudes. Consequently their comedy hour was generally of high quality and frequently presented points of view that seemed daring in terms of what television humor generally had been during the preceding 20 years.

The new climate of freedom for television humor brought about two kinds of material formerly presented rarely on the medium: (a) off-color humor and (b) social commentary and satire. The first category grew partly out of the nightclub tradition and partly out of the mysterious unconscious of man, generally self-repressed, but of late given voice because of the new permissiveness. Since presumably no one would urge unlimited freedom for television humorists, the question presents itself as to what forms of restraint would be most appropriate to the new occasion. Anarchism has an appeal considered as an ideal, but in practice invariably it seems to prove unsuitable for the human race—as it presently behaves or is likely to behave in the immediately foreseeable future. Self-restraint alone, therefore, can scarcely be considered the answer. Those comedians whose primary experience is acquired in nightclubs invariably develop a certain insensitivity to standards of taste appropriate to television, there being enormous differences in the audiences for the two media. This is particularly true for nightclub comedians, whose most dependable response derives from their most vulgar material. Since it is a rare entertainer who will willingly sacrifice the funniest parts of his presentation when working in television, if instructed only by his own conscience, it follows that a degree of censorship must be imposed, either by network officials or—which is preferable—by the production staff of the program involved.

Network officials, in any event, are scarcely a reliable barometer of taste since their own views are affected largely by a given program's ratings. This was first dramatized by Arthur Godfrey, who, during the days of his great radio and television success in the early 1950's, frequently resorted to surprisingly vulgar material but was nevertheless permitted to go his way uninhibited because CBS officials were unwilling to risk the enormous profits his programs brought in. Fifteen years later the Smothers Brothers were generally immune from network interference until their ratings began to falter, after which it became only a question of time as to which of the contending forces would finally prevail.

It is not enough merely to disapprove of vulgarity and obscenity; it is important to understand them. Both forms of communication have a psychological function, whether in an individual or in a society. Where is the most vulgar and obscene humor encountered? It is found precisely in those social contexts characterized by sexual frustration or deprivation: in prisons, military barracks, fraternity houses, boarding schools—wherever people are unable to enjoy free access to company of the opposite sex. What is odd about the present cultural situation, however, is that vulgarity is more common just at the time when freedom of expression is being greatly expanded.

It is possible to detect a difference between the vulgarity a 20-year-old will engage in and that which preoccupies an older man. An obscene joke told by a 45-year-old—assuming the individual's general mental health—may express a momentary outburst against conservative self-repression, but obscenity of the sort exemplified in the tribal-love rock musical 'Hair' seems more a matter of wishing to shock, to challenge the established order. The nudity, sexuality, and vulgarity of such shows are not employed for erotic purposes but rather as gestures of impudent defiance. The question is related to one of the points of origin of formal comedy, in the theater of ancient Athens, when the art grew out of religious exercises celebrating Dionysus, the carefree god of pleasure.

Matters of definition aside, almost all of us are illogical when it comes to humor. Consider the example of the *Reader's Digest,* a conservative, establishment-oriented periodical, which has for many years published off-color jokes about brassieres, girdles, toilets, breasts, and other things, the joking about which would seem inconsistent with the magazine's philosophical orientation.

Since there is today a greater receptivity of television audiences to social satire dealing with delicate issues such as the Vietnam conflict, race relations, birth control, abortion, political reaction, the free-enterprise system, and religion, the humorist is in a more secure defensive position when he demands greater freedom than when he asks only to be vulgar. My own view is that the willingness of television audiences to permit the broadcast of the newer jokes and sketches is perhaps less than has generally been assumed. Just because a given program has a high rating does not logically establish that those watching it approve of all they see. Humor has indeed swung gradually to the political left during the past five years, and presumably will continue in the same direction during the 1970's, but it is too early to assess what the ultimate popular response will be. At the moment all that can be said safely is that the audience that is pleased by the liberal tendency is the youthful audience—apparently now in the numerical, if not yet influential, majority—which traditionally has been more progressive or radical than the establishment or the less imaginative middle class.

The Reactionary Response

But a powerful countermovement to the leftward swing of the social pendulum began to make itself felt as the 1960's drew to a close, as the millions of presidential votes cast for George Wallace in 1968 made clear. Out-and-out conservatives, or less principled reactionaries, are probably no more numerous now, relatively speaking, than at any other point during the past quarter century, but of late they are making many converts in the lower middle class, which traditionally had identified itself with the laboring man and the rights of immigrant minorities. The Italian, Polish, Irish, and German crowds who violently attacked nonviolent freedom marchers in Northern cities during the late 1960's added strength to the reactionary groundswell. It is safe to say that recent undisciplined outbreaks by radical representatives of the New Left, Students for a Democratic Society, Black Panthers, and other revolutionary groups aroused far more popular fervor for conservatives than for their own far leftist causes.

If it were possible for the political amalgam of red-neck, reactionary-conservative forces to have its own humor—its own equivalent of a Smothers Brothers Comedy Hour, Laugh-In, or What's It All About, World?—it is probable that the networks would be willing to strike such a balance. The fact is that such a thing is impossible. The American right absolutely loathes the new humor, but its resentment is compounded in that it is incapable, by definition, of putting a counterforce into the field. The reasons are neither specifically American nor political; they are ancient, historic, and psychological. Creative, artistic people—in most historic instances—have generally been found to the left of center of the political spectrum. The eye of the artist, the social critic, the humorist, intuitively perceives certain realities behind political facades some time before they become apparent to the masses. What the artist has to say, therefore—be he composer, dramatist, or poet—will frequently be unpalatable to the powers that be. The overwhelming majority of American entertainers are at the very least affiliated with the Democratic party, their social sympathies incline to the left rather than the right. American conservatives—since there can apparently be no such thing as a right-wing Lenny Bruce, a reactionary Mort Sahl, a Birch Society Woody Allen—must content themselves with the amiable, traditional sort of folk humor they derive from The Beverly Hillbillies, Gomer Pyle, Mayberry RFD, or Green Acres. Such programs are actually *non*political, but at least they do not trespass upon the ancient verities or question middle-class American prejudices.

The heightened interest in popular humor today then is at least partly a matter of serious reactionary response to what many viewers regard as unseemly license on the part of some comedians. Behind much of the present demand for censorship—if not out-and-out banishment of the offenders—is an ignorance concerning the nature of the raw material out of which comedy is constructed. That raw material is tragedy. Consider the content of most jokes, which generally concern how stupid people are, how intoxicated they were last night, how high they got on marihuana, how broke they are, how sexually frustrated, how sinful, how lazy, how cross-eyed, how deaf, how ill, how embarrassed, how trapped by circumstances. It is therefore absurd to assume that there can be such a thing as subject matter totally off limits to the humorist or comedian.

Certain areas are, to a degree, forbidden to the television humorist, but, as the current excesses make clear, this is not the case for American humor generally. Lenny Bruce, Mike Nichols, Elaine May, Mort Sahl, Dick Gregory, Pat Paulsen, the Smothers Brothers, and David Frye, among others, have had much to say that was pithy and penetrating. That they could not say all of it on television is not attributable to a prohibitive government nor to narrow-minded network executives, but simply to the fact that a considerable percentage of the U.S. television audience is made up of small children and others who do not wish to be exposed to humor that will offend or shock. But the unfettered word can still be spoken in nightclubs, coffeehouses, motion-picture and legitimate theaters, college concert halls, and record albums, and written in the medium of print— all proof that we live in a relatively free society. The humorist cannot function fully under dictators like Adolf Hitler, Joseph Stalin, Mao Tse-tung, Fidel Castro, Rafael Trujillo, or Francisco Franco— something that American comedians given to moments of paranoia sometimes neglect to remember or to appreciate.

The New Humor

The primary difference between the humor of the 1970's and that of half a century before is that today's humorous material is largely *performed,* whereas in the old days it was designed to be *read.* In the 1920's the humorist saw himself as continuing the tradition of comic literature, following in the steps of Mark Twain, Artemus Ward, or Josh Billings. He hoped to produce funny books, magazine articles, or short articles, or perhaps write a column for a newspaper. The tradition gave rise to such great humorists as George Ade, Irvin S. Cobb, Stephen Leacock, Robert Benchley, S. J. Perelman, Frank Sullivan, Corey Ford, Don Marquis, Ring Lardner, and James Thurber. It was the mushrooming popularity of radio toward the close of the 1930's that produced a change in the styles of American humor. Young men who discovered within themselves an ability to create jokes and sketches began to dream, not of writing the great American comic novel, but of becoming rich devising— however anonymously—jokes for Eddie Cantor, Jack Benny, Bob Hope, Burns and Allen, and other popular comedians of the period. As a result, the mainstream of American humor flowed out of the realm of literature and into the business of assembly-line jokes. Some of the individual witticisms produced were quite the equal of epigrams conceived by the earlier humorists, but the totality of the new work, because it was mass-produced, was for the most part briefly enjoyed and then discarded like yesterday's newspaper.

Another cultural influence that has produced a change in American humor was the long change from vaudeville—via radio and motion pictures—to television. In the 1920's a fledgling funnyman started in obscure theaters—usually doing something other than comedy to get his foot in the door (juggling, rope twirling, dancing, singing)—and then spent years in relative obscurity perfecting his craft, meanwhile looking forward to becoming a vaudeville head-liner or moving to the stage in a legitimate Broadway theater.

Today's young comedians, on the other hand, are relatively handicapped in that, since the training ground of vaudeville is no more, they are obliged to acquire their early experience in small nightclubs and coffeehouses. They enjoy one enormous advantage that the old-timers never had, however, in that today's young people have grown up in a culture almost constantly brainwashed by mass-produced humor. Literally all of his life, today's 25-year-old comic has known as a constant companion in his home the dominant television comedians and wits: Sid Caesar, Jackie Gleason, Milton Berle, Groucho Marx, George Burns, Lucille Ball, Martha Raye, Jerry Lewis, Red Skelton, Jack Benny Phil Silvers, Ernie Kovacs, yours truly, and others.

But if television, because of its size and appetite, has created its own supply of young wits and given them opportunity, it has also presented them with the dramatic problem of an accelerated, tele-scoped professional history. The successful comedian of vaude-ville, radio, and motion pictures could generally count on a long career. But a television series can be enormously popular one year and forgotten the next, because networks continue to broadcast only those programs that receive high ratings. Consider the misfortune that befell such gifted and amusing professionals as George Gobel, Red Buttons, Wally Cox, Herb Shriner, Danny Kaye, Fred Allen, Bob Newhart, Ernie Kovacs, and more recently the brilliant Jonathan Winters and Don Rickles as well. Each of these comedians was as funny the day he received the back of television's hand as on the moment he originally appeared on the scene with brass bands and firecrackers. It was the public that changed.

The modern professional comedian must contend with another difficulty which troubles few other professionals, in that every citizen considers himself a lay expert on an art form at which few are, in fact, essentially qualified. Neither brain surgeons, plumbers, television repairmen, nor income-tax experts receive an appreciable amount of critical advice from those outside their fields. We may complain about the prices they charge us, but we do not regard ourselves as qualified to take issue with them. In contrast, we all apparently consider ourselves expert on the subject of comedy.

Lastly, in commenting on the "new humor" one must observe that much of it appears new only to the very young. Older readers and viewers often recognize the sources from which some of the present generation of comedians and writers derive certain of their ideas.

"Sock it to me, baby" was not originated by Laugh-In but was a common phrase in the Negro and music-oriented culture of the 1940's. "Here come de judge" goes back to Negro vaudeville comic Pigmeat Markham in the 1930's. Certain of Laugh-In's comic devices were borrowed from Peter Sellers and Ernie Kovacs. The program's most frequently employed comic construction, the lightning-quick series of cartoonlike sight gags (originally called Crazy Shots), was first introduced to television in 1954 on the National Broadcasting Company's Tonight show—a point Laugh-In's producer George Schlatter cheerfully concedes.

Youth and Tomorrow's Humor

Nevertheless, Laugh-In's creators deserve credit for perceiving that the communications explosion had created a new breed of young

Americans whose attention spans were apparently shorter than those of earlier generations reared in more leisurely environments. Although those over 45 could still savor a three-minute story by Danny Thomas, a long, slow "take" by Jack Benny, or a "slow burn" by Jackie Gleason, the new 10-to-20 age group wanted, and could absorb, rapid-fire jokes, loud rock music, and dazzling images—all at once.

One of the still-puzzling questions about the emerging humor of the 1970's concerns the almost complete lack of creative participation in that humor by the hippie or underground, beat, bohemian culture. Reading the underground press, one finds that the funniest contribution is the work of Jules Feiffer, who—though a gifted, progressive, and perceptive humorist—is very much a member of the over-35, button-down-shirt, responsible-citizen category. It is fascinating that the youthful street rebels are almost never purposely, professionally funny. The hippie world has produced some lively journalism, innovative art, freshly vigorous music, and interesting social philosophy, but its contribution to formal, marketable humor is minimal. Perhaps the rest of us require the services of professional humorists because our lives are so essentially serious, if not tragic. It may be that in living a more carefree existence, avoiding rather than coping with troublesome responsibilities, today's more bohemian young people do not have the emotional need for the escape valve that humor apparently represents to a generally more puritanical society. Young comedy writers and comedians are being produced in goodly supply, but those young people who have the true comic gift generally disdain the pot-smoking, long-haired, barefooted way of life.

The Courage of Conviction

Some years ago Phillip L. Berman wrote to a number of people in public life soliciting a brief statement of their basic beliefs. I dictated a few observations and sent them to Mr. Berman. At that point he wrote requesting that I revise my statement so as to include reference to one or more instances in which what I believed and/or assumed had been reflected in my work. Hence the references to the PBS television series "Meeting of Minds."

Steve Allen (b. 1921)

"TV's Renaissance Man" is one of the terms often used to describe the multi-talented Steve Allen. At one moment he can be blurting out a hilarious off-the-cuff one-liner; at another he can be decrying the plight of the downtrodden. His lucid and open mind enables him to move easily from the most complex subjects to zany comedy. He uses it like a mine on a twenty-four-hour-a-day digging schedule, finding ideas literally awake or asleep. Always ready to extract them, he has small tape recorders everywhere: in his pock-

From *The Courage of Conviction,* edited by Phillip L. Berman (New York: Dodd Mead, 1985).

ets, by his bed, in his car. This system supplies the raw material for the numerous Allen activities.

It is sometimes difficult to get the man in focus. He is, for example, a television comedian of thirty-five years' standing who has written a scholarly treatise on migratory farm labor, a volume on white-collar crime, and a study on China. The actor who has starred in plays and films is the same man whose poems have appeared in the *Atlantic Monthly* and *Saturday Review.* Steve Allen, the composer of more than six thousand songs, is the same man who is the author of forty-eight published books.

In 1977, the Public Broadcasting System presented the first season of Allen's "ultimate talk show": the award-winning series "Meeting of Minds." Created, written, and hosted by Allen, the witty and wise programs (as well as their book versions) brought together famed historical personages for stimulating conversations.

When asked how he can turn from comedy to the serious problems of life, he responds, "I was a human being and a citizen before I was a comedian. And it is in those primary capacities that I take an interest in important social questions."

* * *

Much of my professional and private activity during the last thirty-five years has been motivated by the awareness—dim at first, but coming gradually into sharper focus—that there is no natural justice in the universe. There is justice in the conduct of our affairs, though not nearly enough of it, but such as it is, it is all created by human beings.

To state this truth in even simpler terms, life is unfair. I first felt this in a personal sense because I enjoyed far more than my proper share of good fortune. My health has been generally good, my fellow creatures have, for the most part, treated me very kindly, my work has been generously received, and I have been well compensated for my efforts. But all about me there are thousands I see—and distant millions I shall never see—who enjoy no such luck. Some are doomed physically at the moment of conception by genetic accident. Others are injured while in the womb. Still others are crippled while undergoing the process of birth. Millions more are struck by injury, disease, or death while still young. And always, all about us are the poor, the very old, the ill, the brain-damaged, the insane, the blind, the hungry, the countless hordes who suffer in places where the heat is crushing or the cold painful. Much of their suffering is caused by no human agency, though humans, by such institutionalized forms of cruelty as war and terror, add greatly to it.

I consider it foolish to believe that such tragedies are imposed by a vengeful deity. Such beliefs are an insult to God, rather than a way of paying proper respect to Him. And if portions of the more ancient Scriptures assert—as they do—that God is bent on bloody revenge and violence, so much the worse for the Scriptures.

But if all this is so, then every human is obliged to oppose it. Every one of us is absolutely required to do what pitifully little we, as individuals, can to set the scales of justice in better balance. This means, in part, that insofar as we are able to control our actions, we ought never to harm another human being, which conforms to Cardinal Newman's definition of a gentleman.

It is easy enough to recommend ideals, whether of modern or ancient creation, but some of us, observing that ideals are rarely achieved, proceed to the error of considering them worthless. Such an error is greatly harmful. True North cannot be reached either, since it is an abstraction, but it is of enormous importance, as all the world's travelers can attest. Even though we shall never be perfectly virtuous, we should still strive to be more virtuous. Even though we can never be perfectly courageous, we should strive to be more so. Even though we cannot be faultlessly compassionate, we should persevere as far on the road to that ideal as our moral frailties permit.

Another common error in thinking about morality concerns the timeless question as to whether there is an all-knowing, all-loving, all-powerful God. This, of course, is the inconsistent triad referred to in philosophy. Affirm any one, and it holds that one or the other divine attributes is false or limited. The question itself, obviously, has never been resolved to the satisfaction of the world jury, nor is it the case that only virtuous people believe in the deity and only sinful individuals do not. Most of the world's crimes are committed by people who accept the existence of God. But some, the faith of their childhood having been weakened, assume that if there is no personal, conscious God, there is no particular reason for persisting in our efforts to lead moral lives.

Dostoevsky, for example, believed that if there is no God then anything is permitted. He was mistaken. The debate on the point need not be continued in the abstract for we have evidence of two of the largest societies of all time—those of the Soviet Union and China—which are officially atheistic. Despite their widespread assumption of the nonexistence of a personal God, we observe that it is simply not the case that everything is permitted in these two nations. But the truth goes farther than that, for, in fact, much less is permitted than in societies that are free and largely democratic.

In any event, if there is a God, holding all power, then He can certainly do a great deal to increase virtue and diminish suffering in the world. But if there is no God, or His power is limited, then the entire task is up to human beings. And even if God does exist, it should be clear by now, after hundreds of thousands of years, that he is quite content to leave the necessary work of improvement to his human agents. The deity has never yet miraculously introduced into the human drama a hospital, orphanage, convent, church, synagogue, temple, cancer research institute, or any other helpful social institution. He leaves that to the more compassionate of his creatures. May their tribe increase!

I believe in mystery, not in any dark-shadows-and-incense way, but as a matter of fact. The world seems to me absolutely based on mystery. The three most important philosophical questions—those concerning God, Time, and Space—remain questions, which is to say no answer to them has ever been proposed that convinces all interested parties. Each has, or seems to have, aspects of either–or-ness. The difficulty arises from the fact that these three pairs of alternatives, the six individual answers, are essentially preposterous, so much so that it is easy to think of objections to them.

For example, if there is no God then we are left with a profound puzzle as to how the fantastically massive and intricate machinery of the universe came to exist. But if there is a God, a thousand and one troubling questions at once present themselves, since the vale of tears in which we live is hardly consistent with the premise of an all-loving, all-knowing, all-wise creator with his eye on every sparrow. In reality, all sparrows suffer and die. The creatures of nature survive largely by eating each other alive.

As for Time, either it began one morning, say, at 9:27—which is obviously ridiculous—or it never began, which appears equally ridiculous.

As for Space, either one can go out to the end of it—which is absurd—or it has no end, which is equally absurd.

It is possible to do what millions have done, with varying degrees of satisfaction: accept one prepackaged philosophy or another and try to live by its precepts. A few individuals, over the centuries, have led edifying and productive lives by such means. But all the saints who ever lived could convene in one meeting hall of modest dimensions. And no philosophy, sadly, has all the answers. No matter how assured we may be about certain aspects of our belief, there are always painful inconsistencies, exceptions, and contradictions. This is as true in religion as it is in politics, and is self-evident to all except fanatics and the naive.

As for the fanatics, whose number is legion in our time, we might be advised to leave them to heaven. They will not, unfortunately, do us the same courtesy. They attack us and each other, and whatever their protestations to peaceful intent, the bloody record of history makes clear that they are easily disposed to resort to the sword.

My own belief in God, then, is just that—a matter of belief, not of knowledge. My respect for Jesus Christ arises from the fact that He seems to have been the most virtuous inhabitant of Planet Earth. But even well-educated Christians are frustrated in their thirst for certainty about the beloved figure of Jesus because of the undeniable ambiguity of the scriptural record. Such ambiguity is not apparent to children or fanatics, but every recognized Bible scholar is perfectly aware of it. Some Christians, alas, resort to formal lying to obscure such reality.

But if we are forever doomed to a state of less-than-perfect knowledge, if many of our beliefs are, in fact, only assumptions, none of this justifies a resort to either anarchy or apathy. Just as we say, in the context of modern science, that it is not necessary to reinvent the wheel, it is equally not necessary to reinvent or redis-cover the classic ideals. The greatest minds of the ages have concentrated their attentions on such questions. The tragedy is that most of us go to our graves without ever having been exposed, however fleetingly, to the wisdom of the philosophers, saints, and seers around whose heads at least some helpful illumination has shone.

Having said all this, I should certainly not want to give the impression that I am an especially virtuous individual. I am, in fact, more impressed by my failings, ignorance, and sins than my pitifully few moral achievements. I can, nevertheless, refer to a few instances when I have practiced what I preached. One was the creation of the twenty-four programs of the "Meeting of Minds" television series, which a critic has called the ultimate TV talk show, whose guests were such as Thomas Aquinas, St. Augustine, Martin Luther, Socrates, Plato, Aristotle, Francis Bacon, Adam Smith, Mohandas Gandhi, Susan B. Anthony, Florence Nightingale, and Thomas Jefferson. Such individuals' ideas and labors have greatly influenced our world. I thought that by expressing their views in conversational form I could provide an example of the sort of rational and informed dialogue that is in lamentably short supply in the modern world, except among scholars. Even though these visitors from the past were misguided in many of their views—as in the cases of Karl Marx, Machiavelli, the Marquis de Sade, or Attila the Hun—I felt it was necessary to become familiar with their teachings simply because they are still so influential in the world.

Because I had long argued that our society should undertake a formal commitment to reason, and nurture a respect for wisdom rather than attaching so much credit to blind belief, I wrote and produced a record album for children called *How To Think* (distributed by the *Gifted Children Newsletter*), as well as the thinking game, *Strange Bedfellows* (with educator Robert Allen).

I hoped, by those practical examples, as well as a good many lectures and published articles, to suggest the primacy of intellect and the moral sense. Man was not, after all, put on this earth primarily to buy philosophical merchandise before examining it, just as he was not put here to turn out hit record albums, or to be utterly irresistible to the opposite sex, to use cocaine, or to wear the tightest possible jeans.

From lecture platforms and in personal contacts, and even in speaking on television, I have taken every opportunity to defend rationality and to discourage the idea that it can be achieved with a minimum of effort.

We should not be deluded that all that is needed is a return to good old-fashioned common sense. While no one would deny the shortage of common sense, we need more than that.

I have tried to be specific in encouraging respect for reason, by pointing out, for example, the crucial difference between conclusive and consistent evidence. Consistent evidence argues only that we are still on the right track. Conclusive evidence shows we have reached the terminal of that particular track.

I have also attempted to arouse educators and parents to add a fourth "R" to our formal process of early education. The four would be readin', 'ritin', 'rithmetic, and reasoning. It might be objected that you cannot introduce a six-year-old child to logical thinking of a subtle and sophisticated nature. Indeed you cannot. By the same token you cannot introduce a six-year-old child to calculus or advanced geometry. But no one ever uses that fact to argue that we ought not introduce young children to arithmetic.

As I argued in *Beloved Son,* a book about my son Brian and the subject of religious communes and cults, one result of proper early instruction in the methods of rational thought will be to make sudden mindless conversions—to anything—less likely. Brian now realizes this and has, after eleven years, left the sect with which he was associated. The problem is that once the untrained mind has made a formal commitment to a religious philosophy—and it does not matter whether that philosophy is generally reasonable and high-minded or utterly bizarre and irrational—the powers of reason are surprisingly ineffective in changing the believer's mind. We must acknowledge that the factual record is inconsistent with a significant part of religious belief, though not with morality. If we arbitrarily limit our historical research to the last five hundred years and examine the particulars of every factual argument that pitted the church against science, we find that science has represented the more reasonable and correct side of the debate. Consider the pope's recent apology to Galileo.

But formal instruction in the techniques of reason, beginning at the kindergarten level, is only half the solution because the inability to reason is only half the problem. The other half is the deterioration of the American family, the soil from which each new generation grows. I recommend that from the same early point our schools, churches, and other social institutions provide instruction on personal human relationships. They ought to teach how to love, as well as how to reason. Just as there are millions who do not think very well, so there are millions who do not love well. They may constitute the majority.

I believe it is not enough merely to preach formally the supremacy of love, as the Christian and other religious traditions have done for thousands of years. Such abstract recommendations accomplish nothing. Indeed, they may achieve the opposite of their purpose in that those who hear such lessons may nod in philosophical agreement, assume that our acquiescence automatically puts us on the side of the angels, and then leave our churches and lecture halls only to resume our spiteful or vengeful activities. We must never forget that the monstrous atrocities committed by the Germans under Hitler were perpetrated by a populace overwhelmingly Christian. Nor must we forget that the Germans at that time were the best-educated people in Europe. Despite their frequent church attendance, scholarly studies, and interest in the arts, they succumbed to the appeal of hatred disguised as patriotism. This did not happen because they were German; it happened because they were human.

It can hardly be argued that such sadistic policies and acts were the result of either education or religious indoctrination, but they certainly were the result of the wrong kind of religious and secular instruction.

Since we Christians have slaughtered each other regularly for the last two thousand years, it can hardly be historically surprising that we would slaughter the Jews; and indeed, Hitler could at least claim that he did not invent such an outrage. A philosophy is necessary within which reason and religion reinforce each other and in which not merely nominal belief—in either God or science—would suffice, but in which the results of belief are emphasized. This, by logical necessity, leads to an emphasis on practice, which is to say, morality. That this is quite difficult to work out, I know from personal experience, and again I do not lecture my fellow humans from any position of moral superiority.

I believe that we cannot, in any event, learn about love in isolation, as we might take up other studies in solitude. Almost all religions preach that love is the supreme virtue. A few spiritual teachers, perceiving that we are a gifted at loving what pleases us, teach that the highest, most edifying forms, which might ultimately save the world, involve our regard for those it is difficult to love, some of whom are our enemies.

We have assumed that the ability to love is naturally nurtured in the home, and the home continues to be the ideal place for teaching it. But the American home, I repeat, is now a partly failed institution.

It is tragic that we train young people for practically everything except the two most difficult assignments they will ever face: marriage and parenthood. We train them in reading, mathematics, science; we train them to type, work machinery, pull teeth, maim, and kill—to perform a remarkable variety of manual and intellectual tasks. But for marriage and love, a complex, troublesome, and perplexing business for all its rewards, we prepare them practically not at all.

I am hardly the first to recommend formal courses to ready young people for the roles of husband, wife, father, and mother. But preparing fifteen-year-old boys or girls for marriage is starting at least ten years too late. Better late than never, assuredly, but the sooner we can get such courses into our schools and churches, the better.

I would not presume to suggest the specific content of such instruction. Specialists know what should be taught, and they have already perceived the wisdom of demanding the support of the church, legislators, and educators.

This will require the preparation of suitable texts. If a four- or five-year-old can be taught to read "See the dog. See the dog chase the ball. See the ball bounce," why could he not learn reading and loving at the same time, from a book that would say, "See the dog playing with the little boy. See the dog lick the boy's face. The dog loves the boy. The boy loves the dog. See the boy run with his father. The mother gives the boy a new toy and hugs him because she loves him"?

Human nature has grounds for hope, because love, in a sense, is inexhaustible. I expressed this insight once, years ago, in a poem.

God is love, you said. Or God is
electricity.
I do not know what God is. All I hope
Is that He knows what I am. Electric force
can be both measured and diminished.
Love cannot, at least not in that way.
When the first child was born, I
loved it.
But when the second child was born I found I
loved
Not half as much but just as much.
And when the third arrived, he, too, received
full share. So love's a magic force that
Knows no laws, a well without a bottom,
a purse that's never empty. Use your
own cliché
Just so you get the point.

And one point more remains to make:
that like
The other faculties, the physical,
The musical, the social, and the rest,
Love swells in action. Will sets it
aflame;
It grows in height, direction, depth,
and kind.
It is the wise and wholly just investment.

Published Articles

How to Attack a Liberal

A, er, Liberal celebrity addresses the conservative community on how we should deal with him—what's fair, and what isn't. Proceed with caution . . .

One of the most interesting things that Thomas Aquinas said when he appeared as a guest on the "Meeting of Minds" television series was that he had learned a great deal from his enemies, by which he meant his philosophical opponents, some of whom were Islamic. Many of us today, I fear, seem unaware that we not only can but should be subject to instruction by those who differ from us. For my own part I am aware of having benefited by critics ranging from the political right to the left. But many conservatives who criticized one or another of my opinions during the 1950s and early '60s did a very poor job so far as the requirements of coherent communication and simple accuracy are concerned. William F. Buckley was kind enough to accept and publish—in his *National Review*—the following response.

Audubon Society members interested in the *Golden-Throated Warbler,* the *Red-Breasted Robin,* and the *Great Horned Owl* must detect a familiar ring in those hardy denizens of the political forest, the *Black-Hearted Communist,* the *Die-Hard Reactionary,* the *Moss-Backed Conservative,* and the *Fuzzy-Minded Liberal.* In any event, the hunting season appears more open than ever and arrows fly in all directions.

William F. Buckley, Jr., in his syndicated newspaper column, recently raised the question as to what methods were ethically permissible to conservatives who wish to diminish the political influence of prominent Liberal entertainers. Wisely, he pointed out that whatever weapons were deemed suitable for this purpose could also be turned, by Liberals, against conservative performers. Since I address a conservative audience in these pages, and write in my capacity as a Liberal, I shall say no more about the two-sidedness of the argument but shall restrict myself to general comments pertaining to morality and logic. One reason for this is that the argument is not symmetrically two-sided anyway. There are, as it happens, only a handful of conservative actors, whereas hundreds of our nation's most gifted performers identify themselves as Liberals. This is not surprising, of course. Down through history creative people of all sorts: painters, novelists, poets, playwrights, musicians, composers, sculptors, and actors, when they have been socially conscious at all, have almost always been to the left of political center. This, of course, *proves* nothing, although it *suggests* a great deal.

Now conservatives are certainly entitled to attempt to weaken the political effectiveness of Mort Sahl or Shirley MacLaine or Marlon Brando, but they are not entitled to employ unethical means of doing so. Their own moral code, for example, forbids them to call a man a Communist when he is nothing of the kind. One of the great ironies of contemporary history concerns the sections of those conservatives who on the one hand assert a willingness to defend a code with their lives while on the other ignore the same traditional morality on grounds of political expediency.

Precision of Attack

But even short of this extreme, conservatives sometimes err in attacking Liberals because they have not taken the trouble to get their targets into precise focus. I agree with Mr. Buckley that my own case is appropriately illustrative. In relating some of its details I shall not resort to documenting my twenty-five-year record as a militant anti-Communist: the record is there, and such men as Senator Dodd and J. Edgar Hoover have drawn attention to it. "Some people," Averell Harriman recently observed, "think it is only if you are ready to involve our nation in atomic war that you are a patriot." Obviously those who think that Robert Welch* is *more patriotic* than Dwight Eisenhower are truly in need of psychiatric advice, although how they are to get it when they also suppose that the mental health movement is a Communist plot I do not know.

Much political mischief and nonsense, of course, is traceable not to malice but to a clumsy use of labels. And even when labels are used correctly they tell very little about a man. A socialist, for example, is not *only* a socialist. He may also be a violinist, a Unitarian, a chess-player, a husband, and a comforter of the afflicted. And when you kill the socialist you also kill the violinist, the Unitarian, the chess-player, the husband, the father, and the Good Samaritan.

Those who believe they have precisely indexed and labeled me when they have identified me as a *Liberal* are mistaken. To explain their error I will assume two points of view, the first of which is limited and common, the second of which is wider and more profound. Many conservatives err in believing they have correctly sized me up because, like most American Liberals, I am to a great extent conservative. In other words I respect the Constitution, the flag, our national tradition, and the political philosophy of our forefathers. As much as any conservative I despise Communism—as I despise every other form of tyranny—and I yield to no one in regard to appreciation of the beauty of the ideal of human freedom.

Furthermore, I am not only a believer in the free-enterprise system of capitalism, I am myself a wealthy man and a capitalist. In all of this, of course, I am not particularly virtuous; on the contrary, I

---

*Robert Welch founded the John Birch Society, an ultraconservative, anti-Communist organization that reached its peak in the 1960s.

am nothing more, politically speaking, than the average American. But above and beyond this average-common-denominator position, I am personally an individualist and always have been. I am registered as neither a Democrat nor a Republican but as an independent. During my school days I bridled at all manifestations of inconsiderate authority or bureaucratic habit-thinking and tended to do things in my own way and at my own rate of speed. In my professional life I have never been suited for the job of Organization Man. Like most creative people I have found it impossible to be servile and have functioned most effectively when I was granted the greatest possible freedom. Even the techniques of my craft bear this out: I prefer spontaneous to scripted comedy (I could not resist ad-libbing even in a Broadway play), play jazz piano by ear (an exercise of freedom), and am restless when restricted by TV "format." In other words, emotionally, viscerally, I am the very model of your freedom-loving, individualistic "conservative."

But if this is so, you may ask, how did it come to pass that I became identified as a Liberal in the first place? Actually the thing happened to a great extent without my being aware that it was happening. Out of nothing more than concern about and careful study of particular issues I came to adopt certain positions. To give a specific example, I made a study of the question of capital punishment, with the result that I changed my mind on the subject and became convinced that the death penalty represents nothing more than institutionalized revenge.

Another example: I became aware that all over the world theologians, philosophers, political theorists, military experts—in sum: the intellectual elite—were warning mankind of the catastrophic dangers of nuclear war. I studied the question and became convinced that unless certain historic trends were reversed our world faced eventual nuclear holocaust. (My solution, by the way, is not unilateral nuclear disarmament.)

I arrived at these positions not as a lifelong Liberal (my early background was Father Coughlinite reactionary*), not as a doctri-

---

*Father Charles E. Coughlin, a Roman Catholic priest, began regular radio broadcasts in the 1930s. As his audience grew into the millions, he advocated increasingly radical social and economic policies. In 1935 Coughlin founded the National Union for Social Justice and later he supported the pro-Fascist Christian Front. He was silenced by Church authority in 1942.

naire representative of any group, but as a free American who, having taken the pains to study certain questions, had arrived at conclusions. Once I had adopted these views I made so bold as to *act free.* Living in a nation that prides itself on freedom of speech I had not, in my naiveté, anticipated that there were certain risks attached to practicing a political virtue of which all my countrymen boast. I was not long, however, in learning the political facts of life. Not only did I promptly receive my lumps but I awoke to find that a large label reading "Liberal" had, so to speak, been pinned to my chest.

Now that I have learned the consequences, of course, I shall persist in speaking my mind. To hell, I say, with political cowardice; it is already stifling our society.

The Scientific Posture

Now let us return to the second point of view from which I promised to point out the error of those who react to labels rather than individuals or, as Korzybski* puts it, to maps rather than actual territories. No two things are ever alike. Therefore it follows that no two Liberals in the world are identical, even as regards their liberality. But more than that, no one thing is ever the same at any two moments in time. It follows therefore that Steve Allen, the Liberal, on May 15, 1960, is not the same thing as Steve Allen, the Liberal, on May 15, 1963. Any way of thinking that overlooks this "obvious" truth is likely to lead to error. After all, there is a veritable infinity of individuals on your own side of the political fence, all of whom are clumsily labeled conservative or reactionary. But some of these men are intelligent and fair-minded individuals while others are bigoted ignoramuses. So, if we must use the labels, let us admit they are fuzzy and imprecise.

What I am urging, of course, is the scientific posture. The traditional or Aristotelian view set great store on labels and categories. The scientific philosophy—while it obviously retains all meaningful classifications—nevertheless goes beyond them to a fresh appreciation of the particular.

---

*Alfred Korzybski, an American semanticist, originated "general semantics," a linguistic philosophy based on the "time-binding capacity" of humans to transmit ideas from generation to generation.

Reality changes constantly, as the truly modern man realizes, and any political philosophy which does not take this fact into account is doomed to frustration if not disaster. Change has always been a part of human existence, but in recent years the pace of it is on the increase. Only those are unnerved by change who are unwilling to admit its inevitability. Unfortunately very few, even in our day, are encouraged to appreciate the nature of social evolution. On the contrary, the educational pressures of all societies seem to perpetuate traditions for their own sake, whether or not they are relevant to the solving of new problems. The child is rarely taught to think for himself; he is usually urged to conform to the ways of the tribe. If there were only one tribe swarming over the face of our planet this might conceivably be a defensible position. The fact that there are thousands of tribes with thousands of traditional codes suggests its essential absurdity.

But despite the forces of reaction the world does change, whether we like it or not. If the conservative force had always been dominant, neither Christianity nor the American Revolution, to mention but two examples, would have flowered.

There are indications that philosophical approaches more appropriate to the realities of human existence are beginning to be influential, although it is too early to be optimistic about this. But here and there signs emerge that individuals are beginning to understand what has always been "known," that societies mature just as do individuals and that, as Wendell Johnson observes in *People in Quandaries,* attempts to deal with the problems of maturity according to the methods appropriate to infancy represent a maladjustment.

The new view, I assert, is the *Liberal* view; the old attitude is the *reactionary.* Why do I say *reactionary* and not *conservative*? Because the true Liberal will recognize that he stands upon the shoulders of the giants who lived before him, that the growth of a society is not a matter of throwing out everything that is old and accepting everything that is new but rather a steady, healthy expansion along the growing edge, accompanied by a corresponding sloughing off of whatever is dead, impractical and irrelevant in terms of present reality.

I consider myself equally the friend of any true Liberal or true conservative. But, while I would hope always to be scrupulously just to the reactionary, I say to him nevertheless that intellectually I am his enemy, just as I am the enemy of the tyrant of Communist or Fascist persuasion.

Air-Tight Logic

In raising the question: do right-wingers have the moral right to boycott the sponsors of non-Communist Liberals (to deny Liberal entertainers, one might say, their "Right-to-Work"), Mr. Buckley admits that the affirmative contention leaves him "terribly, miserably uneasy."

To make sure that the issue is understood he spells out the argument:

> If our opponent is a politician, our resource is relatively simple: we vote *No* at the polls. But if he is something else, how do we register our dissent? . . .
>
> The reasoning is as follows:
>
> If Steve Allen did not have a national reputation as an entertainer, would he have been given such a high position as he holds in the hierarchy of the Left-Liberal establishment? If Steve Allen delivers a lecture on nuclear disarmament . . . do the people go to hear him because they are curious about the views of a professional student of public affairs? No, they are, most of them, curious to see the great Steve Allen, the entertainer.
>
> But who gave him the reputation as an entertainer? We did, Mr. and Mrs. Spelvin say, and we are therefore partly responsible for the attention that is given him when he shuts his piano and lectures on nuclear disarmament and amicable coexistence.
>
> Therefore . . . we have only this resource available to us if we would diminish his political influence: we must boycott him as an entertainer.

Referring to this logic, Mr. Buckley in one instance describes it as "pretty tight" and in another uses the phrase "air-tight as it *seems*." (Italics supplied.)

The fact is, the logic contains several fallacies big enough to drive a Greyhound bus (former sponsor) through, and although Mr.

Buckley may not have been able to put his finger on them his sub-conscious apparently suggested that the logic was not *absolutely* tight, which would seem to be the reason why ruminating about the problem left him "terribly, miserably uneasy." As for the fallacies:

1. The first lies in the implication that working to get a Liberal entertainer fired is the moral equivalent of simply voting *No* at the polls or—to put it another way—voting for the opponent or politi-cian of whose views one approves.

Nothing could be farther from the truth. There is no precise moral equivalent of the political nay-vote in this instance. Some-thing that comes workably close is for the right-wing viewer to refuse to watch my television program (which practice, if it became widespread, could lower my rating), or—rather than just turn off the set and go to bed—watch my NBC competitor, Johnny Carson. This—if it became widespread—could raise Johnny's rating as compared to my own and, in the competition for sponsorship, could conceivably work to my disadvantage.

2. To the question, "If Steve Allen did not have a national rep-utation as an entertainer, would his political views be particularly noteworthy?" Mr. Buckley suggests that the only possible answer is *No*. But this cannot be logically maintained. The answer, obviously, could go either way. After all, I am not *only* an entertainer. I am also the author of eight books and numerous articles and stories. The ninth book, soon forthcoming, is about politics. It might well have been the case, therefore, that even if I had never gotten into radio or television my interest in thinking and writing about political and social questions would have led me to a position of some public influence.

Political students, after all, are not born. Mr. Goldwater, when I knew him in Phoenix several years ago, was just a nice chap who ran a clothing store downtown. And, unlike the esteemed senator and most of his congressional colleagues, I write all of my own political speeches, books, and articles.

Theory of Justification

3. Who gave me my reputation? " 'We did,' Mr. and Mrs. Spelvin say." If the reader is not careful he may interpret the word

we in this context as meaning *the public*. In fact, however, Mr. and Mrs. Spelvin do not represent the public. (I believe I remember the Spelvins; friends of Westbrook Pegler's, aren't they?) Mr. and Mrs. Spelvin are conservatives or reactionaries. Let's say *Mrs.* Spelvin is a conservative and *Mr.* Spelvin is a reactionary. As such they represent a small minority of the population of the United States and therefore may by no means arrogate to themselves credit for establishing my reputation as an entertainer.

4. Mr. Buckley's *seemingly* airtight argument might lead the careless reader to assume incorrectly that the public alone is responsible for my reputation as an entertainer. But this could not possibly be the case. Talent, if I do not unduly flatter myself, is not bestowed by popular acclaim; it is God-given. I have been granted the gifts of being able to make people laugh, to play the piano, to compose music, to act, to write, etc. My reputation, therefore, is merely a matter of public acknowledgment of the existence of these gifts. The public is doing me no favors whatsoever; it is simply buying the products of my creation because it considers them of some value.

5. "Therefore," the argument concludes, "we have only this resource available to us if we would diminish his political influence: we must boycott him as an entertainer." The fallacy here lies in Mr. Buckley's use of the word *only*. As I suggested above, right-wingers who wish to diminish my political influence have various alternatives. (According to one point of view, it suddenly occurs to me, they may have no effective alternatives at all since it does seem that each political attack upon me, oddly enough, serves to *increase* rather than diminish my political influence.)

In any event I assert that the entire Spelvin argument is *post-facto* rationalization and will not even occur to the majority of those who attempt to prevent my employment. What motivated the writers of the angry letters ("We will never watch 'What's My Line?' again if you persist in hiring such Red subversives as Steve Allen") is—the proverbial six-year-old child could see it—the good, old-fashioned, bitter lust for revenge. But the boycotters could not look themselves in the face if they admitted as much; hence the development of a theory of justification. The psychological process here is so familiar that it would be presumptuous to say more about it.

Lastly, I submit that many high-minded conservatives would not dream of stooping to the tactic.

I am indebted to Mr. Buckley for removing from the hands of the more irresponsible representatives of the Right one alternative weapon for diminishing my influence which may have had some effect. This is the immoral assertion that I am a Communist. For those who might have missed Mr. Buckley's article I quote:

> The fact is: Steve Allen is an anti-Communist. The campaign to brand him otherwise is a part of the national tendency to break the syllogistic sound barrier. . . . I have read just about everything he has written about world affairs, and if there is a pro-Communist sentence in that literature, I'll join the [American Democratic Association].

This one tool: the lie, the smear which violates the Commandment "Thou Shalt Not Bear False Witness Against Thy Neighbor," is too frequently resorted to, as J. Edgar Hoover, among others, has observed.

Blackmail is not a pretty word, nor a pretty thing, and Mr. Buckley is to be congratulated for being honest enough to employ it when he considers the possibility that "every conservative who opposes the view of Steve Allen were to retire him from television by blackmailing his sponsors. . . ."

The American consensus about blackmail has long since been handed in and I believe ought to be duly considered in this context.

I have not space within the confines of this article to defend my views on foreign policy, concerning which Mr. Buckley has expressed misgivings. I will say only that for the most part they are views which—to judge by a dozen Gallup polls—are endorsed by the overwhelming majority of American citizens. This does not establish their validity, but it does suggest that they are not nearly so radical as Mr. Buckley's statements of opinion might have led the reader unfamiliar with my views to assume.

Let's Brainwash Our Criminals

One of the sadder aspects of the story of modern America is that the branch of the criminal justice system which deals with the formalities of punishment—chiefly imprisonment—has basically failed to accomplish its original philosophical purpose. About the best that we can say for our prisons at present is that they do keep a certain number of violent offenders off the streets, although the great majority of them are, of course, eventually given access to our streets and, all too often, our homes.

The whole idea of prison—and/or capital punishment—as a deterrent has not been very successful. As I have previously argued, for at least two thousand years large segments of human society have firmly believed in the existence of a literal, concrete fiery hell. And yet that belief, fearful as it is, does not seem to have had any beneficial effect whatever on human conduct. Obviously if the idea of being roasted in actual flames for all eternity has never prevented a single sin or atrocity, it is unlikely that the threat of imprisonment or execution will have much effect. In any event it was such considerations which led to the proposal outlined below. There's no way of knowing in advance

From *Science Digest* 63, no. 4 (April 1968): 34–40.

if it will produce any more beneficial results than have other approaches, but the only way to find out is to make the experiment.

If Chinese communists could brainwash our GIs to an alien philosophy, why not use similar techniques, plus the best modern educational methods, to imprint reason, honesty, and decency on the minds of criminals?

Many people who deplore criminal violence seem to have an insatiable appetite for it, to judge by the popularity of television and radio programs, motion pictures, books, and periodicals that depict murders, kidnapings, assaults, rapes, and burglaries. Society, I suspect, would feel cheated if someone were to invent a pill that could convert a murderer into a decent, law-abiding citizen.

Well, society had better get interested in a change soon. The present crime wave is going to assume tidal proportions in the years ahead. Hiring more policemen and making penalties more severe will not solve the problem. The typical American prison is anachronistic and harmful.

For thousands of years society has punished neurotics and psychotics. The sicker they were, the more severe the punishment. It hasn't worked. But society has rarely given up practices simply because they haven't worked. The truth is, we tend to overlook the fact that a crime is essentially an irrational act.

Does punishment deter irrational acts—crime? The rate of repeatism in the federal prison system increased from 61 to 67 percent between 1949 and 1958. It has been argued that a young man who has never been punished by society might somehow feel immune from retribution. But the same cannot be said for a man who has already spent several years in prison. He knows the nature of the punishment that faces him. He has had ample evidence of the misery, the degradation, the monotony, and general horror of prison existence. Nevertheless, he is irrational enough to go back to a life of crime as soon as he is released.

Man, in general, reasons more poorly than he supposes. We are creatures of strong physical and animal needs from the moment of birth. Only gradually and painfully do we learn to reason. Most of us, unfortunately, do not learn very well. Even at our fullest intellectual development, we still carry within us a tremendous burden of factual ignorance, erroneous information, superstition, prejudice, fear, hostility, and other detrimental baggage.

These powerful emotional undercurrents enable us to stifle concern over possible detection, conviction, and punishment. If detection and punishment were certain and immediate, formal deterrence might work. Tell a thirsty man that if he drinks a cold glass of water placed before him he will be shot on the spot, and he will not drink it—unless he becomes maddened by thirst. He may then suspect that you do not really mean what you said about shooting him. Or he may gamble that your courage will fail. Or he will decide that the momentary satisfaction of assuaging his thirst is worth dying for.

But, in reality, deterrence always has been pretty much a failure. Millions of people believe in a real, material hell, with actual flames that burn actual bodies. Yet their conduct does not appear to be statistically different from those who do not share such a belief.

Some will argue that if threat of imprisonment is no deterrent, then prisons ought to be abolished. I see no reason why the assumption must lead to the conclusion. It could still be argued that prisons protect society simply by keeping dangerous people off the street.

No society has ever justified its prison system purely on this thesis, however. Prisons have sprung up as the result of a tendency to do something "civilized" with offenders. In early times evildoers were torn limb-from-limb, drawn and quartered, eaten alive by animals, burned at the stake, skinned alive, boiled in oil, stoned, crushed, impaled on spears, crucified, strangled, shot, and so forth.

For lesser offenses, eye-for-an-eye "ingenuity" was employed. A man who lied might have his tongue torn out, a spy might have his eyes gouged out, a thief might have one or both hands chopped off. This last punishment persists to this day in parts of the Arab world.

Parenthetically, these barbaric atrocities have not been inflicted by demented criminals, but by the authority of the state, frequently with the blessings of the church.

Death or Banishment

We in the West like to believe that human rights are more precious to us than property rights. But when we turn from pious theory to practice, something gets lost. As the European masses broke from feudalism, attacks upon private property increased. More than two hundred offenses were punishable by death. Not every criminal could be killed under the new enlightenment, so more were locked up. Some were put on sailing ships and banished—not always to Australia, either. Many were sent to America.

The first English prisons were the workhouses. It would be impossible to exaggerate the horror of them. They housed not only criminals, but the insane, the impoverished, lepers, women, and children.

In the United States, Dr. Benjamin Rush, a signer of the Declaration of Independence, proposed that criminals be classified and segregated. Gradually two philosophies of imprisonment emerged. One, the Pennsylvania System, was based on solitary confinement and hard labor. The other—the New York, or Auburn, system— held that absolute silence would improve the prisoner. Both were nonsensical and cruel. Eventually they employed beating, flogging, straitjackets, chains, thumbscrews, and other forms of torture.

Every penal system in turn has come to be recognized as generally a failure. Certain side-approaches had value: probation, parole, democracy within the convict population, the industrial prison. Finally the idea of offering the prisoner a few educational opportunities emerged. After that the ideal of psychological counseling was introduced. I use the word *ideal* to suggest that little has been done to develop the kind of sweeping program that is really required.

My own prescription is a revolutionary and radical one.

The field of psychology has yielded up a considerable body of knowledge and theory concerning the impressionability of the human mind. Chinese Communists apparently were able to take perfectly average GIs, brainwash them for a few months, and produce important changes in their basic outlook. Think of it! In a few months of daily indoctrination—without resort to torture or drugs or any James Bondian devices—men who had lived twenty or twenty-five years in one culture were induced to accept ideas of another in which they had spent only a short time.

These same techniques, among others, ought to be used in a new kind of model institution to promote reasonable and socially useful ideals and attitudes.

The success of the Chinese admittedly was less than is popularly supposed. But this does not mean that nothing can be learned from the experience. Communism is an unattractive philosophy to Americans. Communist purges, slave labor camps, subversion, firing squad executions, Berlin Walls, etc., have produced in most American minds an unsympathetic image of communism. Let's assume we are trying to sell worthwhile products—reason, honesty, decency, and other civilized virtues. The results might well be different and better.

The Synanon experience in rehabilitation of narcotics addicts, and the effectiveness of Alcoholics Anonymous, have given a number of interesting results. One reason is that the addicted individual is approached by someone who has successfully overcome the identical predicament, rather than someone who simply lectures from a position of virtuous, inexperienced authority. Our model institution, therefore, should include some staff members who are former convicts. Synanon has succeeded not only in curing addicts but in imbuing them with a desire to help other troubled people. This suggests that it might be possible to select and train individuals from the prison population.

Experiments could be conducted in sensory deprivation, or sensory restriction. Studies undertaken in 1957 at Princeton University showed that immediately following periods of isolation the capacity of subjects for learning certain kinds of material was improved. Here is something that deserves further study. Experiments in sleep deprivation may also hold clues that would be valuable.

It has been determined that one of the most important factors connected with indoctrination procedures is isolation—not only physical isolation, but separation from one's culture group. There is an opportunity in prisons to initiate experimental procedures which, regardless of the degree of their effectiveness, are clearly preferable to the treatment presently accorded a majority of those incarcerated.

Since monopoly of influence is desirable, a *small* institution is better than a giant one. At present, a state prison inmate spends most of his time in the culture of other prisoners, whose values may contradict those that the authorities are trying to inculcate. He is faced with a conflict between his new desire for civilized conduct and his previously established sense of loyalty to the rest of the prison group, to which he feels he belongs. Even in the absence of any such sense of group loyalty, there is sometimes the fear of retaliation or contempt from the peer group for being a "stool pigeon." These considerations support the idea, not only of a small total inmate group, but its subdivision into even smaller and more manageable teams.

Actually, advantage can be taken of a susceptibility to "go along with the group." A good example is the experiment in which an individual is told he is one of a group of five being tested. In reality, the other four apparent subjects are cooperating with those administering the tests. A simple question is asked, to which the four "shills" deliberately give an incorrect answer. In a high percentage of cases an individual will deny what he knows to be the correct answer simply because the majority response makes him doubt the validity of his own initial response. Why shouldn't the same principle be applied to the rehabilitation of antisocial minds?

The learning process is already going on in our prisons. After spending a year or two in a prison in the company of more experienced criminals, a youngster comes out knowing exactly how to jimmy a door, where to go to buy or sell narcotics, how to hold up a bank. Therefore we are not concerned to debate the question: Should a man learn anything in prison or not? He *is* learning something. Much of it is bad. It is, I admit, possible for a man to acquire some formal education in arts and crafts in prison today, but present programs represent a drop in the bucket.

One of the tragic lessons being learned by the Head Start Program is that, while dramatic improvement can be made in the learning ability of small children who live in poverty areas, these same children tend to fall back into their former condition. Powerful influences in home and neighborhood tend to defeat the influences available in the schools. The hard truth seems to be that we can't properly educate young people who continue to live in a ghetto. In a totalitarian society you solve this by ordering the children out of the ghetto and into boarding schools. But we are not a totalitarian society.

There is one situation, however, when at least a small percentage of socially deprived young people are forcibly taken out of their slum homes and neighborhoods. That is prison. What an opportunity to educate and indoctrinate a captive audience! What are we waiting for?

But what kind of teaching am *I* talking about? Two kinds: Standard academic teaching, and intensive, out-and-out brainwashing designed to produce important personality changes. I am not competent to map out a complete program. As for grade school, high school, and college curricula, I should think them essential.

For mind-changing indoctrination, I would rule out practically nothing. Closed-circuit television would be a must, as would tape-recording and playback equipment, with earphones available for individual concentration. High-quality public address equipment for simultaneous communication to all hands is possible. Lectures and informal talks by prominent authorities should be part of the program. The presence of public figures would suggest to patients that society is interested in them and cares.

The institution should be provided with teaching machines and programmed instruction books and devices. Instructions in remedial reading and speed reading would be essential. Videotapes and motion picture films that were not only instructive but interesting— even entertaining—would be important.

Fundamentals of psychology and a course in general semantics might do wonders. General semantics programs already have proved strikingly effective in a few prisons. The patient would be photographed, and shown the pictures, tape-recorded and made to listen to the sound of his voice, patterns of his speech, the techniques of his thinking. He should be given standard psychological tests. The results should be discussed with him in whatever way medically qualified supervisors deemed best to bring the man into realistic focus in his own eyes. For probably the first time in his life the patient would be given an enormous amount of personal attention, made to feel a sense of dignity and importance. There have been startling conversions of hardened criminals through religion. It should be tried.

Restore Self-respect

The kind of institution I envision would set out deliberately to "coddle" inmates—but not in the literal sense. Inmates would *not* be served breakfast in bed, offered a choice of dinner entrees, given manicures or massages, or driven to nearby golf courses. The institution would, however, make up to the inmate for the deprivations, raw deals, and shortchanges that society has generally meted out to him since his birth. This might include good food, instructions about proper diet, the prescribing of decent medicines used in a normal home environment, a complete athletic program, an educational system, a library, a music room, the privilege of wearing something other than a prison uniform on special occasions. By such means, "authority" would be saying, "You have committed a crime and been deprived of the freedom to live in your accustomed environment. But you have not been sent here to be beaten, intimidated, starved, ignored, rejected, or brutalized. We have one objective: to help you to help yourself."

We have ample evidence that the best efforts to control or alter human conduct rely on developing self-control and self-direction in the patient, not on authoritarian, external control.

It's a Family Affair

It is commonly assumed that the home is the place where sound attitudes toward social responsibility, sex, marriage, and parenthood are learned. There is increasing evidence, unfortunately, that it is within the American home itself that much serious social trouble originates. The rehabilitative program I recommend, therefore, should have as one of its parts a method for involving the inmate's home environment through consultation and participation.

Primitive man commonly asked the question "what?" (What is that light in the sky? What is the stranger—friend or enemy?) Later, he asked "how?" (How can I tie these sticks together? How can we make fire?) Finally comes "why?"

Today we consider ourselves civilized and intelligent. We should be asking "why?" about a lot of things. *Why* does a prison look like a prison? The architecture carries an eighteenth-century influence, when prisons were designed to keep dangerous people in. They were copied, at that time, from structures that were designed to keep dangerous people out—castles and fortresses.

It is no longer necessary that a prison resemble a medieval

fortress. We have better means in this age of electronics for maintaining effective security. The prison of the future should look as little like a prison as possible. Nor need it be isolated from the community. Is it because we don't want to face the reality of our mental hospitals and prisons that we hide them from our sight behind the nearest mountain range, or on a bleak island? The chief result of this stupidity—whatever the reason for it—is that patients or inmates are deprived of the important benefits of easy contact with families and friends.

What I propose is visionary and utopian. Such rehabilitation for criminals will not be constructed tomorrow. But what I propose is easier than creating nuclear weapons or putting a man on the moon.

What would a pilot institution cost? I don't know or care. More than two and a half million offenders move through our prison system each year, many of them recidivists. State and local governments spend roughly one billion dollars a year keeping convicts locked up, but less than a fifth of that trying to rehabilitate them. Fewer than 4 percent of prison staff people are concerned with treatment; more than 90 percent are zoo keepers.

My idea is better than that.

Turkey Stroganoff and China's Bomb

William F. Buckley's recent column—one syndicated, alas, in far more newspapers than will ever carry reference to my response—suggesting that I stand shoulder-to-shoulder with him in recommending an immediate nuclear attack by our Strategic Air Command against Communist China's nuclear installations, has stirred up a great deal of comment, as well it should.

In reply, I wish to make clear first of all that those who now find themselves seriously concerned with my views on foreign policy may find them expressed at considerable length in three books. So far as I am aware there has been no change in my general position except in the sense of the growing sophistication and increased familiarity with detail that normally comes with long study of such complex issues.

For the benefit of those readers who might not have seen Mr. Buckley's column—and who might therefore have acquired a distorted impression of its content—I quote from its key paragraph on my position:

This essay originally appeared in the February 1965 issue of *The Progressive*. Reprinted by permission of *The Progressive,* 409 East Main Street, Madison, Wisc. 53703.

"I was recently in conversation with Steve Allen. . . . I put to Allen a week ago a concrete proposal, and was gratified to have an answer which he gave me permission to publish. Namely, that he would join me in approving a nuclear strike by our Strategic Air Command against the nuclear installations in Red China which have recently ground out an atomic bomb."

Since the publication of this remarkable pronouncement I have been receiving letters from two groups: (1) fellow peace-workers who suspect that I have taken leave of my senses; and (2) right-wingers who congratulate me for having, as they suppose, come around to their nuclear point of view, whatever that might be. I deserve—as it happens—neither the blame nor the praise I am receiving.

Is Mr. Buckley, then, telling a bald lie of the sort for which Robert Welch of the John Birch Society is so infamous? Not at all. Mr. Buckley and I did indeed have a conversation about this mat-ter—a conversation about which it is clear there needs to be a fuller report.

The Buckleys, like the Kennedys and other well-educated fam-ilies, are given to dinnertime conversation that deals with matters more weighty than changing hemlines, gossip about the private lives of movie stars, and the latest sports scores. They so enjoy stimulating debate, indeed, that I sometimes suspect it is largely the fact that they have achieved a somewhat numbing family consen-sus that has driven Bill out into the cold, liberal world to argue his sometimes archaic but never boring propositions. Since everyone at the family board agrees with him he must—if he is to be sustained by the heady wine of controversy—either bestir himself or else invite to the Buckley home such itinerant liberals as myself.

Responding to such an invitation during Thanksgiving week, I was transfixed—between forkfuls of wine-spiced Turkey Stroganoff—by Bill Buckley's question: What would I think of destroying Communist China's nuclear capability if no loss of life were involved?

The first reaction that crossed my mind was the phrase: Why not?—a query which, whether it was ill-advised in this instance or not, I think we all ought to form the habit of asking ourselves daily, since we might otherwise tend to become immobilized in the concrete of our assumptions and prejudices. Certainly, all men of good will in the West, and probably the majority in the Communist camp, too, would sleep better if the Chinese were *not* developing a nuclear armory, or if they accidentally blew up the one they are now building.

To the best of my recollection the conversation immediately thereafter went somewhat as follows:

BUCKLEY: Let's assume we would give two hours' warning, so that it would be clear we were interested only in destroying equipment, not people.

ALLEN: Are you talking about a nuclear attack?

BUCKLEY: Not necessarily. Assume the attack were made with nonnuclear weapons.

ALLEN: Well, then, I consider the idea an interesting one that I find myself approaching by way of the question: Why not? The advantages of keeping the Chinese out of the nuclear club by this means are obvious enough, while the disadvantages are not quite so readily apparent. My own participation in the peace movement is motivated simply by a desire to keep men from killing each other, the same desire, of course, that makes millions of people uneasy about the existence of nuclear weapons.

BUCKLEY: And such an attack would destroy—or prevent the construction of—additional nuclear weapons, would it not?

ALLEN: Precisely, which is why the idea, at least considered as an intellectual exercise, has definite attractions. I do perceive, however, problems, such as the great hue-and-cry that would go up from many other nations, not all of them Communist by any means.

BUCKLEY: How important is that consideration?

ALLEN: I consider it more important than I believe you do. But what would you say to our making a magnanimous gesture coincidental with, the attack—for example, offering to send to the Chinese mainland several shiploads of American grain, as a gift, to make it clear to the world that our actions were truly intended to benefit the Chinese people and to establish that we had no designs on Chinese territory?

BUCKLEY: (After a moment's reflection and a brief consul-

tation with his brother Jim) No. To do that would suggest that
there is something unvirtuous about the original act itself . . .
and that we ought not to concede.

After accepting another helping of Stroganoff, I said, "Well,
whatever the merits or drawbacks of your proposition—to deal
with reality for a moment—I can't imagine its ever being carried
out. Besides the problem of world opinion, there arise such questions as whether a declaration of war would be involved."

BUCKLEY: There would be no necessity to declare war. First
of all, the attack would come as a surprise.
ALLEN: Except for the two-hour warning announcement.
BUCKLEY: Yes, but above and beyond that we wouldn't be
contemplating a war. We're talking about this one act only:
destroying the Chinese nuclear capability.
ALLEN: Of course the Chinese might have their own ideas
as to what would constitute an appropriate response. By the
way, I find myself suddenly wondering if this possibility would
appeal to Chiang Kai-shek.
BUCKLEY: (Somewhat cryptically) It would.

It was at this point in the conversation, as I recall, that I first
began to get the impression that my hosts were entirely serious about
what I had assumed was one of those how-many-angels-can-dance
propositions of the sort that so intrigue and divert the Buckleys.

I therefore said: "If by any chance you were serious about the
matter, I assume you can appreciate that the one thing you
absolutely ought not to do is publish a formal call for such a course
of action, for by public revelation of the idea you bring at least two
things to pass.

"First, you give the Communist Chinese a warning that would
provide them with ample opportunity to develop counterthreats and
arguments, thus almost certainly rendering your chess move impossible.

"Second, in the unlikely case that the Johnson Administration
might have sympathetically entertained your notion—had it been
dropped, so to speak, in the State Department's suggestion box—

you would, by publication of your idea, be flying in the face of the
natural and strong reluctance of a ruling party to base important
policy upon suggestions from the opposition."

From the broad smiles that greeted this observation, I tenta-
tively concluded that the Buckleys were, indeed, not serious about
their proposal.

"If you were in earnest about this," I continued, "you would not
advance your proposal in the pages of *National Review*; you would
whisper it in the ear of Senator Dodd or submit it to your contacts
in the Pentagon."

*   *   *

Mr. Buckley's subsequent publication in his nationally syndicated
column and in *National Review* of the proposal itself, as well as an
account of our dinner-table discussion of it, I take as tending to confirm my assumption that the whole thing was an intellectual exercise, a playing with game-theory meant to cause mischief and
embarrass the administration rather than an instance of responsible
policy-planning.

There was more to our conversation. Buckley said: "You say
that if the attack were made without nuclear weapons, you would
feel that the possibility has certain attractions."

ALLEN: Yes.
BUCKLEY: May I quote you?
ALLEN: Certainly.

I was naive enough to think that the quotation would be by
word-of-mouth, but had it been made clear that publication was
involved, I would not have answered differently. I would, however,
have gone much further to assure that my point of view be rendered
more fully, and I would also have insisted upon a much more
detailed consideration of the drawbacks of the Buckley proposal.
My admittedly awkward position in regard to this matter is rather
like that of Barry Goldwater who, in discussing various suggestions
that had been made for dealing with the problem posed by Viet
Cong supply routes in Vietnam, said "Defoliation of the forests by

low-yield atomic weapons could well be done." When it was later claimed by the senator's opponents that he had *recommended* or *approved* such use of atomic weapons, he heatedly denied that this was the case, explaining that he had merely meant to refer to a possibility, the virtues of which were at least worth exploring.

Fortunately, neither Mr. Buckley nor I are candidates for office, and therefore my carelessness in this discussion, which I frankly concede, may be interpreted as a phenomenon common enough among policy theorists whose imaginations roam freely—precisely because they carry no responsibility of the sort that so rightly inhibits those whose word may become flesh.

Buckley said next: "Now what if the attack were nuclear?"

I answered: "With the addition of that factor the proposition becomes decidedly less worth considering. If no loss of life is involved, and if 'clean' bombs that cause practically no radiation damage were employed—assuming such a thing were possible— then I would have to advance reasons why, in the absence of damage to humans, a nuclear weapon is any worse than a nonnuclear weapon. Of course, we're playing a complicated game here. How could you guarantee that there would be no injury to humans? The Chinese might decide to stay and attempt a defense. And what of those non-Communist scientists who have been forced to go along with their government's plans? Have we the right to kill them?"

On the basis of this casual pass at problem-solving, Buckley evidently assumed that I would "approve a nuclear strike by our Strategic Air Command" against China.

I can offer no such approval. The main complications of Mr. Buckley's proposal, it seems to me, are of the sort that only secondarily relate to matters purely nuclear. There are indeed grave dangers attending such a resort to violence.

For one thing we have, as I have earlier suggested, no way of knowing—really predicting—what the Chinese response would be. It would seem reasonable to assume that such an attack would render it impossible, in our lifetime, to ever develop a *rapprochement* with the Chinese. Their attitude toward us is already frequently harsh, but such an attack would replace contempt or envy with pure hatred and would presumably close forever pathways that might have led to some sort of coming-to-terms short of war.

Second, we have no way of knowing what the Soviet response would be. Mr. Buckley seems to feel that the Russians would not be quite so dismayed as their subsequent public statements might seem to suggest. But we do not know. Such an attack might succeed in driving the Chinese and the Russians back into each other's arms, a circumstance which would clearly be to our disadvantage.

Third, we have no way of knowing what the effect might be upon the war in Vietnam, which is already disastrous enough. The Chinese, to vent the anger caused by loss of face, might decide to humiliate us in Vietnam. Short of opening full-scale hostilities against them, there is perhaps not a great deal that we could do by way of retaliation. Certainly we could punish them fearfully from the air, but I know of no responsible American military figure who would feel anything but horror at the prospect of an American infantry invasion on the Chinese mainland. Only *retired* admirals and generals seem to find such madness appealing. And even our heavy air attacks would succeed largely in killing the innocent, non-Communist Chinese millions that we piously claim to be interested in liberating, not incinerating.

Lastly, the propaganda value to the Red Chinese of a nuclear attack upon their territory would be enormous. One can easily envisage their approach: "The Americans—who have previously attacked Asian soil with atomic weapons—are at it again. They are the only nation ever to use these weapons and their repeated resort to their use puts the lie to their claims to peaceful intentions." Whether such an argument is justified is utterly irrelevant. The point is it would be enormously attractive to Asian ears.

These are only a few of many considerations that would have to be taken into account before anyone—even such a foreign policy romanticist as Mr. Buckley—could wholeheartedly endorse the attack plan. Before undertaking such startling moves it would seem the better part of wisdom to explore the possibilities of a greater effort by the United States, Great Britain, and the 106 other signatories of the nuclear test ban agreement to bring France and China to an acceptance of its provisions.

Should we not now also encourage attempts to include China in disarmament negotiations? Moderation on the part of China's leaders is certainly something we would welcome. Have we attempted to promote it? I, for one, do not see what good it does us to prevent our journalists from visiting the interior of China. Would we be worse off with *more* information? Is it wise to found policy upon ignorance? Even Clare Boothe Luce says we should give China food; so, it may come as a shock to some conservatives to discover, does Chiang Kai-shek, a bit of news for which I am indebted to Mr. Buckley, so it shouldn't be a total loss.

Now some conservatives might suppose that the bomb-run proposition was purely a Buckley family matter, for which, therefore, the conservative camp in general ought not to be held accountable. I wonder. If there is anyone of the *National Review* camp who thinks the United States ought not to bomb Chinese nuclear weapons installations, let him speak now or forever hold his peace. Whether such an individualist among Individualists actually exists, one is certainly entitled to wonder, if not doubt. But several far more fascinating questions now suggest themselves:

1. Since the *National Review* group (Buckley, L. Brent Bozell, James Burnham, Russell Kirk, Frank S. Meyer, Ernest Van den Haag, et al.) is—or was Senator Goldwater's brain trust, *would the Senator have advanced this dramatic proposal had he been elected commander in chief of all United States armed forces?* Never mind what I think about this; somebody ask the former senator. There may be a bigger story here than Mr. Buckley anticipated.

2. Mr. Goldwater has spent the past few years criticizing practically everything done by the Truman, Eisenhower, Kennedy, and Johnson administrations in the context of the cold war. As president, therefore, he would have had to come up with alternatives that were off the beaten track. Is it possible that the bomb-China idea is only one of a full bag of venturesome projects that might have been undertaken in the event of a conservative victory, such as, for example, *National Review*'s repeated suggestions that we invade Cuba and break down the Berlin Wall?

Even considering the Buckley proposal as pure game-theory, a far superior means of achieving the destruction of Peking's H-bomb potential—if such a course were agreed upon—would be *to entrust the bomb-run—one made with nonnuclear weapons—not to our Strategic Air Command but rather to Chiang Kai-shek's Nationalist Chinese air force based on Taiwan.*

Or—if one wanted to be terribly James Bondish—one must ask: Is it possible that Chiang, in his inscrutable though still leashed wisdom, might have created this idea himself and commissioned his China Lobby friend, Mr. Buckley, to initiate a public debate designed to lead the rest of us to the very conclusion to which I have just referred, which would involve our turning over the reins of responsibility to Chiang for an important attack upon the Chinese mainland?

But even the let-Chiang-do-it gambit would have results and the possibilities must be faced. Peking would almost certainly retaliate by some form of aggression against Formosa. If this happens, our formal obligation to defend Chiang would force us into a battle that could easily turn into World War III.

Or did all of this start because the attractive Mrs. Buckley put too much wine in the Turkey Stroganoff?

Allen on Buckley

A number of my liberal, Democratic, and Republican friends profess puzzlement as to how William F. Buckley and I can remain personally on the most cordial of terms while disagreeing on so many philosophical specifics. Their puzzlement—it seems reasonable to assume—is no greater than that of those conservatives and/or reactionaries whose affection for me is considerably less than is that of Mr. Buckley.

I admire Mr. Buckley in part because he is an entertaining fellow; he puts on such a good show. He has always been amusing because of his refreshing and somehow winning arrogance. His natural air of superiority—that quality so cherished by H. L. Mencken—is such that I presume it bars him forever from elective office, if that is any comfort to liberals dismayed at the entry of other rightist entertainers into the political arena.

It has long seemed to me that the combination of Mr. Buckley's flair for the drama plus his plutocratic elan makes him, in a sense, a far more romantic and classically tragic representation of The Conservative than the *aw-shucks* Mr. Goldwater. Contrary to the point of Vice President Hubert Humphrey's joke about the Arizona senator's making a movie for 18th Century Fox, Goldwater is truly a 20th Century type, the King of Kiwanis, the likable, somewhat bumbling Babbitt who, though he entertains a number of 1928-ish notions, is nevertheless one-of-the-boys of our age.

Buckley, on the other hand, seems to me truly a man born in the wrong time. I see him in a flowery silk shirt, brandishing a rapier, gallantly defending an about-to-be-deposed monarch of another era.

His graceful prose seems very quill-pen and his practical policy suggestions often have an air of romantic desperation about them. This, of course, does not establish that they will invariably be ill-advised but it may, nevertheless, help to put his foreign policy recommendations into improved perspective.

The Happy Jack
Fish-Hatchery Papers

In which the Messrs. Steve Allen, Dalton Trumbo, and Arthur Schlesinger, Jr., debate the true meaning of liberalism

Mrs. Beata Inaya   February 26, 1969
Los Angeles, California

Dear Mrs. Inaya:

Thank you for your letter of February 25th which I am answering five minutes after reading.

I'm sorry to report that I'm already committed for the evening of Friday, March 14th and will therefore not be able to have the pleasure of attending the party that evening in honor of Mr. Bradley. As I believe you know, I *am* participating in another affair in his honor on March 1st.

It is absolutely none of my business that the March 14th affair is being held it the home of Mr. Dalton Trumbo, but I am assuming that those of you who are working so hard on Tom Bradley's behalf must know that Mr. Bradley's reactionary opponents will certainly

---

Reprinted from *Esquire*, January 1970 (published by the Hearst Corporation).

make capital of the fact that Mr. Trumbo's home is the setting for this particular occasion.

I know absolutely nothing of Mr. Trumbo's present political convictions, nor have I any particular interest in what his political affiliation might have been, say, a quarter of a century ago. I *assume,* however, that at one time he was indeed a Communist. I have also been told he is a very likable individual personally and his position as one of our most talented screenwriters is widely acknowledged. It would in no way affect my own admiration for Mr. Bradley that Mr. Trumbo might be one of his supporters but— to go over the ground again—*if* (a) Mr. Trumbo is today of the Communist persuasion (something he has every right to be), and if (b) this fact is publicized by Mr. Bradley's rightist political opposition, then (c) the March 14th affair will almost certainly be used in such a way as to cost Mr. Bradley a perhaps significant number of votes in this not-always-politically-enlightened city. I am perfectly willing to have you show this letter to Mr. Bradley, or to Mr. Trumbo for that matter, should you feel inclined to do so.

If Mr. Bradley's present campaign is, let us say, similar to William Buckley's in New York, in that winning is out of the question, but the race is run merely as a public profession of political principle, then, of course, my observations here will be irrelevant. But they do indeed have a relevance if Tom Bradley and his supporters are interested in winning the political contest.

Cordially yours, Steve Allen

[Undated]

Mr. Dalton Trumbo
Los Angeles, California

Dear Mr. Trumbo:

The Arts Division of the American Civil Liberties Union inaugurated its first Annual Playwriting Contest open to all students in any college or university in Southern California. The response was overwhelming and enthusiastic, and we now have the two award-winning student plays. They will be presented at the Stage Society Theatre in Los Angeles for four performances only, on Sunday afternoon, June 8 (preview performance for students), and on Monday, Tuesday, and Wednesday evenings, June 9, 10, and 11.

It is because I am certain that you share my interests in both encouraging young, fresh talent and the free expression of ideas that I am asking you to participate as a sponsor in this unique project with me. Only $25 from you not only helps to underwrite the cost of these productions, but it will also make it possible to invite two students to the preview performance on Sunday.

Furthermore, your name will be listed on the program as a sponsor and you will receive two tickets for whichever evening performance you prefer. Please indicate your preference when you send your check made payable to the Arts Division, ACLU—which I hope you will do now.

Thanks so much for your support.

Cordially, Arts Division

Arts Division   May 7, 1969
American Civil Liberties Union
Los Angeles, California

Gentlemen:

Not so long ago, Mrs. Trumbo and I gave our names as sponsors for a liberal cause which I shall not mention here, and somewhat reluctantly agreed to throw our house open in its behalf to a fund-raising party for 150 persons.

Unknown to us, Mr. Steve Allen, who appears to be the doyen of the Hollywood liberal community, wrote a letter to the organization charging that the use of my name would provide rightists and reactionaries with an opportunity to defeat their organization and the cause for which it stood.

Although no one had mentioned the matter to Mrs. Trumbo or me, and the invitations were already at the printers, the party was canceled forthwith, and we, quite after the fact, were notified of our undesirability. I did not like it, and I am resolved it shall not happen a second time.

I shall be glad to sponsor the Arts Division, ACLU Playwriting Contest provided you can secure Allen's written consent for my name to appear on your list. I know this seems odd, but it's the only way I can think of to avoid another spasm of nastiness and, perhaps, disavowel.

I enclose my check for $25 as a straight nonsponsoring contribution.

Cordially, Dalton Trumbo

cc: Mr. Steve Allen

Arts Division, American Civil Liberties Union   May 13, 1969

Gentlemen:

Mr. Dalton Trumbo was kind enough to provide me with a copy of his letter of May 7th to you. I shall naturally accord him the same favor in attempting to clarify the misunderstanding to which an earlier letter of mine has apparently given rise. I can quite understand Mr. Trumbo's personal displeasure at the cancellation of a party for which, in the first place, he had agreed to serve as a somewhat reluctant host.

Secondly, I concede that he is correct in placing on my shoulders the primary blame for the cancellation of the party, although in referring to me as "the doyen of the Hollywood liberal community" he greatly exaggerates my influence upon liberal affairs in our community. Nevertheless, my letter of February 26th did indeed recommend against the holding of the fundraising party in Mr. and Mrs. Trumbo's home.

To make my motives in this instance perfectly clear, I quote here the relevant portions of the letter to which Mr. Trumbo objects:

"It is absolutely none of my business that the March 14th affair is being held at the home of Mr. Dalton Trumbo, but I am assuming that those of you who are working so hard on Tom Bradley's behalf must know that Mr. Bradley's relationary opponents will certainly make capital of the fact that Mr. Trumbo's home is the setting for this particular function.

"I know nothing of Mr. Trumbo's present political convictions, nor have I any particular interest in what his political affiliation might have been, say, a quarter of century ago. I *assume,* however, that at one time he was indeed a Communist. I have also been told he is a very likable individual personally, and his position as one of our most talented screenwriters is widely acknowledged. It would

in no way affect my own admiration for Bradley that Mr. Trumbo
might be one of his supporters but—to go over the ground again—
if (1) Mr. Trumbo is today of the Communist persuasion (something
he has every legal right to be), and if (b) this fact is publicized by
Mr. Bradley's rightist political opposition, then (c) the March 14th
affair will most certainly be used in such a way as to cost Mr.
Bradley a perhaps significant number of votes in this not-always-
politically-enlightened city. I am perfectly willing to have you
show this letter to Mr. Bradley, or to Mr. Trumbo for that matter,
should you feel inclined to do so.

"If Mr. Bradley's present campaign is, let us say, similar to
William Buckley's in New York, in that winning is out of the question, but the race is run merely as a public profession of political
principle, then, of course, my observations here will be irrelevant.
But they do indeed have relevance if Tom Bradley and his supporters are interested in winning the political contest."

Now may I draw your attention to something in Mr. Trumbo's
letter of May 7th which is possibly critically significant in this context. In his first paragraph he chooses not to identify Mr. Bradley's
campaign but refers only to "a liberal cause which I shall not mention here. . . ." While it is conceivable that Mr. Trumbo omits
Bradley's name because he has decided to base his argument on
principle rather than on specifics, it seems to me more probable that
he is motivated by a generous reluctance to draw Mr. Bradley's
name into this discussion at a moment in the mayoralty race when
it is unwise to rock boats. If the latter hypothesis is the valid one
then perhaps, in choosing not now to link his name with that of Mr.
Bradley, Mr. Trumbo may be motivated by precisely those considerations which dictated the writing of my letter of February 26th.

Mr. Trumbo seems to feel that the party at his house was cancelled on my *instructions*. Such was not the case. I simply brought
certain considerations of political expediency to the attention of
one of Mr. Bradley's campaign workers. Apparently my letter was
forwarded to higher-placed members of Mr. Bradley's staff; presumably it was these workers who issued the cancellation order. It
is clear, I would think, that only someone more formally associated
with Mr. Bradley's campaign would have the authority to dictate
such a cancellation. I have no such authority. It is unfortunate that

the reasons for the party's cancellation we're not explained to Mr. Trumbo before rather than after the fact, and again I say that his emotional response to the manner in which the situation was handled is quite understandable.

Mr. Trumbo is a witty and trenchant writer and I stand properly amused by the irony of his suggestion that he will sponsor the ACLU-Art Division's Playwriting Contest provided only that the organization can secure my written consent for his name to appear on its list of sponsors. I have, of course, no more authority to prevent his association with the Arts Division-ACLU in this instance than I had to prevent his public association with Mr. Bradley's campaign in the other. To this point my comments will probably have seemed unexceptionable to you, but concerning what I have now to say a raised eyebrow or two would be understandable. Can it indeed be the case that I have the temerity to recommend Mr. Trumbo's rejection a *second* time, to rub salt in his wounds, to attempt, in my capacity as doyen, to banish him into that exterior darkness into which, from time to time, in recent history, various representatives of the non-Communist left in America have attempted to push their pro-Soviet or pro-Marxist associates?

The question is, alas, impossible to for the reason that I haven't the slightest idea as to what Mr. Trumbo's present position on the political spectrum might be.

At which you should pin me to the wall and demand to know, in certain terms, what my recommendation in this matter would be if it could be absolutely certified—or even assumed for purposes of debate—that Mr. Trumbo is today a Communist and proud of it.

In which case I concede my strong anti-Communist bias. Since there are those seriously afflicted by the either–or disease—a malady apparently as common on the political Left as it is on the Right—I am therefore obliged to state that my opposition to political tyranny does indeed take in all 360 degrees of the circle that stretches to the political horizon, which is to say that I am also revolted by Nazism, Fascism, and McCarthyism. It is all very well for Communists to resent the criticisms of Liberals and Democratic Socialists; the hard fact remains that Liberals and Democratic Socialists in power do *not* send Communists to execution chambers and political prisons; whereas Communists in power—in country after country—do indeed exercise a barbarous vengeance against those members of the non-Communist Left whom the Communists correctly identify as their true rivals for the political affections of the masses.

It would be to a degree irrelevant and presumptuous here to review the political history of the first half-century but I cannot conceive how any true Liberal, being familiar with that history, could be anything but anti-Communist. As a Liberal, I am in favor of freedom of the press, freedom of speech, and of freedom of assemblage. But I know of no Communist society in which such freedoms exist. I am also opposed to the death penalty, as are most Liberals, but it is clear that Communist societies cannot function without the threat, and frequently the reality, of state murder. As a Liberal I am suspicious of official censorship, but I observe that it is harshly dominant in all Communist cultures. As a Liberal I do not think a college student should automatically be considered a criminal if a marijuana cigarette is found in his possession, but we know of the utter ruthlessness with which Communist societies stamp out such instances of bourgeois decadence. The civil liberties the ACLU so courageously defends are not the foundation-stones of any existing Marxist society. The litany of specifics need not be continued; certainly the point is clear enough.

I concede—indeed, I fervently hope—that all of this may be utterly irrelevant in Mr. Trumbo's case. If it is, I would be greatly relieved and—assuming the man has not forsaken one tyranny for another—would therefore be willing to be associated with him in a worthwhile social endeavor as I would with any other law-abiding citizen.

I have frequently been a stern critic of American society and expect to function as such in the future, but for years I have consistently maintained the position that it does not profit the non-Communist political Left to be formally allied with those who will endorse a Liberal cause only when to do so coincides with the purposes of Moscow or Peking in Vietnam, for example, what I hope for is *peace*; therefore I cannot cooperate with those who are motivated primarily by hopes of victory for Ho Chi Minh.

I leave you, gentlemen to determine the relevance, if any, of these observations to the case which Mr. Trumbo's letter has brought to your attention.

Most cordially yours, Steve Allen

cc: Mr. Dalton Trumbo, Mr. Eason Monroe, Mr. Tom Bradley, Mr. Burt Lancaster

Mr. Steve Allen   May 19, 1969
Encino, California

My dear Stern-Critic-of-American-Society-Who-Expects-to-Function-as-Such-in-the-Future:

Thanks for the copy of your May 13th Epistle to the Thespians. It soars. One must stand back to gain perspective. After just two readings I am a much better citizen than I really wanted to be.

Beyond adding three splendid new names to our circle of readers, you have also cast a dazzling light on that gritty little cancelled campaign party by placing it in bold juxtaposition with the political history of the first half-century, the non-Communist left, pro-Soviet or pro-Marxist associates, Communism, anti-Communist bias, the Left, the Right, political tyranny, Nazism, Fascism, McCarthyism, Liberals, Democratic Socialists, execution chambers, political prisons, vengeance, the masses, the true Liberal, freedom of the press, freedom of speech, freedom of assemblage, the death penalty, state murder, official censorship, the marijuana laws, ruthlessness, bourgeois decadence, civil liberties, Marxist society, American society, Moscow, Peking, peace, Vietnam, and Ho Chi Minh. Unhappily my fuller comment must be deferred because of a pledge I made to refrain from using certain names connected with the matter under discussion until after the election. Pending that time, however, allow me to toss a few of my own hang-ups into the pot which you have so generously provided, to wit:

The French withdrawal from NATO, British entry into the Common Market, abolition of the statute of limitations in West Germany, the prevalence of Huntington's chorea in the Sultanate of Muscat and Oman, equal access to the southern fishing banks of Iceland, the plight of West Irianese refugees and the Free Papua Liberation Command, the population explosion among North European elvers, the theft of four paintings from the collection of the Ninth Earl of Linster at Rudford Castle near Cockermouth, the demotion of Sophronia as patron saint of toothaches, the effect of the Spitz-Holter valve on hydrocephalic children, Portnoy's Complaint, the Schism of Photius, the Black Panther Party, tax relief, treasury notes, family foundations, tapped telephones, pornographic pictures, mandragora, nerve gas, vervain, air pollution, euthanasia, law and order, academic freedom, mace, the pill, yohimbe root, penis envy, stainless stealing, fire-buggery, Aristotle Onassis, Eldridge Cleaver, Abe Fortas, Patricia Nixon, Prince Abdul Rahman, Cesar Chavez, Andy Warhol, and Brenda Holton, 23, who died two weeks ago in Canterbury, England, of a diet restricted to honey, cereals, and dandelion coffee.

I am passionately concerned with every one of these issues, some of which are more sinister than they sound, and confident that our forthcoming discussion of them, and those which you have introduced, cannot fail to provide our accumulated pen pals with much nourishment.

Sincerely yours, Dalton Trumbo

cc: Mr. Steve Allen, Mr. Eason Monroe, Mr. Tom Bradley, Mr. Burt Lancaster, Mr. George Plimpton, The Hon. Mr. Lyndon Baines Johnson, The Ninth Earl of Linster, Estate of Mr. Harold Bell Wright

Mr. Steve Allen   May 21, 1969

Dear Mr. Allen:

In my note of May 7 to the Arts Division, ACLU, the word disavowal was spelled *disavowel.* My secretary's mistake. In my letter to you of May 19 I identified St. Sophronia as the dethroned patroness of toothaches. The personage referred to was actually St. Apollonia (her day is February 9). My mistake.

In your May 13 Epistle to the Thespians the following line was quoted from your February 26 letter to Mrs. Beata Inaya: "I know nothing of Mr. Trumbo's present political convictions. . . ." The original letter, of which you forgot to send me a copy, reads: "I know *absolutely* (my italics) nothing of Mr. Trumbo's" etc. Your mistake.

History is watching us, Mr. Allen. We serve larger purposes than our own. Let's show our best profiles by keeping the record straight.

Faithfully yours, Dalton Trumbo

P.S. I discover in this morning's mail that Senator Cranston and Congressmen Bell and Rees are bugging me for a contribution to you-know-who's campaign. My name on a check? Don't they *know,* for God sake?

cc: Mr. Eason Monroe, Mr. Tom Bradley, Mr. Burt Lancaster, Mr. George Plimpton, The Hon. Mr. Lyndon Baines Johnson, The Ninth Earl of Linster, Estate of Mr. Harold Bell Wright, Mr. Haroldson Lafayette Hunt, Mr. Gus Hall

Mr. Steve Allen   May 22, 1969

Dear Mr. Allen:

I hate to interrupt your meditations at a moment when the campaign approaches its climax, but my God, Mr. Allen, I've got another crisis. Before I tell you exactly what it is, I think I owe you an explanation of what led up to it.

Some time ago, when your concern for America and me was less apparent than today, I chaired a public dinner which sported, in addition to a congressman or two, more municipal and superior court judges than I'm really comfortable with. I thought the thing went off rather well: the only guest (an assemblyman) who put his feet on the table had clean shoes, nobody hoicked on the chicken *supréme,* nobody snerched too loud, and everything seemed real nice.

For some reason I'm not quite sure of (perhaps because my presence in the chair drew no attacks from right-wing reactionaries and the rest of that scum) somebody must have spread the word that I was a hell of a chairman, because not long afterward I was asked to chair another dinner in honor of somebody else, and I've got to confess that but for a previously scheduled pilgrimage to various shrines and cadavers of the sonofabitch side of the Iron Curtain, I'd have accepted. That I did not is probably the finest thing which ever happened to that particular honoree, although he himself has never acknowledged my part in his good fortune or even thanked me for it. On the other hand, how can you expect a man to be grateful for escaping an accident he wasn't in and never heard of? You can't. You just have to forget the whole thing and keep on living, which is exactly what I did and still am.

And then this thing happened that I've got to tell you about: last evening, in that hour which finds all highstrung chaps awash with pick-me-up, I was requested by telephone to chair a dinner honoring Mr. Julian Bond. The request was almost as importunate as that of Miss Beata Inaya to grab our house in behalf of you-know-who, and I, perhaps because of pick-me-up, perhaps because of that restless, feckless, reckless streak which keeps running down the middle of my back to dilute my character and befog the luster of my name, accepted.

However, on awakening this morning to the full glow of sunlight and sobriety, I fell at once into a kind of intellectual sweating fit, or whatever it is you call that particular condition which is induced by the collision of a bad conscience with a faulty nervous system. I said to myself, you fool, I said, Mr. Allen is every bit as interested in the triumph of Mr. Bond's cause as he is of you-know-who's, and when Mr. Allen is interested in something, he doesn't just sit around like some crumbum the way you do, he *acts*; things *happen.* Sooner or later he'll find out about what you did last night, compute the evil that's bound to flow from it, and five minutes later—bang!—another torpedo zoops off the old launching pad.

And as if that weren't enough, *you,* poor fool, will know nothing about what's zeroing in until that penultimate moment when (loins neuterized with dusty philters, armpits sweetened, black tie only slightly askew, spirits already afloat on wings of imaginary applause) you find yourself diving through cold thin air with the wind in your ears, shot down once more for the fallen angel you never deserved to be.

What shall I do, Mr. Allen?

Shall I tell them I was drunk when I accepted? I could, of course, if you think it best, but if I say that too often people will get the idea I'm fried all the time, and for a man who needs steady work that isn't a good image to have projecting itself around the community.

Shall I say I'm going to be too sick to show? The trouble with this is that they've scheduled the gala three months in advance, and to say *now* that I'll be sick *then* may suggest that I got lucky and hit Big Casino, and this isn't too good from my point of view either, because health is very big these days and we live in a town that needs cancerated writers about as badly as a bull blowfly needs a second squirt of Black Flag. There *could* have been the possibility of asking them to clear it through you at the outset, but I tried that with the Arts Division, ACLU, and what happened? Your Epistle to the Thespians, that's what: cc's flying through the air like pessaries at a campus love-in, pregnant problems aborting in practically everybody's backyard, grim-faced ideological buzzards flapping home to roost in the most improbable places, sacred geese rocketing at full quack through esplanades and public squares, befouling with their startled excrement the fairest freeways in all our New Jerusalem—*well,* Mr. Allen, I sure don't want much more of that and I hope you don't either. But how shall I go about avoiding it?

Would you advise me to turn myself in like a man (which is not in my nature)? Go back where I came from (which seems a reproach on my people who split the joint over two hundred years back)? Pretend I've been brought to bed with Huntington's chorea (which at least has the virtue of rarity)? Get myself hauled up before some Committee so the real truth at last may be known (which, to survive, requires the kind of luck I haven't got)? Square the whole thing off by blowing out my brains (which probably takes sharper shooting than I'm up to)? Or should I just sort of hunker down and let her blow (which depends a good deal on the condition of your hunkers)?

In any event, Mr. Allen, the man doesn't live who can say I've been sneaky about this thing or insensitive to the consequences of my existence to the dedicated community over which you stand your lonely, solitary, but not always silent guard. I've told you frankly, honestly, and exactly where the bear sits in the buckwheat. All I ask in return is your advice on how to bag him or get the hell out of his hunting range.

Please send me your thoughts as soon as possible, because the pot is simmering here on the back of the stove, and she's tighter sealed than a bull's you-know-what in choke-cherry season, and something's bound to blow a lot sooner than I want it to.

Sincerely yours, Dalton Trumbo
cc: Mr. Eason Monroe, Mr. Tom Bradley, Mr. Burt Lancaster, Mr. George Plimpton, The Hon. Mr. Lyndon B. Johnson, The Ninth Earl of Linster, Estate of Mr. Harold Bell Wright, Mr. Haroldson

Lafayette Hunt, Mr. Gus Hall, The Rev. Dr. Billy Graham, Al-Ibrahim Institute for Control of Huntington's Chorea

Mr. Steve Allen   May 23, 1969

Dear Mr. Allen:

Well, here I am again. The problem may not seem very important to most of our correspondents, but that makes it no less a problem, and I hope I've dealt with it in a way that will make you proud of me.

The Ninth Earl of Linster, who has been shacked up in Chula Vista these past three months house-guesting on a bewildered pair of old family retainers, informs me that although your letter of February 26 was addressed to *Miss* Beata Inaya, my note of May 21 referred to her as *Mrs.* He feels that the difference between those two forms of address involves a rather substantial difference in the kind of person any lady actually is, and begs me to clear the matter up at my earliest possible convenience, which, luckily, is right now.

I have replied to him as follows:

"My Dear Ninth Earl:

"The marital situation of the lady in question is absolutely none of my business. I know absolutely nothing of her present marital status, nor have I any particular interest in what it may have been, say, a quarter-century ago. I assume, however, that at one time she was indeed a single woman.

"It would not in any way affect my own admiration of you-know-who that the lady in question might be one of his supporters, but *if* (a) she is today a single woman (something she has every legal right to be), and *if* (b) that fact is publicized by you-know-who's reactionary rightist political opposition, then (c) her connection with you-know-who will almost certainly be used in such a way as to imply that his feminine support derives exclusively from virgins, maidens, and spinsters, thereby costing him a perhaps significant number of votes amongst that large bloc of married, divorced, or widowed females, which has long infested this not-always-politically-enlightened city.

"It was, perhaps, my unconscious desire to avoid such a split which caused me to refer to the lady as *Mrs.* I leave it to you to determine the relevance, if any, of these observations to the case you have brought to my attention. Most cordially yours, etc., etc."

I hope you will agree with me that this prompt response to Linster of Radford near Cockermouth (who is, in any event, an alien) clarifies more issues than at first glance it would seem to.

Sincerely yours, Dalton Trumbo

P.S. I solved that other problem re: being bugged by Cranston, Bell, and Rees re: you-know-who by sending a small check signed with my accountant's name rather than my own. I pray, however, that we've got a loyal campaign staff, because you know as well as I do that in these critical times the gander's pragmatic virtue almost always turns into the goose's subversive conspiracy, which means that all hell is bound to break loose if my caper is leaked to our opponents of the extremely reactionary right. Right?

cc: Mr. Eason Monroe, Mr. Tom Bradley, Mr. Burt Lancaster, Mr. George Plimpton, The Hon. Mr. Lyndon B. Johnson, The Ninth Earl of Linster, Estate of Harold Bell Wright, Mr. Haroldson Lafayette Hunt, Mr. Gus Hall, The Rev. Dr. Billy Graham, Al-Ibrahim Institute for Control of Huntington's Chorea, Princess Conchita Pignatelli, Estate of Miss Brenda Holton

---

Mr. Dalton Trumbo   May 29, 1969

Dear Mr. Trumbo:

Mr. Allen is presently in Indianapolis and will be leaving directly for Northern California for a few days. However, he will be back in town next week.

In the meantime, Mr. Allen wanted me to drop you a note acknowledging your recent letters, and he wanted me to let you know that he will be answering them as soon as he returns.

Most cordially, Betty Brew, Secretary to Steve Allen

Miss Betty Drew   June 2, 1969
Secretary to Mr. Steve Allen
Encino, California

Dear Miss Brew:

Thanks for informing me of Mr. Allen's absence from the city and his intention to answer my letters when he returns. I must tell you, however, that from my point of view his Indianapolis and Northern California commitments have not come at a convenient time.

He won't believe this (at first I didn't either) but Sunday evening Mrs. Trumbo and I were invited to dine person to person and face to face with he-knows-who in the house of a mutual friend. Knowing how gross an abuse of free speech and assembly my presence at such an affair would constitute, dreading the impact of a second apostolic interdiction while not yet fully recovered from the first, I heard a voice remarkably like my own begging off with the idiot's excuse that we were departing the city Friday noon for a Mexican holiday which hadn't entered my mind until that moment.

Since a chap in my position has to be even more scrupulous with the truth than Caesar with his wife's, or vice versa, there was nothing for it but to transmute my lie into its opposite by immediate proclamation of a southbound hegira to begin no later than Friday noon, June 6, 1969.

Mrs. Trumbo, I'm sorry to report, didn't take the news at all well. For some years she has been doing whatever she can for a group of young preteenage and hopefully prepregnant sub-Aquarians who foregather throughout the mating season (June 1 through August 31) each Saturday afternoon at Happy Jack's Fish Hatcheries, 8041 North San Gabriel Canyon Road in Azusa, where they receive much enlightenment from pisciculture in general, and in particular from unblinking observation of the relatively chaste techniques which characterize the breeding habits of even the most concupiscent among the fishes.

At their last meeting (end of August, 1968), in a somewhat rowdy but nonetheless moving demonstration of gratitude and loyalty, the youngsters unanimously chose Mrs. Trumbo to be Vice-Den Mother for their 1969 season which begins, as anyone with a calendar at hand can see, on Saturday next.

I had written for the occasion a rather stirring First Inaugural Address (based in part on Mr. Allen's Epistle to the Thespians) which can be rattled off in just under forty-seven crackling minutes; and Mrs. Trumbo, having memorized and come to believe it, thought poorly of a command holiday which was bound to spoil what she has lately taken to calling—sentimentally, perhaps, but not unjustifiably—her Vice-Den Mother's Day among the pisciculturians.

Ethics, however, is ethics, and my honor, when it comes to a showdown, invariably takes precedence over hers. Result: we depart Los Angeles International Airport on Western Airlines' Flight Number 601 on Friday, June 6, 1969, for Mexico City, where we shall be met by chartered car, driven forthwith to Cuernavaca, and lodged at Privada de Humboldt 92. Our mailing address, however, will be Apartado 1292, Cuernavaca, Morelos, etc. We can be reached by telephone almost daily between the hours of three and six-thirty A.M., central standard time, at Cuernavaca 2–31–38.

And why, do you ask, have we been put to all this hurly and scurly and involuntary aggravating unexpected burly? Because I, in Sunday's moment of mistruth, had no stern critic at hand to straighten my morals and narrow the range of my political and social pretensions. So much for NCLers who rush off to rival Communists for the political affections of the masses without preschooling their own acolytes in the mysteries of honest unilateral action.

Most respectfully, Dalton Trumbo

P.S. The Ninth Earl has somehow leapt to the untidy conclusion that Burt Lancaster is under house arrest as a carrier of Huntington's chorea. Although I have done everything in my poor power to explain that no man on earth can carry a pestilence like H's c (he has to haul it), I might just as well have spent my time hollering down some neighbor's empty grain barrel. He has filed an emergency application with the Chula Vista branch of Travelers Aid for immediate transport to the Control Institute in Oman and Muscat, and compels his entire household, including two of the most dejected old family retainers you've ever seen, to wallow with him thrice daily in tubs of boiling Lysol hugely adulterated with white lye, sheep dip, and magnums of granulated loblolly *flambé en brochette.*

Raw-wise, the skins around that house have passed the point of no return, and for some reason I can't fathom old Linster has tried four nights running to deposit the whole begrutten mess (the Sixth Earl married a Scotswoman described by a contemporary as "begrutten of face, large of wen and warp but small woof") at my doorstep. For all his breeding, which I am told has been prodigious, the big L shows every sign of becoming, as we say in my middle-class but hopeful precinct, just one more unwanted and ungrateful *anguis in herba.*

cc: Mr. Eason Monroe, Mr. Tom Bradley, Mr. Burt Lancaster, Mr. George Plimpton, The Hon. Mr. Lyndon B. Johnson, The Ninth Earl of Linster, Estate of Harold Bell Wright, Mr. Haroldson Lafayette Hunt, Mr. Gus Hall, The Rev. Dr. Billy Graham, Al-Ibrahim Institute for Control of Huntington's Chorea, Princess Conchita Pignatelli, Estate of Miss Brenda Holton, Happy Jack Fish Hatcheries

Mr. Dalton Trumbo   June 13, 1969

Dear Mr. Trumbo:

I had a nightmare the other evening. It seemed that at some distant point of future time an enterprising publisher released a portly volume titled "The Trumbo-Allen Letters." The book opens with your clever message of May 7th to the Arts Division of the American Civil Liberties Union, which is followed, of course, by my ponderous rejoinder of May 13th. The third letter is your brief note of May 21st, which clarifies a few points of minor significance. But then, where the reader might expect my response, he instead encounters your letter of May 22nd, your letter of May 23rd, your letter of May 24th, your letter of May 25th, your letter of May 26th, your letter of May 27th and so on—God help us—ad infinitum, ad nauseam, ad wolgast. Right to the end of the book.

At this point the scene quickly shifted, the way it can in dreams—where no stagehands are involved. I not only asked myself, "Where do the polls have Tom Bradley?" but "Where do the Cubans have Eldridge Cleaver?" and "Where do the Nielsen's have Gomer Pyle?"

I awakened with my heart beating mightily, concerning which I have no complaint, for the day will surely come when it will not beat it all. But be that as it may, and I see no reason to be sure it is, the explanation of the dream must be that I was beginning to fear I would never have time to answer your several letters. Or perhaps I was asking myself: is this whole misunderstanding just another example of what can happen when entertainers get involved in politics?

In any event, I have not only had no time to write to you about the Tom Bradley Dinner incident, I have not even had time to write to Mr. Bradley himself; a particular shame since I had planned to suggest specific positions for him on the crucial issues of the day.

Reporter: "Mr. Bradley, what do you think about police brutality?"

Tom B.: "I think people are being entirely too brutal to the police."

Reporter: "Do you think we should recognize the Red Chinese?"

Tom B.: "Well, they all look alike to me."

Reporter: "As a former police lieutenant, what would you say to Mayor Yorty if you encountered him face-to-face at this moment?"

Tom B.: "You're under arrest."

What a pity, as I say, that all this, and more, never reached Tom because of the demands of my schedule.

But, you may retort, what doth it profit me to make such easy jokes when I have a flair for them?

Wrong. I have a typewriter for jokes. I use my flair for other purposes.

But all seriousness aside . . . it ill-behooves us to be joshing like this while our city crumbles about us. Whoever governs this disorganized metropolis, what does he propose to do about such problems as the recent parade held to commemorate Fire Prevention Week, a parade that blocked several fire trucks attempting to report to a nearby conflagration?

Which—fire trucks being red—brings me back to the question of your political affiliation.

You have me, of course, at a considerable disadvantage in that I am unable to know to what extent the straw-man Dalton Trumbo I have criticized corresponds with the *real* Dalton Trumbo. All I know about you is that you are one of our industry's best screenwriters and that at one time you were involved in a public confrontation which led to my including your name in a list of imaginary orchestral aggregations such as *Andy Kirk and his "Clouds of Joy," Horace*

Heidt and his "Musical Knights," Harry Horlick and "The A&P Gypsies," Earl Warren and the Supremes, Red Nichols and "His Five Pennies," and Dalton Trumbo and "The Unfriendly Ten."

I am reminded at this point (and I'm glad to be reminded, too, because this letter could use a good, funny line right now) of Billy Wilder's observation that of the Unfriendly Ten "only two were really talented; the rest were just unfriendly." I'm sure you were one of the two. If you'll tell me who the other one was, I'll check and see if he had anything to do with Tom Bradley's defeat.

It is most generous of you to pretend to honestly solicit my opinion as to whether you should withdraw from or honor your other forthcoming social commitments. On all of your specific questions I must simply beg off. I say again that I don't know if you are presently a Communist. I *do* know that the ACLU was rent by a controversy about this general issue some years ago, and I suspect there are still at least two points of view on the question among members and officers of that admirable organization. I am obviously more-or-less cemented into my view that Communists—*acting as such*—cannot be trusted. Nor—I readily concede—could I be trusted if, holding my present political views, I were a citizen of a Communist society. I am afraid I would be in rather constant abrasive—perhaps even treasonable—contact with the state because of my conviction that it was embarked on a disastrously erroneous course. But I am not only willing to make the distinction between a man's political function and his function as husband, father, neighbor, dentist, screenwriter, golfing companion, or what-have-you; I absolutely insist on that distinction. Which is to say that while your letters testify to your wit, charm, and good grace, I would nevertheless be forced to oppose you—to hamper you—in your political capacity were you indeed a Marxist.

The fact remains that, while you and I have been composing witty letters to each other, poor Tom Bradley has lost the mayoralty race. All Yorty had to do to defeat him was confuse perhaps 5 or 10 percent of the electorate as regards the issues of racial intemperance and Communist influence. Gus Hall's incredible stupidity in recommending support of Bradley to his followers at a formal Communist party meeting—however supposedly private—is consistent with the long history of such mistakes on the part of CP functionaries. It is true that at present perhaps a larger percentage than usual of embittered youth are so disillusioned with the American system that they are willing to entertain a Marxist alternative. I suppose some of them would be willing to rally around the banner of Attila-the-Hun if some fiery spokesman for that cause would insult our present leaders colorfully enough. But with this one exception, Communists are now—as they have been for decades—about as popular with the American electorate as Nazi storm troopers at a Bar Mitzvah. There can be no question that the Gus Hall incident cost Bradley a number of votes in this peculiar community. Certainly the polls show that Bradley lost the race in the last few days, since he was far ahead for several weeks before the contest went to the wire.

While—as I previously made clear—I can understand your feeling hurt at being treated as something of a pariah, I ask you honestly what public capital you think Mr. Yorty would have made out of your hosting a dinner on Mr. Bradley's behalf, had information about the affair come to his attention. As regards my not knowing whether Beata Inaya was a Miss or Mrs., I stand corrected, which is understandable, since I'm wearing surgical hose at the moment. To tell you the truth—inasmuch as the lady signs her letters simply "Beata Inaya"—I didn't even know for sure she was a woman until I met her. I suspected hers was one of those African or Muslim names presently sported by so many of our black brethren along with colorful, flowing robes and "natural" hairdos. In reviewing my own correspondence with the good lady I find that I addressed her on February 26th as Mrs. and on April 3rd as Miss. For all I know, she may be some kind of a Communist, too, who one day acts like a Mrs. and the next day as a Miss, just to throw me off the track. It is clear that the name itself sounds suspiciously un-Waspish. Beata Inaya, indeed! Personally, I've never beaten an Inaya in my life and at a time when the pope is reneging on beatifications right and left, it ill-behooves a woman arbitrarily to beatify herself.

Well, enough of the chit-chat, which I was about to call Tomfoolery, but will not, out of respect to Mr. Bradley. I repeat, we have our nerve kidding about all this when conditions in the city worsen day by day. Last night the police in the Griffith Park area got a call for help. From three muggers. And just try to bring other actors to line up seriously in support of one worthy cause or another. Polly

Bergen cares more about her turtle oil. Debbie Reynolds cares more about her Girl Scouts. George Jessel is so old he's concerned only with his infirmities. At the moment I believe he is suffering from bleeding Madras.

If you'll forgive me, I must close now as I am overdue in getting out to local authorities a report of an accident I witnessed this morning on an off-ramp of the Ventura Freeway. It seems a Coupe de Ville gave the coupe de grace to a pedestrian.

Yours in haste, Steve Allen

cc: Burt Lancaster, Lance Burtcaster, Burnt Flycaster, Bald Broadcaster, Aristotle Onassis, George Givot, Euripides Pants, Stannous Fluoride

Mr. Steve Allen   July 17, 1969

Dear Mr. Allen:

I was out of the city when your letter of June 13 arrived. Although it was forwarded to me, the pressure of working away from home prevented me from answering it as promptly as I'd have liked to.

I must now clean up a few matters that accumulated during my absence, after which I shall address myself to a response.

Sincerely, Dalton Trumbo

Mr. Dalton Trumbo   August 12, 1969

Dear Trumbo:

I thought you would want to add to your Allen-Trumbo files the enclosed copy of a letter Mr. Allen has just received from Mr. Arthur Schlesinger, Jr.

Cordially yours, Betty Brew
Secretary to Steve Allen. Enc. (1)

Mr. Steve Allen   August 4, 1969

Dear Mr. Allen:

I have just recently returned from Europe and only now have had an opportunity to read the letters to the ACLU Arts Division.

Your letter seems to me clear and correct, and I would be in strong agreement with it. I have never understood how people who defend communism could consistently associate with an organization dedicated to civil liberties.

Sincerely yours,
Arthur Schlesinger, Jr.

Miss Betty Brew   August 28, 1969
℅ Mr. Steve Allen
Van Nuys, California

Dear Miss Brew:

I think I shall never forget Friday, August 15, 1969, as the day I opened an envelope bearing Mr. Allen's new return address and discovered therein, clipped to your thoughtful note, an enclosure which carried the Great Seal of the City University of New York's Albert Schweitzer Chair in the Humanities, the upholstery of which, it said on the back, is stuffed with honeysuckle pollen and twenty-dollar bills.

"Dear Mr. Allen," I read (thinking how much warmer 'Dear *Steve*' would have seemed), "I have just recently returned from Europe and only now have had an opportunity to read the letters to the ACLU Arts Division. Your letter seems to me clear and correct, and I would be in strong agreement with it. I have never understood how people who defend communism could consistently associate with an organization dedicated to civil liberties." And then, with noble simplicity: "Sincerely yours, Arthur Schlesinger, Jr."

I confess to you, Miss Brew, that I was more than stunned by what that letter was than by what it seemed to say. Although Mr. Schlesinger is perhaps the most prolific correspondent of our time, his and the pope's thoughts are generally considered too precious to waste on individual citizens or even small groups of them. Because of this, a vast number of Schlesinger judgments, opinions, disavowals, affirmations, admonitions, exhortations, and bad tidings by-pass the addressee altogether and go directly to the engraver for mass distribution.

However *my* letter (or rather mine and Mr. Allen's) is what the people at Sotheby's call a "private" Schlesinger. Bells clang all over the place when one of them shows up and the director himself protects it with a ten-guinea bid for openers. It follows that even the Xerox copy of such a find has more cash than sentimental value.

Please be circumspect about having sent it to me. If Mr. Allen discovers that it has fallen into my hands the consequences can be so terrible that—well, for now let's not think of them. We can worry about crossing that particular bridge when we come to it. If worse turns to worst, as it usually does when *my* happiness is at stake, perhaps Mr. Schlesinger, who knows a great deal more about bridges than he pretends, can be persuaded to lend us a hand.

And please, Miss Brew, don't let either of them know that I have written you about bridges or anything else. Mr. Schlesinger has rich and powerful friends on every side of any ocean you choose to cross; Mr. Allen is the most beloved poet, wit, essayist, author, raconteur, comedian, actor, TV personality, stern critic of American society, and potential congressman our democratic way of life has yet produced. Such men are easily offended: their wrath, if aroused, consumes continents.

Let us therefore consider this a private letter from me to you. Since it was, after all, your friendly intercession which made Mr. Schlesinger's views known to me, that fervid spirit of reciprocity which saturates our free society calls for some response in kind. But only for you, Miss Brew—only for you, and strictly between ourselves.

Unhappily for both of us, Mr. Schlesinger, when not speaking *ex cathedra,* is one of those soupy writers who requires translation. One must separate what he seems to say from what he says, and then what he says from what he means to say. Not until the broth has been thoroughly clarified is it fair to judge the quality of the ingredients that went into it or the flavor their blending has produced.

The meaning of his first sentence seems relatively clear: I wrote one letter to the ACLU Arts Division and, to the best of my knowledge, Mr. Allen wrote no more than one. Thus when Mr. Schlesinger says he has "had an opportunity to read the letters to the ACLU Arts Division" it is logical to assume that he has read my letter and Mr. Allen's response to it. By changing the end of the first sentence to an *opportunity to read Mr. Trumbo's letter to the ACLU*

Arts Division and your response to it we know exactly where we stand.

But we don't know yet exactly where *he* stands, do we? The difficulty, I suspect, resides in that almost imperial *would be in strong agreement,* which, by pairing a volitional auxiliary with a volitional verb, does something that isn't very nice if we accept the convention that any well-behaved volitional verb wants to mate with an auxiliary of simple futurity such as *should*: hence "*should* be in strong agreement."

Yet the letter form, however soothing to pedagogues, fails to enlighten the commonality because it raises in their less cultivated minds two questions of substantial importance: one of simple futurity (*when* would/should he be in agreement?) and another of conditional futurity (*in what circumstances* would/ should he be in agreement?)

They are so subtly related that a proper response to one is almost bound to answer the other. For example: "Your letter seems to me clear and correct, and *if asked to take a position on what it says, I should* be in strong agreement with it." Or—do you see what I mean?—something that goes even better than that.

Yet that isn't too good either. What we desperately want to know is not whether Mr. Schlesinger *will* agree with Mr. Allen's letter in some future time, or in some unspecified future circumstance, but whether he agrees with it today, this minute, right now. A conscientious translator trying to solve this typically Arthurian riddle must rely on reasoned analysis of the intent of the full sentence, and, indeed, of the letter, as a whole.

Viewed in this light, it is logical to assume that Mr. Schlesinger intended his letter to convey the bracing views that he *did* agree with Mr. Allen's clear and correct statements the instant he read them, and still does. Our translation therefore reads, "Your letter seems to me clear and correct, and I *am* in strong agreement with it." Or, more simply and less passively, "I *strongly agree* with it."

Now we have it, haven't we? Mr. Schlesinger finds Mr. Allen's letter clear and correct and strongly agrees with it. His feelings about mine, as suggested in his next sentence, are antithetical.

But oh Miss Brew, that next sentence! Stand back for a moment. Regard it: "I have never understood how people who

defend communism could consistently associate with an organization dedicated to civil liberties."

The first thing that strikes us here is the coupling of present
tense *defend* with past tense *could*. Let's dismiss it as misfired ele-
gance, and substitute a *can* for the *could*: "how people who defend
communism *can* consistently associate." That helps, doesn't it?
Well, yes; but not as much as we hoped. We still have that *consistently* to reckon with.

Mr. Schlesinger doesn't understand how people who defend X
can consistently associate with people who are dedicated to Y. Why
doesn't he? Why can't they? What holds them back? *You* know,
Miss Brew, and so do I, that it's perfectly possible for anybody to
join the ACLU and consistently support whichever of its quarrels
he has time for, consistently attend its meetings, and consistently
pay its dues. This being incontestably true, we must conclude that
Mr. Schlesinger doesn't use *consistently* in the sense that one consistently attends church, consistently adheres to a course of action,
conducts his life in a consistent manner, or behaves with persistent
uniformity. If I know my Schlesinger—and, rather more than less,
I do—he is trying to say that there is something inconsistent or
incongruous about people who defend communism (and therefore
wish to destroy civil liberties) associating with an organization that
is dedicated to defending those liberties.

Let us, therefore, change *consistently* to *without incongruity* (or
something better of your own choice) and see if it helps: "I have
never understood how people who defend communism *can without
incongruity* associate with an organization dedicated to civil liberties." That gets us a little closer, don't you think?

But not close enough when we pause to consider the meaning
of *communism* with a diminished *c*. Although the rules of capital-
ization are as variable as a pimp's virtue, and every writer is a law
unto himself, in most dictionaries—the 12-volume O.E.D., Webster's Third Unabridged, Random House Unabridged—the first
definition of communism with a lower case *c* describes a philosophy or system which cannot possibly be considered inimical to the
defense of civil liberties. Now if Mr. Schlesinger refers to this
good, lower case, non-incantatory kind of communism his letter
makes no sense at all.

This becomes particularly apparent if we recall that when he was a much younger man, ardently mindful of Senator Vandenberg's advice to "scare hell out of the country," convinced even before Russia had the bomb that she'd be content with "nothing less than the entire world," playing to the hilt his role of John the Baptist to Joe McCarthy's unexpected messiah, warning his too-complacent countrymen against the "awful potentialities of the totalitarian conspiracy" ("It is we or they; the United States or the Soviet Union; capitalism or Communism. . . . We must not be restrained by weakness *when* [italics mine] the moment of crisis arrives . . . we must act swiftly in defense of freedom"), Mr. Schlesinger *always* gave bad Communism a capital *C*.

Not only did he capitalize it, he often characterized it with great specificity as Soviet Communism, Russian Communism, Soviet totalitarianism, etc. Yet now, despite the *New York Times, The New Yorker, The Atlantic,* and the dictionaries (Random House Unabridged capitalizes it, Webster's Unabridged regards it as a word generally capitalized), he has lately begun to invite all sorts of confusion and misunderstanding by demoting it to a simple, commonplace, lower case *c*.

Although no one can be certain when dealing with a mind as subtle and well-connected as Mr. Schlesinger's, I suggest that his reasons are romantic and ideological. He is so fed up with Communism that he has zapped it into the lower case out of sheer pique, and who can blame him? Certainly not I. Was it not, after all, Lyndon Baines Johnson during his troubles with De Gaulle who commanded the Government Printing Office to place quotation marks around France?

Whatever the truth may be, I think we shall come closer to Mr. Schlesinger's vision of it by changing his lower case communism to upper: *people who defend Communism.* Although it is true that we can't be sure whether the people he is putting the hex on defend Russian, Chinese, Yugoslavian, Czechoslovakian, Hungarian, Albanian, Rumanian, or Cuban Communism. I think it is just clear (and vague) enough to serve Mr. Schlesinger's purposes.

This leaves only *defend* to worry about. Does Mr. Schlesinger use the word in its sense of protect, ward off, or repel? In this sense, the ACLU for many years has defended the legal rights of Communists to be Communists and of the Communist party to exist. Surely he can't object to that, since he himself is an absolute wowser on civil liberties and Mr. Allen is wowsier still.

But, one must ask, when the ACLU and Mr. Schlesinger and Mr. Allen defend the civil rights of the Communist party and its members, don't they actually help the party to stay in business? If so, is not their defense of its rights a form of assistance, their assistance a form of support, and their support, in any practical sense, a defense not only of Communist rights but of Communism itself?

No. This must not be. It cannot be because it *should* not be. If it were, members of the ACLU wouldn't be able to associate with each other, and Mr. Allen would be cutting Mr. Schlesinger cold on the street if Mr. Schlesinger didn't cut him first.

Perhaps, then, Mr. Schlesinger's *defend* takes the meaning of uphold by speech or argument, to maintain, to vindicate. That seems a lot more likely, don't you think? For his sake, then, as well as clarity's, let us change *defend* to *uphold*. Then, carefully underlining the changes we have made, let's assemble the whole thing and see how it looks. To wit:

"Dear Mr. Allen:

"I have just recently returned from Europe and only now had an opportunity to read *Mr. Trumbo's letter to the ACLU Arts Division and your response to it.*

"Your letter seems to me clear and correct, and *I strongly agree with it.* I have never understood how people who *uphold Communism can without incongruity* associate with an organization dedicated to civil liberties.

"Sincerely yours, Arthur Schlesinger, Jr."

Since we have followed the form and structure of the original, our translation is not graceful, but the tenses are all straightened out, the purport of the words is clear, and I'll take an oath in any Federal Court of his choice that it exactly reflects the meaning which Mr. Schlesinger wanted to convey when he wrote it.

We emerge from the maze with three small facts: Mr. Schlesinger has read Mr. Allen's letter; he finds it clear and correct; he strongly agrees with it. Our next step is to determine whether the letter with which he agrees makes sense. Let us accept, as our standard for judgment, the idea that reason is the guiding principle of the human mind in the process of thinking; that a logical statement must conform to the laws of correct reasoning; that logic is the process of valid inference; that an inference is valid only when justified by the evidence given to support it; and that any violation of the rule of valid inference (or correct reasoning) produces a fallacious, or illogical, conclusion.

Let's brood for a moment on the following quotations taken in sequence from what I shall henceforth call the Allen-Schlesinger thesis: *(1) I know absolutely nothing of Mr. Trumbo's present political convictions. . . . (2) I assume, however, that at one time he was indeed a Communist. (3) . . . if Mr. Trumbo is today of the Communist persuasion . . . (4) . . . if it could be absolutely certified—or even assumed for purposes of debate—that Mr. Trumbo is today a Communist . . . (5) I haven't the faintest idea as to what Mr. Trumbo's present position on the political spectrum might be. (6) I concede—indeed, I fervently hope—that all of this may be utterly irrelevant in Mr. Trumbo's case. If it is, I would be greatly relieved.*

Question: "What is the subject of the Allen-Schlesinger thesis? Answer: "Mr. Trumbo's present political convictions," which thereafter are linked with everything from ruthless marijuana laws and political tyranny to state murder and a strong hint of treason.

Question: What qualifies them to write on this particular subject? Answer: Their confession at the outset that they know absolutely nothing about it. In this respect they are more percipient than a Zhdanov or Goebbels but, in consequence of their percipience, less rational. Everything in their thesis which flows from this anarchic demolition of valid inference and reasoned thought is, by definition, fallacious, illogical, irrational, and, for men of such enormous integrity, morally degrading and intellectually disgraceful.

Dare we now admit, against our best hopes and even our prayers, that Mr. Allen and Mr. Schlesinger between them have written almost 1,500 deeply patriotic words (not to mention Mr. Allen's later effusions) on a subject about which they know "absolutely nothing"? We not only dare, Miss Brew, I'm afraid we must.

Can the words of men who haven't "the faintest idea" of what they're talking about be classified as anything but gabble? They cannot, Miss Brew: sheer mindless gabble; garbage, as some call it; dreck; pure merde.

What is it that impels a ranking intellectual like Mr. Allen and a Schweitzer humanitarian like Mr. Schlesinger to write all this gabble or dreck or whatever one calls it? That vincible companion of sloth called ignorance, Miss Brew; that infallible solace of closed minds which has sometimes been called "the voluntary misfortune."

The pity of it is that all their ignorance could so easily have been dispelled. Unlike Mr. Allen, who shows every sign of offering himself one day for public service, and Mr. Schlesinger, who has always had one foot in government and the other in somebody's mouth, I am a private citizen to whom the idea of anyone seeking public office has always seemed faintly ridiculous. As past or future politicos, Messrs. Allen and Schlesinger must be prepared at all times to make full disclosure of their professional, political, economic, military, and even marital histories: as a private citizen, my political affiliations, whether now or a quarter-century ago, are exempt from such disclosure.

By exempt I mean private. By private I do not mean secret. Hundreds of friends, associates, colleagues, chance acquaintances, employers, and adversaries have discovered from my own lips exactly what my political thoughts and affiliations have been from my twenty-first birthday through every change or lack of it to the present time—not only what they were or are, but when and exactly why they were made or changed.

They are secret only to casual sensation hunters and those who hope to extort information about them under threat of legal or economic reprisal. In that sense they are as secret today as they were twenty-two years ago on that bright October afternoon in Washington, D.C., when I first refused to make public disclosure of political affiliations which I had voluntarily made known, in advance of assignment, to every producer for whom I had worked at Metro-Goldwyn-Mayer during the preceding five years. In every other sense they are as open today as they have always been.

Had Mr. Allen approached me for enlightenment on a subject about which he stood in total ignorance, I should cheerfully have told him all my secrets and blessed his warm, inquiring heart. Had he confided to me his misgivings about the effect on the Bradley campaign of a party at my house, I should have consented at once to its transfer from my address to his. Not because I share his fears or admire him over-much for harboring them, but because as a rational man I should have been compelled to recognize the objective fact of their existence and to deal with them on that basis.

Do you begin to perceive what I mean, Miss Brew? This part of my letter you may reveal to Mr. Allen and Mr. Schlesinger in any words you choose, for I am offering them the key to their mystery. Whenever they wish to establish a friendly acquaintanceship with me for the purpose of exchanging ideas on subjects of mutual interest (including my past, present, and possibly future political opinions and affiliations but not excluding all else), I shall be happy to accommodate them. At my house. Over my whisky. And, since they are the supplicants, at my convenience. "Ask, dear colleagues," shall I say unto them, "and it shall be given to you; seek, and ye shall find; knock, and it shall be opened."

But do you know something else, Miss Brew? I don't think either of those aging and obsessed evangels will come tapping at my door, because knowledge is the killer of faith and they are of the faithful. They have hallucinated God as the greatest anti-Communist of them all and been completely unhinged by the sight of His glory. It is no longer important to them that they know what they're talking about. It is important only that they talk, since in their theology the act of speech proves the truth of what has been spoken.

Trapped thus between nightmares of qualified good and unqualified evil, they have become what they hate. For such there can be no surcease of gobble, guano, merde, or whatever it is that gushes from their lips and typewriters until the fevers pass and logic resumes its lonely reign. Thus, as the man said, are sweet reason's children strangled in the womb, and noble minds laid low.

Most gratefully yours, Dalton Trumbo
cc: Mr. Eason Monroe, Mr. Thomas Bradley, Mr. Burt Lancaster

Mr. Dalton Trumbo   September 23, 1969

Dear Mr. Trumbo:

Doing six ninety-minute television shows a week has placed such obstacles in the path of my properly fulfilling my obligations as your correspondent that at this point I must beg off, accept your kind invitation to continue our exchange over an amicable glass, and relegate these paper records of our misunderstanding to our respective heirs, assuming our rival philosophies will ultimately permit the continuance of our species on this planet.

Your witty letter of August 29th to my secretary, Miss Brew, obliges me to attempt a response, but I shall not pretend that what follows is anymore than a half-hearted attempt to tidy up a few loose ends. At this point, as often is the case in matters of controversy, so many elements have been introduced, above and beyond the original grain of contention, that even if either of us had the luxury of an extended exchange of letters, I suspect we should find it difficult to limit the number and scope of our concerns so as not greatly to confuse any others who might read this correspondence—not to mention each other.

Now, then.

1. You raise what well may be a fair question with your observation that a considerable amount of confusion might have been avoided had I approached you about the matter in the first place. You say, "Had Mr. Allen approached me for enlightenment . . . I should cheerfully have told him all my secrets and blessed his warm, inquiring heart."

This reminds me, though, of the occasion when, as a sixteen-year-old runaway from my Chicago home, I found myself, one chill October afternoon, in front of the Bluebird Café in Del Rio, Texas, with a compulsive hunger that drove me to the lunch counter and forced me to gorge myself though I had not a penny in my pocket. When, after the meal, I confessed as much to the proprietor he called the police and then asked me—as we sat listlessly waiting for the law to arrive—"Why didn't you just *ask* me for something to eat?"

Although I couldn't bring myself to say as much, I think a fair answer would have been, "Because, sir, you would have told me to get the hell out of your restaurant."

In any event, what's past is past.

2. Since you know yourself to a degree that I do not, you naturally have me at a disadvantage when the object of our mutual scrutiny is Dalton Trumbo. When you speculate about *me*, however, then the advantage is mine. It is a simple matter to develop factual evidence about an individual, but when we attribute motivations

supposedly explaining his behavior, and indulge in purely theoretical speculation about his beliefs and opinions, our testimony will generally be considerably less reliable. You attribute to me, for example, the view that Communism is an "unqualified evil." Nothing human can be totally evil. The worst atrocity ever committed was an ill-wind that produced some positive result, however slight and however out-of-balance with the enormity of the crime itself. There has never been nor will there ever be the totalitarian dictatorship—whether of the Right or Left—which could not point to certain social achievements; is there anyone beyond the age of ten who would deny it? The near-total law-and-order of totalitarian societies has its attractions, to be sure; the historically crucial question is: are these few material benefits purchased at too high a price when the coin that buys them is the sacrifice of freedoms of belief, speech, assembly, the press, and travel?

3. Three single-spaced typewritten pages of your letter of August 28th are devoted to a reinterpretation of Mr. Schlesinger's letter, yielding the unsurprising conclusion that the man's statement is to be taken at its face value, that he means exactly what he *seems* to mean, which is to say that he is puzzled how people can on the one hand defend Communism—which in all times and places, as a matter of public policy, violates civil rights and liberties—while on the other hand they profess allegiance to organizations—such as ACLU—which are sworn to defend these same rights and liberties.

A crucial word, of course, in Mr. Schlesinger's observation is "consistently." Obviously it is *logically* inconsistent to proclaim civil liberties in one nation while denying them in another. But there is another sense in which such behavior on the part of American Communists is neither inconsistent nor puzzling, a situation directly analogous to that in which the Catholic Church concedes on the one hand that Protestant rights in Catholic Spain have been infringed upon, in law and in deed, while at the same time insisting that Catholics in the United States are entitled to the same rights as other American citizens.

It is entirely reasonable for Communists-USA to endorse the American Bill of Rights since it proclaims the essential political rights of all Americans. But when Communists assume control of a nation then the rules of the game are radically changed and rationalizations are advanced supposedly justifying limitations upon the civil rights and liberties of *non*-Communists.

You delay an approach to the essence of our argument by raising the irrelevant question as to whether Mr. Schlesinger would distinguish, in his disapproval, among Communism of the Russian, Chinese, Yugoslavian, Czechoslovakian, Hungarian, Albanian, Rumanian, or Cuban sort. That no two of these are precisely similar is obvious enough, but the large question is no more necessary than would be the question as to whether, in your disapproval of Fascism, you would be more or less tolerant of it in its German, Italian, Spanish, Japanese, or Argentine guise.

It is irrelevant to our purposes—or to mine, at least—to waste time considering the different dictionary meanings of "Communism," the first letter capitalized or not. Obviously there is always a difference between the purely theoretical statement of a philosophy on the one band and its flesh-and-blood embodiment on the other. In every historical case the ideal is superior to the practice. I see no purpose, therefore, in debating the abstract philosophy of socialism or Communism. What I am here interested in is the undeniably clear record of Communism-in-practice and with—more specifically—the activities of the American Communist party, a political instrument which over the years is on record as endorsing the Hitler–Stalin pact, justifying the Soviet attacks on Poland and Finland, opposing Lend–Lease aid to Europe and assistance to Great Britain before Hitler's surprise attack on Russia, attempting to sweep under the rug of history Stalin's slaughter of millions in his domain, bitter opposition to Franklin Roosevelt during the period of the Soviet–Nazi pact, opposition to the Marshall Plan (Communists wanted Western Europe to collapse, not recover), serving as apologists for the Moscow trials, the crushing of the Hungarian rebellion, the Soviet invasion of Czechoslovakia, and all the rest of the sickening list.

4. Liberals may or may not be opposed in principle to the *economic* theory of Communism (though they will look in vain for evidence of its concrete realization). But by the very definition of the word *liberal* they are logically obliged to oppose the omnipresent despotism of Communist *political* practice and belief. A liberal, as such, may be an atheist, or a devout religionist. But the one thing

he cannot possibly be is an apologist for the ruthless imposition of Communist minority party rule that for more than half a century has characterized the exercise of Marxist authority.

That is not to say that Communists, or socialists of other kinds, are wrong in all their criticisms of capitalist practice, or of American foreign or domestic policies. For many years Western capitalism has propped itself up with a certain amount of socialist timber, and Western democracy has come to understand that—mutual annihilation by either nuclear or conventional weapons being an unacceptable alternative—it will have to come to some sort of terms with the Marxist powers. The more responsible elements in each camp, then, may hope that the other side will mellow and evolve.

Against that hope, there are those who so contemptuously speak the word "revisionism." The young nuts of the Progressive Labor Party and Revolutionary Youth Movement—haunted, I suspect, by the dawning awareness of their essential irrelevancy to the American social experience—actually consider China and Albania the only right-thinking Marxist states and view the Soviet Union as revisionist, if not overtly capitalistic and antirevolutionary.

What these fierce but inexperienced dogmatists have yet to discern about the human adventure is that man is *by nature* a revisionist creature, the only conscious one, in fact, that walks our planet. While other species may have their behavior modified by the slow, inexorable force of nature, man is able to take quicker voluntary adaptive steps to bring himself into a more harmonious relationship with his environment. Addiction to rigid dogma and habit, I assert, is an emotional disease that over the course of time greatly incapacitates those individuals and groups that fall victim to it. Not all evolutionary or social adaptations prove beneficial, but utter inability to revise behavior to conform with changing circumstances is a sentence of slow death. The Soviets are by nature neither more nor less dogmatic or revisionist than the Chinese; the Russians simply started their revolution thirty-two years before the Chinese did. It is therefore to be expected that the pace of their political evolution would have wrought greater changes than China has made since 1949.

As a liberal I selfishly hope, of course, that SDS firebrands become even more fanatic and dogmatic. It will make them still more socially irrelevant, even to the most dissatisfied American blacks, poor, and young.

The last thing I will say on this point, for the present, is that even if a liberal were unable to perceive that reason demands his opposition to all forms of tyranny, he ought to be anti-Communist simply because Communists are antiliberal. When Stalin's armies enlarged the Soviet sphere of influence at the conclusion of the Second World War they almost ignored Conservatives, Reactionaries, Nazis, and Fascists in the areas that came under their control. These pathetic souls had already been defeated, slaughtered in great numbers by the process of war itself, or done in by their own underground movements. The few remaining were in disgrace as having sympathized with Hitler and accordingly posed no threat to Stalin's legions and indigenous Communists. The true threat came from non-Communist socialists and liberal democrats who—though anti-Nazi to the core—enjoyed a popular following and therefore were rivals for the affections of the liberated masses. It was these unfortunates who suffered most tragically at the hands of the Soviet "liberators."

Let us fantasize widespread American dissatisfaction in, say, 1975, a growing rebellion of blacks, Latin-Americans, Indians, poor whites, the unemployed, the antiwar young, and then some idiotic repressive act on the part of Wallace-Reagan-Goldwater-J. Edgar Hoover types, leading to popular uprisings, a coup, and a Communist takeover. Would the party be seriously worried about the Far Right? No, it would need the Extremist Right as a punching bag. The one group it could absolutely not tolerate would be non-Communist leftists who would share popular disaffection but not countenance official terror campaigns. The non-Communist Left would once again be the first to be sacrificed to the Red firing squads.

5. The cleverest portion of your letter is in the following sentences:

". . . when the ACLU, and Schlesinger and Mr. Allen, defend the civil rights of the Communist party and its members, don't they actually help the party to stay in business? If so, is not their defense of its rights a form of assistance, their assistance a form of support, and their support, in any practical sense, a defense not only of Communist rights but of Communism itself?"

The question is—as I say—clever, even a bit playful. So let us play with it for a moment. One might as responsibly ask, "When the ACLU and Mr. Trumbo defend the civil rights of the Nazi party and its members, don't they actually help the party to stay in business? If so, is not their defense of its rights a form of assistance, their assistance a form of support, and their support . . . a defense not only of Nazi rights but of Nazism itself?"

The paradox, of course, is apparent rather than real. All true libertarians are prepared to defend the *civil rights* of a variety of antisocial or subversive or totalitarian groups which they personally abhor. In the process of defending these rights there is no question but that actual material benefits fall to Communists, Nazis, Ku Kluxers, Minute-Men, John Birchers, and political knuckleheads of all sorts. One may feel the *emotional* temptation to say, "To hell with it; civil rights and liberties ought *not* to be extended to such political idiots; it is really too much to assert that a Communist or Nazi, a Mafia murderer, a Black Panther sniper, a Ku Klux lyncher, ought to be accorded the same constitutional protections as decent, law-abiding American citizens." But of course that is the precise point upon which the rights and liberties of all of us are balanced. The minute we make the mistake of saying that all Americans are entitled to civil liberties and rights *except* Communists or Nazis we have opened a floodgate which it would almost certainly prove impossible to close. Others would care to add to the list Fascists, Pacifists, Liberals, Conservatives, and so on back into the bloodsoaked jungles from which we all sprang.

6. You have taken me to task, albeit gently, for having referred to myself as a "stern critic" of American society, perhaps under the misapprehension that the phrase was a fearsome mask held before my face and that what I proposed to criticize sternly was your own political record. No. I meant to suggest that I see much in American *non*-Communist behavior to criticize—from the picture, *"Big Deal"*—for who does not? Today we are all critics, but I was such when it was a somewhat less popular pastime. After visiting Vietnam in 1963 I did a television documentary saying we could not win a military victory there with less than one million American troops and that, since we were clearly unwilling to make such an investment, we ought to begin getting out. At the time I was already

a veteran of the nuclear test ban debate, the capital punishment controversy, and other scuffles in the marketplace, for all of which activity I was publicly accused by Conservatives—this will make you laugh—of being a Communist!

7. In conclusion, a word about your assumption that I plan one day to run for political office. I do not. In 1961 Norman Cousins advised me to prepare myself to run for the office of U.S. Senator from California. A great many other Democratic party people, chiefly but not solely of liberal persuasion, have since made similar suggestions. For several years my answer, was "No, thank you."

Then, in 1965, Congressman James Roosevelt retired, accepted a post at the United Nations, and left ten months of his term to be filled, which called for a special election in his district. I was again urged to run. Since only ten months were involved, I agreed to make the experiment, having received encouragement from Hubert Humphrey and Bobby Kennedy, whose advice I solicited.

A poll showed I would have won handily, but after campaigning for a few weeks I discovered that an obscure clause in the California election code law made it impossible for me to become the Democratic candidate, because I had registered as an Independent. I thereupon withdrew from the race and do not plan to repeat the experience, although I would not have missed it for the world.

8. Lastly, something weighty still seems to block the path toward your understanding of the meaning of my original point. At the risk of boring even myself, let me state it once again, as concisely as possible: (a) at one time you were a mightily active Communist; (b) I do not know whether you are presently a Communist; (why don't you tell us, by the way, and hang the suspense?) (c) if—at the time of the Bradley-Yorty mayoralty campaign in Los Angeles—you *were* still a Communist, then it would have been politically disadvantageous to Mr. Bradley's cause to have it become publicly known that a fundraising party on his behalf had been held in your home.

No doubt upon occasion over the years I have unwittingly vouchsafed public observations that were obscure or ambiguous. This is not one of those occasions.

Most cordially, Steve Allen

Mr. Steve Allen   October 13, 1969

Dear Mr. Allen:

Aside from the owner of the Bluebird Café, who'd have thought that hungry, vagrant, shivering little tyke in Del Rio, Texas, would grow up to be the sort who'd sneak a peek at Miss Brew's mail? Well, I for one. On the off-chance she doesn't snoop yours, please tell her I've just discovered Mr. Bradley didn't know that goddamn party had been scheduled until two weeks after it wasn't held. This means that your spirited croak against free speech and assembly at my address can't properly be called delation because you delated to nobodies, and that doesn't count.

Even were it otherwise, I still feel that the Bishop of Norwich and Exeter held his hackles a bit high when he called informers and delators "an infamous and odious kind of cattle": almost every member of the tribe *I* uncover turns out to be just one more lost, home-loving, duty-driven civil-Samaritan of absolutely paralyzing sincerity, whose only fault is a headful of wind littered here and there with small particles of badly organized misinformation. You can't hate a man like that, you can only try to help him.

To that most Christian end, my secretary is preparing a quick-information kit to set you straight on almost everything from marijuana penalties in the USSR (fifteen days for a first-caught user) to the reasons why what you call your black brethren (whose lives will be 176,000,000 years shorter than ours) sport those funny robes, wear those "natural" hairdos (your quotation Marx not mine), and foolishly prefer two names, as in Muhammad Ali, to the five in Stephen Valentine Patrick William Allen. The whole lot, weighing just under three pounds, will be shipped post-paid in a plain brown wrapper.

As for defending the head humanitarian of CUNY, take one look at that cold, governmental smile, and then head for home. He slings the fastest gun in town and you can't shoot back without blowing Old Glory full of holes. I run a kind of nervous check on him every now and then because when you back him into a serious corner called Bay of Pigs or Congress for Cultural Freedom his talent runs to diddling with the truth instead of telling it.

All that jive about would/should/volition/futurity was, of

course, part playfulness, which you suspected, and part gallantry, which you didn't. Any fool can spot the verb of "would be in strong agreement," but "be," for God sake, is copulative, and I certainly wasn't going to say a thing like that in front of Miss Brew.

Sincerely yours, Dalton Trumbo

P.S. I almost forgot the best news of all: the 1958 edition of March's *Thesaurus-Dictionary,* editorially supervised by the same Norman Cousins who tried to roust you off the tube and into the Senate, restricts its "c" listing under EVILDOER to *caitiff, cannibal, Communist* and *cut throat.* Your pot.

Steve Allen and the Historians

Some of the happiest times of my life have been spent at the Center for the Study of Democratic Institutions, the think-tank headed by that impressive gentleman, Robert M. Hutchins, former president of the University of Chicago. While I was originally invited to his beautiful Santa Barbara, California, enclave as an observer, within a few years I was taking part in discussions following presentations by scholars and then—eventually—chairing certain sessions. On one occasion, the Center kindly convened a number of historians who gave me the benefit of their comments on the television series "Meeting of Minds," which I was at the time writing and hosting for the PBS television network. The participants were Otis Graham, Jr., Cissie Bonini, Mark Poster, Sears McGee, Donald Cressey, Donald McDonald, Keith Berwick, and Walter H. Capps. Unfortunately their comments were so lengthy as to not be conveniently quotable here. I was, needless to say, greatly indebted to them.

I wish, in fact, that television viewers in general had been as hospitable to the "Meeting of Minds" series as were the nation's scholars, historians or not. I do not mean that the programs were negatively criticized, in fact, they received an overwhelming congratulatory response.

The problem is that the average TV viewer is, sad to say, not very interested in philosophical discussions. Thank God for PBS. The following response was, of course, unprepared and spontaneous.

From *The Center Magazine* (January/February 1979).

*   *   *

In 1976–1977, Steve Allen, the American entertainer, realized a long-held ambition: his "Meeting of Minds" television program on the Public Broadcasting Service brought together, in a series of hour-long dialogues, great historic figures and their ideas, as portrayed by professional actors. The series excited considerable interest, acclaim, and discussion across the country. It was renewed in 1977–1978, and again this year.

Otis L. Graham, Jr., Center Associate and Professor of American History at the University of California at Santa Barbara, invited Mr. Allen—who wrote and moderated the series—and four historians to join with Center staff members in a critical examination of "Meeting of Minds." Their opening statements and ensuing discussion are reported on the following pages.

In Television the Clock Is the Ultimate Master

There are a number of categorical headings under which my responses seem to be tending to group themselves in my mind. One, certainly, is gratitude. I use the word, I assure you, out of no considerations of social grace, but simply as a means of conveying, as honestly as possible, the dominant emotion that flows from me in response to what all of you have contributed. Besides gratitude, I also feel sorrow in that I wasn't given the benefit of this sound advice before the ball game. But other ball games are coming up.

Otis Graham touched on one of the considerations that impelled me to this large effort. That is the great gap between the messages that ought to be conveyed and the people who ought to receive them. Inasmuch as I can, fairly easily, get at seven, or eight, or nineteen million people at a time, every so often, it actually had occurred to me when I first got into television that somehow I ought to take advantage of that fact, at least within the context of my own prejudices and philosophical assumptions. After the telecasts of the shows, those of us who put this program together learned that considerable good did, in fact, result from our efforts, despite the inadequacies. People have told us that. One young man, for example, said that he had learned more history from one hour of our first show than he had in three years of formal instruction in history in college. I emphasize that that is a particular from which no generalizations need or ought to be drawn.

Ms. Bonini understands why I selected for one of the first women in our series someone who was frivolous, rather empty-headed, a light character, certainly by no means one of the most important people in history. In terms of what Marie Antoinette was able to accomplish, she would rank close to the bottom of any list. But before you can sell the customer, you must pull him into the store. I have never denied—in fact, I have volunteered the information from the start—that such considerations, crass as they may seem from the academic point of view, are important in my mind. Marie Antoinette was chosen simply because she was glamorous and well-known. In other words, she was a "commercial" character.

There were also more respectable reasons for choosing her. After all, she has elicited the professional interest of such people as Stefan Zweig and Hilaire Belloc,* among others. Although she herself was a light personage, she did play a role in one of the most important dramas in history. So we employed her to say something from a point of view not commonly consulted about the French Revolution and the life of royalty in Europe.

There are a great many other more important players in the whole drama in the collapse of the French monarchy and the onset of the French Revolution, such as, among others you mentioned, Turgot and Necker.† They simply could not be brought in because of limitations of time.

One thing I would be indebted to you for is telling me the equivalent, in American dollars, for the French livre. That is the kind of information which is sometimes hard to get. And, of course, in a book or program designed for Americans, one always must

*Stefan Zweig, an Austrian author, was well known for his psychoanalytical approach to biography. Hilaire Belloc, considered a master of the English prose style, wrote primarily for newspapers and magazines and also served as a member of the British Parliament. Zweig's biography of Marie Antoinette was published in 1932, Belloc's in 1910.

†Anne-Robert-Jacques Turgot and Jacques Necker each served as France's director-general of finance prior to the French Revolution. Each attempted to reform taxation by distributing the burden of taxes more justly, but neither was fully capable of achieving his aims. Necker's dismissal by Louis XVI, July 11, 1789, was an immediate cause of the storming of the Bastille.

make such translations; otherwise you are in the position of the average reader of the Bible who is told that something was fourteen cubits and a hockey puck big.

Now, Mark Poster's comments about Karl Marx. First, on whether there were socialist revolutions in the nineteenth century, I picked that up off a page, somewhere. Unfortunately I do not keep a bibliography when writing these scripts. I should explain that no one else is to blame for errors. So far, I have written all the scripts myself. I can, however, pass the buck, in a sense, to the authors of the many sources I have consulted—and there have been hundreds—in preparing the twelve scripts I have written to date.

Again, since I have no academic credentials whatever, I have not been in the least scholarly or orderly. I have simply grabbed books, sometimes literally at random. I will go to a friend's house for dinner, and I will zoom in on a book on the shelf, simply because it relates to a character I have already decided to work on. I will borrow the book for a week or two, pick stuff out of it, and return it. As I say, I don't make a note as to what book I got what facts or theories out of.

Mark Poster also put his finger on an important underlying question: that is, what are my principles of selection? They exist somewhere hazily in my own mind. I am aware that principles exist, that what I feel is not simply wind blowing in an empty cave. Undoubtedly my selections are related to my own experience and interests. But even if I had the soundest selection principles in the world, it would still be impossible to satisfy even as small a group as the one here today. What is important to one person will not seem as important to others who may be equally qualified to judge such matters.

Professor Poster is also sound in suggesting that it might be more profitable in some instances to do a whole show on more or less one theme. That was my original concept back in 1958, when we first tried to get the show on NBC. I realized I had to pick a subject which would be "commercial," so I discarded some of the most basic issues in the history of human thought, such as peace, freedom, faith. I did not dream then of taking up any fundamental philosophical questions, such as being. If I had, I know a lot of people would have said, "I wonder what Ed Sullivan is doing now?"—

I was on opposite Ed at that time. That is why I chose the subject of crime and punishment. Almost all the philosophers in one degree or another have dealt with that theme, and yet it is also of interest to the average person. But when I finally got to doing the ninety-minute version, several years later, with Cleopatra, Thomas Aquinas, Thomas Paine, and Theodore Roosevelt, I realized that it would simply not be right to limit those characters to one subject. There are certain things you will discuss with Aquinas, certain things you will discuss with Tom Paine.

I might add, without mentioning his name, that I submit my scripts to a professional historian for his comments, counsel, and suggestions. He accepts payment for his services, but not public credit. He has said to me, "You are covering a great deal of information here. As qualified as I am, I do not know everything about all you are covering. There may still be some mistakes in this script that I haven't caught. If my name is up there on the screen, I'll get blamed for them. Don't put my name up there." I think that is a reasonable way to approach that problem.

I agree absolutely that Karl Marx's views on alienation might profitably have been introduced. Again, the clock is the ultimate master. We had only two hours for the two programs with Marx, and even if we had Marx there for a one-on-one interview—that is, as the only guest at the table—we could not do him justice in two hours. There is no ultimately satisfactory solution to that problem. Some very important questions and chapters of historical reality are dealt with simply in the form of a passing comment or in a parenthetical phrase tucked into a sentence about something else. That is a shame, but there is no way to get around it, short of deleting seven pages of something else to make room for seven pages on, say, alienation. Had we done that, someone would now be sitting here saying, "But you shouldn't have taken out that section on exploitation."

One of the difficulties—an inherent part of my task, which I recognized very early—is that the more abstract the reality with which I am dealing, the more difficult it is to convey it in terms that are intelligible to the audience whom we are addressing. That audience does not—in contrast to one assumption expressed here by Mark Poster—consist either entirely, or very largely, of remarkably well-informed people. Such people hardly need any assistance, in any event. I am addressing Just Plain Folk, capital J, capital P, capital F. So, I have this problem.

We had that problem with Plato. I laugh to think of my nerve, dealing with his ideas anyway, and giving them whatever time we had, about a half hour or so. In one section, we just picked up little bits and dealt with those, and then told the people, "Go read a book if you want to learn more." We dealt with the question of being, and Plato's theory of ideas. We did give that fairly extended discussion; but the more extended that was, the less we could devote to anything else. On the second of the two Plato shows, we got to his criticism of the Sophists, but that is really all we could do with Plato, which means we dealt with probably a fraction of 1 percent of his thought.

Professor Poster was absolutely on the mark regarding our summary treatment of China and the Soviet Union. We hope, by the way, to have Stalin, Lenin, and Trotsky on subsequent shows. We will also have the Dowager Empress of China, Tz'u-hsi, on a future show, so we will get into the China question. The Dowager Empress perceives Mao Tse-tung as simply another emperor. You will learn a great deal about the misery and wretchedness which made inevitable, in my view, the events of the last quarter-century or so in China. We have another script I am beginning to put together on Sun Yat-sen. The drama of modern China is obviously of such importance that we are dealing with it in four separate shows. That should help.

As to the question of the extent to which Marx is responsible, if at all, for the crimes of Stalin, that is an issue concerning which the world jury is still out, and probably always will be. As Marx himself says, in dealing briefly with the question, "If you want to talk about this, let's talk about the extent to which Jesus Christ is responsible for the Inquisition." Obviously there is a connection, but whether there is responsibility is another matter.

We do plan to have John Stuart Mill, and we do plan to have Adam Smith. I should mention—as might be suggested by the presence of the Marquis de Sade on one of our programs—that by no means all of those at the table are invited because of their charm or heroic stature. One character who greatly appealed to our viewers was Attila the Hun. We seated him next to Emily Dickinson. She was, of course, a sympathetic character, and he was a bit of a schmuck. But that is why I wanted him there. If I could possibly have a heavy on every show, I would have one. Of course, there are a number of such in history, so the task is not hopeless. Again, the idea is to add emotional components to the intellectual clash of ideas, make more people sit on the edge of their chairs and say, "By God, that's telling 'em, Mac! Hit 'em again!"

But even such monsters as Attila can teach us something, either out of their monstrosity or because they call us to account for our own hypocrisies. I don't want to flatter myself unduly—since I had to write all Attila's lines, there being none of the real ones available—but he made a very telling point when he responded to the shock of those at the table over the number of dead at the Battle of Troyes. It was something like a hundred or two hundred thousand. Attila said, in effect, "Just a damn minute here, folks. You want to talk about how many people died in your Second World War?" As the resident dummy at the table, I said, "How many did?" He said, "Forty million. Now, you want to compare these two chunks of arithmetic and talk about barbarism?"

I should say that there is no reason why any of these people cannot return. If the show goes on forever, it is almost inevitable that Marx will return, and we can then clear up a great deal of additional ground.

Regarding the question of the ample literary precedent for this kind of show, I have created nothing new here. I did think of it unaided, and simply dropped it into television. That was my only creative contribution. As somebody said, there have been many such instances: the Dialogue of the Dead, *Van Loon's Lives,* a rather humorous work called *Houseboat on the Styx,* another book called *Heavenly Discourses.* Someone mentioned that even some of Dante's constructs embody this idea.

I think my most serious errors were in relation to the character of Sir Thomas More. Some of this, as I say, was simple error; some was just a matter of the problems already mentioned, limitations of time and so forth.

This relates to the question, what are the ideals of such a construct? It would obviously be ideal if every single statement by every single character consisted, either precisely or approximately, of an actual quotation from the spoken or written words of the person involved. But, like all human ideals, that one cannot be achieved. Nevertheless, it must be held as an ideal, and it must be kept in mind.

But in falling short of that ideal, one of the liberties I have permitted myself is occasionally to put into the mouth of a character—and here I realize I have to be very careful—something that seems reasonable to assume he would say, simply because he was "a Catholic," or "a Marxist," or "an Italian," or whatever. This calls for very delicate treatment. I am sure I have not satisfied even my own requirements in this regard. It seems to me that one of the statements that I put into the mouth of More—my memory is too hazy on this—is something I drew from Hilaire Belloc, who was also Catholic.

Discussion

SEARS MCGEE: Belloc is almost entirely unhistorical in his use of material from this part of English history. Belloc's stuff was about half fiction. He was a royalist writing about a period that, particularly in the seventeenth century, was pretty bad for English kings. Belloc is a fanatical defender of, for example, the Stuarts.

STEVE ALLEN: You touch here on another one of the inherent, therefore inevitable, difficulties that one faces, once one undertakes such a task. That is—and you historians would know this far better than I—the remarkable degree to which even the most respected authorities differ. That this would be true as regards questions of philosophy is self-evident. But it is frequently true as regards questions of fact. I discovered on the question of the number of Maria Theresa's children that one encyclopedia gave me one figure, and another gave quite a different figure.

OTIS GRAHAM: I am alarmed by this, Steve, but I may misunderstand you. The more history the undergraduates take, the more they develop an absolutely poisonous skepticism. They say, "This professor says one thing, and that professor says another. They gave me three books to read, and I find four different theories. So all truth is relative. It doesn't make any difference what one holds, so I'll just pick this version."

I can understand their feeling. Of course, facts will always be in dispute. But it is not true that, over time, a demonstrably better position will not emerge on these disputed questions. Admittedly, Mark Poster doesn't agree with all of his colleagues on every point. Nor does Cissie Bonini, nor I, nor Sears McGee.

But I would think that all of us would agree that Poster is right when he says that alienation is important in any discussion of Karl Marx's views. There are some things that historians quibble about; but there are other things on which we don't. Thorough-going relativism regarding historical truth would be a bad mistake. I am not charging you with that. But I do say it is a shoal on which many of my students pile up.

ALLEN: Such a skeptical frame of mind is one I personally am uncomfortable with, no doubt for personal reasons, perhaps even because of a character weakness. The authoritarian streak in me wants things to be neater than, in reality, they often are.

CISSIE BONINI: I think that one of the areas where the academy could be most helpful to you would be the biographical. For example, Sears McGee says that Hilaire Belloc's biography is historically unreliable. That kind of help can be given quickly by a historian. We deal all the time in the historical romances and the popularized versions of history. Some of them are good, some are terrible.

GRAHAM: And the historians' judgment on Hilaire Belloc is consensual.

BONINI: If you ask, "Should I rely on this author?" and if it is just flat-out wrong, we can give you a fast answer, so that you won't waste your time.

JOSEPH J. SCHWAB (*Center Associate*): When I first saw the list of people Otis Graham had invited to this discussion, I thought we were pulling a dirty, tyrannical fast one. They were all historians.

And it would have been a tyranny, had it not been for at least two of you—Mr. McGee and Mr. Poster. Everybody in the academy knows that historians tend to have just one notion of authenticity, just one notion of where the meaning of a life or the meaning of a text, lies; namely, in its broad historical context. Everything that has been said here today, with the exception of comments by McGee and Poster, tends in that direction. It is as if this were a "history show." But as a matter of fact, Charles Darwin, Joseph John Thompson, and Heinrich Hertz are not just nineteenth-century figures, they are biologists or physicists; and John Locke and Karl Marx and Jeremy Bentham are not just nineteenth-century figures, they are economists, political scientists, political philosophers, jurists. And, by God! these people have a meaning, a context, and an authenticity which lies in the region of the perennial issues which they attack. There is no reason in the world why mere historical authenticity—and I am deliberately provocative in saying "mere"—should be Steve Allen's goal.

ALLEN: That is not my primary goal. My primary goal is to make people think. There has been a collapse, not only of intellectual standards, but of intellectual performance, in our country. There is statistical evidence for this in the continual lowering of college entrance examination scores, an increase in functional illiteracy, that sort of thing. I think things will get worse before they get better.

At present, our society is rather far removed from what our founding fathers had in mind. The Jeffersonian assumption was that the people—at least those who were to some decree educated and who had some property and some social substance—ought to be able to govern themselves, simply because they were taking the trouble to familiarize themselves with the issues. By the very nature of that familiarity and their dedication, the people, it was felt, could play an important social role.

But it hasn't worked out that way over the last two hundred years. Today, we have a long list of important problems, the problems themselves are increasingly complex, there is a depressing lack of factual knowledge, and there is much less philosophical speculation about the issues. If a person does not know what he is voting for, it is at least fair to ask whether he has any right to vote.

I take all of this seriously, which is why I have bothered about this whole thing in the first place.

DONALD R. CRESSEY (*Professor of Sociology, University of California at Santa Barbara; Center Associate*): You said that television viewers who want to know more about the issues you raise on "Meeting of Minds" should go out and read a book on them. It occurs to me that they are not going to do that. They can't. You just gave the reasons why. That puts more and more of a burden on television to teach people things. The question that I had when I first saw the Marx episode is whether there is any evidence that the viewers know any more about, say, the theory of the surplus value of labor now than they did before they saw your program.

ALLEN: I would think that a survey would show that they do know something more about it. As to how much, of course, that would be a question. And, of course, these same viewers would have been exposed to other sources of information, say Galbraith's series on economics, so that it would be difficult to identify their source of knowledge.

MARK POSTER: Why not roll a few book titles at the end of your show, readings people can pursue?

ALLEN: An excellent idea; a quick bibliography.

SCHWAB: I want to emphasize what I said earlier. There are dozens of contexts within which a life can be understood or a text can be read. There is the general historical set of events. There is also the progress of a problem from hypothesis to solution—or nonsolution—in, say, physics, or chemistry, or political science.

DONALD MCDONALD (*Editor of* The Center Magazine *and* World Issues): If the overall objective of Steve Allen's program is not history per se, but the play of ideas on perennial issues, then the contextual question begins to recede a bit, doesn't it?

KEITH BERWICK: It doesn't for me, for precisely the reason that any idea, or set of ideas, is the product of a peculiar and unrepeatable set of historical circumstances. I do not for a moment deny that there is a dialogue through time. I am sorry to have communicated so little of what I have in mind to Mr. Schwab, because I don't think that these are mutually exclusive propositions at all.

SCHWAB: They're not.

BERWICK: Establishing the relevance of a past articulation of ideas to present and continuing dilemmas of the human condition requires, first of all, that we take the man in his historical context and see what was unique about that. Any damned fool can see analogies. I have never understood the value of analogies tests. Down through time, one can see the analogy between the age of Andrew Jackson and the age of Franklin D. Roosevelt. It takes an act of genius to see what was unique in the challenges that confronted Roosevelt in 1933, and then to establish its place on the continuum. This is the kind of dialogue that is the high ideal of the Center for the Study of Democratic Institutions.

I want to urge Steve Allen on to an even more audacious enterprise, something that goes beyond, as it were, the uninstructed, but inspired, efforts to bring these historic figures into our presence. So I am very much in sympathy with what Cissie Bonini said about seeking the help of historians who are utterly sympathetic to what you are trying to do. Someone like Mark Poster could have come in before you started and said, "Look, don't pay much attention to Hilaire Belloc. Belloc is fantasizing. He will lead you astray." That would have saved you countless hours. The random-research enterprise, it seems to me, disserves you.

WALTER H. CAPPS (*Professor of Religious Studies and Director of the Institute of Religious Studies, University of California at Santa Barbara; Center Associate*): I recall Erik Erikson telling us about critics of his book, *Young Man Luther.* They were, he said, of two kinds. There were historians who said that he had mixed up the facts, and there were theologians who said that he had played around with and denigrated religion. Erikson's response was, "You must remember what I was trying to do. I was not trying to teach the historians or the theologians. I was trying to teach psychologists that they have to take the historical dimension seriously." So, the purpose of a thing is what gives formation to its content. What Steve Allen is involved in doing is, in a way, creating a new genre. The rules belong to the genre, and it's difficult to judge the matter from outside the genre. The genius of it is bringing all those people into the same room, bringing them out of the past and putting them into the present tense. My only difficulty is that I am not sure that some of those folks can make that transition. I am not sure Martin Luther can.

ALLEN: He does seem to be a psychological and philosophical anachronism today. Almost everything he said strikes people today as silly or laughable. During one of our tapings, some in the audience laughed at things Luther believed very seriously.

McGEE: Let's take Luther. There is a whole other Luther that is not the Luther you have in your program. It is clear from the context in one of Luther's works that he expects the father in a family to change the baby's diapers. But that doesn't come across at all in the woman-hating Luther as portrayed in one "Meeting of Minds" episode. Luther's point is the theological one about the value of doing what you do in a spirit of love of God. Luther says it is not priests going around priesting and butchers going around butchering, and so on, that sanctifies tasks in the sight of God. Rather it is the spirit in which these things are done; all labor is sanctified if it is done in the proper spirit, including a father changing his baby's diapers. That is Keith Berwick's point about calling upon historians and asking for some good books on, say, More. That would help solve the problem I raised about the relationship between More and Henry VIII.

POSTER: On the problem of context, I think I would disagree a bit with Keith Berwick. One of the crucial things you have to decide is what is our context today. Then the historic figures fall into place. Luther or More might be outside of one's chosen context, but they could still be interesting and useful because they were in a different context. But then it would be clear that they were, in fact, in a different context. If you say our context is the context of an industrializing society, and that our big goal or project is modernizing the world, then a number of different positions are relevant to that. There is a liberal position, there is a socialist position, there may be an anarchist position, and, perhaps, a technocratic position. There are a limited number of positions; therefore, it is valid to go back to John Stuart Mill and to his ideas about what is going on, as compared with, say, Karl Marx's notions. So, I think those people *are* in our context. They are not purely historical figures of the 1840s. In one sense, we are not only of our time but also of the 1840s.

GRAHAM: Historians know that one of the most powerful currents running in our discipline and in related disciplines is an intensified interest in people who are not the great men and women. Steve, you have mostly great men and women in your "Meeting of Minds." Have you thought about the advantages—while not ignoring the possibly inherent difficulties—in occasionally introducing to your table one of those whom we now facilely call the "anonymous," those who saw history from the bottom up, those who did not leave the usual records, those who were acted upon rather than acting? Historians are belatedly discovering the importance of this. I believe that would add much to your series.

ALLEN: A marvelous idea. We do have one obscure figure, Cesare Beccaria, in another episode. Beccaria is almost totally unknown to the average person. I love your idea. If we were to find a document tomorrow—an autobiography of, say, an Egyptian slave—I would be eager to have him at the table and ask him, "How was it?"

POSTER: You can take a peasant woman in Burgundy in 1750. We know a lot about that. We have a profile of how an average peasant woman lived in that place at that time.

ALLEN: A great idea. If they will let me keep up with this, I'll do it.
    I wanted to say a bit more about our format and alternative formats. I saw an absolutely superb program about Leonardo da Vinci on the Public Broadcasting Service three or four years ago. A narrator simply wandered around talking to us right in the camera, an Alistair Cooke sort of thing. That was beautiful. I wish that was on

the air morning, noon, and night. I wish "You Are There" was back. I'd like to see Eric Sevareid, or anyone else, interview an endless series of people, one at a time. Another series was done in Canada for only a few years. It was called "Witness to Yesterday." These were thirty-minute programs, which is not long enough, but they were good. There can't be enough such programs to satisfy me as a viewer. But at present I am locked into my format.

In terms of what Mark Poster said in his opening statement here is something I had written for another occasion which may be relevant. Mr. Poster asked what I am trying to do on "Meeting of Minds" and what level of audience I am trying to reach. I'll just read a part of this statement:

"I perceive myself as occupying a middle ground between scholars and the people. At the moment, however, the middle ground seems very thinly populated. It might be likened to a no-man's-land or barrier, which prevents, rather than facilitates, communication between the academy and the street, between gown and town. Through the at least personally fortuitous accident that I am chiefly employed in television, I am therefore in a position to share with a large number of individuals such information as I acquire in the process of my own education. There is frustration in this, of course, in that there seems some sort of vague, hard-to-define spirit—as insubstantial as Robert Frost's something that doesn't like a wall—some force in television that doesn't particularly like what I'm doing. For the most part the industry takes little notice."

But the viewers' response to "Meeting of Minds" has been most gratifying. We have literally thousands of letters from grateful people.

Before I forget, I want to comment on the point about consistency in the characters we portray. Man is almost by definition an inconsistent animal. As Walt Whitman said, "Am I inconsistent? Then I am inconsistent." You can always quote someone today, and, two years later, say to him: "You've changed your position!" Seven years later, he may return to his first position. In the case of Luther, there is much more actual quotation of him than of others in our scripts. He left behind a lot of words which we can pick up and use.

And the idea of a bibliography is excellent, as I said before. That could be included not only on the screen, but also as information in publicity stories and magazine articles on the program.

A tremendous problem, obviously, is that we are portraying mountainous characters and barely scratching their surfaces. I am beginning to think that when I have Aristotle as a guest, I might have only three people at the party instead of our usual four. That would enlarge the possibilities for each of the three. I think that will be necessary. I have been very conscious, particularly in dealing with Plato, that short shrift is inevitable. Plato got as long a shrift as anybody else, but it wasn't enough. He deserved so much more. We did pay Plato the honor of mentioning that all of the other guests who had appeared on the series would almost certainly consider him the single most important member of their number. But that was only a compliment. It didn't address the problem. We are going to give Aristotle a better break.

There is another reason why we must get Aristotle soon. A remarkably large number of the other guests who have come on the show have been quite critical of Aristotle. Galileo almost frothed at the mouth when he thought of Aristotle. Francis Bacon was very anti-Aristotelian. So were some of the others. We will give Aristotle a chance to speak in his own defense.

As regards the wisdom, or lack of it, of using a television talk show as our theater, well, for one thing, we are stuck with it; and, two, I happen to think it's a better idea than some of you obviously do. There has been a twenty-five-year conditioning of the American television audience to respond favorably to that format. I think that is a more important factor than perhaps you do.

At one time, I thought of bringing in the four characters without me or any other narrator, letting them appear in some never-never land and start talking to each other. On some of the early shows, the set was not as you now see it, a sort of uncomfortable-looking, nineteenth-century drawing room, with a fireplace and bookshelves. Originally it was more like a combination of the outdoor area of the Center here, the Academy in ancient Athens, and heaven, as conventionally imagined. We had a blue "eye," as it is called, a cyclorama which just seemed to fade off into nothingness, all blueness and clouds. You didn't know where you were. We had some Greek columns to lend a little class to the whole thing. It was never specified where we were. We just seemed to be in the great beyond. Finally we got a little more down home. We got into a room, walked down actual steps, through actual doors.

Glamour Is No Drinking Companion

I have never encountered a woman writer who devoted more than a few sentences to expressing respect and admiration for the amount of alcohol a man could consume without making a fool of himself. But men who write, whether they themselves drink or not, seem to be impressed by an excess, which in reality clearly has the most tragic effects.

The habitual use of liquor is annually responsible for suffering many times greater than that occasioned by AIDS. Thousands of innocents are killed yearly in accidents caused by driving while drunk, countless crimes committed, barroom brawls and sexual offenses, not to mention the gradual destruction of living tissue that at any given moment is sending millions to their deaths.

Why, in the light of this unremitting wave of destruction and foolishness, anyone should express any emotion beyond sympathy for an alcoholic friend has, since childhood, been something that I could not understand.

There is nothing of the holier-than-thou in this judgment. My own mother was a partial alcoholic, as were some of her brothers

This essay was originally published in the *Lost Angeles Times,* April 22, 1988.

and sisters. Although alcohol was not the only cause of destruction of the fabric of my mother's family, the Donahues, it was high on the list of contributing factors.

When I was young, I used to take an occasional drink and have, in rare instances, become as intoxicated as anybody else in my social circle. But in every instance, I behaved like a boob and later wished I had not done so. Again, I am no saint and have no wish to legislate others' morality. If people wish to drink themselves into an ongoing series of bouts of asininity, not to mention eventually the grave, that is their problem and there are wonderful organizations such as Alcoholics Anonymous that stand at the ready to help them.

My argument, then, is not a matter of looking down on the unfortunate drinkers of the world—they have my sympathy. What I object to is the romanticizing, the mindless glamorizing, the endless stories as to who can "carry his liquor." The answer to that one, gentlemen, is nobody at all. Just because a man might be able to walk more or less steadily across a room or not slur too many words in a conversation after several drinks is not to argue that alcohol has no negative effect whatever on him.

As an authority on comedy I am aware that one of the easiest ways in the world to make people laugh is either to pretend to be drunk or to tell stories involving the exaggeration of someone's state of intoxication. This is dependably amusing because, as I've mentioned in other contexts, comedy is about tragedy.

I am never favorably impressed when I hear how much Jackie Gleason, Errol Flynn, or some other semiaddicted individual could ingest without falling asleep or throwing up. I loved Jackie's comedy but I wish he hadn't drunk nearly so much. He'd probably still be amusing us today if he hadn't spent so much time as a barfly.

As for Errol Flynn, there was an impressive, handsome, and intelligent gentleman. I had the pleasure of booking him as a guest on my comedy program twice late in his life, and now that he is gone I can comment for the public record on what a pathetic spectacle he presented at the time.

Some of this reality has been revealed, in a comic way, in the motion picture *My Favorite Year,* based partly on Flynn's adventures on the Sid Caesar show and on my own one year when he came to New York to earn a little quick television money to help with his financial problems, problems partly caused, in fact, by his long history of irresponsible drinking.

A drunken driver once almost killed my wife, our eight-year-old son, Bill, and myself by careening wildly onto the busy California coast highway directly into heavy traffic coming from right and left. Bill and I were on my motorcycle driving behind Jayne in her station wagon, from Santa Barbara to Los Angeles, when I suddenly saw a parked car lurch forward, cutting across traffic.

Jayne, thank God, slammed on the brakes and swerved. As soon as I saw the smoke coming from her braking maneuver, I pulled my motorcycle off the road, came to a quick stop, told Bill to remain where he was and ran forward at top speed to apprehend the driver, who had, in the instant, been hit by a Volkswagen driven by an unfortunate young woman who was badly battered in the crash.

As I raced up to his car and pulled his door open, demanding to know what the hell he thought he was doing, he looked up in bleary-eyed panic, stepped on the gas again, and this time hit another car. Parenthetically, I later learned the man was not prosecuted for the peculiar reason that he was an off-duty police officer.

Again, my sympathies to the poor alcoholic and what must be the long-suffering members of his family. But such brain-numbed drunks kill thousands every year, and injure a far greater number, sometimes ruining them for life. So it's not all that amusing or macho, gentlemen, to be told how much old Bill Holden or Humphrey Bogart could put away. Far too many actors have had their lives and careers partially or totally ruined by heavy drinking. John Barrymore was touched by the muses—what a fascinating gentleman on stage and screen—but alcohol turned him into a pathetic, old, sick bumbler.

Another form of behavior—often sadly addictive—for which some men seem to enjoy praising others, if you can believe it, is gambling. I'm no bluenose about that behavior pattern either. I not only have performed in the gaming clubs of Las Vegas and Atlantic City, I occasionally place a bet myself. The other night at dinner Telly Savalas and I made a $100 bet on the outcome of the Tyson-Spinks fight.

But when I was working in Las Vegas I used to see those poor furtive losers step out of the bushes, knowing that I was making many thousands of dollars a week, and put the bite on me for "just a twenty or a fifty, Steve, so I can get a bite to eat" or "until I can get back on my feet." I always gave it to them; it would have been pointless to preach to the gentlemen about the stupidity of their behavior. They knew all about that, but they couldn't help themselves.

And even those who are not quite so compulsively addicted to the gambling pattern often suffer severe financial losses just because they think it would be "too chicken" to walk away from a craps or card table when they're heavy losers. This is macho? This is how to prove your manhood?

This is the same kind of idiocy as overdrinking. Did you ever notice that it's usually insecure actors, neurotic writers, or other kinds of losers who are the object of such admiring stories? Don't look for any Nobel Prize winners, near-saints, intellectuals, scientists, brain surgeons, or other winners to be trying to act tough by shooting craps.

One of my uncles, Bill Donahue, had his life partly ruined by getting into a street crap game when he was fifteen and winning more than $1,000, an amount which in those days, early in the century, would be the equivalent of about $10,000 today. It ruined his life because he could never give up the foolish hope that lady luck would smile upon him similarly again. She never did, needless to say. Oh, he won an occasional few dollars. The unluckiest gamblers of all time always do win at least that much.

A very clever comedian who died some years ago was terrific when it came to making us laugh. But he was a dummy in the card games and at the gaming tables, as a result of which he left his poor widow with a line of gambling and other debts that she had to work a long time to pay off. Let's stop praising this kind of behavior. Call the addiction to gambling—severe or mild—what it is, a character defect.

This is no argument against your neighborhood bingo game or office Super Bowl pool. People who want to gamble will go ahead and do it, even if it's illegal.

Again, what I'm objecting to is the style of writing in which a journalist, perhaps unconsciously, tries to show us how tough he is by writing about an inveterate gambler in a tone of admiration more fitting a dissertation on a great athlete, military hero, or quiet philanthropist.

What Book Do You Wish You'd Written?

Over the past thirty years or so, I have produced many books, and no doubt at the time of death will not have completed all those I have contemplated writing, given that I am now sixty-seven years old. But there is one I would be interested in reading and, since I am not aware that anyone else has dealt with the subject matter, perhaps eventually I will have to turn to the task myself.

The subject is cruelty, a form of behavior that grows out of anger. Anger is, in its simplest essence, a perfectly "reasonable" form of human emotion as, for that matter, is fear. While we would be very unfortunate indeed if we were always angry and fearful, the two emotions, nevertheless, serve a life-sustaining purpose. But everything human produces both good and evil results. Anger and cruelty have, since long before the dawn of history, brought about an amount of suffering so enormous that our limited imaginations are unequal to the task of even measuring, much less contemplating it. While in most respects the human animal may be superior to all others, he is clearly inferior to them in certain regards. One is

From *The Critic,* 43, no. 4 (Summer 1989): 33–36. Reprinted by permission of *The Critic,* 205 W. Monroe Street, Chicago, Ill. 60606.

that man may be the only animal creature that kills his own readily, constantly, and in massive numbers. All the other creatures, even those we regard as fierce and dangerous, seem to kill only when hunger forces them to do so, when defending their own lives, or protecting their young. But man goes far beyond this limited deadly range. Men will kill others simply because of anger, even in the total absence of the likelihood that any material gain will result from the criminal act.

But since all of this has long been recognized, why should I perceive the need for a book about it? The answer is that I detect a certain recent expansion in that latent viciousness which has always lurked in the human heart. I refer now only to American society. This is not to suggest that the problem is uniquely ours; it clearly is not. But because I am most familiar with American experience, I am therefore most concerned and depressed about the fact that the resort to violence now seems to have become common and casual. And even in the absence of overt killing and physical assault there is something new about the ugliness of spirit in our society.

The first instance in which I detected this happened about thirty years ago when an unfortunate man, threatening to kill himself by leaping to his death from a window ledge of a New York skyscraper, stood for hours undecided, teetering on the brink. There were, of course, those decent citizens—police and a clergyman— who tried to save the poor fellow's life. But at the same time as these efforts were being made, there were many, in the crowd that had gathered below in the street, shouting—God, I shudder to think of it again—encouragement to the poor soul standing on the wind-swept ledge so close to death.

"Come on, jump, you jerk," one man shouted.

"Let's get it ovah with," someone else said.

Newspapers at the time reported this. I shall never be able to forget the horror that the story evoked in me. Here were dozens of men—apparently no women—standing below, having not the slightest idea who the poor sufferer was but encouraging him to jump to his death anyway. What sort of homes did these men come from? Were they chiefly members of one religious denomination or another? They were presumably lower-class or lower-middle-class residents of New York City. They were all of the Caucasian race.

Perhaps they represented various economic strata. But how do we account for their disrespect for life itself? For that is what they were demonstrating since they could have held no animosity for a man totally unknown to them. They actually wanted to witness death. They wanted to see a hideous spectacle, that of a tender, sensitive human body plummeting, at increasing speed, onto the pavement below.

It is doubtful whether any of them would have given voice to such cries were they alone. Something about the mob-factor made these men less than human, depending on what one thinks the word *human* means.

In any event, one of my first reactions to all of this distressing reality was to devise a short story in which the scene of the would-be suicide is presented on the first page. But then—a switch. A squad of about twenty men move quickly and efficiently through the crowd. In pairs, they one at a time quietly approach the shouters, handcuff them and take them away. It was not made clear as to what the fate of such sadists would be but, if I insert myself into this fantasy, I would very much like to sit down with those men, first one at a time, and then perhaps in a "therapy" group, and ask them questions. I would like to know if, even after the fact, they could be brought to feel the slightest guilt, or whether they would seek to justify their vicious insensitivity.

Another development of the story, still found among my notes, would stipulate that the man who threatened suicide was actually protected by an invisible wire fastened to his belt and was, in fact, an *agent provocateur,* assigned to exhibit himself as a way of drawing out of the waters below, so to speak, the killer sharks who infest our society.

Whether I shall eventually write a book that addresses this problem I do not, at the moment, know. First, there are at least four others I must complete, but there is a problem here that needs to be addressed. It needs to be addressed by the churches, by the art/science of psychiatry, and by our philosophers.

Almost every indicator of violence seems to have worsened in recent years. As of 1989, four thousand women in America each year were being killed by their husbands. The statistics on child abuse are horrendous, war among our criminal gangs has made our streets more dangerous than ever, life in our slums is ever more precarious. There are so many guns in the hands of private citizens now, including murderous rapid-assault weapons, although never enough to satisfy the National Rifle Association, that gun control may be a lost cause. Even life in our prisons is more dangerous than it has been in the past.

And there is a mysterious increase in the kind of killing that used to be described as "senseless." In the past, robbers, burglars, and thieves might carry guns chiefly for the purpose of intimidation. Now it is common for victims to be shot even after they have given up their money, jewelry, or other belongings.

Language itself has become more debased and vicious. Thirteen- and fourteen-year-old girls now use language of the sort that in earlier years was encountered only in military life or among the lower class.

In our schools both students and teachers are physically assaulted, sometimes with weapons. On the American Far Right you can almost detect a bizarre greenish glow over the spectacle of paramilitary groups, parties of vengeance, training in terrorist and "survival" techniques. We see a resurgence of activity by the Ku Klux Klan and even more violent organizations. Even comedy is now debased, defaced, abusive, and critical to an unprecedented extent. The writers of popular music flaunt violent images.

Violence enlarges constantly, moving like a blight or deadly viral disease across our society. Simple social courtesies are rarer now. In a word, ours has become a strangely sick society. Much of this, accompanied by other evidences of physical and moral collapse, has happened during the recent eight years in which a doddering old smile-specialist has reportedly been making us "feel good about ourselves."

The Lesson of Clarence Thomas

No one, apparently not even God himself, has ever expected per-fection of his human creatures. Even as a philosophical abstraction the ideal of perfection can be applied only to God. To state the same thought another way, not even the saints were perfect. But all human law, including the moral law, is based on the premise that perfection will be respected as an ideal.

No ideal has ever been achieved, but ideals are of the greatest possible importance, because they provide a moral compass.

No one has ever achieved true North, either, but the abstraction is of great practical importance, as all the world's travelers can attest.

In an age when, for better or for worse—and usually both result—the church is frequently embarrassed by revelations that certain of its sons and daughters have not always practiced what they preached, it's easy enough to say that this is true of humankind generally. Indeed it is. But there's one crucial difference, and that is that the church, especially in its formal representatives, is called to a much higher standard than the human race generally.

Reprinted with permission. Originally published by America Press, Inc., 106 West 56th Street, New York, N.Y. 19919, in *America*'s November 9, 1991, issue.

215

If priests are no better than lay people, who needs them? It would be better to be guided in our own conduct by those who are simply virtuous, compassionate, and wise, whether or not they are priests. But it is simple, and more orderly, to train young Catholics for the priesthood in such a way that they *will* be morally better than those they lead and minister to.

But the church's relative failure to eradicate racial, ethnic, and other hatreds from the hearts of the faithful has led to the tragic result that certain Catholic communities of this sort are providing a number of young men to our seminaries, with predictable—and deplorable—results.

May I be so bold as to suggest that the time for a scholarly, disinterested approach to this problem is long past? May I further recommend the following brief lecture of indoctrination to the prefects of all the world's Catholic seminaries, and most immediately those in the United States:

Dear Students:

In the months and years to come you will be absorbing a great deal of information. Some of our training by-and-large has been very effective over the centuries. It has produced remarkable men, many of whom have done remarkable things.

Recently, however, it became clear that one particular message has not been properly taught. I refer to a quite specific moral lesson, the kind of thing we usually classify under the heading of "It-goes-without-saying." Well, if it ever did go without saying, it does not so go now.

That's why I'm not only saying it, but saying it first, right at the top, before we get to anything else.

Here's the lesson, and may I suggest that you pay damned careful attention to it.

There is no place in the priesthood for racism.

Simple enough? Actually there's no place in the Catholic church for racism—just as there's no rightful place for sin or evil of any kind.

The church has established mechanisms for dealing with sin: discouraging it in the first place and forgiving it when it does occur. Some sins involve a simple succumbing to temptation. It may be difficult, in a given context, to resist the temptation to give in to the sins of the flesh, to financial corruption, or to the sin of anger, to mention only three categories.

The behavior motivated by racism doesn't even have that justification. You are not tempted to be anti-black, anti-Jewish or anti-any other division of humanity. Racism is not a matter of temptation, it's a matter of stupidity, and—again—there's no place for it in God's plan for the redemption of us all.

At the risk of boring you by making the same point repeatedly—*there will be no place for it in the seminary.*

I hope you're familiar with the story of Supreme Court Justice Clarence Thomas. The distinguished gentleman—whether you agree or disagree with his views on one question or another—once studied for the Catholic priesthood. Perhaps if the young men who attended the same seminary where he was being trained had heard a lecture of this sort Clarence Thomas might today be a Catholic priest.

Do you know why he decided to chuck that ambition and check out? It was because in the Catholic seminary, the very sort of place where you might expect to encounter Christian and Catholic behavior at their best, Clarence Thomas was exposed to racism of a particularly mindless sort.

Now some of you—originally through no fault of your own—may have come from political camps, from neighborhoods or even—God help us—from families that were anti-Sematic or anti-black. That's tough. You're not going to get away with that kind of bull here.

I'm not using any big words, and I think any reasonably bright ten-year-old child could understand what I'm saying, so I'm sure there won't be any trouble as far as you gentlemen personally are concerned. As you now approach and, ultimately, we hope, achieve the honorable status of Catholic priest, you will be permitted no such moral lapse. The reasons are obvious.

The first one is that if you had to compress the message of Jesus Christ into one word, that word is *love*. Second—and I deliberately repeat this point—the dominant feature of racism is its utter stupidity. As Catholic priests you will have enough problems. You don't need deliberately to court a reputation for stupidity as one of them.

An American humorist once said that it is asinine to despise another man purely on the basis of his race or religion. What you should do, the wit said, is get to know that individual. Learn what makes him tick. And quite often, if you study that man carefully, you can learn some *sensible* reasons to despise him.

Naturally, I'm not recommending any such course of action, nor was the humorist who made the observation. What he was concerned to show was the inanity of disapproving of another individual solely on the basis of his nationality, race, or philosophical views. You are perfectly at liberty to oppose those views, but that's quite another matter.

Although I'm addressing you in your capacity as future priests, what we're dealing with here is a failure of the church—which may well go back 2,000 years—a failure to apply the ideal of Christian love and compassionate understanding, not just as an abstraction, since that is obviously morally appealing, but in concrete application.

It's bad enough—and embarrassing enough to the church—that after 2,000 years of preaching Christianity there are still millions of Christians and Catholics who are quite comfortable with their hatreds. They seem to feel no guilt about them at all.

That, as I say, is bad—indeed tragic enough—but that there should be Catholic priests so morally misguided is intolerable.

Let's again repeat the point—it won't be tolerated here.

Some men—and some very good men, too—have over the ages left the Catholic priesthood because they could not resist their attraction to women.

Apparently, there have been no cases of men who have left the Catholic priesthood because they could not resist hating members of other philosophical, political, or ethnic tribes. Perhaps one of you will be the first.

Thoughts on Gifted Education

Those who are already aware of the importance of special treatment for gifted children require no further encouragement to support so vital a cause. The real target audience is that 99-plus percent of the human race that has yet to even become aware of the problem, much less convinced of the necessity to address it. And, sadly, the misfortune of those trying to help the gifted is that their campaign is being conducted in a time of general social disarray, one manifestation of which is that literally all of those working to keep our society together are faced with funding problems. There would be no point in listing the various components of the difficulty. Every part of the large machine requires financial oiling.

Gifted Education and Ethnic Minorities

I choose next to make a few observations about the dilemma of the gifted as it relates to racial conflict in American society. That general social justice for our nation's African Americans and Hispan-

Reprinted by permission from *Gifted Education Press Quarterly* 8, no. 1 (Winter 1994): 2–7.

ics has not yet been achieved is clear enough. Those Anglos who try to be helpful in this connection can be motivated either out of simple compassionate concern or by the perception that all of us suffer if our disadvantaged citizens suffer. History demonstrates that quite regardless of color the masses of the poor will not forever supinely accept the fate imposed on them. Surely we do not have to wait for the next revolution to become aware of something so self-evident. Already a significant portion of our tax money is committed to shoring up the social structure of inner-city and rural black and Hispanic communities.

Tragically, despite efforts that are formidable if not our potential best, the news for the American poor, of all races, continues to be depressing. One glimmer of light in the surrounding gloom, however, is that certain blacks and Latinos—by no means only entertainers and athletes—do somehow contrive to become educated and to achieve success in the workplace, not only at blue-collar jobs but in the professions. Although a few individual blacks and Latinos view all whites as the enemy, their attitude is just as misguided as that of white racists who have contempt for all minorities. The average American white is overjoyed at any evidence of minority success. It is clear that our corporations have by-and-large been diligent in their search for qualified employees, regardless of race. All of this, of course, is directly related to the special problems encountered by those who are blessed with superior intelligence of one sort or another, in that it is now generally appreciated that even if we are doing a generally lousy job of helping the poorest members of our nation's minorities, it is at least possible to do something more practical for the small percentage who are fortunately endowed.

A fascinating question is: To what extent are those who are sometimes openly hostile to special education for the gifted in our public schools themselves of black or Latino background? I would not be surprised that some are, although it does not follow that their negativity is the result of envy or any other unseemly emotion. The primary reasons may simply be: (1) an awareness of the dreadfully inferior educational opportunities available to the majority of poor children, and (2) competition for already scarce funds.

Fortunately for purposes of clarity, no one has ever argued that we ought to help only the less fortunate or only the brightest. Arguments are about degree, not essence. But if there are any citizens, regardless of color, who cannot see the necessity for helping the best and brightest minority children, then it must be explained to them they should change their minds on the issue, if only out of group self-interest, for where will the next generation of African-American and Hispanic leaders come from if all poor children receive an inferior education?

Funding Gifted Programs

As regards the funding crisis, something relevant happened recently when I was addressing an audience of several hundred people connected with the San Diego Anti-Crime Commission.

Rather than making a conventional address I responded to questions put to me on the spot. Someone had just asked, "How can we get more cops on our streets?" I said, "Well, to approach the question logically it's clear that at the moment we have two alternatives—either to get more cops or fewer streets. Given that it is unlikely that we will actually start closing up certain neighborhoods, it therefore follows that we will get more policemen in our neighborhoods the same way we get anything else in this world—by paying for it. Civic expenditures of that sort are, as you know, provided by the taxpayer, so it boils down to this: you're not going to get more cops on the street until we all stop whining about our taxes and assume responsibility for funding the many programs that our very survival demands." To my surprise, the response was hearty applause, and from a largely conservative audience.

As applied to the controversy about gifted children, this means that our national leaders—all of them—the president, members of Congress, our governors, and local leaders are going to have to stop trying to make political capital by sounding like Ronald Reagan on the subject of tax-paying. At present, funds for all sorts of valuable educational programs are being cut on the quite understandable grounds that there isn't enough money to pay for them. But that is outrageous. We've got to get the money for the programs that hold America together—but that means that there should now be, in the conservative intellectual camp, an exchange of ideas on the narrow

subject of taxation. Obviously, no conservative, capitalist, or libertarian argues that taxes themselves should be outlawed. It follows
that there's nothing essentially wrong with taxation—the question is:
How much is too much? Who says so? According to what principles?
Do we want a strong military? Do we want at least reasonably good
schools? Do we want a sane health-care program? Do we want security on our streets and in our homes? Damned right we do; therefore
conservatives are going to have to ask themselves about the practical
effects of their budget-cutting. At what point do cuts become counterproductive? Obviously lowering an individual's taxes enables him
to acquire a few more CDs, take a trip to Las Vegas, or buy a slightly
more expensive car. But if these expenditures are made at the cost of
deteriorating education for our children, should his intellectual advisors point out the cause-and-effect relationship to him?

By the way, I would not want to suggest, by these observations,
that conservative intellectuals, as individuals, do not support programs for the gifted. I assume that most of them do. But all the
more reason, then, for them to enlighten those in a position to influence the providing of funds for programs that are not luxuries but
crucial necessities.

Influences During My High School Years

I attended five high schools in all (something I do not recommend),
but as I look back at those years, of which it took me five rather
than the traditional four to complete the process, I recall something
that might be helpful in the present context. I refer to clubs. I
remember, particularly at Hyde Park High School in Chicago, that
there were Latin clubs, chess clubs, math clubs, and other special
groupings that brought together students who shared assorted interests. Perhaps the word "gifted" itself ought not to be used because
of its effects on other students not so fortunate, but it should be a
simple matter to form a "creative thinking" club that would draw
together students who are, in fact, gifted.

As I recall, there were no academic credits offered for club
activities in the schools I attended; involvement was voluntary. But
I have little doubt that bright young people in a given student body
would gravitate to such stimulating opportunities.

While I have never described myself as gifted, I suppose that I was blessed, by the accidental roll of the genetic dice, with a number of abilities that set me apart from most of my fellow-students. But there were in those days—the 1930s—no formal programs specifically for intellectually fortunate children. Some might argue, therefore, that since I have obviously done well as regards my professional activities without the benefit of involvement with a gifted children program, it follows that other bright youngsters also need no special encouragement.

No, it does not so follow at all. While it is true that there were no programs by which I could benefit, there were, in fact, two individual teachers who gave me the sort of special attention and encouragement that often proves to be so decisive. One was a Catholic nun, Sister Mary Seraphia, at the St. Thomas the Apostle School in Chicago's Hyde Park neighborhood. Having become aware of my ability to write, she made me the editor of a little schoolroom newspaper, supplied me with books, and in every possible way encouraged me to exercise my gift. Years later, in gratitude, I dedicated one of my early books to her.

The second teacher to whom I will always be grateful was Marguerite Byrne, who taught English at Hyde Park High. She encouraged me to enter an essay contest, in which I won a prize; made me the poetry editor of the school magazine; carefully graded my essays and test papers; and in every possible way made me aware that there was something special about my ability to communicate coherently.

These two women, then, provided the very sort of encouragement and attention that at least a few fortunate children today can get from organized programs. It might be counterargued that there will always be certain teachers so sensitive and well-qualified, ever on the lookout for students who can profit by special attention. Indeed there will, but today the problems of our schools are so notoriously difficult that, even if a few such teachers exist, their tender concerns have little opportunity to be exercised given that so much of their energy is devoted simply to keeping the peace in their classrooms.

Having done a bit of teaching myself, I know that it is a simple matter to quickly identify the brightest students in a class. School principals should cooperate with teachers in this connection so that extracurricular programs of some sort can be developed, not over the dead bodies of administrators but with their full encouragement.

Obviously there will be subdivision. Some children, for example, may have a remarkable gift for music but possess intelligence that is only in the normal category.

An Effective Way for Encouraging Gifted Children to Think

Next, I refer to a teaching gimmick I recently employed, with what I perceive as success, in communicating with two of my nine grandchildren, Bobby (age six) and Bradley (age eight), chosen simply because they live near me, whereas the rest of my descendants are scattered about the country.

As all teachers and parents know, it is difficult to get children to concentrate on almost anything for long periods of time. But just a few nights ago these two little fellows spent about an hour and twenty minutes eagerly participating in an experiment that occurred to me on the spot.

I pointed out to them that because they lived in a comfortable home and were lucky enough to have a father who was well-paid for his professional services, they took for granted a good many things that the majority of the world's children didn't have at all. At that point my purpose was simply to make them appreciate the scores of objects that are a part of their daily environment. But then I said, "Also you'll find that you'll be much more interested in things—all sorts of things—if you play a little mental game about them." At the mention of the word game their eyes lighted up. "What's the game?" Bradley said.

"Just pretend," I said, "that you personally have been asked to make one of the objects that you see all the time, as distinguished from just going to a store and buying it."

There was an antique Chinese ceramic food dish on the table next to us as I spoke. "Look at this particular object," I said, picking it up. "Now let's suppose that somebody asks you to make one of these. Do you think you could?"

"I don't think so," Bradley said.

"That's an acceptable answer," I said. "But now let's add another factor to the equation." (Yes, I use such adult language with my grandchildren, as I earlier did with my four sons when they were growing up. How else are they to develop a vocabulary if grownups weed out the kinds of terms they employ in communicating with each other?) "Let's pretend that I offer you a thousand dollars if you can make one of these. Now would you be interested?"

"Sure," they both said.

"Okay, then let's get started. Tell me how you might make one of these things. But before you answer, study this one. Look at both the top and the bottom of it. Notice the various colors that some artist has painted on the flowers and other decorations. Now, what do you suppose the person started with in making this dish?" Their faces were blank.

"Let's try what they call the process of elimination," I said, taking a moment to explain what the phrase meant "For example, would you make one of these dishes out of peanut butter?" They both giggled.

"All right, would you make it of cottage cheese or bubble-gum?" They giggled again.

"Since it obviously wouldn't make sense to try to make a dish out of anything of that sort, or hundreds of other things we might mention, what do you think you could use to make a dish?"

"Some kind of clay?" Bradley asked.

"Exactly," I said.

For the next fifteen minutes or so we discussed what sort of tools might be used to draw pictures on the clay, what paints we might use to add color. Eventually we went over the same kind of ground, referring to a small, silver-trimmed, wooden box; an Oriental lamp-base; and then, in the next room, some sculptured busts.

When they gave bright or at least reasonable answers to my questions, I complemented them lavishly. When they gave not-so-bright answers, I gently explained why such thoughts weren't on-target. I explained to them, as we went along, that I wasn't giving them a test, that I wasn't putting to them the sorts of questions that had only one right answer. I told them that the whole point of our conversation was to have fun by exercising their minds and brains. I told them that at times even a wrong answer can be helpful because if we can be made to understand why the answer was wrong we will then tend to think more relevantly and creatively about the question at hand.

No doubt it would have been technically possible to teach the same lesson by simply doing all the talking myself, but of course the children would have squirmed and wanted to get away after just a few minutes of that. By making my points chiefly by the use of questions, I was, obviously, teaching the children not what to think, but how to think, as the saying goes.

My oldest son, Dr. Steve Allen, is a family physician who lives and practices in New York state. But he also spends a good deal of his time lecturing, in various parts of the country, on stress reduction, something he does with great good humor and marked success. In teaching his sometimes uptight audiences to relax and have fun he gives them a bit of instruction on how to juggle colorful silk scarves. One of the basic moves, he explains, is "the Guilt-Free Drop," the point being that obviously anyone starting to juggle will spend most of his time dropping the objects he is trying to toss about, and that it is therefore necessary to get rid of self-critical reactions to such temporary clumsiness. In some of my own teaching, I stress the importance of guilt-free errors. Errors must, needless to say, be identified as such, but this can be done in a way that does not dampen the child's enthusiasm but rather encourages his freedom to speculate. I sometimes explain, in such connections, that although Thomas Edison invented the electric light, he was able to do so because he had made a long list of earlier experiments that failed. I say, "I don't know the exact number, but Mr. Edison might have made about fifty mistakes until he finally arrived at the correct answer. But I'm sure he didn't berate himself or get discouraged by all those mistakes. He was wise enough to learn from them, and often we don't know quite what we should do, which means that it's extremely helpful to learn what not to do, or what answer not to accept."

My point here is certainly not to advise professional educators, who know far more than I about methods of stimulating the thinking and creativity of bright boys and girls. But I would hope that nonspecialists reading this article will see, from the modest example given above, what sorts of educational approaches work particularly well with children whose minds are unconsciously waiting to be exercised.

An Effective Method for Encouraging Gifted Children to Accumulate, Classify, and Use Information

Back in the 1950s I stumbled over a method of information-gathering that has been wonderfully useful ever since. The discovery grew out of my sense of outrage at the degree to which organized crime—chiefly Mafia-related—controlled the city of New York. Working with the New York City Anti-Crime Committee, I prepared a two-hour television documentary on the subject, during the process of which I was granted access to the committee's files. At that point I simply began to develop my own, which at first consisted of copies of material already gathered by the committee. At the first stage all the items, chiefly articles on the public record, related to Organized Crime in a general sense. The papers were gathered together in black, three-ringed leatherette binders, filed both alphabetically and chronologically. After a few years this large category began to be subdivided into separate areas in which organized gangsters were operative. There were entries such as the Teamsters Union, the New York and New Jersey waterfront unions, the recording industry (including jukeboxes), professional boxing, the garment industry, narcotics, gambling, etc. Eventually the boundaries of these categories were passed so that at present the library, which now consists of well over a thousand separate volumes, came to cover almost every significant social issue of our time. Among the categories, for example, are abortion, birth control, communism, capitalism, religion, prisons, poverty, and hunger, to name only a few. I see no reason why children cannot be taught to collect articles from newspapers and magazines that relate to subject matter they're already interested in, whether that might be electricity, football, space travel, gun control, and other urgent issues. They can be encouraged not only to read the materials they accumulate, but to underline significant passages, even to make neat marginal notes. Obviously such a learning method can easily be adapted to individual circumstances and settings, but I assume that if it has been so invaluable to me it must be of at least some use to others.

Conclusion

Ten years ago, in an article for the *New York Times,* I suggested that it would be a very peculiar state of affairs if our society took the position that children who are found to possess remarkable musical aptitude were, nevertheless, not to be given any special consideration or instruction. And it would be unthinkable if we argued that young people blessed with superior athletic ability should not be encouraged to develop their gifts.

But when it comes to students who are only intellectually superior, we are remarkably indifferent. There are, to be sure, individuals concerned with the special needs of gifted children, and some of their responses are organizational. But there is by no means a consensus concerning the wisdom of providing special nurture for those who, partly by the mysterious roll of the genetic dice, are intellectually superior.

Does this mean we care more about athletic than intellectual achievement? I'm afraid it does, insofar as we can be judged by our actions. But is there any way that we could be made to even begin to imagine that the mind and spirit are more important than the biceps or the hamstring? The trick might be turned if we could plug this particular computer program, so to speak, into the national ego-circuits. There would certainly be justification for such a connection, because in the long, historic run it is a damned sight more important, and dangerous, that we are mentally inferior than that, in some instances, we are physically inferior.

To approach the problem from another angle, we must all somehow be made aware—as quickly as possible—that as of the last twenty-five years or so, the American people have been getting demonstrably dumber. We were shocked, some years ago, to be told that "Johnny can't read." Indeed he can't, at least not as well as he should, nor can he write, do simple arithmetic, or even think very well.

In the face of such negative factors, there is a depressing stupidity in our refusal to offer proper encouragement and nurture to the small percentage of our children who are performing well. A number of super-bright young people do somehow contrive to get a reasonably good education and to enjoy professional success. But a good many others of equal competence are falling through the tattered net of public and official ignorance and neglect. That we cannot afford.

Although there is an urgent need for active programs that respond to the needs of gifted children, it does not follow that all such efforts will be properly conducted. Well-intentioned parents can be counterproductive if what they perceive as special attention is construed by the child—perhaps accurately—as a high-pressure message saying, "You'd better succeed, or else."

Concerned parents, therefore, must assess their own motives. Otherwise they may become as destructive as the notorious stage-mothers who, in the theatrical context, sometimes do permanent damage to their children's hearts and souls because of the intense critical pressure they put on them to succeed as actors or performers.

The most successful programs of encouragement for superior children strike a reasonable balance between special instruction on the one hand, and warm, friendly encouragement on the other. I recall from my own somewhat chaotic educational experience that if I liked a teacher, I tended to do well in her class. If the teacher was cold, insulting, sarcastic, and/or impatient I learned little.

This issue, of course, exists within the context of a larger and unresolved philosophical debate concerning suitable relationships between what might loosely be described as the haves and have-nots of society.

As regards superior intelligence, the issue would at least be simpler to understand if all the strikingly bright boys and girls lived on the "right side of the tracks," and all the below-average children on the other side. God help the unbright ones if that were the case, because perhaps no society in history has morally distinguished itself by its treatment of the poor or otherwise disadvantaged. But intelligence may spring up in a rural shack or a slum apartment.

A classic example is that of Charles Kettering, whose achievements as an inventor are rivaled only by those of Thomas Edison. Many of Kettering's remarkable discoveries and developments were related to the automobile industry. His incredible gifts might have been easily overlooked, given that as a child he attended a very small rural school. Fortunately, two young teachers noticed his aptitude and gave him special attention. Had they not done so, the development of nothing less than the American economy itself might have been delayed or handicapped.

If, as I assume, the primary factors of giftedness are physical and genetic, it then becomes a matter of the most crucial importance that the unusually bright ones in poor neighborhoods be identified as early as possible. Otherwise the initial natural gifts are wasted, swamped by the harsh realities of being brought up in conditions characterized by poverty, crime, inadequate diet, parents who may be either absent, tragically ignorant and uneducated, and socially unstable, if not criminal. It is, then, all the more necessary that efforts be made to identify gifted children in the below-the-poverty-line segment of our society. It is no exaggeration to say that if it were the case that an appreciable and ever-growing segment of our society were, in fact, becoming less well educated, less prepared for life in the marketplace, less socially responsible generally, this would be a grave threat to the stability of our nation. It is painfully clear in the rising statistics concerning violent crime that the poor will not forever supinely accept their fate. If they cannot legally secure the benefits of life in the world's richest nation, some of them will simply break and enter, grab and run, even assault and kill to get what they want. The problems of our society do not exist as a series of more-or-less separate issues. They are all part of a large, ugly, interconnected machine. It is the height of social stupidity for the white, affluent descendants of former peasants and laborers to say, "If they want something, let them work for it," at a time when there are no jobs for 10 percent of America's workers and when, moreover, our poverty-stricken neighborhoods are producing millions of young people largely unqualified to accept such low-paying jobs as might otherwise be available to them. Education is obviously important as a means of uplifting the human mind and spirit. But it also has a profound importance in the context of social and economic considerations. It would be an exaggeration to say that a large, continued, and strikingly successful program of identifying all gifted children and offering them proper nurture could in itself resolve our larger problems. But not doing so will certainly make these problems more severe.

The News of His Demise
Was Greatly Appreciated*

I am writing to congratulate *The Advocate* on being the only newspaper to correctly report the fact of my recent death, in your story of January 2, 1993, apparently originating from the *Chicago Tribune*, headlined "Recalling the Artists, Musicians, Actors, and Entertainers Who Died in 1992."

In this connection you were kind enough to run a photograph of myself and another of actor, Denholm Elliott. Although a depressingly long list of notables left us during the year just past, only Mr. Elliott's photograph and mine were used to add visual interest to the obituary notices.

A number of your readers have written with the suggestion that I might want to demand a correction.

As a matter of fact, I think *The Advocate* deserves great credit for perceiving the fact of my demise, which a good many other newspapers had missed.

*Steve Allen, who has been a living legend for years, was kind enough to write this for *The Advocate,* which mistakenly published his photo instead of one of entertainer Peter Allen, who unfortunately did die in 1992.

I actually passed away two or three years ago, but, due to the fact that so much of my television and film work is constantly being reshown, apparently the illusion that I was still alive was somehow sustained.

While because of certain contractual agreements I am not at liberty to share with your readers details of my experiences while on The Other Side, I can at least confirm what might be your own suspicions that, in a certain statistical sense, things are not much better there than they are here.

There is indeed, you will perhaps be glad to hear, a place called Heaven—but so few people have qualified for entrance into it that, given my urban background, I couldn't stand the quietude, much less the solitude.

I was next permitted to visit the other major alternative, but despite the fact that I immediately recognized many of my former friends and acquaintances, I found the heat unbearable, even though I spent some of my early years in Arizona. The infernal regions themselves, I am now able to report, abound with more or less what one might expect—blatantly tasteless and lascivious behavior, an endless barrage of profanity and vulgarity, a total lack of interest in virtue, and—well, basically everything that characterizes modern entertainment.

Oddly enough I did run into Mark Twain, who, despite the fact that he was not dead when he was first reported so, did eventually leave us.

In any event, I'm back now and though I suffered the inconvenience of having missed most of 1991 and '92, I'm pleased to report that I have a busy schedule of obligations for 1993. Despite the fact that I almost died during my opening monologue at a recent comedy concert booking in Boston, it appears I will be quite active during at least the short-term future.

Madonna

As an entertainer myself, I have felt some discomfort in criticizing another practitioner of the trade. But as regards the rock
vocalist in question, my hand was freed by the fact that from the
beginning of her career she has deliberately courted criticism and
controversy by purposely flaunting her disregard for even the
minimum rules of decent behavior. No one ever expected that
people like Mother Teresa would work in the theatrical profession. Indeed in centuries past, the church in Europe would not
even permit entertainers to be buried on consecrated ground, so
degraded were the performing arts considered.

Another reason I felt it was time to speak out was that we live
in a time where depravity and license have not only become the
norm but have often proved to be the path to riches and public
adulation. Though I am far from having achieved the state of
sanctity myself, it is possible even for a sinner to be shocked at
the behavior of others, just as in prisons there is a status-order
among criminals as regards their offenses.

The true and serious harm the Madonnas of our time do lies

From the *Journal of Popular Culture* 27, no. 1 (Summer 1993): 1–11. Reprinted
by permission of Popular Press, Bowling Green State University, Bowling
Green, Ohio 43403.

in the fact that some of them are particularly popular with children and teenagers.

Madonna scrawls graffiti on the national dialogue. The saddest aspect of the present situation is not that she herself is the problem, any more than the Prince of Filth, Andrew Dice Clay, is the problem of the vulgarity and general ugliness that characterizes much of modern entertainment. These two pathetic individuals—and the scores like them who now market not beauty, the traditional province of the artist, but ugliness—far from being objects of contempt, as they would be in any truly civilized culture—are eminently successful in the marketplace.

Mr. Clay, at least as of several months ago, was able to fill Madison Square Garden, something that probably no other comedian, however gifted, could do at the time. Just so, Madonna's services are more in demand than those of other popular singers or entertainers who far surpass her in talent, a fact that speaks volumes about our social predicament.

There is one point of crucial moral importance, that appears not to have impressed itself upon either the public consciousness or the circle of professional critics. No one assumes that there was ever a Golden Age of personal rectitude among creative people. The statistics about alcoholism, drug addiction, sexual promiscuity, and emotional instability in the general population are tragic enough. They have always been higher in the arts, and particularly so in that branch of them referred to as show business. When, therefore, we say the present degree of moral turpitude is shocking and depressing, we are not being naive enough to compare it to some sort of moral never-never land in which our singers, musicians, and entertainers were as righteous and heroic as the roles they played or the public images they manufactured.

But the sinners and offenders of earlier times at least attempted to keep their transgressions private, if only for selfish reasons. The popular comedian Fatty Arbuckle, in the 1920s, never worked again in the motion picture business after his arrest in connection with an incident in which a prostitute died, apparently because Arbuckle, in a sexual context, had inserted into the poor woman's body a Coca-Cola bottle, which broke and cut her internally, after which she bled to death. If such a thing were to happen today, I would not be surprised if Arbuckle ended up doing a TV commercial for Pepsi.

It has become almost impossible to shame our public figures, given the general social sickness of our society and culture.

In the American past there was always, under the combined facade and reality of the sort of happy home depicted in the old MGM Andy Hardy films, a strain of social and moral illness, but formerly sexual perverts, sadists, masochists, and assorted other psychos and whackos at least scurried for cover when the lights were turned on, as do cockroaches and other insects in the middle of the night. Today, by way of contrast, the offenders, though they may become the butt of a few random jokes by late-night television hosts, are promptly surrounded and defended by those who stand to make money from their professional activities, and we are quickly told that even the most vile on-stage excesses are permissible because they are protected by the rights specified by the First Amendment in that most noble of documents, the American Constitution.

I do not take lightly the question of creative rights, and I'm certainly no abstract philosopher viewing the question from an impartial distance. I am myself the creator of a large body of poetry, short stories, novels, nonfiction books, plays, musicals, and songs, as well as an actor, vocalist, and pianist. But it would never occur to me to argue that simply because of my creativity I am entitled to introduce into the marketplace literally anything at all, however revolting.

The point here—again—is not that the present flood tide carrying us all into the sewer is to be properly contrasted with a state of moral perfection. Even Shakespeare occasionally inserted a bawdy comment or joke into his magnificent plays. The Bible itself has passages that could hardly be considered suitable instruction for children.

The fundamental question as to the proper place of sex within the context of any even remotely civilized society is simply one of those ongoing dilemmas about which the ablest philosophers continue to differ. Relations between the creative community and the state, which through its laws is somehow supposed to represent the will of the people, have always been uneasy. But I deliberately return to the point, since it seems not to have been generally grasped, that we are by no means presently faced with one of those historic balancing acts. In the past no artist has ever argued that literally *anything* is permissible. Henry Miller* was not a complete moral anarchist. Today, however, *anything goes* seems to be the operative principle.

Am I exaggerating here? It is of the most crucial importance to understand that I am not. The marketing of the most depraved and disgusting material is now not only permitted—which would be bad enough—it is philosophically defended and dominant in the commercial marketplace. Millions of Americans have died, in various wars, presumably not on the classic justification that our borders needed to be defended—largely because of our two oceans, our mainland has traditionally not been in that sort of danger common to European and other nations around the world. That those millions of American deaths were justified as a defense of our economic system—which practically all Americans prefer—is part of the problem. Major national and international corporations are now making no distinction whatever between a dollar earned by marketing moral poison and a dollar made by marketing toothpaste or automobiles.

When, in the past, at least a segment of the public became aware that some of their favorite entertainers left a great deal to be desired in their simple capacities as human beings, they at least could respond, "Well, I wouldn't want my daughter to marry the fellow, but I like his singing (clarinet playing, acting) so much that I'll just turn a deaf ear to his personal faults." And indeed, this is a perfectly reasonable attitude as regards individuals possessed of true artistic talent.

Although I understand the reasons behind the U.S. government's campaign to ban Bach, Beethoven, and other great German composers from our airwaves during our wars against Germany, it was always my private opinion that there was something stupid in the practice. It is, after all, possible to thrill to the music of a German genius while still despising the Nazis, or to enjoy an Italian opera while still loathing Mussolini and his Fascists.

---

*Henry Miller, an American author, was noted for his sexually candid, autobiographical novels.

But such equations do not apply to our present predicament, and this is nowhere as clearly illustrated as in the case of the young woman who calls herself Madonna, for the simple reason that her talents are quite modest. She has never been considered a great singer, and she is certainly not a gifted dancer. She has a certain modest ability as an actress, but given that so do many three-year-olds and other untutored individuals, including a few animals, she is not noteworthy at that capacity either. Many performers achieve success because of their remarkable gifts. Barbra Streisand, Meryl Streep, Robert De Niro, Al Pacino, and Robert Duvall come to mind in such a connection.

Madonna does not. She has succeeded for a reason that reflects no credit upon the rest of us. She has succeeded because of her neurosis, her moral weaknesses, her willingness to prostitute herself for fame and money, to shame her family. She is not, like the rest of us, simply someone who almost daily falls short of the moral standards we sincerely profess. She does not hide but flaunts her disdain for those standards. No doubt there are women working in offices, restaurants, or other workplaces who are equally depraved, but *they are not role models to millions of impressionable teenagers.*

It is precisely at this point that the terrible work of the Madonnas of our time is done. I now hear seven-year-olds using vile terms and references that not so many decades ago did not enter into the American consciousness and vocabulary until the age of fourteen or fifteen. It has never been suggested that Madonna is solely to blame, but it cannot be denied that her name is high on the list of those responsible.

In this general connection I am reminded of the evening, some years ago, when at a small dinner party in her apartment in New York, former congresswoman and social critic Clare Boothe Luce, who was an admirer of "Meeting of Minds," a television show I had created for the PBS network, recommended that I consider booking the Marquis de Sade as a guest. ("Meeting of Minds" was a television talk show, though scripted and rehearsed, in which important figures of history came together to engage in philosophical debates.) For a moment I thought that Ms. Luce was joking. "Oh, no," she said. "I'm quite serious. Sade was the most despicable person imaginable, but his views are very influential in today's society." Ms. Luce was quite right, needless to say, and the two one-hour shows in which Sade was permitted to advocate his depraved positions were both stimulating and sobering. Madonna is the Marquis' ablest and most influential present defender, although because she has been poorly educated she may never have consulted his works.

*   *   *

One clue to the profound seriousness of our present predicament concerns the term *deviant behavior.* The concept, which for centuries has had legitimate application among social philosophers, is obviously based on moral distinctions between more or less common modes of behavior, not all of them necessarily highly virtuous, and other forms of conduct that represent dangers to society. But that classic and commonsense difference is not, in the public consciousness, as clear-cut as it formerly was. Indeed, those guilty of blatantly deviant behavior are now unapologetic, even defiant, and if they happen to be celebrities, their very fame seems to provide at least a degree of immunity from public criticism. Some such criticism is there, of course, though largely because there is an unappealing appetite for scandal. But there is so much of it, such a daily flood, in fact—the public's attention span apparently now being comparable to that of a gnat—that there is not only little likelihood that the offenders will suffer professional harm, it is quite likely that they will profit by rather than suffer from their escapades.

Although it would not matter to me in the least if I were the only person in the entertainment field to express such views, the important thing is that I am not.

Although standards of beauty are notoriously personal—as are judgments as to what constitutes sexual attractiveness—Madonna cannot be sensibly defended on the ground that, through no fault of her own she is simply a highly desirable creature to members of the opposite sex. There are women of whom this is true, Marilyn Monroe being a classic example. Although I met Marilyn on only one occasion (she had just started work in her last picture), I had long admired her work in films. She exuded that always mysterious trait referred to as "star quality," and was, in person, as breathtaking as she appeared to be on screen. Because of the tragic circumstances of her early upbringing, she always seemed to me a helpless puppy desperately in need of attention and love. It makes no sense whatever to marry such individuals, as Joe DiMaggio and Arthur Miller were to learn to their sorrow, but they are naturally lovable. Dolly Parton, Sophia Loren, and a few of today's young actresses might also be cited in this connection. But as against this real sexuality there has always been the pseudosexuality of the professional prostitute. It may come as a shock to fifteen-year-old boys, but the fact is that the average prostitute does not enjoy sex, and certainly not with the parade of johns who purchase her temporary services. In the film *Klute* Jane Fonda struck just the right note, in the role of a whore, when, pretending to be emotionally moved by one of her clients, she suddenly look at her wristwatch as if to say, "How soon can we wrap this up?" It was a moment of both high comedy and important insight. Madonna's sexuality is, to put the matter quite simply, that of the professional prostitute. She does not really look like Marilyn Monroe. Her hair is black and her features considerably less than ideal; she simply *imitates* Monroe's true beauty. As contrasted with Dolly Parton's cute, ultranatural country girlishness, Madonna presents a hard, tough attitude. She may make legitimate claims on our sympathy, since we all emerge from the shell of childhood as products of genetics and environmental conditioning, but there is no reason for the rest of us to accept as genuine the illusory merchandise that has been so cleverly marketed. Even as a sex object the young woman is simply not the real article.

There is a clue to this in the sort of wardrobe and costume she affects. There is nothing in it of the sweet, feminine, even Victoria's Secret sort, in which the purpose is to glorify and enhance the natural factor of womanly beauty. What we see in Madonna, by way of contrast, is much use of black and of leather, of the sort associated with sadomasochism. Then there are the absurd conical, metallic-looking brassieres, a dehumanizing element when contrasted with the natural beauty of the well-formed breasts with which some women are gifted by nature.

To sum up, Madonna has not become arguably the most commercially successful performer of her time because of her ability to sing, dance, or act; in all three categories her gifts are minor. Nor has she become successful because of her beauty, the illusion of which is largely a matter of the contributions of makeup people and hairdressers. She has become successful because of her willing-ness—even eagerness—to resort to the grossest sort of vulgarity.

*   *   *

There has never been any such thing as a universally popular enter-tainer. The only American who came close was the brilliant and naturally lovable Will Rogers. It is therefore not particularly note-worthy that Madonna has her detractors. But it is instructive to con-sider what it is, very specifically, that makes her repulsive to mil-lions. A few examples:

On the night after a throat ailment caused her to cancel a con-cert she announced to an audience in the Washington, D.C., area, "I don't care what anyone says, I'm f—— hot tonight."

In the presence of a performer dressed as a Catholic priest, Madonna not only starts to disrobe but smashes a crucifix—the most sacred of symbols to hundreds of millions of Christians—to the ground.

Asked why she chose to use a sacred religious symbol as a trademark/logo, Miss Class actually replied, "Crucifixes are sexy because there's a naked man on them."

After nude pictures of her were published in *Playboy* and *Pent-house,* she explained, "It was like when you're a little girl at school and some nun comes and lifts your dress up in front of everybody and you get really embarrassed." (Were there no journalists present to ask for the identity of the nun and the name of the school where the alleged incident took place?) . . .

A concert in Texas included one number about sadomasochistic spankings and another in which masturbation was feigned.

Another number features seven cross-dressed male dancers wearing brassieres.

Given that no other entertainer in modern history has con-sciously conveyed so many destructive and perverted messages, is it perhaps possible that the young woman's own intentions are vir-tuous but that she has fallen under the influence of some evil guru of the sort connected with the infamous "Children of God" cult?

The answer is *no*. It's difficult to dig out clear answers to certain kinds of questions, but not in this instance. The evil done by Madonna is entirely of her own volition. As her close associate, songwriter Stephen Bray, has put it, "This is a woman who is in complete charge of her life. She calls her own shots." This is perhaps the one point about her that is not a subject of controversy.

Despite the entertainer's success, which is formidable, her eager willingness—no, determination—to shock does occasionally affect ticket sales. When she appeared in Italy in the summer of 1990, sales were low, and one performance in Rome was canceled after Catholic spokesmen, quite correctly, termed her show blasphemous.

The ancient debate pitting The Past against The Future is meaningless except as regards specifics, but even then the debate is impossible to resolve because it is not so much a matter of science as of opinion and taste. Literally every professional critic on earth could assure us that the music created by Jerome Kern or George Gershwin is vastly superior to that of this week's shocker-punk group, but to those who simply prefer the latter such unanimity of opinion would mean nothing. There are, however, certain factors of the large argument that have nothing to do with opinion and are therefore demonstrable as matters of fact. It is simply the case that in earlier decades entertainers achieved success largely by having actual talent. Sometimes other elements contributed—dumb luck, physical beauty, connections, sleeping with a studio executive—but talent was dominant. This is no longer the case.

The greatest art has traditionally appealed to the best elements of human nature. It did not disguise the reality of evil. Quite to the contrary, it called evil by its right name. What Madonna presents— one can certainly not call it art—is very much the opposite. She appeals to sickness, to perversion, to the worst elements of human nature. In one of her 1990 concerts she stomped her female dancers, again and again. Was the crowd shocked into silence as sometimes happens to comedians or talk show hosts who have "gone too far?" Sadly, no. The crowd *approved* of what it was seeing and, in fact, as critic Richard Goldstein put it, "went wild."

Says Goldstein "At another point, she stopped the show to give a speech about Keith Haring, a friend she admired for his candor about being gay and having AIDS. Polite applause."

And Goldstein, I must make clear, is no Michael Medved. He is not only not neutral about the chiefly male performers he calls sexual outlaws; he greatly admires them. In his defense it should perhaps be explained that he is talking about theatrical representations, since it is obvious enough that judged purely as human beings— which is to say as faithful lovers, husbands, fathers, citizens—such people are utter failures. I am afraid that to critics like Goldstein the ideal of sex within the context of romantic love and/or marriage simply eludes them.

It might be instructive for Time-Warner executives to consider a few of the audience-segments the woman called Madonna has alienated:

Feminists do not like her.

Eighty percent of Americans report being affiliated with one Christian denomination or another. Catholics, in particular, despise her because she has directly attacked the church and its symbols. But Protestants, too, strongly disapprove of her. Explains Christian columnist John Lofton, "The opening excerpt from [one] video shows some scum bag of indeterminate sex, sucking on the face of a blonde woman. And this androgynous something mounts this woman and as sexual intercourse is simulated we see, fleetingly, pressed between these two riding bodies, a cross with the crucified Christ on it . . . what we're seeing here is plain, old-fashioned, blasphemous sacrilege. . . . Just how bad is this video? Well, it's so bad, so slimy and sleazy, that it's been banned by MTV—the cable network that, twenty-four-hours-a-day, is already an open sewer."

Since the Jewish community has historically had relatively elevated cultural tastes and has distinguished itself by its support of the true arts, the Jews have, understandably, not been conspicuous among Madonna fan-clubs. In January 1981 Rabbi Abraham Cooper, Associate Dean of the world-famous Simon Weisenthal Center in Los Angeles, described a track of Madonna's "Justify My Love" CD as "dangerous and an insult to every Jew."

The passage in question is from the Revelation of St. John and is commonly translated as "and the slander of those who say they are Jews, but they are not, they are a synagogue of Satan." "The notion," Rabbi Cooper said, "that an icon of American pop culture should, for whatever reason, zero in on the most notorious anti-

Semitic quote in the Bible is totally unacceptable. . . . The idea of the synagogue of Satan was a very powerful weapon used against Jews in the Middle Ages, and the Nazis depicted Jews with horns in the image of the devil."

The Anti-Defamation League, commenting on the case shortly thereafter, said that lyrics of the song and anti-Semitic slurs spray-painted on three California synagogues in December, bear a "painful resemblance."

In a letter to an executive of Warner Brothers Records, which released the CD, the ADL expressed the "hope that the influence that you and your company have on the shaping of American youth can be used to impart a more positive and hopeful message."

I would not advise that any of us hold our breaths until the record industry starts to take that recommendation seriously.

* * *

Over half a century ago James Thurber wrote a prescient short story that had not a funny line in it but made, in a bitter, Swiftian way, a powerful point that, had Thurber not shared his insight with us so early, would almost certainly never have occurred to those modern critics of culture who would appear to have abandoned whatever taste they might originally have had and permitted it to be replaced by a lemming-like submission to the dominant mob-mood of the present.

The protagonist of Thurber's story is a young hero-of-the-moment who has attracted the attention of the nation by making a remarkable airplane flight. So hysterical is the acclaim that greets this achievement that a number of national leaders convene in a room, high in a Manhattan skyscraper, to share the young favorite's company. Unfortunately they discover that the daring young fellow is, to use the simplest possible language, a total jerk who appears to have not one redeeming feature that might justify and sustain his incredible fame. The shocking ending of the story comes when the high government officials, perceiving that the young fellow—by a combination of his social idiocy and popularity—is actually a threat to the nation, contrive, by unspoken agreement, to push him out an open window.

Thurber was, of course, not seriously recommending such a course of action, but the story is instructive because it is based on the sobering realization that the world would really be better off had some people never lived, whatever the degree of their momentary popularity. Today, so compulsive have we become in our adoration of The Celebrity that Thurber's solution to the problem, even as a purely literary exercise, would simply never come to mind. The result, God help us, is that the pantheon of American heroes has now admitted so high a percentage of jerks that we are—well, getting the culture we deserve.

In the 1950s and '60s there were hundreds of critics, in their middle years, who had no doubts whatever that Cole Porter, let's say, was vastly superior at the songwriting art to, oh—Mick Jagger or Bob Dylan. Why, then, did they so rarely say as much? I submit that the reason was a sort of social cowardice. The critics, though they knew better, held their tongues because they did not want to seem un-hip.

I make a distinction here between middle-aged, generally well-informed critics and the teenage fans then attending rock concerts. The young people could be forgiven on the classic grounds that they simply didn't know what they were doing. They were not consciously rejecting Porter, Kern, Gershwin, and the other representatives of the glorious Golden Age; they simply had never consciously heard them in the first place. Eventually a small minority of the younger generation who happened to be, for the usual mysterious and genetic reasons, gifted with the ability to write, used the ability to express their taste, vulgar as it was.

The point is that even these aesthetically compromised modern critics have turned against Madonna.

But Madonna seems not to understand the essential message her critics are now transmitting. When asked by the "Today" show's Bryant Gumbel about the barrage of public criticism to which she has been subjected, Madonna referred only to "bad reviews," showing that she either entirely missed Gumbel's point— or pretended to.

By the time of the release of her film *Body of Evidence,* in January of 1993, quite a distinct phase of Madonna's career had been entered upon. Even the usually tolerant popular media had begun to treat her not so much as a femme fatale socially dangerous because of her willful assault on conventional morals, but as a laughing-stock. *People* magazine, a Time-Warner subsidiary, unwilling even to take the film seriously, ran a feature headed "Madonna's Movie Misadventure," in which it was pointed out that film critic Roger Ebert gave the picture half a star, Susan Stark of the *Detroit News* called it "trash," and in Peoria, Illinois, "52 people gathered in a 237-seat theater and giggled." At a Loew's theater in Cambridge, Massachusetts, the audience reaction was "belly laughs that dwin-dled to snorts and cackles." One theatergoer was quoted as describ-ing the picture as "stupid and confusing." An audience in New York City, according to the feature, applauded when Anne Archer called Madonna a "coke-head slut." It is important to grasp that audiences all over the country were not so derisive simply because the film was of such low quality; scores of pictures every year may be so described. What audiences were contemptuously rejecting, even with laughter, was precisely the merchandise that is Madonna's stock-in-trade.

No society can long endure that has abandoned its ideals. Granted that ideals are rarely achieved, they are nevertheless vitally important compass-points. It might even be argued that in a society of liars, Truth and Honesty are needed more than ever. The rele-vance of this to Madonna's unhappy story is that for a very long time, and by no means only in Western nations, one purpose of social education was to prepare young people to assume the status of lady or gentleman. Granted that there has never been any short-age of sluts, whores, pushovers, rogues, and rakes, it was neverthe-less considered important that a society produce as many actual ladies and gentlemen as surrounding circumstances permitted.

Madonna and her kind run precisely counter to such an honor-able tradition. It would be as ludicrous to refer to her as a lady as it would be to describe her as nun or princess.

Traditionally theatrical criticism relates to specifics—singing, dancing, acting, playing an instrument, or, at the more creative level, writing, composing, directing. It is important to understand, in this context, that no performer ever lived who was not occasion-ally negatively criticized. But no professional critic, theatergoer, or television viewer ever made much of a fuss about the simple quality of a performance. In any event, such traditional considerations have nothing to do with the barrage of criticism to which Madonna has been quite properly subjected. What outrages millions is not the quality of her singing, dancing, or acting. This particular young woman is criticized because she has made a conscious, calculated decision to debase herself. There are those who work as whores, but we may safely assume there has never been a case in which a young woman, having had the opportunity to choose among dozens of professions and trades, decided that the best of them all was prostitution. As regards those who work in what are called strip joints, the same may be said. They are uniformly women with no particular talent, with nothing, in fact, except impressive bodies. If they could make good money working at McDonald's or the neighborhood dime store, they would no doubt be quite willing to do so. But that's not where the big money is. So they go where it is; it's that simple.

In the case of Madonna, she's a megamillionaire and indeed at present is probably making so much money she herself doesn't have an accurate accounting of it. She has, therefore, no excuse whatever for deciding to become a public slut.

Those presently reaping enormous profits from deliberately marketing anything-goes sex and violence are, judged morally, as loathsome as purveyors of tobacco or cocaine, although the latter can at least be excused of hypocrisy in that they know that they have made a conscious choice to become criminals, whereas tobacco companies, in common with the marketers of much popular culture, actually attempt to justify their trade.

Woman's Right

It is fascinating that the purest form of the respect-for-life philosophy that motivates at least some antiabortionists is consistent with the general thrust of Humanist thinking over the last couple of centuries, but it relates scarcely at all to much Christian behavior of the past 2,000 years.

Two basic questions are: (1) What is life? (2) When, in the human context, does it begin? While at first the answers appear obvious, the relevant realities are complex. For some time it has been possible to keep human tissues, separated from bodies, alive. They need only be placed in an aqueous environment and provided with such nutrients and methods of waste-disposal as their individual cells require. We can, then, point to a brain, a heart, a lung, or other portions of a once-conscious body and state, quite accurately, that it is alive.

Yet if someone were to destroy such an organ, would it be reasonable to accuse him of murder? There is no question that he was destroying living human tissue. But it is equally clear that the indi-

Originally published in *Steve Allen on the Bible, Religion & Morality* (Amherst, N.Y.: Prometheus Books, 1990).

vidual organ was nevertheless not a human being. Why? Because it did not have a mind. If then, it is only the existence of brain-function and/or mind that establishes the existence of a human, it follows that the termination of a fetus that is just a few days old can hardly be equated with arbitrarily ending the life of a six-month-old child or of an adult.

On this point, incidentally, there is invaluable relevant information in Exodus 21:22, which refers to two men who engage in physical combat and who, in thrashing about, bump into a pregnant woman who suffers a miscarriage as a result. In both rabbinical and early Christian commentary there is a clear distinction between punishments thought suitable for two outwardly similar crimes. If the fetus that dies is unformed, the common opinion was that the guilty individual need not receive the death penalty. But if the fetus is formed—which is to say in the late stage of development—then that is a much more serious matter and the death penalty is considered appropriate punishment. This makes clear that, quite aside from the question as to whether it is ever appropriate to refer to the medical disruption of a developing fetus as *murder,* it was not correct at one time to use such a term if the unborn individual was in a very early state of development.

For an excellent analysis of this question, see "Two Traditions: The Law of Exodus 21:22–23 Revisited" by Stanley Isser in the *Catholic Biblical Quarterly* (January 1990).

As noted above, a growing segment of the Christian Right openly advocates that the proper solution to present-day social problems is to make the United States formally and legally a Christian nation with a government entirely under Christian domination and guided by the laws and principles of both the Old and New Testaments. This would require repeal of the First Amendment.

Needless to say, such Christians are members of the prodeath-penalty camp. If (1) they succeed in their ambitions, (2) abortion is outlawed because it is considered murder, and (3) all murderers must be executed by the state, then it logically follows that the many millions of American women who would beyond question continue to have illegal, secret abortions would have to be put to death if detected.

Concerning certain aspects of the abortion controversy, there is surprisingly little disagreement or debate. Statistically speaking, few people think it is permissible to end the life of a fetus in the last several weeks of its development. This is so simply because a baby in the eighth or ninth month is clearly a human being and is therefore entitled to all the rights that society is prepared to accord a newborn or any adult citizen. (An interesting sidelight on this point is that in Nationalist China, America's ally against the Communists, the practice of infanticide was widespread among poor families, particularly if the children were female. When the Communists assumed control of that country in 1949, they legislated against the practice.)

Fundamentalists have, of course, attempted to justify their stand against abortion by citing the Bible, just as an earlier generation of fundamentalists used scriptural texts to try to justify their opposition to new birth-control devices or their acceptance of slavery. Among the passages used to oppose abortion are Ephesians 1:4, 2 Thessalonians 2:13, and Jeremiah 1:5. These and similar texts emphasize divine foreknowledge and election by stressing that God knew his prophets and apostles when they were in the womb.

Fundamentalists have pressed these texts further in the service of their metaphysical conjecture that the entity in the womb, from the moment of conception, is a person. What they failed to note was that their premises led them into the heretical doctrine of reincarnation. According to the book of Jeremiah, the Lord said to his prophet, "*Before* I formed you in the womb I knew you." (italics added)

According to Hebrews 7:9–10, Levi the priest was within the loins of his great-grandfather, Abraham. If one used Jerry Falwell's exegetical methods in interpreting Scripture, one might conclude that Levi existed as a 100 percent person in Abraham's loins. This suggests that Abraham would have been guilty of manslaughter or negligent homicide if by fortuitous nocturnal emission he had allowed the innocent Levi to escape his loins. (See Joe E. Barnhart, *The Southern Baptist Holy War* [Austin, Texas: Monthly Press, 1986], pp. 159–60.)

According to Luke 1:42, another antiabortion passage employed by fundamentalists, when pregnant "Elizabeth heard the greeting of Mary the babe leaped in her womb." Elizabeth herself is then quoted as saying "the babe leaped in my womb for joy" (1:44). But this does not prove anything, because a pregnant woman, feeling the fetus moving, can attribute any emotion she wants to the baby she is carrying. Most women simply speak of the baby's "kicking."

Barnhart also notes:

> For many years, a number of [fundamentalist] preachers like Jerry Falwell and W. A. Criswell raised no prophetic voice against the known brutalities of racism or unjust treatment of women. Now suddenly they have turned into bleeding hearts over almost microscopic zygotes. With little sustained concern for the civil-rights movement when it had to do with conspicuous persons of minority status, some of the antiabortion preachers have recently begun to deliver impassioned and eloquent speeches about the civil rights of the fertilized egg.

There is the general perception that the new organism, which in its early stages is a small blob of matter, can hardly be referred to as a human being, consisting, as it may, of only a few dozen cells. Nature itself daily aborts millions of such creatures and, in fact, not only at early stages. The majority of those who take a clear-cut, no-abortions-under-any-circumstances position naturally wish to make it impossible to terminate the life of even these forms.

Most opponents of abortion seem unaware of the fact that the European and American successes in legalizing the practice during the last half-century grew largely out of public concern about the thriving market in criminal abortions. Few of these were performed by licensed medical practitioners. Not surprisingly, the results were often horrendous, so far as the life and health of the unfortunate mothers were concerned. Informed citizens eventually said, in effect, "It makes no sense to continue to permit so much death and suffering. If abortions are going to take place, as they obviously will continue to do, then the procedure ought to be performed under controlled circumstances by qualified medical professionals." This is certainly not the only rationale for legalized abortion, but since it is part of the larger argument, it must be taken into account.

To the great number of those who have not yet taken a formal position concerning the difficult question of abortion but who have at least been exposed to arguments from both sides, it may seem that at one end of the field are those who think that abortion is, generally speaking, a positive and justified act, and those on the opposite side who believe that it is a simple act of murder.

If there is a single person on earth who views abortion as favorably as he views playing tennis or reading a good book, he would be in urgent need of psychiatric attention. Abortion, like many medical procedures, is a sad business.

As for my own position—with which I would not trouble the reader except that I have frequently been asked to state it for the record—I am opposed to abortion in the sense that I can envision an ideal state in which no such medical procedure would ever be necessary.

And it is not difficult, after all, to at least imagine, if not bring about, a utopian situation in which almost no further abortions would be desired or performed. Such a situation, of course, would involve far more widespread use of methods of birth control than is practiced at present. The debate as to whether there is an overpopulation problem has never, in the present century, been worth the attention of any serious or informed person because everyone sensible agrees that there is. Even the Catholic Church acknowledges that there are too many people in certain places for the available food supplies to sustain.

Many sincere and intelligent Catholics are so disturbed that their church only acknowledges the population problem and resists serious efforts to alleviate it, that they simply ignore Catholic doctrine on birth control and make their own moral decisions. Nor do they have much difficulty in finding priestly confessors to tell them that they are entitled to let their conscience be their guide on such difficult questions.

Among the many prominent Catholic thinkers who are at odds with their church on the question of contraception is James T. Burtchaell, C.S.C. The details of his argument on the question may be found in *The Giving and the Taking of Life: Essays Ethical* (1989). Father Burtchaell is professor of biblical theology and ethics at the University of Notre Dame, and his collection of essays was published by the University of Notre Dame Press. Moreover, the book is referred to in respectful tones by the Jesuit magazine *America* (October 14, 1989). None of this would happen if Burtchaell's was simply the voice of a lonely heretic. It is my assumption that, on this question, the majority of Catholic intellectuals are on the side of common sense and therefore in opposition to their church.

One of the reasons that millions of abortions will continue to take place, regardless of the views of American conservatives, is that, though great numbers of eggs are being fertilized, not all the potential children are *wanted by either or both of their parents.* In a large percentage of the cases, this is because the parents are not married. In some instances, they are married, but to other individuals. And in cases where a married mother and father are the parents-to-be, they too, by the millions, are deciding, for whatever good or poor reasons, that they do not want the particular birth that will result if nothing is done to interrupt the cellular development in the womb.

Life is difficult enough for even the more fortunate among us in the present day. For those new arrivals who are not welcomed by loving parents, the eventual results are almost invariably horrifying. This relates, in a very direct way, to the problem of child abuse in American society. In one city alone, New York, over a hundred children are killed by their own parents each year. Nor is such a death a sudden, swift release. It usually results from a long series of savage beatings, sometimes—the very soul shudders—accompanied by sexual abuse.

The future society that was serious about trying to diminish the need for abortion would incorporate a vigorous program of instruction on sex, starting at the appropriate early grade-level. There is a tendency to assume that because modern America is inundated by sexual themes on a morning, noon, and nightly basis, high school freshmen have absorbed so much information about the subject that they do not require further formal instruction. However, research has shown that the same old historic ignorance of sex prevails and is one of the factors contributing to the present unhappy picture.

Should instruction about sex restrict itself to a description of the plumbing, so to speak? Absolutely not. Should it incorporate moral and ethical considerations? Certainly. The only sort of moral component that is automatically ruled out in American public schools is that which represents a strictly sectarian religious viewpoint. In other words, the Catholic Church, which still feels that masturbation and birth control are grave sins, clearly ought not to be permitted to impose that view on the American process of public education.

The sort of moral considerations that could quite properly be incorporated into a program of instruction are those indicated by common sense, social custom, and practicality. Young boys, to give a specific instance, must be taught that they have no right to force their sexual attentions on anyone else, that to persist in doing so is called rape, and that it is a grave crime, punishable by imprisonment, in our society. Furthermore, it should be explained to immature boys that rape is wrong, not simply because it is illegal but also because it is a cruel violation of the Golden Rule.

Young men and women should also be taught that until they are absolutely certain they want children, they shouldn't even think of having them. The present situation would be an outrage if only one unwanted child was born, but we are talking about millions.

It must be stressed that for those teenagers, especially the older among them, who would, despite moral advice, continue to lose emotional control in certain instances, largely because of the dictates of nature itself, there would have to be a great deal of information provided concerning methods of birth control and, for the unmarried, birth prevention. This returns us to a key and dramatic factor in the on-going public dialogue on the ancient problem of irresponsible sexual activity.

Nature itself has always provided one means by which intercourse may be avoided. That is masturbation. But the largely Christian participants in the antiabortion camp belong to churches which are very clear in their condemnation of the practice of self-stimulation. Many of them are also, though with less unity, opposed to all practical methods of birth control. As a result of these two views, those who would do away with abortion in fact contribute to an increase in unwanted pregnancies and therefore a demand, on the part of millions of young women, that those pregnancies be terminated. We see, therefore, that among those elements of society that worsen the problem are the forces that want to make abortion unavailable for everybody.

Another feature of the better society in which abortions would be unnecessary would be a humane and civilized adoption program in which every child who was either unwanted by its natural parents or who became suddenly orphaned would be taken into a new and loving home. But such visions are, of course, fantasy. We are unfortunately forced to address the problem in the context of present reality, which is deeply depressing. Millions of children are presently being born to parents who either have little or no interest in them or who, if they do feel some rudimentary form of love for their newborns, are themselves so socially handicapped that they are simply incapable of responsibly assuming the role of parents. There are few orphanages either and a tremendous shortage of foster-care homes.

Another crucial requirement in any society prepared to outlaw abortion would be a massive and well-funded program of health care for the poor, day-care centers for infants whose mothers must work, family-counseling services, and other such agencies. Unfortunately these are in painfully short supply at present, largely for the reason that the conservative elements of society refuse to underwrite such compassionate programs with their tax dollars. Moreover, when, despite their wishes, a certain amount of tax revenue is allocated to such benign programs, conservative spokesmen complain vociferously about these expenditures. They cannot have it both ways. If they are serious about bringing about a sharp revision of the long-standing legality of abortion, it follows that the number of births will rise by the millions. It would rise even more, of course, were it not for the inescapable fact that armies of women will continue to insist on abortions, and will get them, if new laws are passed, generally from the same type of back-alley practitioners who have provided such services for centuries.

There is evidence that at least a minority of antiabortionists realize this, and we find, in the field of Catholic social services, for example, admirable instances of willingness to lend additional support to orphanages, adoption agencies, and day-care centers. One hopes that if the wishes of the conservative minority prevail in law and abortions are, in fact, outlawed or sharply curtailed, then the victors will not simply turn their backs on the millions of unwanted infants. This will, of course, require antiabortionist forces to stop complaining about taxes and start making clear that they care about the poor in America in ways actually detectable to the poor.

TV Humor:
Barbarians Are Storming
the Gates . . .

The following two articles, published in the *Los Angeles Times,* simply involved my speaking out in protest against the incredible tidal-wave of vulgarity that had, starting in the 1960s, gradually come to dominate American comedy. Since, like most Americans, I'm leery of any sort of formal censorship imposed by either government or church, I had repeatedly suggested that the radio and television networks, as well as film studios, should consider self-censorship without which—I felt—the real thing might eventually be imposed. After the first of the following articles was published, I received congratulatory calls from comedians Mort Sahl and Gary Morton and jazz pianist Jimmy Rowles, which simply reflected the fact that even most people in the entertainment industry are shocked by the degree of emphasis on sex that has become common. From other evidence I conclude that about 80 percent of the American people disapprove of the sort of ugliness presently so common.

The producers of a new sitcom, incapable of creating actual wit of the sort weekly provided by "Cheers" or "The Cosby Show,"

Reprinted from the *Los Angeles Times,* September 17, 1990.

255

decide to go with the current flow, despite the fact that that flow is carrying us all along right into the sewer. They make an innocent five-year-old say, "It sucks." The very sort of language parents forbid their children to use is now being encouraged not only by anything-goes cable entrepreneurs but the once high-minded networks. We may therefore paraphrase the ancient moral admonition about money to read: Love of Ratings Is the Root of All Evil.

We're not just talking about television here. Much of modern entertainment already involves vulgarians addressing barbarians. But the underlying questions are vastly more important. Why are ratings important? Because they translate into dollars. The bankers, corporate executives, and country-clubbers who own network stock, plus advertisers, far from resisting the present aesthetic and ethical collapse as their class would have in times past, are actually abetting the ugliness.

Marketplace factors are already largely responsible for having thoroughly debased popular music, a billion-dollar industry, since the tastes of poorly educated teenagers with discretionary income dominate the field. Most of today's punk and heavy-metal lovers have yet even to hear such names as Gershwin, Porter, and Rodgers. Forget Beethoven.

The best humor, when it is not simply purely playful, says something witty and wise about the issues it confronts. Among the horrifying problems of American civilization at present is the collapse of the American family, which has assumed such proportions, that many now react to the word *family* as if it were just another noun like *roller skates* or *television*. Humans can do without roller skates or TV but they literally cannot long survive, as a rational, emotionally healthy species, without a secure family structure.

The reason, to belabor the obvious, is that the family is the soil in which each year's new crop of humans grows. It is mostly the failed family, therefore, which has produced our present millions of prison inmates, rapists, drug addicts, burglars, muggers, sexual psychopaths, nonprofessional whores of both sexes, and general goofolas.

Very well—agreed; that is the problem. The solution of today's comedy specialists, with few exceptions, is to make vulgar light of what is, in reality, tragically heavy. As for those trying to treat as deep a wound as our society has ever suffered, far from encouraging them, today's comics deride them. That even those who acknowledge the right rules of social conduct will often fail to live up to their own honestly professed codes is sadly clear.

But what the dominant voices of a culture—with their access to popular music, radio, TV and the comedy concert circuit—now are saying is "F—— virtue."

If you think our society is sick now—stand by.

This relates, of course, to the debate about censorship and the question as to whether the large segment of American society that perceives the moral dangers in totally unrestricted artistic expression has any say at all concerning the use of public funds by the National Endowment for the Arts. The question is a perfectly fair one. Though artists have the creative right to produce work that may express racial, sexual, or religions hatred, does the state have the correlative obligation to endorse such expression with already inadequate taxpayers' money?

The matter is by no means justly resolved by reflexive condemnations of censorship, which in any event already exists, in law, or are slander and libel perfectly acceptable?

Even the maligned networks do censor their programs. When the Prince of Filth, Andrew Dice Clay, appeared recently on that bastion of free speech, "Saturday Night Live," several of his more revolting remarks were, quite properly, censored.

High time.

It's Time for Comedians
to Clean up Their Act

When I entertain, I almost invariably spend the first twenty minutes or so responding to questions submitted by members of the audience. In one recent instance, at a business luncheon awards ceremony of a Toastmasters group—in other words, people who are experienced public speakers—three different people brought up the same subject matter.

A Christina Hsiao asked, "What's your opinion of current-day comedians who mostly shout and insult the audience and have no intellectual or entertaining ideas?"

A Norman Riggs of Thousand Oaks asked, "Has humor gone too far?"

A Mern Reaves of Torrance wrote, "You've spoken of certain infamous public personalities who 'scrawl graffiti on the national dialogue.' How do we let these people know how far off base they are? How do we get them to cease and desist?"

It's also relevant that when that same day, in the process of telling a story about a guest on one of my television shows who, back in the 1950s, accidentally used a vulgar term, I said, "Perhaps

Reprinted from the *Los Angeles Times,* May 22, 1995.

I should explain to you younger people here today that while television now permits almost any sort of vulgarity, especially on its talk or comedy shows, for most of television's history nothing of the sort was permitted. We just laughed at Sid Caesar, Jackie Gleason, Red Skelton and those other wonderful comedians because they were funny."

And then I added, quite casually, "It might be interesting sometime, just as an experiment, to go back to that system."

To my surprise, the result was thunderous applause.

Perhaps the time has come to determine, by standard polling methods, what percentage of the American audience actually relishes the incredible daily barrage of vile language that has come to be so characteristic of modern comedy. Note that I am not referring here to the sort of innocent and cutely naughty humor that was common in old burlesque, although never in vaudeville, where it simply was not permitted.

It has been possible for American viewers to see instances of this sort of humor, almost always involving baggy-pants comedians working with pretty young women, because of the availability on our television sets of that delightful production "The Benny Hill Show." Mr. Hill was in the grand tradition of English music hall in which there has always been a great deal of comic leering at attractive showgirls, almost invariably by comedians with naturally funny faces, but our burlesque entertainers never used vulgarity of the sort that one hears now even on daytime television, which is to say where children can and do see it.

It is certainly relevant to consider that those regarded as the great comics of the century did not resort to the gutter-language heard today in every comedy club in the land. We simply laughed at Charlie Chaplin, Stan Laurel and Oliver Hardy, Buster Keaton, Fred Allen, Victor Borge, and the others. Even the most depraved individuals never appealed to our great comic entertainers to deal in obscenity and language that would shame a drunken sailor.

Show business is, of course, a business, in some respects like any other, and if American taste generally has fallen to such a low estate that millions of dollars can be made by catering to it, then it would be difficult to address the large problem constructively or to hope for much improvement. But the will of the majority is also an important factor in our political and social system. Let us assume that polls and surveys would reveal that most Americans are disgusted by the degree of ugliness in modern comedy. Wouldn't it be reasonable to demand that the fact—if it were so—would be reflected in that marketplace?

For that minority who apparently could not get enough vile concepts and terms in their popular entertainment, perhaps a submarket could be established for their convenience; something like "Filth Night: Monday, Wednesday, and Friday" could be advertised at comedy clubs. And "Clean Nights" be made available on Tuesday, Thursday, and Saturday.

The various rating systems, of course, are an attempt—though weak—to do something about the otherwise constantly descending level of vulgarity to which we are presently subjected.

The Press of Freedom:
Jack O'Brian and the Art of Criticism

Of all the articles the editors have collected for the present work, the following is the least historically important. I honestly do not know, as of the moment I dictate this note, whether the journalist I wrote about so long ago, in the 1950s, is still alive. He was never of national prominence, but in New York City—because it was the television capital—he had enormous power. There is nothing wrong with that; O'Brian's problem was that he shamelessly abused such power. His field was television criticism, which meant he was daily called upon to praise what was admirable and criticize what was deplorable, amateurish, or otherwise inferior. The hundreds of other television critics in cities across the country were perfectly capable of expressing their dislike for a given telecast without indulging in personal attacks. O'Brian could not resist the temptation. Some of his criticism had nothing whatever to do with how well or poorly a given performer played the violin, did comedy, tap danced, sang, or acted but was based instead on O'Brian's dislike of their political views. He was roundly disliked within the entertainment community, needless to say, but, as is often the case with bullies, his

From *The Village Voice Reader,* ed. by Daniel Wolf (New York: Doubleday, 1962).

critics were afraid, because of his power as a journalist, to speak their minds. Finally his offenses became so notorious that something had to be done.

Nothing I have ever written has occasioned such an outburst of cheers. Letters poured in form major television figures—Ed Sullivan, Arthur Godfrey, Frank Sinatra, and others, as well as from dozens of smaller figures who the columnist had treated unkindly.

At least fifty times during the past several years I have heard television people say, "Something really ought to be done about Jack O'Brian."

It should be explained at the outset that this article is not a simple instance of a performer taking personal issue with a reviewer. There are few more pathetic spectacles than that of an actor pulling critical barbs out of his skin and demanding naively to know what right the press had to attack him. One of the first things a performer must learn is to take the bitter with the sweet.

It should also be made clear that this protest concerns Mr. O'Brian alone. With rare and isolated exceptions, all other television critics have been eminently fair with me, as they are with other entertainers. No, O'Brian is unique. He alone, among his hundreds of colleagues, has so abused his position and power that a statement concerning him must be made, and publicly. I say publicly by way of establishing that the majority of New York television people are privately willing to express their contempt for him at length.

Recently I dined with a group that included one of television's biggest comedians, one of our top singing stars, and a popular emcee. O'Brian's name happened to come up and, as if reacting automatically to the stimulus, each performer in turn had shocking stories to tell of unfair treatment at his hands.

That there has never been a public protest about him before is explained by the fact that most performers are conditioned, and correctly, to feel that it is pointless to become involved in controversy with critics, and by the fact that *were* any actor tempted to speak out, he would be advised that O'Brian could retaliate daily in his column. I am well aware that O'Brian's response to this piece will more likely be a series of personal attacks on me than a response to the charges against him, but I feel that my discomfort is a small price to pay in this instance. Mr. O'Brian has assumed the role of the neighborhood bully. His conduct demands attention. There is a job to be done. No one else has seen fit to do it.

There has never been a scoundrel on earth, of course, who could not rally a certain number of people to his support, but the fact remains that by far the greater number of TV people openly disapprove of O'Brian's professional methods. And I propose to limit this article to those methods, to what can be learned of the man from his written word. Concerning his personal life I shall say nothing, since all men are weak.

But the business at hand is an analysis of O'Brian as critic. Such an examination, I submit, cannot fail to substantiate the opinion that he is derelict in his duty to his readers, unethical in his methods, and beneath the respect of the industry because his column is frequently an outlet for his personal emotional delinquencies rather than a reflection of intelligent, fair, responsible criticism.

It cannot be emphasized too often that the reason performers consider O'Brian anathema is *not* simply that he is from time to time displeased with what he sees on television. Hundreds of other columnists are able to discharge this duty, with varying degrees of finesse, but always with honor and with some consideration of the fact that they are writing about fellow human beings.

O'Brian alone writes criticism that is characterized by clumsy reporting and vindictive displays of pique. He alone has reduced his column to an adolescent potpourri of brickbats for those whom he personally dislikes and posies for those who are, or pretend to be, his pals.

The list of entertainers who are consistently treated unfairly by O'Brian is long and imposing and, significantly enough, largely comprised of the biggest names in the business.

O'Brian's anti-Arthur Godfrey attitude, for instance, is so unbending that if there is not enough bad news he can relate about him, O'Brian will drag Godfrey's name into print for no other reason than to express contempt. Example: "Bill Gargan doesn't own any of his new Martin Kane TV films, and *they're selling like Godfrey used to*."

Another victim of the O'Brian love-'em-and-leave-'em pattern was Jackie Gleason. Initially O'Brian praised Gleason. Eventually he attacked him, at last so rudely that the two almost came to blows one night in a restaurant.

Still another performer unable to receive fair treatment at the hands of O'Brian is Ed Sullivan. If there is any news to gladden Ed's heart you may be sure it will not be brought to the attention of *Journal-American* readers. If, on the other hand, Sullivan's rating happens to slump, or a portion of his program is below par, it is fairly certain that O'Brian will mention it. His hatred of Sullivan is so pronounced that he cannot even bring himself to refer to his hour as a "program." Instead he uses phrases such as "the Ed Sullivan whatsis," or "the Sullivan catch-all."

Whether O'Brian's frequent errors are the results of slovenly reporting or deliberate intent to harm is, of course, impossible to say, but neither possibility reflects credit upon him. I can perhaps best explain what I mean by careless reporting by referring to my own experience. A few years ago my good friend and producer Bill Harbach was being badly overworked to the tune of ten or twelve hours a day on the old "Tonight" show. In social conversation he happened to remark that the show was a man-killer and that he would welcome a long vacation, or words to that effect. A few days later O'Brian reported Bill wanted to get off the show because of "the star's temperament." Since this was an untruth, Bill sent O'Brian a letter explaining that my "temperament" had nothing whatever to do with the case. O'Brian ran the retraction but left the quotation marks off the word *temperament,* which of course exactly reversed Bill's meaning.

Another instance: We took the "Tonight" show to Hollywood once for a two-month stay, and since our crew numbered some twenty people we could not have handled the expenses of the move without working out a "deal" with a Los Angeles hotel. The hotel agreed to put our small army up more or less free in return for on-the-air plugs, in accordance with common industry procedure. You would never have known that, however, from O'Brian's reference to the matter. Omitting all mention of our large staff, he implied that I did plugs for the hotel so that I personally could avoid paying room rent.

There were numerous examples of a similar sort. For a time I contented myself with writing fair and frank letters to O'Brian, providing him with the facts of the matters he had incorrectly reported. A trade-wise publicity man advised me I was wasting my time. "If you contradict him, no matter how politely, he'll kick and scream [like a four-year-old]."

"He can't be that bad," I protested.

Eventually, I was to revise my opinion. Several headaches later O'Brian printed one particular lie that caused me to write him not a peacefully worded note at all but one telling him frankly that I had a good mind to take a poke at him if he didn't correct his untruth and fast. The facts of the case were as follows:

One evening an NBC executive called my office in a state of considerable apprehension. It seems a movie actor had walked off the Perry Como show after rehearsing for a couple of days and left Perry on the spot for a replacement. My agent, Jules Green, asked me if I wanted to fill in for the actor and I said: "Well, it's my night off, but if they're in trouble, naturally I'll jump in." The NBC man said: "Of course Steve will get his usual guest-shot price, $7,500, which is okay because that's Perry's top anyway." Jules told him it was a deal, I did the show, and Perry and I had a lot of fun. Then I read in O'Brian's column that the Como show had been over a barrel because Perry had had a sore throat and that when I was contacted about replacing *Perry* I held the show up for big money, whereas other comedians around town had offered to go on without salary.

My letter to O'Brian about this particular untruth was phrased in such forthright terms that he referred to my denial the next day, but characteristically didn't admit his error, saying instead that the source for his version of the story was an NBC executive.

One of O'Brian's uglier practices is what would seem the deliberate attempt to foster ill-feeling between performers by including in a single paragraph a compliment for one with a criticism of the other. To select one example: "David Brinkley of the NBC-TV news twosome is very good, dry, and interesting; can't say the same for Chet Huntley." Any intelligent viewer can observe that Huntley and Brinkley are two peas in a pod; the apparent reason for O'Brian's criticism is that he suspects Huntley of liberal political inclinations. O'Brian is perhaps the only critic in the nation who judges television fare according to the political opinions of those who present it.

Like many people who are themselves ultrasensitive to criticism, O'Brian has the sensitivity of a mastodon when it comes to the feelings of others. An orchestra leader who has appeared on my program wears a toupee, presumably because he does not want people to know he is bald. O'Brian informed his readers about the musician's baldness. He can be equally cruel to women regarding their physical endowments or the lack thereof. Recently he referred in print to the fact that one TV comedienne wears "falsies." Such insensitivity is hardly the mark of a gentleman.

One reason for the preparation of this statement, incidentally, is my feeling that new, young TV performers will benefit by being warned that destructive evaluations of their talents by O'Brian need not be seriously entertained. By way of example consider the case of Dody Goodman, who appears with Jack Paar. I find Miss Goodman amusing, and so do most of the people with whom I have discussed her. On the program one night several weeks ago she happened to say to Hans Conreid: "Oh, shut up," in a tone obviously intended as playful. O'Brian attacked her cruelly the following day and has done so on many occasions since. One of his more shocking comments about her began: "Dody Goodman—who isn't funny—." I watched the program the night of his initial attack and observed that Miss Goodman was uncommonly subdued and not at all her usual happy, scatterbrained self. Suspecting that O'Brian was to blame, I wrote advising Dody that millions of television viewers knew that she *was* funny, and warning her that the critic for the *Journal-American* was the one TV columnist whose criticisms were beneath respect because of his record of irresponsibility. Her reply confirmed my suppositions as to the reason for her depressed on-the-air demeanor; she told me that a number of other people had given her substantially the same advice.

It must not be supposed that O'Brian's rudeness is directed only toward performers. Many publicity people and secretaries relate stories of his chip-on-the-shoulder attitude if they are first assured that their words will not be broadcast, for they tell you frankly that they fear O'Brian. It is precisely that fact which has had much to do with the preparation of this article. That decent, hardworking publicity and network people feel fear of this irresponsible man is deplorable. Part of that fear is understandable, of course, although not entirely excusable. There exists the baseless impression that O'Brian *is* the *Journal-American,* that to antagonize him is to alienate the Hearst organization. Nothing could be farther from the truth.

Protests will, of course, antagonize the readily combustible and sometimes pugnacious Mr. O'Brian, concerning whose character psychologists would no doubt have an easy time drawing inferences from his choice of verbs in sentences pertaining to the relative ratings of television programs. His column of November 12, 1957, leads off with the announcement that the "Maverick" show "mauled" Ed Sullivan and myself in the overnight Trendex competition. Since "Maverick" topped Sullivan by only 2.8 and since our rating for the same half-hour was 17.6, it will be seen that the verb "to maul" is (a) an exaggeration, and (b) an indication of a wish on O'Brian's part, either conscious or unconscious, that Sullivan and Allen be mauled, either professionally or physically. It is true that any columnist, rushed by a deadline, and seeking a colorful phrase, might employ such phraseology without malicious motivation, but such wordage is not the exception with O'Brian, it is the rule. To describe the difference in rating between programs, he habitually uses terms like "clobbered," "swamped," "buried"—all of which may cast more light on the real Mr. O'Brian than the "clobbered" shows. His most famous boner in this particular area has become something of an industry joke and was perpetrated one week last year when Lawrence Welk had a rating of 21.7 to Sid Caesar's 21 even. Describing this difference, which all television people know is completely meaningless statistically, O'Brian wrote that Welk "walked all over Sid Caesar."

Something else that throws interesting light on O'Brian's character is his attitude toward psychiatry. In his column of November 1, 1957, he expresses approval of the Western series, "Boots and Saddles," but makes use of the opportunity to drag in by the heels the following outburst: "It ['Boots and Saddles'] isn't one of the avant, or nouveaux, double-dome Westerns with delusions of intellectuality . . . it simply is a very good, straightforward film series without the fidgets or idgets of the egghead cowpokes, who too often are not the good, simple, homespun cowhands and nineteenth-century American soldiers of pioneer fortune, but irritating cerebral explosions of the new spate of TV authors who wish to extend lessons learned on their head-shrinker's couches to those among the TV audience who, psychiatrically, are considered members of the great unwashed-brain brigade."

The circumstance whereby the individual most in need of psychiatric aid is discovered to be he who denounces it most vigorously is too classic to require further emphasis.

O'Brian does have his occasional "normal" working days when his modest critical ability manifests itself, but there are others when he can find little to please him in this world. One column, for example, contained thirty-six separate items. Of these *only three could be construed as complimentary.*

Despite all this, the man is not entirely without virtue. If a program is truly inept, O'Brian can sometimes do an accurate, if heavy-handed, job of pinpointing its inadequacies. Upon occasion he has shown that, when he is not emotionally involved in the issues he is covering, he can be a capable reporter.

*   *   *

The case against O'Brian has so many particulars that I have been able to do little more than summarize it here. In doing so there is no question but that I have reflected popular opinion, even among other New York columnists, most of whom openly dislike the man. What is perhaps open to question is the matter of result. What good will have been done by the publication of this article? Well, first, as I have pointed out, performers who are relatively inexperienced will be cheered by the knowledge that O'Brian's destructive criticisms are in most instances unworthy of respect. To be criticized by Crosby, Gould, Van Horne, Minor, and the rest—especially in concert—is to have cause for concern. To be criticized by O'Brian may well be an indication that you have talent.

Will the publication of this essay have any beneficial effect upon O'Brian himself? It is not inconceivable. Perhaps O'Brian's evil has been done all in innocence. Perhaps it truly has never occurred to him that he is the only television critic in the nation who is rude, inaccurate, un-Christian, and vengeful. Perhaps this blunt presentation of the case for the entertainer will, after his initial shock and anger, lead him to consider mending his ways. Ani-

mosity is always unpleasant, and I am sure the hundreds of performers who presently dislike O'Brian because they disapprove of
his methods would much prefer to be on the same sort of polite
terms with him that they are with all other reviewers.

Critique by Nat Hentoff

Steve Allen's prolix shadow-boxing of Jack O'Brian's cars in this journal detonated a small brouhaha. Columnist Hy Gardner noted approvingly that Allen was being congratulated by the trade; Allen noted
approvingly that Allen was being congratulated by the trade; and *Time*
magazine ran a characteristically inconsequential story on the incident.
(*Time* leads all publications, including *U.S. News and World Report,*
when it comes to missing the basic point of any story in any context.)

O'Brian says he is not going to answer the Allen term paper so
I will, although I'm in on a pass. Contrary to appearances, Allen's
essay was not in answer to my column on television critics—in
which I had largely praised O'Brian—but was already written and
was just looking for a home. I find, by the way, that the fact of my
lauding O'Brian has puzzled and occasionally angered several liberal friends of mine who cannot understand how I can approve a
reactionary in any area of his activities. (O'Brian's definition of a
reactionary, incidentally, is a guy whose reaction to any situation
you can predict before the situation even occurs.) I repeat, however,
that although I find O'Brian's gratuitous hauling of Roy Cohnisms
into his columns thoroughly repugnant, I fault him on one score at
a time and don't condemn him in toto. Except for his being the
David Lawrence of TV columnists with regard to politics, I still
think O'Brian is second only to Jack Gould in this city for taste,
courage, and knowledge of the medium he's writing about.

The issue here, however, is Allen's conception of the nature of
criticism and his own approach to criticizing O'Brian. Allen uses a
hoary lawyer's trick toward the beginning when he notes: "Concerning his personal life I shall say nothing, since all men are
weak." (Thanks, St. Augustine.) Allen continues, however: "I
would be remiss . . . were I not to report that this gentleman who so
frequently speaks for virtue in his column impresses many people
as shockingly vulgar in speech and social deportment." There is

more later in the Allen article about O'Brian's "personal life," at least Allen's version of it, so I guess some men to Allen are weaker than others. Aside from Allen's smugness in this vein—he calls O'Brian "un-Christian" along the line, and as a pagan somewhat learned in Christian history I wonder what on earth that's supposed to mean—it seems self-evident, I would think, that a man's personal life and habits have no necessary relation to his ability as a critic or a novelist or a statistician or a TV comic—at least on the surface level utilized by Allen. I care not at all whether or not O'Brian is "shockingly vulgar in speech and social deportment," and in any case, I'd want to know Allen's criteria of vulgarity. I expect Dostoevsky or even G. B. Shaw might not pass.

During the substance of Allen's argument, the main charges seem slim indeed. He objects to O'Brian's consistent harpooning of Godfrey, Sullivan, and others of "the biggest names in the business." If a man is aware of the capacities of a medium, he rightly becomes enraged when that medium is being consumed by mediocrities and fools. It's to O'Brian's credit that he keeps measuring the small talents (has Allen ever read Shaw's music criticism?). Eddie Fisher's manager is another who complains that his charge is a frequent O'Brian target. Fisher, as un-musical a nontalent as has ever been manufactured into a personality, deserves O'Brian's attention. If you care about music, you're being remiss as a critic not to underline the deficiencies of the robots (and Allen doesn't mention that, in terms of jazz, O'Brian is the hippest and most encouraging of all the TV critics).

To indicate O'Brian's inaccuracy as a reporter, Allen submits a few examples which hardly indicate that O'Brian's reporting is all that "clumsy." In one case, O'Brian was absolutely right to call Allen on the "deal" with the Los Angeles hotel for free plugs in return for housing and feeding the Allen entourage. This is a reprehensible practice that I would think the FCC should have been fierce about a long time ago, and O'Brian is one of the very, very few critics to continually fix attention to other applications of the plugola greed that is so prevalent in TV. Allen's other examples are pretty slim ammunition (O'Brian left quotes off "temperament" and got a bum steer from an NBC executive about an Allen guest-appearance on the Como show).

Allen's own skill as a television critic is, I trust, not to be wholly judged by his astonishing statement that David Brinkley and Chet Huntley "are two peas in a pod." As O'Brian rightly has noted, they are almost completely different. Huntley is humorless, not particularly incisive, and, in general, an average, competent "news analyst." Brinkley is drily funny, unusually perceptive—he is almost in a class with Howard K. Smith—and much the warmer of the two personalities. Allen writes that O'Brian puts down Huntley because "he suspects Huntley of liberal political inclinations." Yet it is Brinkley who is the more outspokenly liberal of the two and the more effective antiadministration marksman, and Brinkley whom O'Brian has praised. I'm surprised actually that O'Brian does occasionally have something good to say about Brinkley, and at least he doesn't call the tandem "two peas in a pod."

Allen continues to document O'Brian's wickedness by adding, "One of his more shocking comments about her began: 'Dody Goodman—who isn't funny—.' " I agree with O'Brian. I think she's not only not funny but rather pathetic and no little of a phony in her new guise. (She used to be an excellent revue comedienne.) What does that opinion make me—Jack the Ripper? Allen is quite right later on, however, when he says there is some antipathy to O'Brian in the higher Hearst echelons. That this hostility exists may be to O'Brian's credit, since he refuses to be pressured by anyone and is, in fact, one of the few thoroughly independent writers left in journalism.

Some of Allen's points—O'Brian's adjectival hyperbole in discussing comparative ratings—are valid, but Allen's analysis of O'Brian's choice of verbs ("clobbered," "swamped," "buried") with its implication that they connote that O'Brian needs an analyst is dinner-table psychiatry. If one grants that we all need analysis ("since all men are weak"), to proceed from that assumption to that kind of verb-analysis is to "condemn" every writer from Thucydides to Joyce. The verb, as Allen should know being a writer himself, is the most important motor part of a sentence. The more alive the verb, usually, the more alive the sentence. O'Brian's particular choice of alive verbs may indeed indicate fury, but as I said before, if a critic is deeply concerned with the potential of a given medium, he's a poor critic if he doesn't react furiously to mediocrity and dishonesty. Some of the angriest pieces that have ever appeared in the *New York Times* have been by Jack Gould. Does that make him "sick" too?

The final criterion of criticism with which Allen ends his article is perhaps more revealing than he meant it to be. He wrote that perhaps by some miracle ("since all men are weak") O'Brian may yet repent; and "I am sure," concluded Allen, in what I expect is Christian spirit, "the hundreds of performers who presently dislike O'Brian because they disapprove of his methods would much prefer to be on the same sort of polite terms with him that they are with all other reviewers."

Allen's vision of the world in this context is of an "adjusted" society wherein we are all polite to each other and suppress those of our feelings that are not approved or that might get us—the worst of all penalties—disliked by someone. I would think that if the positive measure of a critic is that he be on polite terms with everyone he writes about, we had better replace Murray Kempton with Norman Vincent Peale, Jack Gould with Charles Kenny, and B. H. Haggin with Harriet Johnson. Allen knows better, I think. His own approach to comedy, the fact that he wrote the article about O'Brian, and some of his short stories would imply that he realizes that the primary danger to our society is the growing queue of the bland leading the bland. Politeness, hell. The need is for more people, including critics, to learn to express their feelings again, to say and write what they feel, not what they hope their audience wants to hear. All men are weak; let's not make them any weaker.

Critique by Steve Allen

Before we start our show, boys and girls, let's bring ourselves up to date on our story. Yesterday, you'll remember, Terrible Jack was getting his Just Desserts when all of a sudden he was rescued by a Mysterious Visitor from another planet, Nat-Hen-Toff. Nat was not actually sent here to defend the likes of Terrible Jack, you understand. His true mission was to attack the Camp of the Flabby Critics. Since Terrible Jack is certainly not Flabby, Nat found himself admiring him for his very Non-Flabbiness. Now go on with our story. . . .

*   *   *

One difficulty in keeping controversy tidy is that ideas will not easily submit to being isolated in watertight compartments. They insist on fission, or osmosis, or some damned thing that will forever bug man as he tries to settle one issue at a time. Since a number of matters more or less extraneous to my original thesis are now jostling each other for stage position, I can perhaps best discuss them in an orderly manner by resorting to a system of numerical listing.

I find first of all that Nat and I agree on a great many points.

1. I agree that much TV criticism is watery.

2. I agree that O'Brian writes a column that is not spineless. The quality of boldness, however, is not necessarily a virtue or a vice in and of itself. *Mein Kampf* was vigorous, too.

3. Nat says: "O'Brian's gratuitous hauling of Roy Cohnisms into his column is thoroughly repugnant." All-righty. But what is a thousand times worse is the practice of criticizing television people *on the basis of their political opinions* rather than on the quality and content of their performances.

4. I agree that if a man is aware of the capacities of a medium he rightly becomes enraged when that medium is being consumed by mediocrities. That bit of philosophy, however, has nothing whatever to do with the point with which Hentoff linked it: my contention that O'Brian's critical integrity is degraded by his refusal to print *anything* good about certain performers who are on his "don't like" list. To repeat only one example of many that could be cited: O'Brian hates Ed Sullivan. Result? He knocks Sullivan at every opportunity. Does Hentoff truly believe that there is *nothing* good, *ever,* about Sullivan's program? His honest answer to that question forces him to admit that O'Brian has been unfair to Sullivan. At the risk of belaboring the point, I now state bluntly: much of O'Brian's criticism is based on his *personal relationships with* performers, not truly on the quality of their programs. Surely Hentoff would admit that such a thing is indefensible.

5. I agree with Nat that I goofed in calling Huntley and Brinkley "two peas in a pod."

6. I agree with Nat that "some of Allen's points are valid." (All right, let's laugh it up; these are the jokes.)

7. Hentoff admits that O'Brian's choice of verbs may indicate fury. A good critic should react vigorously to mediocrity, but here again Nat, it seems to me, has coupled an idea with which any reasonable man would agree to a fact about O'Brian that does not relate logically. When O'Brian says that "Lawrence Welk walked all over Sid Caesar"—when the difference in ratings was a fraction of a point—against what mediocrity is the man railing? When he says that "Maverick" "clobbered" Ed Sullivan and Steve Allen, does he mean that the Sullivan and Allen shows are truly for the most part mediocre or that "Maverick" is superior to them in quality?

8. I agree that in a time of lack of originality nonconformism can be a virtue. Television desperately needs intelligent, informed criticism. But it needs commentary of the sort provided by the Goulds and Crosbys, not the O'Brians. True, Gould has written some very angry criticism, and good for him, say I. He's even written some of it about particular bits of my own program, and good for him again, say I. But his criticism was based on what he saw on his television screen and did not originate out of spiteful feelings. Neglect to say hello to O'Brian in a restaurant and he will knock you in his column: that is the common belief among TV people about the man, and Nat, please note: only TV people can know the score on this particular point. Hentoff would have no way of knowing about the incident in the restaurant; all he would see was the slur in the column the next day. Much of O'Brian's evil is of this hidden-part-of-the-iceberg sort. You saw the letters I sent to you, Nat, letters from important and respected people: network officials, writers, composers, producers, actors, publishers, newscasters, other television critics, all without exception endorsing my original statement and many offering more information. Only these people, I repeat, can tell you of O'Brian's unfairness. The public has practically no opportunity to be informed as to his motivations.

*   *   *

Now: a few points on which Nat and I do not agree, or on which at least we do not understand each other.

A. I was not aware that I was employing "a hoary lawyer's trick" in saying that I would limit my argument to O'Brian the critic rather than discuss his personal life. To begin with, I don't know any hoary lawyers, but "seriously, folks," the point I was making was that O'Brian seems to have established himself as President of the National A-Woman's-Body-Is-Nasty Club, and that while there might be a certain justice in the puritanical attitude coming from, let's say, Ben Gross, the pose ill befits O'Brian. Standards of decency must indeed be maintained, but the industry does not intend to jump to O'Brian's lonely piping. Just this morning I noted a comment in the popular Catholic publication *"Our Sunday Visitor"* to the effect that our television show is a clean one. Let O'Brian go argue with *O.S.V.* Perhaps, though, if Nat misunderstood this part of my argument, the fault was mine in not making my intentions clear.

B. I disagree with Nat's theory that there is something immoral or unethical per se about television's practice of doing "plugs" in exchange for services, merchandise, or what-have-you. A case might be made that by certain standards it is improper for a comic to do an unfunny Smirnoff Vodka joke with the intention of getting a private, personal payoff, but again Nat has coupled a principle with an instance not covered by that principle. Television literally could not function in its present way without the legitimate plug. When the Perry Como show goes off the air, for example, the announcer does a plug for After-Six Tuxedos if such suits were worn by the chorus boys. I say there is nothing whatever wrong in this. The clothier is made happy, the program saves a very hefty costume-rental payment, and the regular sponsors of Perry's show are in no way inconvenienced.

Similar examples abound. Does Nat think that the "$64,000" show pays retail for the Cadillacs it gives away? Is there anything wrong with Ralph Edwards mentioning the airline that flew his guests to Hollywood? Is there anything wrong with "Queen for a Day" plugging assorted vacuum cleaners, mink coats, etc., by way of lining up prizes for some lucky woman? But beyond all that, Nat quite ignored O'Brian's real sin in this instance. I did not object to his referring to the fact that our show was plugging a Los Angeles hotel in return for rent for our large production gang. In fact I would have settled for that. What O'Brian did, however, was quite different. He implied that I was doing plugs so that I *personally* could avoid paying room rent. Surely Nat can see the distinction, and the unfairness.

C. Nat neglects to tell us of his reaction to O'Brian's habit of praising a performer to the skies, then one day doing an abrupt about-face. O'Brian should, says Hentoff, "measure the small talents." Indeed, but is it reliable measurement when O'Brian highly praises, say, Arthur Godfrey until he happens to develop a *personal* dislike for him and then begins to attack him? And in what way is O'Brian measuring talent or elevating television standards when he writes that a close-up of John Crosby showed "his face with a seemingly endless mouth, like Ruth Gordon's, which seems to go all the way round her head, and large lips which when speaking seem to be pulled vertically apart, as if with unseen strings"? This, in my opinion, is not responsible criticism but out-and-out boorishness.

D. I do not agree that my other examples of O'Brian's reportorial peculiarities were "slim ammunition." But whether they were or were not is not important. What is important is that space limited me to the selection of a very few examples. From what I have heard on the phone about O'Brian the past few days, I think that an edition of the Sunday *Times* could be filled with similar ammunition, much of it very heavy indeed.

E. Nat misunderstood my references to the O'Brian–Dody Goodman matter. O'Brian is entitled to be unamused by Miss Goodman, or by Milton Berle, or name who you will. There's no such thing as a universally popular comedian. But is a critic entitled to say "Dody Goodman isn't funny" or "Jack Paar isn't funny" or "Sid Caesar isn't funny" when it is obvious that millions are laughing at the comic in question? Sue me, but I don't think so. I believe that a critic may observe that he personally finds an entertainer unfunny, and I am well aware that it is assumed a priori that a critic is after all only giving his own opinion of things, but there is still something frightening about the power of the press when it is employed unwisely, and I feel therefore that blunt statements like "Jonathan Winters isn't funny" first of all make a critic look unattractively arrogant, and secondly that they are, in the sense that they ignore the relationship between the subjective and the objective, somewhat on a par with statements like "Johnny Weissmuller can't swim" or "Pat Boone can't sing." What such statements really mean is "Johnny Weissmuller doesn't swim nearly as well as he did twenty years ago," or "Pat Boone, according to my standards, isn't nearly as good a singer as Frank Sinatra or Ella Fitzgerald." A statement such as "Dody Goodman isn't funny," therefore, can be understood to be incorrect in quite a literal sense, it being granted that at the time the statement is made a great many people are laughing at Miss Goodman in her professional capacity.

In the sense that Fred Allen was funny, Miss Goodman is not, but in the sense that Zazu Pitts or Butterfly McQueen were funny, she *is* amusing for the quite obvious reason that the outward accidentals of her personality mark her as eccentric, scatterbrained, and, as Hentoff has accurately pointed out, "pathetic." She is precisely the type of square and flighty woman Nat would find himself chuckling at if he overheard her asking directions from a busy traffic cop or addressing a woman's club.

But at this point I perceive that I am becoming guilty of that against which I directed my opening remarks: digression. One thing, it seems, always leads to another. From here on, Nat, let's kick this around over a beer.

Speeches

Concluding Remarks at the National Catholic Conference for Interracial Justice
August 24, 1968

This conference has had a profound seriousness of purpose, and it would be inappropriate to conclude it with nothing more than a few aimless witticisms. It has been suggested, therefore, that my closing remarks pertain directly to the issues that have concerned you.

Since the various speakers and participants of this conference have been very plain-spoken—and rightly so—I will continue in the same vein.

In the background paper supplied to participants in this conference one is urged to consider the question as to how Christ's Mystical Body—the Church—could have been involved in three hundred years of prejudice, discrimination, and preferential treatment in the United States of America. It is a good question, but it is only a fragment of the larger historical question: How could the Church have been involved in almost two thousand years of prejudice, discrimination, and preferential treatment in all parts of what used to be called the civilized world? There have always been, thank God, individual churchmen who were not guilty of such un-Christian behavior, but it has never been seriously suggested that they constituted a majority. It may be fairly argued that the warlike tribes of Europe would have been considerably more barbaric had they not become converted to Christianity, but the fact remains that as Christians, and in their ethnic or national capacities, they have only occasionally shown an inclination towards those qualities of mercy, compassion, meekness, humility, charity, rationality, and tolerance which are supposed to distinguish Christians from those of other philosophical persuasions.

As consistent evidence, consider the present tragic situation in Ireland, North and South, in which we see Christians resorting to the same savage violence that has plagued mankind throughout his history and is so common on our planet at the present moment. That man is part animal we know; the question is: to what extent has Christianity sublimated his vicious impulses? To what extent does it do so on the streets of Londonderry this afternoon? To what extent has it done so throughout Catholic Latin America for the past four hundred years? To what extent are the Christians of Catholic Sicily civilized by their religion? The Mafia culture imported to this country—whatever else it is—is a Catholic culture, God help us all. These are hard truths, hard questions, but it is long past time when they should have been faced.

The problem is not, needless to say, exclusively Catholic. The Protestant cultures face it as well. The members of the Ku Klux Klan have always been God-fearing Christians, have they not? Hitler was voted into power by God-fearing Christians, was he not?

We have all heard of those religious fanatics of India who make incredibly long journeys on their knees. It is not the Indians who ought to travel on their knees but rather the Christians, out of penitence for the way we have combined the ancient savageries with the arrogant blindness of self-righteousness.

Against this, one can naturally reflect upon the achievements of the culture of the West. Artistically and scientifically there have been Herculean works of genius. But morally? The answer does not come as readily. There are the saints, of course, but all of them who ever lived could be crowded into this one auditorium.

Enough of breast-beating about the crimes of history, one might protest. What do we do now, here, in these United States? But the answer is this: first look back into history—both ancient and recent—and ponder well.

A practical suggestion. The churches are going to have to join together and make a concession unequalled in human history. They are going to have to publicly concede what is painfully apparent, that—except for the usual sprinkling of exceptional individuals— they have failed in what was presumably their one basic task: the inculcation of a moral code based on the love of God, the Golden Rule, and the ideal of love for one's fellowman. Is there anyone who would seriously deny it?

Is the failure not glaringly apparent in today's racial crisis? It has been just as apparent, of course, in the Protestant American South for the past two hundred years, as generations of Catholic and Jewish leaders have agreed. But now that the drama is no longer being played out solely below the Mason-Dixon line, it is interesting to note to what extent Northern affiliates of one faith or another have recourse to their moral codes when the social chips are down.

The Catholic Church in America is just now coming to a staggering realization which has brought it literally to its knees in this hour of challenge, the realization that it has so often failed to turn obedient Catholics into practicing Christians. John McDermott, writing in the November 1, 1966 edition of *Look* magazine, draws this shocking picture:

> Terrible evidence of the failure of the Church to teach racial justice came to light last summer, when Negro and white demonstrators from the Chicago Freedom Movement marched through all-white, predominantly Catholic neighborhoods to dramatize the need for an open and just housing market. Hundreds of policemen could not save the marchers, including Dr. Martin Luther King, Jr., from an avalanche of hate: hurled rocks, bottles, and firecrackers. The score of nuns and priests who marched became a special target. "You're not a real priest! Where did you get that outfit?" a heckler shrieked at one priest. "Hey, Father, are you sleeping with her?" a man screamed at a priest walking side by side with a Negro woman. After one march, a Negro priest was dragged from his car and savagely beaten.
>
> Even the nuns were not exempt from obscenities and physical attacks. People cursed and spat at them. A rock felled Sister M. Angelica, O.S.F., a suburban nun who was spending her summer at an inner-city parochial school. The crowd cheered wildly

when she went down. At the hospital, when her bleeding head was being sewed up, she said: "I feel no bitterness toward these people—but it hurts to think we haven't taught them better."

It has always been something of a puzzle why individuals feel pride for what are considered the accomplishments of their total cultures but are usually achievements of solitary individuals or small groups. One naturally has enormous respect, for example, for the achievements of that small percentage of Americans working in our space program, but since I personally have made no contribution to those achievements, I do not understand why the emotion I should feel about them is pride. Certainly the wonders of science and technology, for which a small handful of us are responsible, cannot be said to be typical of our people. Most of us are poorly educated and rarely inclined to think in a scientific or logical manner. In *that* regard we are typical; therefore, an appropriate emotional response to the magnificent achievement of landing men on the moon is not pride but rather shame that the great majority of us are incapable of participating in such accomplishments. In the same way, I do not see why we Christians are entitled to pride because of the personal achievements of Christ, Thomas Aquinas, or St. Francis. Rather we should feel shame and humility that as individuals we fall so far below such levels of moral perfection.

Another key word of the new approach to morality and faith is "relevance," which really relates to the ancient relationship between faith and good works. The Conservatives have told us, consistently enough down through the centuries, that man should concern himself with the salvation of his own soul, if possible with the salvation of the souls of others, but that—to quote a recent statement by Father Gommer De Pauw, president of the Catholic Traditionalist Movement—"Religions and their representatives, clergymen, are *not* supposed to concern themselves directly with social or any kind of temporal problems . . . we priests should leave the social and the other temporal problems to lay people, experts."

The underlying reason for this conservative view, I suspect, is that when you apply Christian principles to social questions, the poor actually get helped. From some reason this practical effect has not much interested most of the conservatives of history. Those who *have* attempted to do something concrete to better the social conditions of the poor and oppressed have in almost all times and all places been attacked as either idealistic dreamers or dangerous revolutionaries. But that particular part of the historic debate has become a bore. It's over. The conservative position on this particular question is irrelevant, no longer even interesting.

The hard fact is that unless the churches can now, in very practical as well as spiritual ways, become relevant to the needs and concerns of the poor and minorities, there are going to be even more defections from the ranks of the faithful by the poor, the young, the alienated, and the impatient. And it is not enough to agree with this in the abstract. It comes down to a question as to what one can say, as a Christian, about a long list of very specific social problems. There are hundreds, but consider, for a moment, just these:

1. What can we do to allay social unrest so that the Marxist alternative will seem less attractive? We must respond rationally to the Communist challenge.

2. The nuclear weapons dilemma still threatens us.

3. Most of the world is hungry.

4. There are now three billion of us on this planet. In thirty years there will be six billion, half of whom will be Chinese, by the way.

5. We claim to be concerned with law and order, but many are unconcerned about the open anarchy that prevails among nations in the absence of a world law to which nations are prepared to pay honest respect.

6. The daily pollution of our air and water resources continues.

7. We are the wealthiest nation, currently enjoying our moment of greatest prosperity, but as many as thirty million of us live in poverty.

8. The Negro revolution rages about us.

9. The sickness of our great cities worsens.

10. The breakdown in family stability continues, and not only among the poor.

11. The explosion in crimes of violence continues.

12. The power of organized crime increases daily.

13. The plight of the nation's farmworkers is a scandal.

14. The sad plight of the American Indian is a disgrace.

15. The predicament of our Spanish-speaking population urgently requires our attention.

16. The breakdown of our schools continues.

17. The increasingly troublesome problem of mental illness is unsolved.

18. The absurdity of our prison system cries to heaven.

19. The problem of narcotics addiction and abuse worsens.

20. The increasingly serious aspect of that old-fashioned problem, alcoholism, demands our attention.

21. The startling dimensions of the puzzle of homosexuality are becoming more apparent.

22. The incredible corruption of the so-called law-abiding, majority segment of American society, a society on-the-take, continues.

23. Twenty thousand Americans are killed each year by guns, but we can get only weak gun-control legislation.

24. The war of Vietnam goes on.

The list could be continued, but let us arbitrarily stop it at this point.

It remains to be seen how the ideal will fare as the present controversy continues. For centuries—and for understandable reasons—the papacy looked with disfavor on democracy as a political form, even for national states, and certainly as regards its own functional structure. But as the Church undertook to do philosophical battle with the forces of Communism, it found that the chief reason for opposing Communism is that it is totalitarian. In the long run, the church's most dependable allies are the relatively free democratic republics. But writers such as Thomas Sugrue became worried as to how reliable an ally the United States was in the struggle for freedom.

"We are not becoming more spiritual," Sugrue wrote in his 1951 book, *A Catholic Speaks His Mind.* "We are growing more materialistic. . . . In America we are greedy, afraid, and sectarian; and we are rich, powerful, and self-righteous. Before we save the world, we may strangle in our own web of evil."

It sounds much like what is being commonly said on all sides today, does it not?

*   *   *

A word of qualification about democracy and the sharing of authority. Democracy is obviously preferable to totalitarian dictatorship,
but it has its own built-in problems and dangers. Majorities will frequently vote for monstrously dangerous leaders, or leaders who
have little more to recommend them than a pleasant face and clear
speaking voice.

There is the loose assumption in this sort of a conference that,
in broadening the base of control of Church funds, the inevitable
result will be to spend funds more wisely and charitably. This is
indeed among the possibilities, but it is by no means logically
inescapable. One may protest against Cardinal McIntyre's philosophy of administrative control, but what if crucial questions were
instead put to the total Los Angeles . . . or, for that matter, to the
total American Catholic electorate? The very question is alarming.

I think it might be productive to try to pry loose that hyphen that
presently is so often found linking the words "capitalistic" and
"racist." Rev. Walker and others at this conference have referred to
our capitalistic-racist society. There is obviously not the slightest
doubt that our society is in some form capitalistic, and to some
extent racist. But it is not totally capitalistic and it is not, thank
God, totally racist. Nor is it impossible for an individual to prefer
the free-enterprise economic structure over that of, say, one of the
Marxist alternatives, and still fulfill, in general degree, his obligations as a Christian to those who are not of his race or faith.

Nor should it be assumed that a Marxist society could not possibly be racist. The mainland Chinese are presently accusing the
white Soviets of, among other things, arrogant racist contempt for
their yellow brothers. And we know of the sad state of the Jews in
the Soviet Union. Not only are their religious rights infringed upon,
but in their ethnic capacities they are also subjected to discrimination and official abuse by representatives of the Soviet state.

The point here is not to say a good or bad word for either capitalism or Communism but merely to observe that the classic human
failings are universal. They grow, not out of any economic or social
philosophy, but out of the confused, partly animalistic, and essentially mysterious heart of man. It is to men and women as human

beings, therefore, that we should primarily communicate our grievances and accusations, rather than assuming that just by changing
the architecture of a social structure we would necessarily greatly
alter human behavior within that structure.

The wisest philosophers have insisted on the dignity of the individual. It would be a tragedy if, in lamenting the crimes against
human dignity inflicted by individual free enterprises, the frustrated
were drawn to systems in which the crimes against human dignity
are demonstrably even more atrocious. Freedom of religion,
speech, assemblage, freedom to publish, freedom of association
and travel are all no doubt frequently debased in our culture. But it
does not follow that the solution is the adoption of a framework in
which these same freedoms are explicitly denied by the state.

We very much require the kind of hard-hitting criticism of our
economic faults and crimes that was provided by the Rev. Albert
McKnight. He is correct in suggesting that our system does not now
need Bandaids but rather major surgery. It is not enough to criticize
Communism. One has the moral obligation to show how our system, as revised, can satisfy the requirements of social justice.

*   *   *

You have considered the question as to how the economic power of
the Church might become a weapon for social justice.

While it is self-evident that, to the extent possible, the economic power of the Church ought to be turned to the benefit of the
poor, one would hope that the factors of the problem are worked out
as clearly as possible, not by philosophers, polemicists, or charitable progressives alone but also by mathematicians, accountants,
and economists.

Whatever else, the question is in part mathematical. Let us suppose, for example, that the Catholic Church announces this afternoon that it will make a contribution of 30 million dollars toward
the benefit of the poor; black, brown, red, and white. Now this
would be a morally admirable gesture, but among its possible practical effects could be the placing of a one-dollar bill into the hand
of each of the 30 million American poor. The dollar would be spent
on the spot; the following morning the poor would be as destitute

as ever, and the Catholic Church would be poorer by 30 million dollars.

As regards the questions of reparations, from either the American churches or the American state, it would be advisable to avoid a semantic hang-up about the word itself, and instead to proceed to debate the question according to the understanding that American Negroes, American Indians, and American Mexicans are indeed entitled to some sort of financial redress of grievances. The proper questions then are: How much? To whom paid? And when paid?

Some unsympathetic whites are no doubt covering their reluctance to pay anything by harping on the question as to which hands should receive payments. But there are other white men, of good will, who realize the question indeed does have to be asked, and answered. Blacks themselves will obviously have to debate the question among themselves. The sooner they do so, I would think, the better, so that they will have an answer ready with which to silence those white who erect the question merely as a delaying tactic.

And the question, inevitably, will have to be related to the entire issue of welfare payments and other government and private programs designed to help the poor in America. One is entitled to frustration at the slowness and inefficiency of such programs, but their existence must still be acknowledged and their arithmetic incorporated into the large debate.

*   *   *

Reared, as I was, in the middle-class Irish, Chicago, Studs-Lonigan world of the 1930s, in which Father Coughlin was accounted a profound political philosopher, and the fortunes of the Notre Dame football team seemed of more moment than anything else I heard about the Church, I am as awe struck by the state of the Church as we approach the 1970s as we all are by the state of science and technology at this same point in history.

When I learn that some 2,700 priests and nuns left their posts in the American Catholic Church last year I am astounded. When I learn that there are Catholics who now hold informal worship services in their own homes, I am astounded. When I hear that 50 percent of American priests are opposed to the papal encyclical on birth control, I am astounded. When I see the very great change in attitude toward those priests who leave the Church or the priesthood, I am astounded. Consider, for example, the treatment accorded the Franciscan, Emmet McLoughlin, some twenty years ago: a vindictive attack which did much to turn him from a superior priest to a dedicated enemy of the church. Contrast that with the considerably more civilized response to the present-day defections.

All this and more about the new state of the Church in this country is strange. Even the vigor and authority of the National Catholic Conference for Interracial Justice is something that one might not have been able to predict a quarter of a century ago. There are new currents, new tides, and they are flowing fast. But perhaps the metaphor is unwisely chosen. We cannot control currents and tides, but we must have some control over our own destiny and that of our society. We can effect such control in part by communication, by putting all possible cards on the table. This has not as yet been done. A recent survey in Worcester, Massachusetts, showed that 55 percent of the Catholics there had never heard of the Second Vatican Council!* Just so, simple ignorance is partly responsible for middle-class Catholic apathy about the problems troubling the Negro, the Mexican-American, the Indian, the farmworker, the poor white.

You have wrestled energetically, and in many cases productively, with these considerations during the past few days. Quite aside from the question as to how many practical solutions you will be able to put into early effect, it is enormously important, and a sign of hopeful days ahead, that you have made the effort.

The questions have even been asked: How productive will this conference be? Is this sort of conference perhaps out of date? I don't believe it is. We do not have enough conferences of this sort. You see, not all white offenses originate out of hardness of heart. Many arise, I repeat, out of ignorance. For example, until recent years there are few black faces seen on television screens. Yet most people in the entertainment profession are generally liberal, progressive, and sympathetic to minority problems. What was needed

---

*The Second Vatican Council, convoked in 1962 by Pope John XXIII, wrought many changes in the Catholic Church. The most easily observed of these was that Mass was no longer celebrated in Latin.

was a black program of public complaint, letter-writing, education. This took place and the TV and advertising industry simply said, "Oh, all right," and began hiring many more black actors, models, and announcers.

Public appeals to the conscience of white America are of vital importance. They must be multiplied, not discontinued.

*   *   *

We have spoken of democracy, reparations, poverty, racism. Lastly a word about *love*. Isn't it fascinating, and significant, that it has been the young people of America who have reintroduced the word in the Christian sense, back into the common language? There is always talk of man-woman love and parent-child love, but brotherly love is something that Americans of my generation ordinarily do not discuss in any meaningful, personal sense. Or if they do, it is with a feeling of embarrassment and awkwardness. The National Conference of Christians and Jews presently employs a rock-and-roll group to sing its message to the nation. You've heard the song "Everybody get together and try to love one another right now."

I feel that this conference, despite moments of communications breakdown, despite moments of recrimination and the occasional static of irrelevance, has been—essentially—an exercise, an expression of love.

If that is so, your time cannot possibly have been wasted.

Graduation Address—
Immaculate Heart High School
June 9, 1970

A few years ago, high-school graduates customarily suffered through speeches by visiting dignitaries, of sometimes questionable distinction—speeches consisting mostly of easy exhortations to civic virtue, vague generalities, perhaps a bit of poetic imagery about distant horizons and brighter tomorrows, and idle compliments.

But the times they are a-changin'. You don't want to hear that kind of a speech. You are of an age that speaks frankly and freely. You deserve to be spoken to in the same manner.

You have the dubious distinction of being alive at the most dangerous moment in human history. And—to hurry past the obligatory cliché—the most challenging.

Our nation is passing through one of its darkest hours.

Our governor has spoken of blood baths, and he is getting them. Blood is shed at Santa Barbara, at Kent State, at Jackson State.* And have you observed the pattern? It is almost invariably the blood of your allies that is being shed. It was John Kennedy, Robert

---

*Antiwar and civil rights demonstrations throughout the 1960s and 1970s often resulted in the deaths of demonstrators at the hands of those trying to disband the protesters. Demonstrations which took place at Santa Barbara, Kent State, and Jackson State are three such examples.

292

Kennedy, and Martin Luther King who were assassinated. In moments of urban strife, it is usually the poor man's blood that bathes the streets, the black man's blood, students' blood.

The response, God knows, is *not* to stoop to the same brutality, not to demand the death of a reactionary for the death of a Kennedy or a King, not to resort to senseless retaliation in kind. The better response is to continue to demand the radical changes in our society that will transfer more power to the people of the United States, more power to the Negro, to the Mexican-American, to the poor white, to the students, to the peace movement. Such changes will make violent confrontations less likely.

In the meantime, we must resist the temptation to respond to fury with fury, to answer violence with violence. Civilization—such as it is—has been slowly and painfully achieved by the appeal of reason, of the essential morality of social justice.

We do not *separate* ourselves from our radical, revolutionary brothers insofar as they are concerned with righting grievous social wrongs. We, too, want peace, and law with justice. We, too, want freedom, and decent jobs, and an end to discrimination.

One is perfectly free, of course, to withdraw from the established system and to join a revolutionary movement in which the weapons are rifles, grenades, molotov cocktails, and bombs. But that is a distinct approach from that of the tradition of progressive social reform, is it not?

There is some virtue, after all, in consistency. Those of us in the peace movement have always said—as the song expresses it—let there be peace on earth and let it begin with me.

And there is a violence of language as well as a violence of act. Hurtful terms are intended to hurt. Consider the wave of criticism to which Vice President Spiro Agnew has rightfully been subjected for his intemperate and sometimes boorish pronouncements. Consider the criticism which rightfully came down on Richard Nixon's head for using the word "bums" in describing student dissenters.

But now consider the language of the revolutionary press. Leaving aside its everyday four-letter words, let us take a three-letter word we *can* use in this company: "Pig."

Are *all* law officers pigs? Or only *some* of them? Are *all* American soldiers or National Guardsmen pigs, or only *some*?

Intemperate language in a moment of passion is something within the experience of all of us. But that is quite different from a daily campaign of verbal intimidation which does not discriminate between decent policemen or soldiers and the smaller percentage of brutes in uniform.

Again, the word "consistency" points toward a solution. Do we really believe in *peace*, in *social justice*, in *freedom of speech*? Then let us be consistent in defense of these ideals.

You are now partially prepared to take your places in society, for even if you move now to the university campus, you are not in the secluded academy of past years but at the very heart of the social struggle.

How can you meaningfully continue your preparation for full citizenship? I make the specific recommendation that you consider enlarging your interest in history. You should do this for several reasons. First of all, you are *part* of history. Let us consider history in a deliberately simplistic manner. Imagine the record of every significant human event as a book of a thousand pages, the last page of which deals with the events of the year 1970. All of you will not have a full understanding of its contents if you do not take the trouble to examine the earlier pages. The saying that "we learn from history that we learn nothing from history" is not meant as a statement of fact but as a bitter joke. It means, of course, that man is so irrational that not only does he rarely learn from his own mistakes, but he usually acts as if he had learned nothing from the mistakes of earlier generations. In fact, we do learn a little, though we learn it slowly. But progress is always established by individuals who *have* learned something from the past. Your present will seem somewhat less puzzling if you can perceive the patterns that emerge from the seeming chaos of historical data.

You will discover, for example, that war is always psychologically disintegrating to a society, that it stimulates all the vices and very few of the virtues, that it encourages killing, lying, hatred, suspicion, intolerance, rapaciousness, and insensitivity. You will discover that the bad moral habits considered necessary to the technological success of war on the battlefield wash back over the civilian society, with easily predictable—and observable—results.

You will discover that European man was no less warlike and

in some comparisons considerably more dangerous than those of other cultures he considered barbarian and savage. You will discover that American man had no dispensation from this tragic weakness of Western man generally. Not a single page of our history is unstained by human blood.

Today—after World War I, World War II, the Korean War, the War of Indochina—we are a generation practiced at killing. What is most deeply significant about the massacre of civilians at My Lai, and similar tragedies, is the *lack* of guilt on our part. When four innocent students were murdered at Kent State University recently, we were saddened by their deaths. But even more deeply depressing was the outpouring of letters to newspapers and magazines suggesting that the killers were blameless, that it is perfectly all right to shoot down in cold blood young people who are in a crowd some members of which are shouting obscenities and throwing stones.

An inexperienced young soldier losing his temper and firing indiscriminately into a mixed assemblage is bad enough. But far more disturbing is the calm, cold-blooded attitude of many that young people *ought* to be shot if they refuse to obey authorities. This is precisely the attitude responsible for the horror of the German concentration camps, the view that the thing to do with troublesome people is exterminate them, the way one would exterminate troublesome insects.

A few years ago, a young soldier, just back from Vietnam, was a guest on one of my television programs. He had escaped from a Viet Cong prison camp and his story was fascinating. He was a likeable fellow, from a small town, apparently an average, middle-class, young American. After the broadcast was over, our production group invited him to join us for dinner at a nearby restaurant, where we continued our cordial conversation about the war in Vietnam.

At one point he expressed the fear that our ultimate problem in that part of the world was not the National Liberation Front but mainland China.

"What do you think we ought to do about that problem?" I asked.

"I think," he said, speaking very casually, as if he were discussing football strategy, "we ought to drop the bomb on them."

"You mean attack China with nuclear weapons?" I asked.

"Yes," he said.

"Do you mean wipe them all out?"

"That's what I mean," he said. "I know it would be a hard thing to do, but the way I look at it, if we don't do just that then we're only gonna have to fight them right here at home in a few years."

So here was the boy-next-door dispassionately believing that it was morally permissible to burn alive 600 million mostly civilian, innocent men, women, and children—because of his dislike of the bluster and threat of the Chinese Communist leadership.

Somehow the moral evil here is so enormous that one is at a loss to know how to deal with it. We have no trouble comprehending the evil posed by one man with a gun, by one man beating a child, by one man assaulting a woman. Such crimes are personal. We grasp them. We disapprove of them. We apprehend the criminals, and we try to punish or reform them.

But this other evil—which seems to be a growing monstrosity in our midst—is of such a magnitude that one tends to respond to it not with argument, not with analytical criticism, but by merely shaking one's head and by fearing for the future of ourselves and our children.

For this madness is not confined merely to the identifiable neurotics and psychotics who people our prisons. This is the kind of stain that rots the soul of a nation, the kind of an evil that does not even lack leaders who attempt to justify it. When Governor Lester Maddox passes out axe-handles to his admirers, we are in the presence of that sickness of the spirit which leads to the systematic denial of justice, to the formalized endorsement of brute violence, to the torture chamber, the firing squad, and the concentration camp.

Among the historical precedents I recommend to your attention, then, is that of Germany in the 1930s. By this comparison I do *not* suggest that the United States is in the slightest immediate danger of a takeover by a combination of reactionary and Fascist forces. But it is not beyond question that such a stage could be reached if we continue on our present path.

Hitler came to power, before his true face had been revealed to most Germans, because he represented strength and determination at a time when the nation was angry, confused and divided. The machinery of the German Republic had become unable to deal with problems of unemployment, inflation, and general social unrest.

The Communists were fighting the Liberals, as they always do when they sense a chance to seize power, and the country was becoming rapidly polarized.

As regards our present moment, we should be sympathetic about the experiences which led Eldridge Cleaver, Stokely Carmichael, Abby Hoffman, and other radicals to the extremity of their position. We should—we must—alter the conditions that drive intelligent men to such distraction. But we must refuse to share the paranoia and fanaticism to which these men have been driven.

Do these people really have much effect on a society such as ours? Yes, but not the effect that some fear. The most pronounced results of their efforts is to jangle the anxieties of the American middle-class and hence move that middle-class—not imperceptively inch by inch, but massively, in sudden lurches—to the right.

There will always, in all political contexts, be a certain audience for demagogues of the Right who wrap themselves in the flag, who sell a great deal of heat and very little light, and whose appeal is not that of reason and charity but that of anger, sometimes outright hatred. Study carefully some of the speeches of Lester Maddox, George Wallace, and Spiro Agnew. Your initial reaction will perhaps be despair that there are so many who are attracted by such vulgar appeals.

But what some of the left-wing revolutionaries preach is precisely a resort to the methods of Fascism. It was therefore no surprise on logical grounds when Stokely Carmichael told us recently that the historic figure for whom he has the greatest admiration is Adolph Hitler.

Civilization, you see, is an edifice built upon very thin ice. Man has been irrational and impulsive for hundreds of thousands—perhaps millions—of years. He has been reasonable and civilized only recently, and still readily relapses into savagery. Even many of those who think they are interested in law and order are not. They are simply desirous that the affairs of the world be conducted according to their prejudices.

You can enlist a crowd of hard-hats on a moment's notice in any parade behind banners that bear the words *law* and *order*. But should that parade chance to encounter those of alternative political persuasions—let us say, college students, young people with long hair, pacifists, Negroes, Jews—why, then you discover at once how empty are the claims of respect for law and order, as the hard-hats physically assault those whom they have already sinned against by despising.

So I urge you to pick your way carefully between the savages of the Left and the Right. But I draw your attention here to a fascinating distinction. The barbarians of the Left are on the far outer fringes of the left. The barbarians of the Right, however, occupy a vastly larger ground on their side of the political spectrum. That the avowed Nazis, Minutemen, and other such are criminally dangerous is acknowledged by every respectable conservative. But there were no Minutemen, no Nazis, marching with the hard-hats in New York city recently. It is not American Nazis who give George Wallace his power. It is not the true Fascists who fuel the machine of Lester Maddox. It is not only the out-and-out barbarians who applaud the boorish invective of Spiro Agnew. It is a large segment of middle America that responds to such appeals.

Last year I happened to be driving, with my then eleven-year-old son, Bill, through some of the all-black neighborhoods in Central Los Angeles. We saw some interesting posters and novelties in a sort of hippie shop and stopped in to do a bit of shopping. One of the posters we purchased was the by-now classic sketch of President John Kennedy, Senator Robert Kennedy, and the Reverend Martin Luther King.

These three men were most deeply mourned by young people, by Negroes, by the poor generally. The political philosophies of the three were essentially the same. They were liberals, believers in the possibility and advisability of social progress, in nonviolent approaches to difficult domestic problems. It is sad that if they were still alive today they would be under attack from some who wept at their loss such a little while ago.

The deep emotion of loss and love that moved so many young people—black and white—to tears at the passing of these three leaders was a better emotion than the hatred which now motivates some among us. . . .*

---

*Because lecture audiences differ, public speakers often focus on similar or identical topics, especially when the point they wish to make is particularly important. Steve Allen is one of those who employs this practce. Therefore, to avoid repetition, duplicate material has been deleted from this and other speeches included in this volume. Ellipses have been used to indicate where text which is included elsewhere has been removed.

Of the many issues with which you *must* concern yourselves there is one that is most important. It concerns your own function in this world as human beings, as *wives* and *mothers*. A happy home and family life is far more important—to you and to your society—than other kinds of achievement that at the moment may seem more appealing. No matter what you might achieve in your profession or art or in public service, it cannot truly compensate for the discord and inner suffering that comes out of an unhappy home. If as parents you can bring a child into the world and teach him how to love, how to feel, how to think, giving him the kind of wholesome, loving nurture that produces secure adults, you will have accomplished a difficult but marvelously satisfying task, not just for yourself and your loved ones but for the social environment in which we all live. I sense that your generation realizes this and that you perceive the failure of my generation in this regard.

Marriage and the raising of children has many rewards, but it is *not* just something that comes naturally. It is an incredibly complex assignment and one that requires your constant attention. The old saying that charity begins at home is far wiser than we commonly assume.

You are a more sensible and sensitive generation than those of the past. You are more beautiful than you know, and your social conscience is better developed. You have become accustomed to think that if not all the older generation constitute your opposition, at least your opponents are to be found within the over-forty group. It is not so. The people over forty, in any event, are dying like flies. Before many more years all of us will be gone, and your nation and your planet will be in your hands. At the end of this process you will discover that your most formidable, long-run opponents are your own age.

May you deal with each other wisely.

"The Eleventh Hour" Speech
Denver, Colorado,
October 22, 1994

Had the present examples of the philosophical equivalent of last wills and testaments been written only a few years ago, they would almost certainly have warned of the quite practical dangers of worldwide nuclear holocaust. Fortunately that specific danger is no longer as threatening as it once was. Note that I did not say "as it once *seemed*"—because the danger, the possibility, was indeed real.

But to say as much by no means implies that the danger is now past. The reason for the improvement on that narrow question was in no way the result of human wisdom or creative contrivance. It was simply the collapse of the Soviet Union. But unknown numbers of nuclear weapons still exist, and there's now the absolutely unprecedented danger that such armaments might fall into the hands of not leaders of states but fanatical terrorist groups, who have all too amply demonstrated a lack of both moral principle and concern for humanity itself.

But even if the nuclear threat were to be totally banished, it would by no means follow that our troubled world was thereby a great deal safer, for the list of worrisome factors is presently longer than it has ever been in all human experience, and the technological potential for extrapolating those dangers into actual conflagrations is not only threatening; it is already here, as we see by the daily accumulations of evidence in the form of world events.

There was a time, on the vast tapestry of history, when certain social problems of the most serious magnitude could at least be accurately described as local or regional in scope. In those days massive expanses of sea and land separated various geographical enclaves. But humans have learned to travel so fast, and to communicate even more swiftly, that when the bell of tragedy rings now it is heard everywhere, so we are no longer protected by our ignorance, nor can we claim it as an excuse for standing idly by while the vilest sort of atrocities take place on a mass scale.

The moral monsters who terrorize either their own people or those of neighboring areas were much more comfortable under the old system, whereby it took so long for news of enormous crimes to reach the world's capitals that by the time the morally concerned were prepared to act the atrocities were often over and done with.

As a result of the change in background circumstances, all humans, everywhere, are now faced with more troubling moral choices than ever. By describing such choices as troubling, I do not mean to suggest that there is the slightest difficulty in separating right from wrong. Even those most blinded by economic self-interest must be aware of the ugly evil of, to give only one example, the Serbian atrocities that presently shame the human race itself. They must be aware of the dark evil of the moral monsters who have for so long terrorized the poor people of Haiti. We know, in quite specific terms, who the evildoers in Haiti are. They are, to put the matter very simply, the rich, and the military forces that the rich pay for and therefore own.

So the question is, as regards these two instances—and dozens of others that could be cited—now that we can no longer claim ignorance, are we prepared to stand by and do nothing while human beings every bit as entitled to justice as we are are raped, tortured, robbed, terrorized, and murdered?

All such considerations give rise to interesting questions about the responses of such of our philosophical advisors as are formally religious. I refer to the members of actual churches.

As regards certain moral issues, one does not have to be a professional theologian to clarify simple questions of right and wrong.

A concerned five-year-old child could do the job. In fact, the child could perhaps do it even better because he is unlikely to be infected by the virus of political and social bias and economic self-interest that so often confuse the moral judgement of those to whom many of us turn for guidance.

This is a point of such profound importance that I must rush right back to it.

Every society, every culture, is enriched and instructed by its literature. One of the most morally instructive examples of the literary art is Ibsen's play *An Enemy of the People*. (Actually, as literature, it is not to be accurately described as of Olympian stature, but the point of the story is one we would all do well to absorb.) As some of you are aware, the story is that of a medical man who works in the area of a popular European resort which is about to celebrate an annual fair, an event that brings in large amounts of money to local merchants. The doctor happens to discover a bacteria in the local water supply, one that will undoubtedly sicken and perhaps even kill either local residents or visitors. The danger is so severe that the doctor does the only thing he can do, as a concerned citizen. He tells the local powers that under no circumstances must they proceed with their plans for the annual event because of the great danger to the public health. He is promptly told to keep his mouth shut. But he protests, "People may die." Without making their argument in so many words, his local critics make it clear that they really do not care that deaths and serious illness are likely to result from the contaminated water supply. They are more concerned about the fact that what the doctor is advising is, as we say, "bad for business."

We would be very ill-advised to assume this is just a fascinating story about a place long distant in time and space. It is as relevant as any story you will ever hear because precisely the same drama is acted out literally every day of our experience.

*   *   *

As regards the limited variety of economic systems available on our confused planet, I happened to be biased in favor of what is loosely called the capitalist or free enterprise economy. The best we can say about it is that it is better than the purely Marxist alternative. But to treat our system as somehow morally sanctified, as holy, is downright dishonest, and also it blinds those of us who work within that system. Our economic system is, to use a term from the history of Christian theology, an occasion of sin. We did not have to wait for Diogenes of ancient Greece to become aware that truly honest individuals are in sadly short supply.

So what happens when you have a generally free economy is that every thief, every economic scoundrel, every robber baron, every out and out crook who can position himself in the marketplace is wonderfully situated to perform his evil work. In the economic history of our nation, we see the most shocking scandals arising not just on a now-and-then basis but on every single page of that history.

The point is not that those with economic power are therefore automatically to be considered evil and opposed. Indeed, for all of our benefits they often must be supported. But they also must be forced to behave in a moral and decent fashion. The meat-packing industry early in the century was one vast scandal in which the major meat packers, to judge by their behavior, didn't give a damn how many of their customers were fed poisoned or contaminated meat as long as the business machine was kept well oiled.

Now what happens, and this is typical—this is traditionally structural—what happens when outrages of this sort take place, as they always have and always will, is the bad news first comes to the attention of those who are qualified to detect it, the doctor in Ibsen's play being one example. Then these informed scholars or scientists or civic leaders begin to share their findings with increasing numbers of concerned citizens. And the word finally works its way through society that the outrageous situation is no longer to be countenanced and that it must be changed, and as quickly as possible.

So far so good.

But what happens when the whistle-blowers do their wonderful work, which—if there is a God—must make the inhabitants of heaven smile warmly? You *know* what happens. Those who try to alert us to the dangers to our own health are immediately verbally tarred and feathered, and their critics would do it literally if they thought they could get away with it.

The fact-finders, the saviors, the good decent reformers—who in any rational society would be regarded as the heroes they certainly are—are treated as—again the phrase—enemies of the people. Depending on the time and place they are called whatever ugly name is currently in bad odor in a given society. For the last seventy-five years or so such social reformers—very few of whom were Marxist—were nevertheless uniformly called *communists*, or they are called *outside agitators*, or *bleeding hearts*, *do-gooders*. My God, how long do we have to suffer before we know that we don't have nearly *enough* bleeding hearts, not nearly *enough* do-gooders?

Now who are these critics that so uncharitably use character assassination as a response to information that originally may be purely scientific or medical? Are they natural evil-doers themselves? No, they tend to be your cousin, the man across the street, your brother-in-law. But what makes them behave in so morally shameless a fashion is nothing more complex than good old economic self-interest. To hell with the deaths, to hell with the suffering, we must not do anything to shake the foundations of business.

There are several reasons you put up with that, but one of them—and I must speak frankly—is the general stupidity that prevails. You don't have to put up with rotten meat, with vegetables or fruits contaminated by pesticides, with devices or medicines that harm, maim, and kill. You do have the power—in your capacity as the American people—to put a stop to that kind of outrage. But you must organize and study and participate in organized campaigns or the old evils will simply continue.

For examples in our time and place we have only to look at the shameful examples of the tobacco and gun industries. Medical science is united in pointing out that at present, in the United States alone, about 400,000 people die every year from the effects of inhaling tobacco smoke! But the leading tobacco executives are equally united in denying all the massive accumulations of evidence and insisting on conducting business as usual while—of course—warning against "big government's" intrusion into the marketplace. The gun manufacturers do the same, going so far even as to oppose the best interests of the police, despite the daily slaughter that occurs in our homes and the streets.

And when you do participate, what you are doing, in essence, is taking your place in the ancient and I'm afraid never-to-end campaign for justice. . . .

Address to the Institute of Social Psychiatry: Summary of Workshop Proceedings

If you are the last speaker on a given occasion, you may be expected to not only deliver your own observations but also summarize, or at least comment upon, the remarks of earlier speakers.

I delivered the following speech to the Santa Barbara Social Psychiatry Workshop in March 1971. Note that although the occasion was obviously a relatively serious one, a few touches of humor, handled properly, were not out of place. The speech was partly written, partly ad-libbed, and partly based on handwritten notes made during the proceedings described.

Thank You, Dr. Auerback, for your generous introduction. Since you raised the question as to whether—my parents being vaudevillians—I ever slept in a dresser drawer, the answer is no—we couldn't afford a dresser.

Well, this has been a most stimulating conference. I arrived here three days ago, refreshed and energetic, eager for what was to come. Now, after three days of listening, speaking, taking notes, studying, and discussing from early morning till late at night, I am utterly exhausted—in which condition I am called upon to summarize these proceedings.

I am comforted by the knowledge that the very futility of my assignment will merit me your sympathy. In this connection I am reminded of a very funny story. But I shall resist the temptation to tell it.

The title of my address, like that of Mr. Rozenfeld, as rendered in the program is inaccurate. It has no title. In a sense it isn't even an address. It's more an exercise in presumption.

Being an expert on nothing that has been discussed here I am, of course, the most qualified to discuss everything because I am uninhibited by those sharply defined professional boundaries that limit the rest of you.

I might be considered, in this context, a lay expert. No, come to think of it, I'm not even an expert on that. I throw in a bit of vulgarity so that you young people will feel at home.

But, in all conceit, I have a few observations, and questions, about some of the things we have heard during these three stimulating days.

Since the discussions themselves did not, indeed could not have, followed a straight, disciplined line of inquiry, my comments on them then constitute chiefly a catalogue of your modest digressions, to which I may perhaps add one or two of my own.

There were countless endearing indications, during these meetings, of our naive humanity, which it is always particularly refreshing to encounter in an assemblage of sophisticated practitioners of one discipline or another.

For example, even here, despite the fame and importance of a given speaker, despite the breadth of experience of members of this audience—and despite the great unlikelihood that the next person to walk into this room at a given moment might have been President Nixon, Mao Tse Tung, or the returned Christ—nevertheless every time someone walked in during an address almost every head turned away from the speaker and glanced, however casually, toward the door.

And despite your depth of understanding and compassion, there were hostile glares directed at those seized by uncontrollable fits of coughing, and even at the inanimate device that is recording these proceedings.

The high-pitched, wavering tone it has emitted this morning I found first annoying, then nostalgically comforting in that it reminded me of the sound of the old radiators that heated so many of the rooms in which I lived as a child.

Dr. Auerback, intending to refer to Sarah Lawrence College, called it *David* Lawrence, and then, in response to your laughter, said, "Make of it what you will." I respectfully suggest, Doctor, that in this professional context what is made of it will have to be what *you* will.

Dr. Erika Freeman has told us among other interesting things, that in a sense England was our mother, France was our mistress, and Germany our teacher. She did not identify our *father,* which would seem to confirm our present low opinion of ourselves.

Her point that we ought to judge ideas on their own merits rather than solely in regard to their source is precisely that which led to the development of a new game (for which I served as consultant) called *Strange Bedfellows,* one of a series designed to teach all of us how to think.

Dr. Tietz's reference to asterisks and the numerous and lengthy footnotes in his paper reminded me of an insight (or at least a crazy idea) that occurred to me some years ago when I participated in the experimental program on the effects of LSD conducted by Dr. Sydney Cohen at UCLA. That was at a time, of course, before the abuse of the drug had emerged as a serious social problem.

I envisioned a page of a book, every word of which was followed by an asterisk, with footnotes. *But* . . . in the footnotes, too, every word was followed by an asterisk.

In a time when many, particularly among the young, have grown increasingly cynical about the competence and dedication of political figures, it is encouraging to hear from so able and dedicated a public servant as Mr. Lanterman.

I was greatly enlightened by my exposure to Dr. Bierer's theories, impressed by his accomplishments, and charmed by his company.

Dr. Bierer believes that the solution to the mental health problems of our times is much too large and complex a job for psychiatrists and the mental health people alone. Dr. Auerback's sobering recital makes the dimensions of the problem alarmingly clear. The collaboration and involvement of a multidisciplinary group of professionals is clearly required. Even if Dr. Bierer were wrong philosophically, he is inescapably right on this point. But his achievements argue persuasively for the essential validity of his approach, for he has contributed many significant innovations to social psychiatry: day and night hospitals, self-determining and self-governing therapeutic clubs, therapeutic communities, and others. Dr. Bierer believes that mental illness as such does not exist. He also believes—as now apparently every informed person does—that our system of legal justice and punishment is ineffective if not irrational.

One of the more interesting subsidiary questions raised concerns the extent to which the political Right, which has long been active in the field of mental health as the force of the opposition to it, is now making use of Dr. Szsaz and Dr. Bierer as weapons with which to attack psychiatry and the mental health movement generally. There are a number of historical factors involved in this rightist paranoia: (1) anti-Semitism, because many psychiatrists are Jews, (2) the Church-versus-Freud, and (3) the suspiciousness characteristic of political fanaticism. Those who *need* treatment but deny the need are pleased to hear Dr. Bierer say, "There's no such thing as mental illness," because it confirms their sense of righteousness.

I am not referring to responsible conservatives here but to the traditional force of know-nothing reaction.

The large question Dr. Bierer raises, being complex, is still unresolved. In recent years, as you know, there bas been a return to emphasis, in some quarters, upon *physical* factors related to mental illness, if Dr. Bierer will pardon the expression. That kind of genetic chromosomal abnormality, for example, which has a correlation with antisocial criminal behavior would be a case in point. There are studies, too, as you are aware, of differences in blood chemistry between those who are schizophrenics and those who are not. And there are the obvious questions presented by the successful results obtained by the administration of such drugs as *lithium* in modifying human behavior for the better.

It was only recently, historically speaking, that we discovered that separate parts of the brain governed separate bodily functions, muscular movements, speech, sight, memory, and so forth. But uncharted horizons now beckon in that specific area of the brain out of which the *emotions* arise. I suspect little is known, too, about such refined areas of specialization as the *mathematical* or *musical* functions. If the strict environmentalists present will forgive me, it has always seemed to me preposterous to assert that if a genius can compose a symphony and play the piano brilliantly at the age of six, the fact is explained purely by the availability of a better-than-adequate music teacher.

I know from personal experience that the gift of musical composition has nothing whatever to do with being taught. The mechanical components of the art can be taught but the essential gift, the ability to synthesize factors in previously unimagined ways, is just that—if one posits a giver—a gift, a puzzling accident, difficult to explain even in terms of standard Darwinian theory, since it hardly is necessary to the survival of the species.

In a book written some years ago I advanced the hypothesis that the gift of religious spirituality, which is clearly more pronounced in some individuals than others, may have its focus literally in brain tissue. I hasten to add that since the firm belief that God made all things logically requires the belief that He created the human brain, the theory is in no way incompatible with religious philosophy generally.

It is interesting that some years later, when we began to receive reports, most of them scholarly and some of them from Dr. Bierer, attesting to either the reality or illusion of religious and spiritual insights under the influence of LSD and similar drugs, I began to feel that my theory was given substantial support in the form of consistent if by no means conclusive evidence.

Dr. Branch's presentation had the appeal we always sense in those arguments that conform with our own prejudices. I was especially intrigued by his reminding us of the importance of the emotional attitude of the therapist in relating to the patient, as dramatized in the story of the practitioner who reported that on five particular days his patients seemed especially cheerful and open. As you will recall, these were the days on which he had taken benzedrine. This is consistent with my own experience in being frequently interviewed over a period of years, in connection with my television activities. I noticed early that the interviewers who were themselves extroverts tended to describe me as lively, witty, and genial, whereas those who were more introverted tended to describe me as shy, withdrawn, uncommunicative, etc.

There were a thousand-and-one tempting digressions, the following out of which could take literally many lifetimes. For example, Dr. Kennedy referred to *glossolalia,* the speaking in strange tongues. I would like to know if tape-recordings of the phenomenon have been made, if written transcripts of these recordings have been rendered, and if both have been subjected to analysis by disinterested linguistic scholars.

Dr. Kennedy's remarks struck a particularly responsive emotional chord. One could not fail to be impressed by his enthusiasm for the campaign to, as he put it, *unscrew the pew.* He expressed the idea with such force, in fact, that I would not be surprised to see him shortly dispense with the negative prefix. But the relevance of the self-treating encounter group to the essential work of the church is clear. Just as Christians civilized the savage tribes of Europe, so the humanist tradition has worked tirelessly for centuries to civilize Christians. It is encouraging to observe that its influence continues unabated.

One of the most touching illustrations drawn by Dr. Kennedy concerned the man who was unable to weep at recollection of his own misfortunes but did so when one of the women in the group told him she loved him for his sympathetic response to her own recital. The tears that flow in response to love are more mysterious than those that help relieve the sense of tragedy. I find that I am moved to tears at the spectacle of the reconciliation of enemies. There is a sudden rush of feeling that comes from the appreciation of the beautiful aspects of human communication.

I found Dr. Brill's presentation of particular interest, although perhaps at our next convocation we might be privileged to see a slide projection of that mysterious picture of him with the two Yugoslavian girls.

His description of the alienation of American youth was most complete and detailed. One must, it seems to me, agree with his conclusion that the state of consciousness of today's young people is different in kind, as well as in degree, compared to the youth of earlier generations. One reason may be that today's technology, TV, radio, films, magazines, videotape and audio equipment, brings our social reality into focus to a degree unprecedented in all history. And, in today's world, to become *aware* is to become *angry.*

One may become angry at the social injustice suffered by others or by oneself.

But it is remarkable how many ancient beliefs are currently relevant and popular among young people. As regards the materialistic biases of our generation, what are the young saying but that the love of money is the root of a great deal of evil? In saying that they want to *enjoy* their work, not just perform it for money, the young are repeating the medieval theologians, are they not?

Unfortunately we resort to the specious as well as to what has been valid from the storehouse of history. Frank Kelly calls ours *The Age of Paranoia.* Who would have supposed it would follow the Age of Reason? And who would have predicted, in a period of spectacular scientific achievement, that the superstition of the Dark Ages, belief in witchcraft, astrology, fortune-telling, and diabolism would culminate in today's very similar wave of occultism and deliberate rejection of rational standards?

To the extent that the young regard the rest of us as enemies, it might be argued that their position is most fortunate. For example, if you could tell the Marxists of the world that all capitalists will be dead in another twenty or thirty years, their joy would know no bounds. If you could assure the West that all communists would shortly vanish from our planet they, too, would be pleased. Well, the young can literally be assured that all of the older generation will be gone before long, after which the young will perceive that their most formidable adversaries are their own age. And soon, all those who have said "Don't listen to anybody over thirty" will be over thirty themselves, and presumably without an audience.

As for the rebelliousness of today's youth, many of you must be tempted to hope that some magical method might be found whereby it could be stamped out. Not only is the hope utterly incapable of realization but, even if the thing were possible, it ought never to be done, for by inhibiting the rebellious instinct we would be running counter to one of mankind's most fundamental drives: the need to identify what is wrong in his physical context, to oppose what he regards as contemptible, and to construct a better social order. I naturally do not suggest that every fourteen-year-old who breaks a window consciously articulates such a philosophy, but rebellious acts as a class grow out of such a need and are consistent with such a philosophy. The rebel without a cause, as the brilliant Robert Lindner suggested, is dangerous. But the rebel with a good cause will be our salvation.

Both Dr. Brill and Dr. Girvetz commented on the problem of violence in today's youth culture. In my view, the underlying danger of violence, above and beyond the obvious physical destruction it causes, the deaths, the maimings, the personal tragedy, is that when it becomes institutionalized and apparently legitimized by philosophers or other spokesmen it unleashes dark, dangerous, poorly-understood forces in the human heart, forces that may leap out and eventually consume those who called them forth.

In World War II we observed the atrocities committed by Germans and Japanese, while ignoring those perpetrated by ourselves and our allies. But the evildoers seemed more than evil in our eyes. All men, after all, are partly evil. Our enemy seemed monstrous. Clearly there were psychopaths, sadistic bullies, and other such wearing German uniforms. But I think most atrocities are committed by very average people, when they have been programmed to kill and absolved of guilt before the fact. The My Lai murders are a case in point. . . .

Dr. Girvetz's delineation of the problem of violence in our culture clearly suggested that it is on the increase and side-by-side with the common view that today there is a greater incidence of mental and emotional disturbance in our society than at any time in our history; it is remarkable that Dr. Bierer's theories relating to doing away with mental hospitals and prisons are being advanced at a time when one might otherwise assume that they would be building *more* hospitals and prisons.

Another vitally important question, suggested by Mr. Kelly, is this: In a presumably *representative* society, who really represents the people? It is not today the easiest question in the world to answer.

Part of the problem is that running for any political office is an incredibly expensive undertaking. Running for high office takes millions of dollars. The sources from which such funds are donated understandably enough expect some sort of return on their investment.

But in response to the growing awareness of this dilemma, there are signs of emerging programs designed to alleviate the distress. Ralph Nader and his organizations are a result of the feeling of helplessness on the part of the average citizen. *Common Cause* is another. So is the *consumer revolution* generally. Ombudsman experiments are springing up. Environmental conservationists are making their influence felt. Radio and television stations are not only editorializing but offering free time to spokesmen of points-of-view differing with those of station management.

I take these as hopeful indications.

At least two of our speakers, Mr. Rozenfeld and Dr. Cobbs, emphasized the destructive effects of inadequate social environments upon those forced to live in them. In the physical sense it has long been obvious that poverty and squalor lead to greater incidence of disease and a higher death rate. But only relatively recently have we learned of the harm that poverty does to the mind and the spirit.

Is it possible, however, that the harm is done in a secondary rather than direct sense, in that the conditions of the urban ghetto, as well as of rural poverty, tend to destroy the family, then bring the collapse of adequate parent-child relationships that directly cripples many children psychologically?

It is fascinating to observe to what extent the psychologically destructive potential of many of our unpleasant social problems is now being emphasized. We have long known that litter, garbage, and sewage are unedifying to observe, but we are now being told that they also contribute to our societal *neuroses.* Perhaps one solution, in the context of our free-enterprise biases, would be to find a way to make sewage and garbage commercially valuable. Then it would be responsibly handled.

Concerning racial confrontation, I found Dr. Cobbs's remarks of very great interest and I plan to read his book *Black Rage.* In introducing him, Dr. Brill observed that although over a million copies of his book had been sold, Dr. Cobbs reported receiving *very little money,* a fact which by itself would make his rage understandable.

One was pleased to hear his recommendation of the Jeffersonian approach to oppression. Almost everyone is opposed to some form of tyranny, but few seem to regard *all* forms as intolerable. Perhaps because most of our forefathers fled from oppression to these shores Americans have long been opposed to all oppression except that which we perpetrated ourselves. But our foreign policy dilemma at present hangs on precisely the question as to how one should oppose oppression. Do we oppose it only within our national borders? If not, how do we respond to the pleas of the oppressed in other parts of the world? Neither of the two large alternatives is entirely satisfactory; consequently we grieve and are uncertain.

Small, revealing things hold a special sort of interest, whether we observe them in the behavior of individuals or groups. I noticed, for example, that the applause for Dr. Cobbs reached a higher volume of intensity than that received by any of the *white* speakers at this conference. This is consistent with my hypothesis that in the entertainment field, all conditions being generally equal, black performers will usually receive somewhat more applause from *white* audiences than will white entertainers.

The facile explanation is obvious: white guilt. But perhaps something more is involved. Perhaps such applause is one of the few gestures of goodwill that whites know how to make toward blacks. It isn't much, but it *is* something.

One of the most fascinating exchanges—as Dr. Freeman has reminded us—came when Dr. Cobbs characterized Dr. Park's concept of the ghettoization of prison populations as *shoddy*.

We do not have time here to take up the details of the controversy itself, but we might learn something from the nature of Dr. Park's response to Dr. Cobbs's verbal attack. *Your* response was not to gasp but to *smile*. Several of you, in fact, turned to *me* and smiled, as if to say, "Get a load of what's going on." I did.

But Dr. Park's response was primarily emotional, perhaps visceral, as evidenced by the immediate breakdown in his sentence-structure. As the tape-recorded transcript will show, he communicated in various unconnected fragments of sentences for a few seconds and then counterattacked, not ad hominem but ad civitatem. What else might one expect, it occurred to Dr. Park to ask, from someone who lived in San Francisco?

It is certainly not my purpose here either to make light of Dr. Park or to force him to relive those few awkward moments during which egos were wounded and exposed. My intention is rather to emphasize the frailty of our capacity for reason. Passion may occasionally inspire men to eloquence but it is more likely to render them less rather than more articulate and reasonable. Dr. Park, then, stands for everyman. Perhaps none of us are truly graceful under surprise attack.

I was myself subjected to critical aspersions and had my loyalty questioned by a woman in the audience I addressed here locally on Friday at noon. My response, too, was to feel a surge of emotion. It was low level but its components were recognizable as fear and anger. So we all carry this ancient animal burden, part protection and part curse. The knowledge should make us more charitable in dealing with those with whom we disagree.

Dr. Girvetz has become a typical figure in the contemporary American political drama, the liberal who, though he does not substantially change himself, feels the ground shift under him, as a result of which social earthquake he comes to rest at a point farther to the right on the political spectrum than he is accustomed to.

Today's liberal is historically symptomatic, however, in a sense that merits him far better treatment than the casual dismissal or outright contempt he sometimes receives from those to his left or those who feel that he has not done enough for them.

For the values and institutions the liberal defends are those that were unknown for countless ages, those that were prayed for, dreamed for, struggled for, died for by a now-faceless mass of valiant souls who suffered under a thousand tyrannies and longed pathetically for the freedom to speak their minds, to write or otherwise disseminate their views, to travel without harsh restriction, to worship or not, as it pleased them, to congregate with others at will, to live in such social conditions that one could at least *pursue* happiness, insure domestic tranquility, and function as both reason and passion have told the best among us down through the ages man was meant to function.

The crimes of the Industrial Revolution rudely cut across these libertarian dreams. Clearly the people deserved a large measure of economic security. It is perhaps the primary task of this century to determine if the inherent contradiction between *freedom* on the one hand and *security* on the other can be reasonably balanced.

Even now the liberal stands between the Radical Left and the Radical Right, who might today be at each other's throats if it were not for his intervention.

The liberal is as open to criticism as everyone else, but in concentrating on his shortcomings we must not lose sight of the herculean achievements of progressive forces over the centuries in advancing human freedom.

Speaking of freedom, a gentleman in the audience expressed a combination of horror and surprise that a recent survey shows that young children voted *against* our constitutional guarantees of liberty, against free speech, against legal rights, and so forth. But I would have thought that children were recognized as notoriously intolerant. They are trained to *receive* love rather than to give it, to receive material necessities rather than to provide them to others. An infant is a squalling, screaming bundle of insistent demands, not a beneficent dispenser of blessings and concern for others.

Faced with the question as to how to deal with evildoers, children almost invariably recommend harsh punishment because they are motivated by their horror of the evil done, not by those sophisticated and tolerant standards which it took adult mankind untold hundreds of thousands of years to develop, and which even now are shakily buttressed by popular sentiment even in the most civilized societies. Because of their exposure to television and films, children incline to believe that the way to treat a bad man is to have Gary Cooper or John Wayne or Jack Webb shoot him on the spot. And they are not alone.

Dr. Bierer wisely draws our attention to the fact that on the one hand we have millions of wealthy or retired people who report that they have little to do to productively occupy their time, while on the other hand almost all necessary social agencies report a shortage of helpful workers. Clearly the idle personnel must somehow be directed toward the areas of need. Perhaps experienced management people, given the opportunity for public communication, could productively deal with this problem.

Something along this line is already being done by the Thiokol Chemical Corporation, for whom I recently narrated a documentary film telling of their very positive and productive program for training hard-core, unemployable young ghetto people, not only for regular jobs or further academic studies, but, perhaps most significantly, training them to do the same work by which they were helped so that they in turn can have a positive, productive feedback in their ghetto communities. This program deserves far more public attention than it has received and I recommend it to your further study.

I am troubled by a certain looseness of language which seems to me symptomatic of our time. In discussing *violence* yesterday one gentleman said "rats are violent." Others make the claim that poverty itself is violence upon the poor. Having lived both with poverty and with rats in my own youth, I know their ugliness. It is disgusting and disgraceful that men should have to live in rat-infested tenements. But to bend the word *violence* to cover this painful-enough reality, it seems to me, confuses rather than clarifies the issue.

In the debate on obscenity one hears it said that *war* is obscene, that *violence* is obscene. Words are imprecise enough to begin with, judged as scientific instruments, without our rendering them even more rubbery.

Lastly we were moved by Judge Lodge's recitation of his experience in visiting Atascadero State Hospital and finding that he was the only judge, out of over five hundred, who had accepted the inmates' invitation to attend a conference there.

Perhaps there is some connection between Judge Lodge's social conscience and his youth. Such men serve for me as yardsticks by which I measure my own passage through time. Partly I suppose because my health is still good I do not feel as old as I am, which is forty-nine. But since I reached the middle thirties I began to notice the strange phenomenon that policemen were starting to look like high-school boys. Eventually clergymen, doctors, and now even judges look like college youths.

In closing, I take it that we would agree that there is no one magic answer, no one philosophical framework within which all problems will be resolved and an difficulties surmounted. Those abstractions, representing concrete enough realities, which elicit hope in our hearts, *education, religion, democracy, freedom, psychiatry, political constitutionalism,* even such attractive ideals are not panaceas.

Perhaps I should mention that I am a Christian so that you will understand my fundamental bias in regard to this question. I stand, in other words, among those who hold that religion in essence is a positive force and one capable of influencing human behavior in acceptable directions. But the fact remains that the pages of religious history are stained with such rivers and seas of human blood, that the record of religious practice is blackened by instances of such massive intolerance and fanaticism, that it cannot possibly be responsibly argued that religion pure and simple is the answer our hearts seek.

Nor can *education* be that answer. Germany in the 1930s was the best educated nation in Europe. The German people were also highly religious, for that matter; at least they were affiliated with the various Christian churches. But this religious and well-educated people nevertheless perpetrated the horrors, under Hitler's guidance, that led to the massive destruction of World War II.

As for *freedom,* we feel its lack sensitively and its loss even more painfully. Obviously it is a good. But it frequently provides operative room in which countless moral atrocities and obscenities are committed.

It is not a proper response to such understanding to turn *against* education, religion, or freedom; we are merely advised against investing overly large amounts of hope in such conditions.

It is perhaps a wonder, or a tribute to our resourcefulness and resiliency, that we know any happiness or intellectual satisfaction at all, given that our existence is quite literally bounded by mystery and death.

Consider the two fundamental concepts by which we locate ourselves, *space* and *time.* Concerning each there are two possible positions, both of which are absurd. Either time began, which is preposterous, since we can easily think of a continuum *before* it began, or it did *not* begin, which we can not think of at all. Either it will end or it will not, both of which are obviously impossible. As for space, either it is infinite, which cannot be the case, or it ends somewhere, which is equally preposterous.

We are born ignorant animals and we die in pain and confusion. In between we can perceive and create things of beauty and value, but part of our tragedy is that they can all be turned to evil ends. Whether we speak of freedom, democracy, education, religion, courage, love, sex; everything that we need to sustain us can also kill us, everything can be abused as well as used.

This association merits great credit for its attempts to induce man to make the wisest possible use of his mental, spiritual, and material resources.

Presbyterian Bicentennial Convention Speech

When, a few years ago, Thomas Aquinas made an appearance on "Meeting of Minds," a television talk show I was then doing for the PBS network, he paused a moment before seating himself at the table, looked around our studio, and said, "Good heavens, what miracles we might have been able to work in my day if we had been able to address millions in an instant, as you can now."

Aquinas was able to spend only two hours with us in the two separate sixty-minute discussions in which he exchanged ideas with President Theodore Roosevelt, Cleopatra of Egypt, and the American revolutionary figure Thomas Paine. During that two hours, the discussion concentrated chiefly on the achievements and ideas of our four visitors and therefore was directed to the past rather than the future.

Had Aquinas and the other members of his group been able to study our society at length, no doubt they would have been depressed at most of the uses to which our incredible powers of communication are actually put.

*   *   *

Access to radio and television obviously presented the churches with a dramatic opportunity to preach their unfortunately hundreds of separate versions of the biblical message. Whether that opportunity has been properly taken advantage of is doubtful. The assorted financial, sexual, and other scandals involving certain prominent televangelists are a case in point, but they by no means cover all the abuses. In ages past, even the prophets never claimed that their every utterance resulted from direct, personal communication with God Almighty. By way of contrast, certain prominent television personalities of the present day are constantly sharing with us messages allegedly from the God of the universe which, if authentic, suggest that where the Almighty was once concerned only with the weightiest possible questions, he has now become willing to partake of the general trivialization of thought that characterizes our society and culture.

That healing by faith can take place is something certainly not doubted, on principle, by any Christian, but when we examine specific instances chiefly associated with the television ministries, we find numerous instances of outright fakery and fraud, and other situations in which there has been no studied follow-up whatever in an attempt to separate those cures which might be legitimate and perhaps miraculous on the one hand from those which are not real at all.

Since our emphasis, in this setting, is on the future, what are we to conclude? Unfortunately, it is that, on the basis of the recent past, it is more likely that abuses will continue than that the perpetrators of fraud and mass-hysteria will be guided by those same moral principles they constantly urge upon others.

*   *   *

Beginnings have always fascinated me, whether related to trivial or important subject-matter. But often, even in our personal lives, we literally do not recall the precise moment at which something eventually important to us first became part of our experience. As regards my interest in *dumbth* (a word I coined to describe the increasing inability of people to use logical reasoning processes, to *think*) oddly enough, I do recall the instance in which the enormity of the problem became crashingly clear.

It was back in 1948 that I came across a series of articles in the

New Yorker written by humorist James Thurber, in which he reported what an extended study of radio soap-operas had revealed to him. After so many years, Thurber's series has gone out of focus for me, except for one particular. He reported that whenever a character on a popular soap-opera died, had a baby, became engaged, or was married, thousands of listeners across the country would send letters and gifts of a sort that it would be reasonable to send to real life rather than make-believe characters.

If a soap-opera character had a baby, she would receive enormous quantities of booties, little caps or jackets, supplies of diapers, cards of congratulations, etc. I was very young when I learned this, but I have never forgotten how the news depressed me. It still does. This particular aspect of the large problem, in fact, is now worse than ever. And it was bad enough in the 1950s, when actor Robert Young, who played the title role of a popular television series "Marcus Welby, M.D.," received an average of five thousand letters every week seeking *medical* advice!

In 1968, when actor Leslie Nielsen played a brutal sheriff in the television film *Shadow over Elviron,* he received over two hundred poison-pen letters. In addition to the naked hatred and anger the letters expressed, Nielsen noted, the language was shockingly vulgar. Perhaps the most discouraging factor of all is that the majority of letters were written by women.

A classic instance of dumbth on a nationwide scale occurred in July 1982, when the ABC television network carried a program titled *Pray TV,* on which actor John Ritter played the role of an evangelist. Incredibly, the stations affiliated with the network received some twenty-two thousand calls, many of which pledged financial contributions.

When I learned this from a column by Marvin Kitman in the New York newspaper *Newsday,* I found it difficult to believe. But a check with Peter Durlin of ABC's publicity department established that Kitman's information was reliable. Durlin reported that the various telephone companies involved had monitored and logged the incoming calls. Just after a scene in which the evangelist said, "We need your prayers," a fictitious toll-free number was flashed on the screen. A number of viewers around the country tried to phone the number to offer prayers and money.

*   *   *

The decline in mathematical ability, though exceedingly unfortunate and certainly dangerous for a modern society, nevertheless is perhaps understandable. But the decline in the simple ability to speak coherently, to read, to write, to spell, to communicate is even more depressing—and surprising—since modern Americans live in the most talkative, talked-to, and talked-about culture in history.

Churches, too, are becoming concerned about the problem and its effects on their members.

According to a 1980 Gallop Poll, 57 percent of Americans believe in unidentified flying objects, 10 percent believe in witches, 28 percent in astrology, 39 percent in devils, and 54 percent in angels.

Those who believe in witches, angels, and devils are, of course, chiefly Christians, since belief in the literal reality of such creatures is part of Christian orthodoxy. But obviously, assuming the statistics are reliable, there is a serious problem for the churches, as revealed by the discrepancy between the 39 percent believing in devils, the 54 percent in angels, and the only 10 percent in witches. The figures for church members—according to Christian doctrine—are supposed to be 100 percent in all categories.

The Christian churches have now had relatively unimpeded opportunity to preach the gospel for some two thousand years. For the last four centuries the availability of printing presses and the greatly increased literacy that resulted have considerably facilitated the large task. New editions of Bibles leap immediately to bestseller lists, the number purchased usually running in the millions. There are religious television and radio programs, Sunday School classes, university courses, adult-study courses, books, pamphlets, tapes, lectures, sermons, ad infinitum. Incredibly enough, such a vast effort, engaged in not only by thousands of individual clergymen but hundreds of separate Christian congregations, has resulted in a general state of biblical illiteracy. As long ago as 1959, the Reverend Thomas Roy Pendell, a Protestant pastor of what he described as "quite a proper congregation in a boulevard church located in the college section of a rather large city," prepared a simple test about Jesus' life for the members of his flock. Reports Dr. Pendell:

The results are staggering. Nearly one-fourth of the adult members of that Sunday's congregation could not identify Calvary as the place of Jesus' death. Over one-third did not know that Nazareth was the town where Jesus was brought up. Gethsemane rang no bell for 43 percent, and Pentecost had no significance for 75 percent. Only 58 percent could identify the Gospels.

There was complete confusion as to the number of converts baptized by Jesus, ranging from none (correct) to three hundred thousand. Jesus was variously listed as living under Julius Caesar, King Saul, and King Solomon.

Concludes Pendell, "It seems plain that biblical ignorance is the rule among members of one particular congregation. If other Protestant congregations are like ours, Christian education still has a long way to go."

It does indeed. And Catholic church leaders have long conceded—and lamented—that Catholics know even less about the Bible than do Protestants.

* * *

As a Christian I am grieved to report that fellow Christians, though chiefly of the fundamentalist persuasion, have been responsible for more than their share of publicly exhibited stupidity in recent years. A notable example concerns the rumor that the famous household products company, Procter & Gamble, is connected with devil worship. Because I perform comedy for a living, you might take the preceding sentence as a joke. It is not.

During the 1981–1982 period, Procter & Gamble was obliged to go to great and expensive lengths to stamp out the rumor, which had taken a variety of forms. The most common alleges that an executive of P&G appeared on either the Phil Donahue or the Merv Griffin show and admitted that the company logo—a crescent with the outline of a man's face looking at a group of thirteen stars—represented the company's formal connection with Satan worship.

To the extent that the realities may be of interest, no executive of the company had ever appeared on either television talk show, and the trademark itself is merely a picture of the traditional childhood symbol, the man-in-the-moon, facing toward thirteen stars which represent the thirteen original American colonies. The logo has been used on P&G products for over a hundred years.

I stress that I do not refer here to a casual comment from an at-liberty mental case or two. In fact, the company began receiving an average of *twelve thousand telephone calls a month concerning the rumor.* In the early stages of this nonsensical drama, P&G responded by issuing press releases and answering phone calls and letters with factual information.

A new phase was reached, however, when P&G employees and their families in the Cincinnati area, in mid-1982, were threatened and harassed by fanatical Christian fundamentalists. According to the *Los Angeles Times* of June 25, 1982, "Employees reported that paint had been thrown on their cars, tires slashed, and workers challenged to fist fights. Children of P&G employees have also been harassed at school."

Once the company learned that certain fundamentalist ministers had actually been spreading the rumor from their pulpits, P&G enlisted the aid of two fundamentalist leaders—the Reverend Jerry Falwell of the Moral Majority, and the Reverend Don Wildmon, executive director of the National Federation for Decency—in attempting to put an end to the bizarre campaign of attack. Said Falwell, "It is unfortunate that such false accusations are made in the first place, but even more disconcerting that they can be spread as rumor by people who call themselves Christians." Added Wildmon, "The facts are that this is a vicious, unfounded rumor, and I hope we can help stop it."

One way that the Reverends Falwell and Wildmon can make such displays of irrationality less likely is by encouraging a respect for reason and evidence across the board.

*   *   *

Since the United States, in the ninth decade of the twentieth century, is facing a longer list of social problems than ever before in its history, do we really need to direct our attention to yet one more?

You had better believe it. And, given that the issue at hand is that of a serious erosion in simple intelligence, we have no choice. The problem exists. Because it is real, it must be faced. To say that

Americans, in recent years, have become less intelligent obviously is not intended to suggest that we have become a nation of mental incompetents, or that every American is less intelligent than he formerly was. There is no need to exaggerate the dimensions of the problem; the actuality of it is serious enough.

Part of the problem is that we *think* very poorly. But how could it be otherwise when few of us have been given any instruction in that difficult task?

Schools teach us how to think? They do not. They teach us *what* to think.

But it's odd that in a time when "expanding consciousness" is at least relatively popular, thinking itself has nevertheless enlisted the support of relatively few defenders, even though it is one of the chief means of expanding the consciousness.

When people use the now-common phrase, they usually refer to consciousness about specific issues—abortion, civil rights, women's liberation, environmental pollution, and so forth. But simply to learn seventeen new facts about these important social questions is hardly an adequate method of achieving the desired end. What one wants is the addition of a philosophical component. It is necessary to *think* about such issues, intelligently speculate about them, reason about them, communicate articulately about them.

This by no means excludes increased awareness of emotional factors. It is good, for example, to be aware of the sufferings of those who fall on the uncomfortable sides of such social dramas. Our hearts should bleed for them, and the injustices they suffer should serve to fuel our energy in the cause of social justice. It would be foolish to choose between (a) being angry or moved to tears about such issues, and (b) thinking intelligently about them. Both avenues should be busily traveled. What we often see at present, by way of contrast, is a combination of apathy and ignorance at one extreme and belligerent fanaticism at the other.

*   *   *

Eliminate trash from your reading. A journalistic form detrimental to the national intelligence is that exemplified by the sensation-and-nonsense papers, sold at hundreds of thousands of supermarkets, drugstores, and newsstands. Their circulation is enormous. Since it is impossible for anything human to be totally negative, such papers are not completely without merit. Occasionally one may encounter nuggets of sound medical or psychological advice, an interesting fragment of information, or an unusual narrative, but the bulk of the material published by such papers consists of brain-numbing stories on Elvis Presley, Mick Jagger, Boy George, and other popular heroes of the moment, gossip about entertainers and political leaders, by no means all of it factual, plus a generous portion of stories dealing with flying saucers, the occult, and unscientific superstition of the grossest sort. Several years ago, one of these papers ran the following story:

> Steve Allen went berserk in Hollywood—and nearly went to jail. The usually mild-mannered Steverino showed up late one night at his agent's office building and ordered a security guard to unlock the door. The guard refused, so Steve kicked in the plate glass door. Alarms went off, the cops arrived, and a suddenly sheepish Steve said he'd merely wanted some keys he'd left inside earlier that day. No charges were pressed, and Steve offered to kick in with a new door.

Needless to say, there was not so much as a speck of truth to the story. After my attorney brought this to the attention of the editors, I received an apology and a published retraction. Some such incident had indeed occurred, but it had involved a man with a name somewhat similar to my own. Parenthetically, the retraction was run, not at the top of page two—where the false story had appeared—but far back in the newspaper. Consequently we may be certain that it came to the attention of far fewer people than had read the original libel.

As for the propensity of such newspapers to print "Twilight Zone" stories, there is nothing the least bit wrong in publishing accounts of actual or alleged instances of supernatural or scientifically unexplainable phenomena. Reputed scientists, in fact, conduct research into such matters and issue reports of their studies; it is important that they continue to do so. But such scholarly or impartial rendering of information is of little interest to the editors of check-out stand publications, for whose tastes there seems to be no story too bizarre or improbable. Photographs are sometimes provided, which, to those who have not learned to think properly, are interpreted as proof of the stories' allegations, with the result that popular but sometimes inaccurate ideas are not dealt with constructively but pandered to. The purpose—as no one would dream of denying—is to make money. Judged by such a standard, the enterprises are eminently successful.

But such periodicals, and the more conventional fan magazines they emulate, sometimes work actual moral as well as intellectual harm. They do this by publicizing, generally in wholly uncritical terms, the depravities or weaknesses of popular figures of the musical or cinematic world. Consequently, while our churches and ethical societies continue to preach the traditional moral verities, the minds of the young and philosophically immature are assailed by messages subliminally suggesting that the important thing in American society is to be not moral, not law-abiding, but only successful, in which case anything goes.

A fascinating aspect of this is that these same publications, as they are weakening the moral consciousness of a sizable percentage of the American population, at the same time cater to such popular religious predispositions as can be turned to the publishers' financial advantage. There are, thus, complimentary references to Billy Graham and other religious leaders, endorsements of the power of prayer, the common occurrence of miracles, and the like. Putting these two mutually contradictory messages together, readers by the millions gather the impression that the most perverted or socially destructive behavior-patterns are permissible as long as (a) one continues to assert a belief in the existence of God, and (b) one is successful at selling recordings, attracting audiences in Las Vegas, hitting home runs, making touchdowns, or becoming a millionaire.

Two questions automatically now present themselves.

First, are the churches—is religion itself in America—to any degree responsible for the unhappy state of affairs we're considering?

There's naturally no suggestion that the churches bear sole responsibility or even a large part, but what *is* reasonable to ask is: Are the churches on the depressingly long list of causative factors? I do not see how it can possibly be denied that they are.

The second question is this: What can the churches, as such, now *do* about the matter? The happy fact is that they can do a great deal.

Obviously Jewish and Christian participation in the simple process of education has taken place for centuries, and there is much of which the churches can be proud in this connection. Great universities have been founded under religious auspices. And the churches have long been concerned with the education of children from the earliest years.

But we should waste no time patting ourselves on the back for what we have done right, since it is obvious that all of this sometimes quite heroic effort has been part of the background social situation which has given rise to the present deplorable state of affairs, in which ignorance and irrationality are so common as to be socially destructive.

Granted that, for Christians, the ideal of education is important, and will presumably always be so; granted secondly, that in our country Christians have ready access to the public media, what are we likely to see in the future as Christians address the problem of dumbth?

Unfortunately, what we are *likely* to see is more of the same.

But that won't do. The churches are going to have to do more than they have in the past. And they are going to have to do some things that they have not done in the past. They are going to have to acknowledge—to be very basic—the existence of the quite common word "superstition."

There's considerable awkwardness for the churches in this, of course. One man's superstition may be another man's dogma. But just as there are certain religious opinions and beliefs that are common to almost all faiths, so there are surely very large areas of agreement concerning which forms of ancient or modern belief may accurately be described as superstitious.

Christianity has held, for long centuries, that astrology is worthless superstition. You will recall that when, a couple of years back, it was revealed that both Ronald Reagan and his wife, both of whom had long proudly and publicly displayed their Christian credentials, were nevertheless so firmly committed to belief in astrology that they actually conducted the official business of the United States under the guidance of certain professional astrologers, the response from Christian spokesmen was strangely muted. As I recall, a leading Christian conservative journalist, Cal Thomas—whom I'm proud to identify as a personal friend—called the Reagans publicly to account for this—shall we say?—discrepancy. But here would have been a marvelously fruitful opportunity for the churches to instruct their hundreds of millions of followers on this simple point: Christianity and astrology cannot be harmonized. After the entire nation's attention was drawn to the controversy, the churches, sad to say, simply ignored the opportunity to strike out against unscientific superstition.

It is not the slightest exaggeration to say that in our culture more people are being influenced in their views about astrology, unidentified flying objects, and other unsubstantiated superstitious nonsense by the supermarket tabloid press than by America's hundreds of Christian denominations.

Is that really the way you want it? One would assume not. So, when will the campaign start to do something about that question?

*   *   *

Looking again toward the future, we must ask—what do the churches, specifically, have to say about the present degree of political and religious fanaticism in the American population or—to look at the other side of the coin—what do they have to say about the current headlong rush away from reason? What do they have to say that promotes reason itself? Well, they can take some credit for instruction offered at the university level.

In the cloistered halls of Christian academies simple words such as "evidence" and "logic" are not considered satanic.

But what about the other 99 percent of Christian impact on American consciousness? What Christian leaders with access to the media are endorsing reason and science in that arena? The answer—we must face all painful truths simply because they are truths—is practically none.

And this failure to address the dumbing of America means that the long overdue counterattack on the problem is left almost entirely to science and to secular humanism.

Now the scientists (some of whom, of course, are religious

believers themselves) and the secular humanists, too, deserve great credit for what they are doing in this connection.

Christians would presumably hope that they do not make the same historically tragic error in this context that they earlier made as regards the large question of economic injustice.

When students sometimes ask me what are the causes of communism, I tell them that capitalism is one of those causes. The point is that the man named Karl Marx, and other political and economic theorists of this type, would have done something else altogether for a living had there not been enormous actual problems—outrageous social realities which cried out to heaven for remedial action, in the same sense in which the prophets cried out to heaven about the injustices of their separate days.

But we know that what has happened, all over the planet, for more than a century, has been that the West has tended to deny the existence of the problems, or to downplay them, and this massive stupidity has left the field open to the Marxists who were quite truthfully able to say to the suffering majority of the human race, "You see who really cares about your suffering? We do. The capitalists do not, and the Christians, except for a few heroic individuals and charitable organizations, do not seriously concern themselves with your state in this world; they try to direct your attention to the next."

Perhaps, if we could replay the history of the last century, the second time around there might be enough Christian revolutionary activity to preclude the necessity of communist involvement.

The Center for a Postmodern World Conference Santa Barbara, California, July 1–3, 1989

... This has been—let me see, interesting—we've agreed that that's a good adjective. Thrilling—how about that?—for these whole proceedings. Really. (applause)

But Frances Moore Lappe, John Cobb, Wes Jackson, the Lovins, and the others I'll be talking about did have an effect that it's going to take me a very long time to even measure in myself.

Like many of you, I've attended dozens of these sessions over the years, in fact a good many here in Santa Barbara. I was a frequent visitor in the days when the Center for the Study of Democratic Institutions was based here, when Robert Hutchins was alive, and in that instance, as well as in many others, I've experienced this sort of proceeding—but this tops *anything* I've been involved with. (applause)

The erudition, the freshness of the ideas that were shared, their insights, the emotions they evoked, the reasonable quality of the arguments—that's a point I'll be returning to—and the inspiration they provided—it was all quite overwhelming.

It didn't, fortunately for your purposes of the moment, stimulate in me the creation of a speech, but it gave me a thousand-and-one disconnected notes which I must now try to connect with my mouth.

One related to an idea in education—a thinking game that an educator named Robert Allen and I put together a few years ago. Before telling you about the game I'm going to play it with you, for just a moment, if I might, by reading something from a magazine called *The Critic*, a Catholic intellectual periodical. It's very short. And I'm going to ask you to imagine what sort of a Marxist wrote it.

The editors had written to a number of us and asked us to respond to the same question: What book do you wish you had written that you did not?" I'm not going to read you my entry, but this is something quite remarkable. It says:

> I wish I had written Secretary Gorbachev's *Perestroika*. First it breaks new ground by calling for human dignity and human rights. It also calls for a totally new attitude towards arms control and peace. Either everyone is secure, or no one is. It calls for the elimination of nuclear weapons, freedom of religion, international cooperation for economic development in the Third World, and many other initiatives that would stand the Soviet Union on its head. Will all this happen, and will Secretary Gorbachev, through *glasnost* and *perestroika*, be able to create a new kind of society? Well, whatever one thinks, this book is a blockbuster, with many paragraphs never before encountered in the books of Soviet leaders, and completely devoid of Soviet cant.
>
> How about this one? One might think it was from an encyclical from Pope John Paul II. This is the quote: "Today our main job is to lift the individual spiritually, respecting his inner world and giving it moral strength. We are seeking to make the whole intellectual potential of society and all the potentialities of culture, work to mold a socially active person, spiritually rich, just, and conscientious. An individual must know and feel that his contribution is needed, that his dignity is not being infringed upon, that he is being treated with trust and respect. When an individual sees all this, he is capable of accomplishing much."
>
> Again, those are the words of Mikhail Gorbachev. The book is available in English, published by Harper & Row.

Isn't it remarkable that the author of this article, in which Mr. Gorbachev is so favorably quoted, is not a Marxist but the President Emeritus of the University of Notre Dame, Father Theodore Hesberg? By the way, Fr. Hesberg would make a hell of a president, if you're looking for one. He's a great man.

But who could have predicted that we would be here, now, even considering such things? Nobody. Nobody did. If anybody had, they would have gotten in trouble.

You will recall that I deliberately distorted your initial reaction to Father Hesberg's comments by suggesting that his argument was that of a Marxist. The gimmick here is one that Robert Allen had noted in some of my writings. In two instances I quoted previously written material which I falsely identified as coming from a Marxist source. This factor alone, I suppose, would lead most Americans to react negatively to the material quoted.

After serving the quotations up to the reader, I only then revealed that the author of the first was Pope Pius XII and the author of the other was Abraham Lincoln. Bob Allen and I proceeded to develop a thinking game based on that idea, which we called "Strange Bedfellows." Its purpose, obviously enough, was to encourage the interpretation of statements on the basis of their content and to discourage either the enthusiastic acceptance or contemptuous rejection of them purely on the basis of their source. You may make such individual use of that idea as you might in the future see fit.

But what David Griffin and Ann and Terry and all of you have done in your separate ways is memorable—There's another adjective I'm sure we'll accept. And, of course, David provided a number of valuable services during the past few days, not the least of which was his repeated announcements early on that the lights had been left on in a Mustang convertible with a Grateful Dead bumper sticker. I checked on that and am able to report to you that the car ended up with a grateful dead battery.

*   *   *

It is reassuring to note how often moral questions were raised during the past few days. The ultimate political problems, of course, are always moral. Is a given political course right—or wrong? That's a moral question, obviously.

But there are obstacles to raising moral considerations about the workings of political machinery, particularly in a materialistic society such as ours. Consider, for example, what Christian theology has for long centuries identified as the seven more serious sins, calling them deadly. Every one of them is now considered a virtue in the context of the American marketplace.

I mentioned the emotions that are evoked by these kinds of proceedings. Among them are spiritual or religious emotions—but it's always a bit dangerous to automatically assume that one is doing God's work because one has felt a lump in the throat.

I'm reminded in that connection of Field Marshall Montgomery, who, for the very young among you, was a great English military leader in World War II. You might recall World War II; it was in all the papers at the time. It is really necessary to make these explanations now, even in a university setting. Anyway, the field marshall was, despite his gifts at his professional assignment, apparently possessed of a remarkably secure ego. This is not a joke. This is something he actually said one day. It was just before a major battle, and he was addressing his men, he said, "Gentlemen, the Lord God has said—and on the whole I'm inclined to agree with Him . . ."

So we have to be careful we don't fall into that same trap, you see.

I mentioned to someone today that were I to share with you all of the ideas, wise and otherwise, that your remarks stimulated in me, we would be here far too long, so I'll just touch on a few more.

Esther King's presentation, suggesting connections between the ecology and feminist movements, something I had not perceived, also stimulated a good many reactions, in all of us, I'm sure. And gave rise to a good many questions. One that occurred is that at this stage, since we're by no means totally civilized as yet, a male president, postmodern or not, could very probably do more for the feminist cause than could an American Margaret Thatcher, for the same structural reasons that a Republican or Conservative president can do more to deal reasonably with Communist leaders than could a Liberal or a Democrat.

If Jimmy Carter had restored the dialogue with China, or even announced that he intended to do so, American conservative critics would have been all over him. So until the day, therefore, that we become civilized enough to elect a president without regard to gender, Ms. King may wish to concentrate on educating all male applicants for the role of president.

Johanna Macey's provocative observations on the subject of time came as totally new to me. As for some of the other comments, I thought, well, that's consistent with my own thinking, but Johanna opened up new doors. She seemed to treat time as if it were somehow more like space than our usual mode of perception permits, and since there's gravity in space, my brain responded by thinking of the phrase *the gravity of time*—perceived as a force that tends to make everything in time slide forward down the hill that leads to the future, so that we're endlessly encumbered with the past, at least all of its main features, with which we then build what is to come.

A number of our participants spoke from a theological perspective. Parenthetically, I've always been somewhat uncomfortable with the word "theology" itself. Its meaning is clear enough. It's not one of those fuzzy-edged words like "postmodern." That meaning is, of course, the science or knowledge of God. But that's just the problem, for it is not clear that we are entitled to say that we know anything at all—in the simple, dictionary sense of the verb *to know*—about God. And this applies even to those of us who believe in or assume the existence of God, however defined.

But to step over that difficulty, on which in any event I may have a patent—a number of our participants, as I say, speak as believers or representatives of one form of orthodoxy or another.

It occurs to me that they can now help this particular cause most by running home and getting their churches behind it. But as I listened to some of those who spoke from a religious perspective, it occurred to me that it is perhaps not the churches that make individuals holy. It is decent, courageous, warm-hearted individuals who make the churches holy.

Religion, over the centuries, has been endlessly renewed and justified by its most charming and warm-hearted representatives, who are often, sad to say, regarded with some suspicion by the communities in whose interests they speak. The name of Dorothy Day came up the other night in this connection. Ms. Day was heroic, but she was subjected, in her day, to fearful criticism from fellow Catholics because of her selfless efforts on behalf of the poor and the laborers.

So it may now be the case that, before our Christian participants can contribute to the present cause, they must first civilize their own churches on the dozens of specific issues that presently perplex our society.

Jim Wallis's presentation was particularly moving. At certain points, the movement was to tears, and at others to anger—the two, of course, not being mutually exclusive. Reports about young ghetto drug sellers and gang members in the news media rarely refer to causes. But even after we learn that for some slum children the choice is between no job at all and making several hundred dollars a week marketing drugs, we often smugly assume that if we were in their predicament we would make no such criminal choice.

As I thought of this, while listening to Jim, I related it to a thankfully brief experience, in my own teenage years, when I had no money. I was sixteen and had run away from home, such as it was, in Chicago. The seven dollars I happened to have in my pocket lasted just a few days, and after that came a profound change. For one thing I became instantly, officially homeless. So I slept on the ground or on concrete ledges in alleys, and that was one immediate shift of behavior.

I didn't think, "I wonder if in three or four days I'm going to be driven to—" I laid right down and did it.

I had only the clothes on my back, so very shortly I looked like the kind of person you would not want to invite into your home.

The biggest problem, of course, to those in such predicaments, is just getting food. So after about two and one-half days of total absence of food, I automatically became a beggar. And there was no thought of shame, there was no embarrassment whatever. My body knew what it needed, and it asked for it.

By this time I was moving through the Southwestern states, where I learned something else that has affected me ever since. And that is that my fellow Anglos, with few exceptions, were of very little help. Some were actually rude as they refused the nickel or dime I'd requested; others just hurried by. In case it has occurred to you to wonder, I did offer to work for the food or the money to buy it, but no one was interested in my services. But to return to the cold shoulder shown to me by people who looked like me, I discovered that the response of the Mexicans I approached was much more charitable. Not one of them turned me down. One man who had nothing himself smiled, pulled out his pockets, and showed me they were empty.

Another fellow asked me to wait where I was, went to a nearby house, itself very poor-looking, and came back with a tortilla full of beans.

Another man could offer me no food, but he went into his house and brought me a cold glass of water. Another gave me a nickel.

I have tried to repay those favors over the years by being of some modest help to a number of Mexican-American organizations. I guess in some cases they don't know why I showed up, but now *you* do.

In addition to becoming a beggar, to get to a more important point, I also became a thief. Before my last fifty cents had run out, I'd gone into a grocery store, bought a loaf of bread and stolen a can of sardines. And just as there was no shame in the decision to beg, I felt no guilt in stealing enough food to keep alive. It was done quite automatically, not as a result of any process of agonized interior debate. Some simple primitive part of me just took what it needed.

Another discovery—not of great importance except to people in this kind of predicament—I finally became hungry enough to eat garbage, and was damned glad to find it. It was a discarded can of pork and beans that I found by the side of the road in California. Inside were a few beans and a good many ants, so I shook the can, got rid of the ants, and enjoyed eating every bean. And each one of you would do exactly the same, because *I'm not talking about myself; I'm talking about you, us, about how human beings act when they're poor and hungry.*

The ghetto children of today also are us. Should we disapprove of such crimes as they commit? Certainly. But our criticism by itself doesn't mean a damn until we make reasonable alternatives available to them.

Once I got to Los Angeles, on that long ago trip, and reached the home of a relative, that kind of problem was over for me. But there are people who spend years like that, sometimes the rest of their lives.

Another sobering realization that emerges from such discussions is that good is not opposed only by evil. It is perfectly possible for one good, one value, to be opposed by another.

Consider, for example, two much-praised concepts—freedom

and law and order. We love them both but rarely perceive that they have an oil-and-water relationship. We certainly must have law—which is to say a list of specific laws, to deal with specific offenses. But every such law is an infringement on freedom.

When Upton Sinclair disclosed the criminal greed of America's meat-packers early in the century, the wave of moral outrage his writings produced led to a demand for legislation. That legislation was absolutely necessary. But it certainly did limit the freedom of Swift, Armour, and Cudahy to purvey poisonous and rancid meat. So it is absurd to talk about a free market as if it were, or even could be, totally free. In the same sense, it is absurd to speak of totally free speech as long as there are laws forbidding libel and slander.

The market must be constrained by moral laws, by moral considerations. It is not enough, even for the most devout, to wait for malefactors of great wealth to be punished in the next world, as we assure each other they will be. Practical believers want to see them punished in *this* world.

*   *   *

It was a pleasure to see my old friend Frank Kelly. We used to see more of each other when I came up here to Bob Hutchins's center. Frank's right in saying that people should have more to say about who gets into the presidential race than they presently do, but it remains to be seen how a larger constituency will be influenced by a factor that presently looms so large—the electability or marketability of a potential candidate. It would probably, even if Frank got what he wanted, still be the case that being a good speaker would carry considerable weight.

Come to think of it, if you carried considerable weight, that would be a disadvantage. Because physical appearance, too, would certainly be considered; whether it should be or not, it would. Albert Einstein was as great and brilliant as you can be, but if somebody who looked like Einstein told you he wanted to run for president, and if you could think of forty-nine reasons why he should, you still probably wouldn't encourage him.

What about charisma, or the lack of it? And what would be the chances of a man or a woman who was absolutely marvelous and ideal for the role but also a pacifist? Or an agnostic? Or an atheist? So I'm sure almost all of us would hope there are ways to move Frank's proposals along, but, again, we have to be realistic and assume that we would not be going from something terrible to something absolutely ideal. It would have to be worked on.

Another question that was raised is "Should progressive-minded people work within the Democratic party, or start a new one of their own?" The group consensus seemed to be that working to reform the Democratic party was the preferable one of those two limited choices, although some expressed little confidence that that could be soon accomplished. But it could. There's a lesson to be learned from the fact that the conservatives quite successfully hijacked the Republican party, took it away from the country-club suburbanites who so long had controlled it. So that sort of thing can be done.

Richard Falk referred to the fact that George Bush has offered us leadership that, to use Richard's word, is rudderless. And yet, connected with that unhappy fact, is another fact: and that is that Mr. Bush is enjoying a high peak of popularity.

It occurred to me, as I considered this, that what I have long known to be true in the context of television talk shows apparently is now the case, too, as regards the presidency of the United States, and that is that although it does no particular harm if a TV talk-show host has talent, talent is, quite seriously, by no means a requirement. Some talk-show hosts have had it, and others have had none whatever, and there have been impressive success stories in both categories. What *is* absolutely essential in the talk-show host is the quality of likability, geniality. (Incidentally, it's not necessary that the master of ceremonies of such a program actually *be* a nice guy, it is only necessary that he seem to be. The illusion is as marketable as the reality.) So, in Ronald Reagan, we may have reached a stage when not talent but just the quality of personability is all that the role requires.

It also struck me, and I'm sure I was not the only one, that though, like most intellectuals, you would deplore Ronald Reagan's policies and the acts which flowed from them—most of them any-way—Reagan nevertheless might serve as a sort of structural model of the kind of postmodern president you'd like to see in office, in that he was an effective salesman who used his practiced actor's and radio-announcer's charm to market merchandise that would have seemed much less appealing if it had been proposed, even in the same words, by say, James Watt or Jesse Helms. Because you liked the announcer.

So if our American presidents then need only be decently attractive, presentable, and genial, this would be consistent with Mr. Falk's view. Perhaps he's right in feeling that we can no longer look to the presidency for strong, knowledgeable leadership, at least in the present situation.

The word *invention* was used by one of our speakers—I've always been fascinated by factories. The question as to what is manufactured in them has only secondary relevance. There's something thrilling about the machinery created by humans for the narrowly specific purpose of cranking out millions of roller skates, plastic paper clips, or hockey pucks, whatever it is. While ours is certainly not the only country to distinguish itself by the genius of its capacity to invent and mass-produce, we are nevertheless eminent in that regard. The achievements of such typically American inventors as Thomas Edison or Charles Kettering are nothing short of astonishing, at least to those who still have the capacity to be astonished, by anything.

I spent two days recently in Kettering's home in Dayton, Ohio. It was quite an enlightening experience. Now, since it could hardly be the case that the brains inside the skulls of American citizens are genetically programmed to be superior in this regard, it must have been something about the accidental confluence of a number of factors that led to the happy result from which almost all of us have either profited or simply benefitted as users or consumers. That list of causes would probably include the Industrial Revolution, the opening up of a new continent, political and social mobility, the intellectual stimulation provided by the Enlightenment, the growing stimulation provided by the Enlightenment, the growing strength of science against the centuries-long dominance of the Church of Europe, which splashed over to us, the ready availability here of natural resources, and the formal guarantees of freedom. All those factors, and no doubt others, constituted the reason for American technological superiority. And it could be argued, I think, that the founding fathers, the framers, were part of this yeasty process. This line of speculation occurred to me in response to the word used, as I say, at the outset of Roger Wilkins's argument, when he suggested that the presidency was the most human of the governmental *inventions* that resulted from our revolutionary separation from the monarchist mother country.

Mr. Falk, during one of our discussions, lamented the present absence of leaders of heroic stature. I had the pleasure, in this connection, not long ago, of spending two days at Thomas Jefferson's Monticello in Virginia, and while there was struck by the inventiveness, the gadgetry, in fact, of that great gentleman, in the home that he not only occupied but largely devised. It's full of tricks and shticks.

In casually reading some books on Jefferson's shelves, I came across an exchange of correspondence between Jefferson and Thomas Paine, and, just as I have been dazzled the last two days by some of the ideas to which I've been exposed here, I was dazzled then by the combined ease and dignity of the language of those letters. The grace, the word selection, the clarity of thought, the simple coherence were wonderfully impressive.

What was it they were writing to each other about? It had nothing to do with political philosophy. It had, in fact, to do with building bridges. Now men build bridges in the present day, but I doubt if there would be such literary interest in an exchange of correspondence between two gentlemen, one of whom might work for the Army Corps of Engineers, and the other for the Bechtel Corporation. And yet, here were these two heroic revolutionary thinkers, quite casually, and at some length, discussing the employment of certain kinds of lumber and metal, the relevant aspects of the laws of physics, the mathematics, the geometry, the grace of design—I was literally smiling as I raced through their letters. Think of it— both Paine and Jefferson knew how to build a *bridge*, as well as how to build a country.

At your own leisure you will no doubt make comparisons about the generalized competence of Paine and Jefferson, and their illustrious colleagues and our political leaders today, but I'm glad that, if you're going to do so, you've finished eating.

To jump to another point: Given the obvious importance of

avoiding war, particularly among nuclear powers, and also keeping the pollution and destruction of natural resources to the minimum consistent with modern technological civilization, it's not surprising that at least two issues tended to dominate the group's thinking. On the one hand it's obvious, but we have to keep being reminded of the obvious, I guess, so we should remind ourselves that the list of serious problems facing us has far more than two components. In a radical revision of our philosophical and political approach to the resolution of modern problems, we'll have to recognize not only the large number of such difficulties but also the distressing fact that many of the items on the list affect a good many of the others. To refer to only one example of that, the problems of education in this country now are difficult enough, but when you realize that millions of those we are trying to educate are also living in abject poverty—well, the point is clear enough.

Another comment on something that Roger said: we should not, in our enthusiasm, be deluded that there will be anything the least bit easy about even one step of the work we're undertaking. The major source of sand-in-the-gearbox is a phenomenon for at least one version of which I have coined the word *dumbth*. It's a world like *length*, *breadth*, *width*, rooted in the word *dumb* obviously. It's easy enough to conceive of some sort of statistically generalized consensus among, let's say, the one hundred American scholars and officials most competent to indulge in such speculative philosophy. It is certainly possible to achieve such a consensus. It would be even easier just to let *you* make such decisions.

But since we're speaking here for the moment in science-fiction terms, let's assume that Almighty God, after having looked at perhaps the fourth or fifth draft of this group's final proposal, heartily endorses it. So far so good. But the raw material upon which such social architects will then have to work would not be machines, institutions, or already existing philosophical formulation. That raw material would be, unfortunately for our most virtuous purposes, human beings. And that brings us to the annoying factor that humans are not very easily trainable animals, granting the usual exceptions.

All of this, of course, relates to the discussed ideal approaches to this question of a postmodern presidency. One thing on the hopeful side of the ledger is that the postmodern society over which such an executive would preside would be characterized by the dominance of moral considerations, if we are to judge by many of the points you've made. Everyone loves morality in the abstract and even, upon occasion, in particular; nevertheless, there's another difficulty here which could all by itself swamp the sort of idealistic hopes, the consideration of which is the rationale for your presence here. I refer to the fact that a state, as such, would appear to be an amoral institution. You know you're going to be dealing with human beings, which we've already established as difficult enough, but a state, as such, will cause you further problems.

It's easy enough to distinguish in terms of pure definition, between things that are *amoral* and those that are *immoral*. It's not always easy to measure the practical results that flow from such a distinction. When we examine the behavior of states, not the things they put up on the bulletin board to be smiled at but the actual behavior apparent in all the states that have ever existed, we find that what is characteristic of them is a willingness to lie, cheat, steal, murder, extort, invade, and appropriate without permission.

Indeed, modern states have actual, formal institutions the sole purpose of which is to carry out such activities. I don't refer to things that happen when people go crazy, I mean that when they're acting normally, such crimes are part of the deal. Modern states have, to be specific, propaganda agencies. No one imagines that such arms of governance are assigned first of all to discern the truth and secondly to preach it. Truth will indeed be used by such agencies, but only when it serves underlying and usually purely selfish purposes.

Propaganda agencies are employed in precisely the same way that lawyers are. Both prosecution and defense attorneys have only an accidental interest in the truth and are, often, honestly unable to determine it. The assignment is simply to win. By any means possible. Now Mr. Falk has described our ideal post-modern president in such admirable terms that the longing for such a leader is greatly intensified, but again, the difficult question is: given (a) the moral superiority of such a lady or gentleman on the one hand, and (b) the notoriously rakish record of nation states over the last few thousand years, how would it be possible for such a philosopher king, or queen, to either influence or manipulate the levers of power of an actual society of the next century?

Socrates aside, while it's by no means a fruitless exercise only to ask questions, even in the absence of immediate answers, it's still helpful to suggest directions in which we might travel in search of such answers. It seems to me that what has, down through history, made states as shmucky as they have sadly been, is that the people whose interests such states allegedly represent and govern are often themselves so fearful, ignorant and unimaginative that they are at least as likely to resist the efforts of farsighted and moral leaders as to cooperate with them.

To refer to our present predicament again, there is, and has been in recent years—twenty, thirty, however many years you want to grab—serious erosion in the simple intelligence of the American people. Every yardstick shows the same thing. Sometimes in, oh, Cleveland, fourth grade will come up two and one-half points—but forget that—the basic direction is going down the steps. So, even if you knew what was to be done, and somebody had decided to let you do it, you have, as I say, this problem. It puts the spotlight back on education, but not the kind of education we've had until now. We need a new kind of education.

So if we are to take this large assignment seriously, and begin to work to bring about the sort of postmodern presidency and society that you desire, the very first factor to be addressed is the role that the people will play in such a political drama, starting with what must surely be the inarguable perception—again I must repeat it—that they will be utterly unable to assume such a role in anything like their present condition of ignorance.

The degree of simple popular factual ignorance now is shocking. It's chiefly encountered in the under-forty generation, and the over-seventy generation is forgetting a lot, so on both sides folks don't know what the hell is going on.

Knowing very little of history, and that's how it is these days, means we're cut off from the enormous span of time of the past, of all that's gone before. Knowing little of geography—and we're even dumber as to where things are—means that we're cut off from space.

I have horror stories, and I'm sure some of you, especially you teachers, could tell millions of them yourself. There was an instance of a geography teacher at the University of Miami teaching almost entirely Anglo students in a geography class, and you wouldn't believe it if I told you how little they knew. Eight percent of them—this sounds like a joke; you'll laugh, but comedy is about tragedy—eight percent of them, in Miami, did not know where Miami is. They knew they were there, but they didn't know where they were. They didn't know where France was . . . or Germany.

And it's not just the University of Miami, it's our whole country. . . .

*   *   *

Over the last forty years or so, as I mentioned earlier, I have had the pleasure of taking part in a good many conferences of this general sort. Invariably I have found the experience intellectually stimulating and philosophically broadening. No doubt all who participate in such proceedings come away from them greatly enriched, whether the specific ideas we bring to such moments are more firmly buttressed or critically challenged.

But it is a separate question as to what extent our actual world is changed by virtue of the presentation of such insightful studies and enlightening exchanges.

That there is some effect seems clear. Political leaders now rarely have any ideas of their own. To the extent that they endorse and promulgate any at all, it is safe to assume that they have absorbed them from people brighter than themselves.

But the degree to which more has been accomplished here than the mere enhancement of the prestige of the conference participants remains, as I say, unclear.

If we look for change characterized by immediacy, we will invariably be disappointed. Great thinkers themselves change their ideas slowly, and then there is the separate stage during which the ideas of thinkers with some degree of access to power can influence those who wield it, and thirdly, the time when those ideas are broadcast with a wide enough reach to permeate the public consciousness.

So over the long pull, it is easier to detect degrees of influence.

An instance from personal experience: When, in the late 1950s, I first began to publicly suggest that the incineration of hundreds of millions of innocent civilians by nuclear weapons could not possibly be morally justified, I found a very narrow audience and was rewarded chiefly with accusations that I was a Communist.

At that point I helped create a book called *God and the H-Bomb*, which consisted of separate statements; letters; chapters; speeches by leading Protestant, Jewish, and Catholic spokesmen, including such notorious Communist sympathizers as the pope, Bishop Fulton J. Sheen, and other distinguished religious leaders.

Little by little such attempts to influence public opinion did have their effect, and it was not very many more years before the formal American position in regard to the atmospheric testing of nuclear weapons, and in fact their possible use as instruments of foreign policy, began to sound remarkably like the arguments of peace activists of some ten years earlier.

The same sort of process later was repeated in the context of the public debate about the wisdom of American involvement with the war in Vietnam.

There, too, the critics were first attacked and then accorded the eventual honor of the grudging concession that they had been right after all.

It was interesting to contrast my personal experience, as an early critic of the war in Vietnam, with that of Mr. Wilkins. He mentioned that his reservations about our emerging plans for Vietnam were rooted not in morality but in practical considerations. That's how it was with me, too. I had come across in, of all places, *National Review* magazine, an observation by a French military authority on counterterrorist activity, who had had long experience with such drama in fighting the native resistance in Algiers.

He stated that military victory, in the traditional meaning of that term, over a local revolutionary force could not possibly be achieved in the absence of a ten-to-one numerical superiority. That meant simply that there was no hope of American or South Vietnamese victory unless we were prepared to place several million American soldiers into the tiny country of Vietnam. Since were clearly *not* willing to do so, the issue was, for me at least, settled in the moment.

Mr. Wilkins suffered for his prescience, he has told us, by being shunted off to less dramatic forms of public service. The price I paid was being called a Communist or Communist sympathizer by conservative critics, despite the fact that I had a documented record of anti-Communist activity stretching back to high-school days.

Mr. Falk has referred to the two interpretations of reason: the Jeffersonian, and the more optimistic, that more-or-less shared by Burke and Voltaire, who, while supporting reason, were nevertheless mindful of those destructive and irrational impulses that are all too typical of human behavior.

This is not necessarily to endorse a theological explanation. It has always seemed to me that the concept that the fall from an originally saintly natural state was a highly imaginative and creative response to the puzzling reality that man all too frequently behaves in an either stupid or destructive manner. In either event, we need not delay our quest by debating such theological concepts. It is evident enough that the forces of irrationality and organized anger—whatever their origin—are dangerous.

We must, then, initiate a wide-ranging public discussion, dialogue, debate about reason itself, which naturally requires us to analytically consider unreason.

An enormously complicating factor, alas, is that in the ongoing campaign to encourage reason and discourage unreason, only an intellectual minority of those who are formally religious will be on what is clearly the better side of that ancient argument.

A sobering aspect of that awkward reality is that part of the present "return to religion" tends to be a return to the more irrational and fanatical aspects of belief rather than a revival of that admirable tradition that regards reason as God-given and for that reason, too, worthy of respect and encouragement.

In this connection, it was instructive to be reminded by Roger Wilkins of the debate on the question of slavery that took place in 1787 and, of course, continued. He quotes John Rutledge, former governor of North Carolina, as stating that religion and humanity had nothing to do with the question.

It was enlightening to be reminded that not all the political leaders of that day were as gifted at simple reason as were Jefferson, Madison, Hamilton, Paine, Ben Franklin, and some of the others. It

was clearly an instance of poor thinking for Mr. Rutledge to say
that religion and humanity had nothing whatever to do with the
question of slavery. The most he would have been entitled to claim
is that such factors were not nearly as important as that of naked
self-interest and the happy economic results that flowed from it.

As for the connection between religion and the debate on slavery, alas, the fact is that references to Scripture were employed
most effectively by those who spoke in *favor* of slavery, since both
the old and newer Scriptures simply accept slavery as a given and
do not speak critically of it unless those who authored certain passages happened, at certain times, to find themselves in the roles of
the slaves. For example, St. Paul, the founder of Christianity,
clearly advises slaves to be obedient to their masters.

It was interesting to contrast the views of Rutledge with those
of George Mason of Virginia, who pointed out that slavery brings
the judgment of heaven on a country. How Mr. Mason presumed to
know the judgment of heaven on that question, given that his views
clearly ran contrary to those of sacred Scripture, would be an interesting and by no means fruitless question to explore.

Please do not imagine that to touch on such a question is a
digression in the context of the purposes for which we are here
gathered. The American mind continues to be profoundly influenced by formally religious considerations. Absolutely nothing, in
either abstract philosophy or concrete prescription, can now be recommended as a means of improving our future that does not make
recognition of that fact.

Address to the Jesuit Convention

The following speech was prepared for a Catholic conference that took place in Milwaukee in 1991. Once I was introduced, however, I spent a bit too much time entertaining and amusing the audience—which consisted of about 600 priests and former members of the order—so that it wasn't possible to deliver the entire address I had brought to the stage. What follows, then, is the text as originally drafted.

Thank you, Father.

And if I am to address each of you as "Father," it would seem reasonable for you to address me as "son." Those of you who have *left* the priesthood—"stepfather."

It might occur to some of you to wonder how—or why—I happen to be here. Well, part of the answer is that I was invited. Another part of the explanation is that I *accepted* the invitation. But I don't accept *all* such invitations, so there must be more to the answer than that. And there is. I like priests. Lest that go to your heads, I also like rabbis and ministers. But because of my own background, I like priests a little more.

Perhaps I should explain that I also have a particular admiration for policemen, firemen, and those who practice St. Ignatius' original profession, all of whom have in common with priests the obligation of cleaning up the dirty business of the world.

Actually, had it not been for the truly bizarre method that either God, or the blind watchmaker—or both—established for the purpose of propagating our species, I might today be one of your number. . . .

Needless to say, I am honored by the invitation to appear at so auspicious a conference. And then, too, those of us who spend most of our time speaking to television cameras, rather than to human beings, frequently welcome the opportunity to get out of the studio and address people face-to-face.

Interesting things happen in this kind of a context that probably wouldn't in a television theater. For example, as I was coming into the building this morning, a middle-aged woman passed me and then spun around and began snapping her fingers and pointing.

"Oh, I know you," she said. "You're . . . don't tell me," she said. "I see you on TV all the time. You're—uh—"

I said, "Steve Allen."

She said, "No."

I hope I have somewhat better fortune in addressing this particular conference than I did some years ago when I served as master-of-ceremonies for a social function at a Catholic church in Los Angeles. The program was of the traditional sort, a brief talk or two followed by some singing, an exhibition of dance, my own contribution of a piano number, and at the end, closing remarks by one of the pastor's assistants, whom we can call Father Murphy.

The problem was that when the time came for me to introduce Father Murphy, he still had not put in an appearance. I made small talk for a minute or two, since the pastor had assured me that Father Murphy would arrive, but finally I began to explain to the audience that it appeared our program was over.

"Father Murphy was unfortunately detained," I said, "and will not be with us this afternoon as he had hoped. But I'm sure that he—"

But just at that moment, the door behind the audience opened, and I saw Father Murphy hurrying in.

"Well," I said, "speak of the devil."

It was one of the biggest laughs I ever got, but for years I've secretly resented the fact that I had *not* been trying to be funny at all.

* * *

Well, you're a wonderfully responsive group and—speaking for a moment just as an entertainer—it would be a pleasure to have the opportunity to perform for you on some other occasion. But this conference has a more legitimate purpose.

An early point of my connection with the Jesuits came when I ran away from home in Chicago, at the age of sixteen, bummed around the country for a few weeks, and ended up in Los Angeles, where my mother's sister entered me into Loyola High School.

During that year, I profited by the kindly personal attentions of a Father Colosimo. Among my other recollections of that period, however, is that of an instance in a religion class where the instructor, whose name I cannot recall, was telling us about the doctrine of papal infallibility, according to which, he explained, it was literally not even possible that the pope, in making an official pronouncement about faith or morals, could be in error.

At the time I saw no reason to doubt that assertion, but a moment later, when our instructor explained that the Vatican is always extremely careful in making such pronouncements and usually, in fact, devotes years of study and discussion before reaching a final decision, it occurred to me to say, "Father, why is such study necessary if, as you've told us, God has personally guaranteed that the Church cannot be in error in such a context?"

That happens to be a perfectly fair question, but our instructor missed an opportunity to share with us additional information on the question. What he *did* say was, "Just shut up and don't be a wise guy."

* * *

Our individual progress through the years, which we measure by particular acts or experiences, sometimes make time seem elastic.

I recall an instance, about twenty years ago, when I spent a day at a Jesuit institution—Springhill College—in Montgomery, Alabama. I was doing some detective work in my search for a half-brother who had been born to my mother out of wedlock years before my time, a brother concerning whom I knew nothing definite until my mother died and left behind a few meager clues.

The young man had attended Springhill, so, acting on a sudden hunch, I flew down from Chattanooga one Sunday morning, without an appointment, walked in the front door, and asked if it might be possible to go through the school's old yearbooks from early in the century. I was welcomed and introduced to an old Barry Fitzgerald-type priest who was the librarian, a Father Mulcrone.

After hours spent poring through ancient records and photographs, I was invited to have lunch with the resident priests.

About a dozen of these turned out to be very young fellows—they looked to me like teenagers—but what astonished me is that they looked more like members of a rock group than the traditional image of Jesuits. In my generation, priests were supposed to look like Spencer Tracy or Pat O'Brian. There was nothing wrong with the appearance of these young men, as far as I'm concerned, but it does remind us that even institutions which seem day-by-day not to change, are nevertheless subject to that evolution that affects all things natural. . . .

*　　*　　*

We have not just been talking about sin here at this convention.

Everyone of us knows, to our sorrow, that it is perfectly possible to *know* what is right and yet *do* what is wrong, believing that if we are truly repentant and that if God loves us, He will forgive us.

That, I repeat, is *not* what we're considering. The issue here is quite distinct from that ancient process.

I am talking about something more serious—patterns of behavior that demonstrate that certain individuals, though they consider themselves loyal sons and daughters of one branch of Christendom or another, have apparently never gotten the essential message in the first place.

Let us draw out this thread and see if it is only that, a thread, the loss of which does not materially affect the garment, or whether, God forbid, its loss leads to a recognition that the garment, as we have inevitably designed it for ourselves, simply does not fit.

One sort of material evidence that must be carefully examined in this context is that connected with the quite specific form of evil designated as hatred.

Hatred is not simply another word for *anger*. Anger, though it clearly leads to an incredible amount of suffering, is nevertheless a perfectly natural human attribute. Even infants—which is to say humans so young that they are incapable of sin—experience and display anger.

It is even one of the more inherently tragic factors of that equation known as the human predicament that anger has survival value. To say as much is certainly not to justify all manifestations of the emotion, merely to concede something the very obviousness of which must make us weep.

How beautiful it would be if God would grant either all His human children, or even any one of them, that absolute clarity of moral thought which would enable us to distinguish, in fiercely sharp focus, the fine line that separates all good from all evil. But again, it is hatred that raises the question as to whether the essence of the Christian message was ever not perfectly perceived—since none of us is capable of perfection in any regard—but even adequately perceived.

And the answer to this shattering question would appear to be that no, that message was not properly grasped.

Scripture tells us that of the long list of virtues of which humans are capable, three of the most important are *faith*, *hope*, and *charity*, or love. It is certainly one of the more astonishing assertions in all the massive accumulation of moral literature that of these three, *love is supreme*.

Given the great number of Christian clergy, and the vast amount of preaching to which their flocks are properly subjected, there must have been sermons on this narrow theme, though I personally have never heard one, and I was a Catholic until I incurred automatic excommunication at the moment of my second marriage. The reason for that apparent lack might be that there is something scary about saying that *love is even more important than faith or hope*.

We should all eventually drop in our tracks were we to persist in considering all the moral and logical implications of this remarkable lesson. Fortunately, such an exhaustive survey is not necessary. Even the mere start of such speculation is disturbing enough, for it follows that if indeed love is more important than faith, then it is perfectly possible for a formal unbeliever to please God by car-ing passionately about social justice and actively manifesting tender concern for the welfare of individual human beings.

Such an incipient digression need not detain us at the moment, though we would be well advised to return to it at our leisure.

What we are considering now is the evidence that hatred—which is anger organized, anger incorporated, anger as an ongoing motivator of social conduct—appears to be far more dominant in the lives of some who consider themselves followers of Jesus than do the traditional Christian teachings about love, compassion, and the desire to treat all of God's children justly.

Parenthetically, I have the impression that this moral dilemma is not a particularly serious problem for adherents of the Islamic religion, the chief appeal of which might be that it justifies certain destructive forms of behavior by simply considering them virtues rather than sins. It is no statistical accident that many of those professional killers accurately described by the word "terrorist" in today's world would not dream of feeling the emotion of guilt at the commission of their assorted atrocities but rather see themselves in heroic terms, and indeed are advised by their religious superiors that, if they should happen to die while engaged in their slaughters, they are assured of the instant and eternal company of Almighty God in heaven. Whatever the virtues of Islam—and all forms of religion have at least some—they clearly do not include the love for one's neighbor that Jesus preached.

War, of course (and how depressing it is to have to say "of course" of such moral concessions), actually depends for its successful prosecution on rooting out tender Christian concerns and replacing them with the most maniacal forms of evil and destruction. And there is certainly no shortage of embarrassment to Christianity in the consideration of that sort of fierce and warlike behavior of which Christians, by the millions, have been guilty over long centuries.

We exhibit a remarkable ease in swallowing large abstractions of this uncomfortable sort. But, it is not so easy to preserve our equanimity when we turn from wide abstractions to narrow specifics.

In today's world, thank God, there are apparently no Christians guilty of perpetrating the massively atrocious evil of slavery. But we do not have to step back very far into Western history before we encounter a scene so hideous that it makes us depressed at consideration of the fact that slavery was, among other things, predominantly a Christian crime, in the simple sense that the vast majority of those who participated in it were Catholics and Protestants.

Now the perpetrators of slavery, during the several centuries of their dominance, were not uniquely depraved individuals who asked themselves the question, "What could we possibly do that would savagely abuse millions of human beings and, in those cases in which they had the temerity to resist, ruthlessly destroy them?" No, that is *not* how such atrocities occur.

The motivation for such sins is usually one form or another of self-interest, in this case economic. The freedom to hire enormous armies of workers without bothering with the formality of paying them for their services represented a temptation that few Christians could resist. Nor, with some exceptions, did their churches during those long centuries morally distinguish themselves by their opposition to such crimes. (In making such observations, we run the risk of being morally simplistic. It is easier now, with hindsight, to see slavery for what it was.) But for those who played roles in that drama, for those born into a world in which slavery already existed, it was vastly more difficult—and frequently personally risky—to deal with the large economic equation by applying moral principles to it.

And, of course, Christian defenders of slavery could point to the clear fact that the human authors of Scripture accepted slavery as a given and *raised no moral outcry against it whatever*. But in our own time and place, it is perfectly fair to raise moral issues as regards our ongoing relationships with our brothers and sisters of other races.

The tribes of the earth, alas, have always distrusted each other, and frequently gone to war, concerning which we can only sadly observe that *the initiation of hostilities has never been delayed by so much as one minute by reference to religious considerations,* but was, moreover, frequently *encouraged* by them.

We've never gone to war against the Jews as a tribe. This, however, is not saying much, because Christians have consistently treated Jews not only as the other, which is, to an extent, understandable, but as the enemy.

From Old Testament times to the present moment, Jews have obviously had enemies other than Christians, but to say as much in no way justifies Christian sins of either omission or commission, for do we not preach, and *believe,* that we are morally different? And we had damned well better be different, otherwise we are still just a mixed assortment of tribes, every one of which has a shameful history, united only by purported allegiance to a set of sometimes vague statements somewhat haphazardly united under the rubric of a religion.

It is all too clear that, as Germans, as Englishmen, as Irish, Spaniards, Italians, and French, we have bloodied every page of our history. This, after all, has been the way of humanity, presumably from the very beginning.

But Christianity was supposed to change all that.

If there are angels, and if they can observe human conduct, can they have been pleased by the spectacle of Christian treatment of Jews, not just in Hitler's Germany, but for the past two thousand years?

My own early background was lower middle-class Chicago Studs-Lonigan Irish, and when I recall the quite casual anti-Semitism of that entire culture, I have difficulty selecting words that properly convey the sense of horror I now feel about it.

I absorbed all that ugliness, as I fortunately absorbed the more edifying and beautiful aspects of my culture, time, and place.

Again, this was not just a sin of which some Catholics occasionally were guilty, as one might be guilty, for example, of now-and-then excessive indulgence in alcohol. There is no philosophy that justifies the idiocy of drunkenness, but there are attempted philosophical justifications for the idiocy of anti-Semitism.

It was certainly not uniquely Catholic, nor Irish. But the most monstrous part of it all is that from the Church, which was my only instructor in those days, I heard not a word to the contrary.

Eventually that changed, thank God.

A particular nun, Sister Mary Seraphia, to whom I would later dedicate an autobiography, introduced me to two magazines, your own *America* and *Commonweal*, from which for the first time I learned of a Catholicism vastly superior to that of the—even then—mean streets on which I grew up.

But we are not referring here to ancient history and moral prob-lems now happily resolved. Not very many years ago, at a Catholic Archdiocesan Seminary in Camarillo, California, it was not possi-ble for seminarians to *read Commonweal* or *America*, though the conservative periodical *National Review* and *The Brooklyn Tablet* were readily at hand. . . .

*   *   *

One of the first shots fired in the present phase of the revolutionary battle for control of the mind of at least the American branch of the Catholic Church was Thomas Sugrue's *A Catholic Speaks His Mind*, published in 1951. At the time it seemed a radical and quite dramatic document, but in the light of events of the present day, it no longer has the shock value it did forty years ago. Sugrue observed that when the United States went to war with Japan and Germany in 1941, self-criticism disappeared for the duration from the public media, with the result that graft, treason, and corruption flourished while the national attention was turned elsewhere.

"When, in the sixteenth century, Protestantism split the western Church in two," he said, "self-criticism vanished from the parent body, the Roman Catholic Church. Four hundred years later, in the latter half of the twentieth century, it was still absent." The damage its exile had caused within the Church, Sugrue argued, is beyond our power to measure.

Sugrue saw the American branch of the Church becoming less Christian as it became more American. "I do not think," he said, "that any group of people, whoever they may be, should be allowed to employ the Church, a Christian institution founded and main-tained for the spiritual task of redeeming mankind, as an instrument for the expression and the exercise of that group's peculiar preju-dices, neuroses, personality imperfections and grudges against life."

One of the remedies that Sugrue urged for the disease that he diagnosed in the Church—the disease of narrow-minded, intoler-ant, reactionary rigidity—was more democracy. It has taken us some four decades to catch up with Sugrue.

All of this leads to a consideration of the Church's relationship with the poor. Or, to put it another way, whose side are you on?

On the proverbial rational planet, the creatures of which could look at the behavior of earthlings from an impartial distance, those societies would no doubt be judged as profoundly foolish in which the suffering and struggling 95 percent of a population seemed willingly to submit to the domination of a selfish and pampered wealthy class who had, for their luckless subjects, either a cruel contempt or a blind indifference, and almost never a good-hearted and charitable concern.

The Church boasts of its martyrs, though it does not always give them full-fledged support while they are alive. But it is a fair if disturbing question as to why—when the Church has had long centuries of opportunity to propagandize and convert the minds of millions in Latin America—it has nevertheless done such a poor job of encouraging dedication to living by the light of philosophical ideals acknowledged even by ancient pagan philosophies. It has not, after all, succeeded in inculcating respect for even those ideals that are considered specifically Christian. The Scriptures ring with repeated denunciations of the selfish rich, and this was true long before the New Testament came into existence. Why, then, have the princes of the Church so often served the interests of the rich and left the poor to the loving attention of those few orders of priests and nuns who morally distinguish themselves by their true, loving concern for them?

The pro-rich bias of some churchmen would be a moral outrage if the poor numbered only 5 percent of a given population. When they number 95 percent, what we are addressing is more than an outrage. It is a massive moral idiocy.

Secular humanism, at its best, can enlist the minds of well-intentioned men and women by its inherent reasonableness. Whether it can enlist their hearts is a still-open question. But the Church has had access to both hearts and minds for two thousand years and yet has obviously failed to inculcate a decent social conscience in the great majority of its adherents, whether they be Catholics or Protestants.

Again, it has clearly failed to create a widely accepted social ethic in Latin America, despite its long near-monopoly there.

The Church has also failed to inculcate such a conscience in that not inconsiderable subsection of Catholicism dominated by the

Mafia, in both Europe and the United States, of which the staggering degree of corruption in our major cities is but one result. People in that milieu actually cheer Mafia leaders. They do not cheer priests and bishops—unless they show up at weddings.

The Church has failed to instill a moral conscience in more than a minority of Christians forced to address racial injustice in this country in the nineteenth and twentieth centuries.

There are reasons for all this, of course, and some of them can be interpreted as excuses. As noted earlier, the Scriptures themselves, after all, have little or nothing to say in condemnation of the vile institution of slavery, and the American Catholic branch of Christendom was hideously embarrassed at what it learned in the 1960s, when Martin Luther King, Jr., and other campaigners for social justice for blacks marched through predominantly Catholic neighborhoods, with courageous priests and nuns at the head of such parades.

Were they welcomed, applauded, cheered? No. They were attacked, assaulted with sticks, bottles, and stones. They were spat upon and addressed in foul and insulting language.

Obviously, the Church had made some sort of monstrous mistake in so seriously neglecting to apply the Gospel of Jesus to the practical realities of Christian living in twentieth-century America. There have always been heroic exceptions. May God bless them and may their tribe increase. But it is painfully embarrassing that they are only exceptions.

There are, thank God, in the American context, sensible and humane countercurrents to all such ugliness, and some of the virtuous work has been done by Christians—and, to your order's great credit—by Jesuits. But this was partly a matter of the Christian conscience having been publicly shamed into a more virtuous mode of conduct, often by non-Christians.

I have suggested, in this connection, in one of my recent books, that the secular humanists have actually done modern Christians a very great service in forcing them to more often practice what they preach, forcing them to be just and humane to Jews, to blacks, to women, to the poor—when for centuries they have often behaved quite otherwise.

* * *

I was a personal friend of John Cogley, at one time editor of *Commonweal* and religion editor of the *New York Times*, a heroic gentleman who, parenthetically, shortly before the end of his life made the conscious decision to leave the Church, although he remained a Christian.

I have never forgotten John telling me one evening that, as a young Catholic and follower of the heroic Dorothy Day,* he sometimes would just sit in his car alone, at the end of a long working period doing what little he could for the poor of New York City, and weep at the massive proportions of the difficulties he faced, and moved, too, by the pathetic sufferings of those he was trying to help.

I think, in this connection, of the shock I felt when, in my twenties, I first heard that term so popular with conservatives—bleeding hearts—applied, with a sneer, to those who, like John Cogley, actually wished to do something practical for the poor. Such a term, of course, used as an expression of contempt, revealed far more about those who uttered it than it did about the targets of their invective.

Conservatives of the world, can't you see that we need *more*, not fewer, bleeding hearts?

The Church is honored and glorified by those who participate in the never-ending campaign for social justice. The Church is dishonored by those who make heroes of such bums as the late Senator Joseph McCarthy. Yes, I use such a term freely. I'm not running for office, and as I have no time at present even to communicate with all those I am honored to call friends, I have no motive for enlarging their circle. And it is no proper response to defend Joseph McCarthy by saying he was an anti-Communist. Hitler was an anti-Communist. At least 98 percent of the American people have always been anti-Communist, to their great credit. But one wants to know not only what a man is against, we must also examine the other side of the coin by asking what he is for.

But—to return to Thomas Sugrue's point—if anything ever muddled the mind of the Catholic church over the past century, it

---

*An American journalist and reformer, Dorothy Day (with Peter Maurin) founded the *Catholic Worker* newspaper, which promoted social justice and aid to the poor.

has been anti-Communism. Under that banner there was never any shortage of churchmen to bless Mussolini's and Hitler's bombers and tanks, nor at present is there any lack of Christian churchmen to take the side of the Latin American dictators and oligarchies with their death-squads and officially sanctioned torture chambers, though Jesuits hardly need to be lectured as to what happens to those in Latin America who take the side of the poor.

Now, are there, or are there not, Christian principles which clearly address such questions? If there are, let Christians act upon them. If there are not, let us hasten to formulate them. Just as we have seen that the banner of anti-Communism is not enough to establish either political or personal virtue, so the banner of Christianity itself is insufficient to that task. The great majority of the German people who democratically and enthusiastically welcomed Hitler and who demanded that he take control of their nation were Christians. Damned poor Christians, true, but Protestants and Catholics nevertheless.

*   *   *

Although the expanse of human knowledge at present is incredibly vast and rich, compared to what even the wisest minds of five hundred years ago knew, yet I have had, since childhood, the feeling that everything known by humanity represents an incredibly small percentage of the reality that might, at some far distant future point, be known. I'm not referring to esoteric philosophical knowledge, but to simple fact and science.

Indeed, it is this insight which chiefly accounts for my reluctance to die. Death itself is of no special importance to me, particularly since I've lived a long and perhaps too full life—but I have a consuming curiosity as to how a lot of things are going to turn out.

It's pointless to speak of their ultimate outcome since there could be no such thing except a moment before the end of the world, if indeed there ever will, or even could be, such an end. I would be relatively content with knowing how things are going to be fifty years from this moment.

Since it is commonplace to observe that whatever even the brightest individuals can know may be likened to a grain of sand compared to the vast Sahara that will in time be knowable, I stress that I am not talking about that, but rather of the knowledge accumulated by all humanity. That, too, must be very modest in amount, compared to what might be its distant stage of development.

Among the million-and-one things that we do not know, one is the mystery as to what makes a saint. I refer, of course, to actual saints, those legitimately so designated by the church, and not to the numerous long-respected personages who, the Vatican itself told us not many years ago, had not in fact enjoyed the primary attribute of existence.

But even after we subtract all such imaginary creatures, and grant that some others who did exist were perhaps not all that morally admirable after all, there is still a remainder concerning whose virtue we must always be deeply perplexed.

One possible way to look at the saints is to be discouraged by their rarity. There are approximately five billion human inhabitants on our planet now, plus other billions—there's no way of knowing their number—who have lived here in the past. And out of that vast horde, the number of saints is so small that all of them could be accommodated in a meeting hall of very modest dimensions.

*   *   *

Perhaps the most striking thing that can be said about Ignatius Loyola's* philosophy is that it is utterly incompatible with the American social ideal.

Loyola taught, as have other moral philosophers before him (some of the Far East), that all physical appetites are, by nature, insatiable and that it is wrong to become enslaved by them, but the American social and economic system actually depends not only on satisfying any and all appetites, but on creating and stimulating them if they do not occur naturally.

Nor is it only the spiritual exercises which stand opposed to the American way of life. Loyola, in common with other Christian leaders over the centuries, gave thought to the seven deadly sins.

---

*Saint Ignatius Loyola founded the Society of Jesus (the Jesuit order) in 1539.

Every one of them is now accounted not only a virtue but an aid to the effective working of our economy.

Pride? We are never at present urged to resist its temptations. We are taught precisely the opposite.

Covetousness—the lust for money and possessions? There are now Christian spokesmen who argue formally that financial success is a sign of God's special favor.

Lust? The American marketplace could scarcely exist without it. The body is glorified. The soul and the mind are scarcely mentioned. The man or woman who manages to remain married to one mate throughout a lifetime is accounted of no special interest for that quite difficult achievement. The popular media and therefore the national consciousness instead honor those who have repeatedly failed to sustain even a love relationship, much less one sanctified by marriage. Scandal was once associated with disgrace and failure. In the world of entertainment, which almost totally dominates our culture, it is now guaranteed to enhance one's prestige, thus increase one's earnings.

Anger? In our time and place, it is admired partly because in films and television it is equated with courage. Most of those perceived as heroes accomplish their ends by violent means.

Gluttony? An entire advertising and manufacturing industry exists to encourage it. Indeed, the only exception results not from a respect for the relevant virtue, but from the fact that those who eat and drink gluttonously often become fat, and fat is not considered chic.

As for envy, if, by some sort of spiritual magic, it were to vanish overnight, the results in the business world would be catastrophic.

Sloth is scarcely mentioned in the present day. The equivalent operative word is leisure. A massive industry is erected to disguise the fact that leisure can often lead to boredom, and most especially when the pursuits it makes possible are trivial.

*   *   *

Religions and churches do evolve, if only for the purpose of keeping up with social evolution generally. All we can hope is that such changes represent improvement.

There is a tendency to think of the debate on the question as to whether priests should be permitted to marry as something quite new. But as this audience well knows, the dialogue on the issue is ancient.

Having seen so many other changes over the last forty years, I would not be surprised if some sort of experiment were eventually made whereby perhaps priests in a given order were permitted to receive the sacrament of holy matrimony.

Unfortunately, I would also not be surprised if—about thirty years thereafter—the Church began to concern itself with the question as to why so many married priests were getting divorced.

While I originally thought of that as a joke, it does, come to think of it, reflect what has happened in the Protestant churches, in which divorce among ordained ministers is now all too common.

There are many variations on this theme, of course. Several months ago, a Brazilian cardinal informed a meeting of bishops convened in Rome that the pope had personally permitted two married men to become priests on the understanding that under no circumstance were they to have sexual relations with their wives. It remains to be seen whether this is either a practical alternative, or the basis for a new situation comedy on the Fox network.

I suppose there would be general agreement, whatever one's bias on the general question, that priests must be more carefully selected in the future. And, as long as this is all considered part of God's work, it might not be the worst idea in the world to appeal to Him in support of the proposition that human beings ought to be more carefully selected before they are permitted to get past the point of creation.

Another problem the church faces, as you know, is the serious shortage of Catholic clergy. Whether this can ever be resolved simply by more vigorous recruitment is far from self-evident, but since the word "shortage" is a relative term, it occurs to me that a solution to the problem would be for the Church to change its mind on birth control, in which case there would perhaps eventually be a greatly diminished proportion of Catholics. And when that larger number reached an appropriate lower level, there might one day be no shortage of priests, whatever their number.

*   *   *

Your order, it seems to me, faces an interesting question as regards its mission. I do not refer to the primary purpose of all religious groups, Christian or not, which is obviously to win souls to their particular version of the life of the spirit. But in addition to this common ground, the Jesuits can be rightly proud of having always placed emphasis on the importance of the intellect. The first happy result of this is that Jesuits themselves are well-educated.

A second fortunate result is that those who are educated by the Jesuits are likely to receive an education ranging from better than most to quite good, granted, of course, that the ideal can never be achieved in your universities, partly because you have only a four-year crack at your college students, with rare exceptions.

But it's time now to take a fresh look at the importance of a Catholic education, and the Jesuit branch of it specifically. The reason this is a more important question than ever before is that, to speak in very plain terms, the American people have, as we enter the 1990s, somehow contrived to be dumber than ever before.

Granted, there is some difficulty in measuring such things. Comparing Americans in 1991 with those of 1891 is not an apples-and-oranges relationship—it's more like apples and roller skates, there are so many variables between the two situations. But those of you who are chiefly educators will already be familiar with the numerous studies that have all too well established the incredible ignorance of today's high school and university-level students regarding even the most basic elements of geography, history, and mathematics, to refer to only three disciplines in which we seem well on our way to becoming the dodos of the modern world.

We live in an age when many young people think that the name Loyola means a basketball team. I dealt with this in a book that came out about a year ago called *Dumbth: And 81 Ways to Make Americans Smarter.** To this point, we are referring only to knowledge of facts. That sort of intelligence can easily be measured, and every time it has been assessed recently the results have led to a great flurry of recriminations, patriotic embarrassment, outrage at contemplation of the comparisons between what we spend on edu-

---

*(Amherst, N.Y.: Prometheus Books, 1991).

cation and what we spend on weapons of war, angry letters to the editor, tears, suicide notes, and God knows what else.

But side-by-side with this large and gloomy problem of our astonishing ignorance—and this, remember, in an age with the most incredibly powerful technological means of communication and instruction ever devised—there is another quite separate problem which relates to the fact that the brain is supposed to do considerably more than remember. It is also supposed to *think*.

The philosophers have told us that function is, if not the only distinction, at least one of the chief differences between humans and other animate creatures. Apparently all other animals can remember, but we are evidently unique in that we possess the glorious and, yes, dangerous ability to bring pieces of information and speculation together in new and intriguing combinations so as to lead to new and intriguing and often desperately necessary ideas; solutions to problems; and remedies for illnesses, whether of the body or spirit.

There have always been those who, because of factors encountered in the mysterious realm of genetic control of our growth and development, have certain, in a sense, accidental elements of superiority. Some of us are gifted, through no credit of our own, with the ability to produce beautiful music, or fresh and sensitive poetry. Some are able, genetically, to manipulate mathematical symbols so as to make important contributions to that particular discipline, and some are apparently just naturally better at reasoning than others.

But what a sad and relatively empty world this would be if we depended for our music only on the Mozarts, the Beethovens, and other true geniuses of that art. What an even more visually tawdry world it would be if we depended only upon the da Vincis, the Michelangelos, the van Goghs, the Picassos for our pictorial art.

No, in all the arts and sciences, we encounter the quite justified supposition that, while not all of us can be geniuses, we are nevertheless not supposed to leave the dialogue and the accomplishment only to such Olympian figures. We *all* have a role to play, major or modest, in such grand dramas.

A clear analogy can be drawn as regards morals. Thank God for the saints, and, as noted earlier, how sad it is that there have been so few of them. But thank God, too, for the near-saints, and for those who at least make an earnest attempt to be guided by their moral example, their courage, their heroic dedication.

And that last point is crucial. What the hell would a saint mean if it were not for the *example* that he or she affords, thus becoming a model for our conduct?

So now, as we return to the question of that dazzling potential of the uninjured human brain, the ability to reason, to think critically, we would surely not argue that it is best to leave such things to the naturally gifted and that the rest of us should not trouble ourselves with anything more than internalizing factual information and doing what we are told, especially what we are told to think.

President Donald Kennedy of Stanford University has said:

> It simply will not do for our schools to produce a small elite to power our scientific establishments and a larger cadre of workers with basic skills to do routine work. Millions of people around the world now have these same basic skills and are willing to work twice as long for as little as one-tenth our basic wages. To maintain and enhance our quality of life, we must develop a leading-edge economy based on workers who can think for a living. If skills are equal, in the long run wages will be too. This means we have to educate a vast mass of people capable of thinking critically, creatively, and imaginatively.

The Jesuits, because of their well-deserved reputation for respecting the intellect and also for realizing that it is essential to dialogue with the non-Catholic, non-Christian, and nonreligious intellectual communities of the world, are well-positioned to make an important contribution in this campaign that is clearly more necessary than ever before. And yet, there is always a certain element of risk in approaching any kind of power, whether it is purely material, as in the case of fire, electricity, steam, and nuclear energy, or whether it takes more abstract forms.

This is especially so as regards religion.

If we were able to take all the religious beliefs in the world and pour them into some enormous blender, then take a sip of what had been produced, we would be sampling a remarkably indigestible cocktail, essentially for the clear reason that when two statements are mutually contradictory, they simply cannot be harmonized.

Matters of discordant emphasis *can* be harmonized. Concessions can be made on both sides, sweet ecumenical sentiments can mollify bitterly opposing views. But some questions are truly in the either–or category. And there is not the slightest doubt that of the literal totality of religious opinion on planet earth, a certain percentage of it is absolute error and intellectual garbage.

Oddly enough, to say as much is *not* to make a particularly objectionable suggestion. In fact, I've never known a religious believer who didn't thoroughly agree. He would almost certainly be blind to that portion of nonsense in his own philosophy, but he would enthusiastically concur that as regards the views of others, a great deal of absurdity is preached and believed.

But certainly no Christian or Jew would be surprised that risks are attached to sampling the fruit of the Tree of Knowledge. And such a tree did not absolutely have to physically exist to teach its solemn lesson.

In the book *Dumbth*, and in assorted lectures, magazine articles, and television commentaries during the last thirty-five years or so, I have suggested that it is not enough to make courses in logic or critical thinking available at the university level. At that stage, they tend to appeal to those who have some natural gift anyway. I recommend that we add a fourth R—reasoning—to the traditional reading, 'riting, and 'rithmetic.

I mean literally that a simple introduction to the brain and its functions should begin at the kindergarten and first-grade level.

Now everyone in this room could imagine being assigned as an attorney, let's say, to either defend or attack that proposition. But I didn't waste time doing that. I simply set about to create an instructional album, aimed at young children, and it has been selling well since the 1960s. It's called *How To Think*. Certainly you cannot introduce a very young child to sophisticated, abstract knowledge about anything. You could not, for example, expect five- and six-year-olds to successfully deal with sophisticated algebra, geometry, trigonometry, or calculus, but you still teach such children to count. You still teach them addition and subtraction, and you continue to build on such basic elements.

I didn't come here today to defend this particular proposal. A number of individual teachers have already picked up that ball and are running with it, but along with such instruction as is being offered there is a sense of what might be considered a moral component, because in encouraging children to become aware of their *brains*, you are suggesting right and wrong ways of using them. You are encouraging reason. You are encouraging fair-mindedness. You are encouraging a sensitivity to justice and its lack. You are raising important moral questions about the relationship between reason and the notoriously troublesome emotions.

The Jesuit order can no doubt play an important role in this particular social drama. It has always excelled at teaching *what* to think. Now it can do more to teach *how* to think.

A Call to Action

In November 1995, I was invited to be a panel speaker at a Conference for Women convened by California Governor Pete Wilson. Although the topic assigned to our panel was the relatively inconsequential matter of enlisting the aid of celebrities for charitable and social groups, I took the occasion to discuss something far more important, a brief history of the reasons the campaign for women's rights had been necessary in the first place.

At the conclusion of my remarks the first question put to me was "What does all that have to do with asking celebrities to help different campaigns?" My answer was "Not a damned thing, but since the purpose of this entire conference was to discuss issues important to women I thought it necessary to review a bit of relevant history."

Your other guest-speakers today may be addressing you on the subject of celebrity involvement in the cause of social justice for women. It's my assumption that they will cover the subject so eloquently that my own participation in that narrow regard is not required. During the few minutes that I can call upon your attention, I'd prefer to discuss something much more important than celebrities, a category with which our society and culture would

370

seem to be over-supplied at the moment in any event. Perhaps, by the way, in some future utopian society we will place stricter requirements on those who seek to become celebrities.

In past ages and in other cultures those who became widely known achieved that status as a result of some sort of remarkable ability or heroic accomplishment. That would seem to no longer be necessary. But I would rather refer to a factor that presently delays progress along a thousand-and-one lines—that of simple factual ignorance.

How can you reliably assume that there will be *more* freedom and justice for women when most of us don't even know that after white American males finally permitted the black man to vote, they still would *not* grant women the same right.

We don't have to go very far back into American history before we arrive at a period when women not only were unwelcome in the voting booth, but had very few of the rights of men across the board. They were, for example, not welcomed in American colleges and universities. They were not welcomed in the professions of law and medicine. Particularly you might profitably familiarize yourself with the case of Myra Bradwell, who died in 1894. America's first woman lawyer, she was—given the bias of her time—literally prevented from practicing in her chosen field. I do not mean only by narrow-minded law association leaders in localized situations. The Supreme Court of the United States itself formally handed down a decision that excluded Ms. Bradwell from practicing law. She was, fortunately, very resourceful. She became the editor of the *Chicago Legal News* and in that capacity argued successfully for the enactment of a great many legal reforms in women's rights, child custody cases, treatment of the mentally ill, and improvement of the legal system itself. All of us today owe Ms. Bradwell a great debt.

Women were not welcomed in many prestigious clubs and meeting-places. They were certainly not welcomed in the political arena.

In their capacity as members of our nation's leading religious faiths, women's assignment was quite simple. They were to serve—and to keep their mouths shut.

To the extent that a few women had the courage and dedication to principle to question their subservient role they were told that their lowly position was recognized not only in civil law but, more importantly, in what was considered the law of almighty God, as reflected in the Bible. And indeed it is simply the case that those gentlemen—if I do not unduly flatter them by the term—who were determined to keep woman in her place had Scripture on their side.

It is sometimes possible to differ in interpretation of one passage of Scripture or another, but on certain issues the record is quite clear, and there was no doubt in anyone's mind—on either side of the argument—that the ancient documents not only said that woman was to be man's servant because of her inferiority, but advised her to acknowledge the lowliness of her station.

Women of that day could not enter into legal contracts. They had no rights in the case of a divorce. The husband made all important decisions, even if he was scum-of-the-earth and his wife was a woman of nobility and virtue.

And in those days—is it necessary to point out?—the minority of women who were permitted in the workplace—naturally, only when their services were needed—would never be so impertinent as to ask to be paid the same salary as men for doing precisely the same work, and sometimes more.

Nor should we ever forget that all of this hideous injustice was by no means a matter of simple oversight. Every bit of it was deliberate and conscious.

More such outrages could be added to this brief list but, because of the shortness of time at the moment, I will refer to just a few other examples.

Today our society is rightly concerned about the physical abuse of women. The problem of brutal assaults on women is at long last so well recognized that organizational defenses have had to be developed. But it wasn't so many years ago that American culture—its arts, its scholarship, newspapers, periodicals—simply did not perceive this particular problem, even though it, of course, existed and always had.

On the difficult question of abortion—very few women, in practice, ever asked for it, though they did in the most extreme cases—those involving incest, rape, or serious illness. But even in such predicaments abortion was simply against the law, and that was that. It's true that law was made by men, but the fact was that women had the choice of bearing totally unwanted children or resorting to the underground illegal market, with all the attendant complications and dangers.

The younger among you may find it hard to believe but when, in the last century, the medical profession made anesthetics available to us men they were actually not permitted to administer them to women, even those suffering the most painful forms of childbirth. While this sounds like simple stupidity on the part of the men responsible, they were, for their own part, again able to quote scripture as reporting that God had said to Eve, "In sorrow thou shalt bring forth children." And, some of the clergy asked, "How could a woman properly sorrow if she was unconscious?"

So we return to the original question—if most Americans are almost totally unfamiliar with this chapter of our quite recent history, how could they possibly form coherent judgments about the continuing campaign to achieve social justice—which is to say nothing more than a simple fairness—for women?

Of course not everyone wants to hear such truths publicly expressed.

By the way, it's acutely important to look back and note who it was that did express the wise and compassionate sentiments that we now perceive were so socially needed. Do you know what kind of people did that? I'll tell you. "Outside agitators." "Dangerous radicals." "Trouble-makers." "Bleeding hearts."

Yes, they were indeed that—and thank God for them, or you women wouldn't have been permitted to enter this meeting hall today.

I thank you.

Miscellaneous Writings

Open Letter to Frank Sinatra

Frank Sinatra, whom I have always felt was the best popular singer of our time, caused widespread consternation on the political left and center when after years of outspoken advocacy of various progressive, prolabor, and propoor causes he suddenly switched his political allegiance and publicly endorsed Ronald Reagan. It eventually emerged that his reasons for doing so had to do with the Kennedy administration and its stand on organized crime. The Mafia and its allies in Chicago had been helpful in delivering votes for Jack Kennedy. Mafia leaders therefore felt they had been "betrayed" when Kennedy in the White House did nothing to slow down IRS and FBI anticrime activity. But little of this was known at the time the following letter was written.

September 7, 1970

Dear Frank:

A great many uncomplimentary things are presently being said about you by Democrats around the country. They can't understand how a lifelong liberal could suddenly switch to the support of one of the leading exponents of conservatism, Ronald Reagan.

The more knowledgeable among your former political allies,

377

Frank, are saying that the really surprising thing about your endorsement of Reagan is that you haven't substantially modified your views at all. They say your hatred of Senator Bob Kennedy was so great—because he kept you away from the confidence of his brother, the president—that you have waited a long time to get revenge and would not even be denied by the Senator's assassination. The word is, Frank, that all you can do now that Bobby is gone is "get even" with his man, Jess Unruh and the Kennedy–McCarthy types who work for him.

I'd like to hear you do a chorus of Irving Berlin's "Say It Isn't So," Frank. Sincerely, I'd like to know that all the current rumors about "Sicilian vengeance" are untrue. No doubt you will tell us that they are. But if so, then consider a few of the social problems that make this moment of our history the most dangerous and perplexing the U.S. has ever known, because we know where Reagan stands on these issues. We thought we knew where you stood, too. But now we're not sure.

I can't believe another story, Frank, which is that you're so poorly informed you don't *know* the political philosophy of the man you're now supporting.

Either way I'd like to run through a list of the major issues and problems and remind you of Reagan's approach to them. And note that I'm not addressing this letter to Reagan. It's a free country. He's a conservative, and he's got a right to his views. Some of my best friends, to borrow the bigot's phrase, are conservatives. As I say, Frank, we all know where Ronnie stands and in a day when many voters will be motivated by nothing more edifying than their fear and hatred of Black Panthers, campus revolutionaries, and "crime-in-the-streets," it may well be enough to get him another ride to Sacramento. He won't be able to *do* anything about crime or social unrest, of course; they've all gotten much worse during his four years in office, but what the hell.

So here's how Reagan feels about the puzzles and moral outrages of our century, Frank. Tell us—do you *agree* with him?

Prison reform. The scandal of the American prison system stinks to heaven, Frank. Our prisons are human zoos where inmates are further trained *toward* criminality, not away from it. One of Reagan's first moves as part of his alleged campaign to trim state spending, was to cut San Quentin's already inadequate budget by 10 percent!

Medical care for the aged. Hospital rooms are now going for about a hundred dollars a day, Frank. If an old-timer is bedded for a month, hospital charges alone can wipe out his meager, or usually nonexistent, life-savings. Hell, Germany had social welfare programs as long ago as the Bismarck regime. They're common all over non-Communist Europe. But American conservatives have fought them off for decades. Reagan has been speaking against Medicare for years. In 1961–62 the American Medical Association distributed a "Ronald Reagan record kit" featuring "Ronald Reagan Speaks out against Socialized Medicine." He has backed down only just enough to disarm his critics among the elderly. When California Rural Legal Assistance challenged Reagan's decision to cut 160,000 old people off the Medi-Cal roles and won its case, Reagan tried to cut its federal lifeline.

Farm Labor. The plight of California's farm workers has long been a moral outrage. The heroic Cesar Chavez, aided by the Catholic Bishops, Senator Robert F. Kennedy, and other progressives, have finally brought the downtrodden farm laborer a measure of social justice. But Reagan has told us that one of his "most joyous moments" was vetoing federal poverty funds for a group trying to help poor farm workers organize.

In 1968 Reagan decertified eighteen of the twenty-four strikes in the Delano area [of California], as a favor to the large growers, permitting the State Department of Employment to send strikebreakers to the struck farms.

The U.S. Judicial Council, Chief Justice Warren Berger, the American Bar Association, the *Los Angeles Times,* key figures in the Nixon Administration, and many legal scholars believe that quality legal services should be provided for those unable to pay for them. But Reagan and George Murphy fought to give the governor power to veto all or any part of such a poverty program.

Concerned citizens all over the nation breathed a sigh of relief when twenty-six leading grape growers in the Delano area recently signed a union contract, signaling an end to the five-year grape strike and boycott. Even growers were pleased. "This is a new era," said their spokesman, John Guinarra, Jr. "Once again peace will come to this valley." But in Sacramento Reagan—characteristically—called it "tragic" that workers had "no choice" in determining if they wanted to be unionized.

Hunger. As a humanitarian, Frank, you know that hunger is a very serious problem for millions of Americans. To Ronnie it seems a joke. In one of his many speeches for Barry Goldwater he said, "We were told four years ago that 17 million people went to bed hungry each night. Well, that was probably true; they were all on a diet."

The Generation Gap. You have long depended heavily, Frank, on the support of young people; you must know how important it is to give them straight talk and to respect their intelligence. When Reagan voted with the University of California Board of Regents to fire Clark Kerr, the President of the State University, protesting students came all the way to the Capitol. Reagan's first words in addressing them were, "Ladies and gentlemen . . . if there *are* any . . ."

Taxes. You and I don't have too much trouble paying ours, Frank, but millions do. Reagan ran for office by *promising* to cut taxes, pledging "sound financial management" and "tax reductions." In March 1967, as *Time* magazine put it, he "had the crust to demand the highest budget ever proposed in any American state, buttressed by the biggest tax boost in California history."

You and I pay a hell of a lot in taxes, Frank, but you know damned well that this country couldn't run for one day without some form of progressive income tax. Says Reagan, "We have received this progressive tax directly from Karl Marx, who designed it as the prime essential of a socialist state."

The Black Man. If ever there was a time in world history when reason and decency among races must prevail, that time is certainly the latter half of the present century, but in 1962 during a question-and-answer period, after addressing a student group on the University of Southern California campus, Reagan—speaking of Negroes—said, "In their own country they're eating each other for lunch." He became embarrassed at discovering that one of his listeners was black.

Campus Unrest. In "explaining" your support for Reagan, Frank, you said, "We must all work together to end the turmoil on the campuses." A few months ago, at a convocation of prosperous growers in Yosemite National Park, Reagan was asked what could be done to support his stand against campus militants. "If it takes a blood bath," Ronnie said, "let's get it over with . . . no more appeasement."

Political Integrity. On August 30, 1967, Reagan was asked about published reports that he would abandon his college tuition plan in favor of an increase in student fees. "Such a report," he said, "was the most bare-faced lie that has ever been told." The next day the University of California's Board of Regents, after defeating Reagan's proposal for a $250 annual tuition, accepted his alternative proposal for an additional "charge" on students. So much for bare-faced lies. I don't recall Reagan ever telling the voters that U.C. students were already paying a $250 annual fee for special purposes as well as $1,800 for room and board.

Anti-war demonstrators. You and I know, Frank, that a few demonstrators are Communist revolutionaries, but far more are good, decent American kids who are honestly convinced that the Vietnam War is immoral and stupid. Reagan's solution? *The United States should consider a formal declaration of war against North Vietnam to facilitate the prosecution of war resisters as traitors!* Ronnie is pretty handy with words like "treason" and "traitors," Frank. He used them after Goldwater's defeat in attacking the millions of decent Republicans who could not vote for the archconservative.

Education. Our educational system faces serious problems. Without federal aid to education the situation would become even more disastrous. Reagan, like almost all conservatives, has been a long-time critic of federal aid to education. One of his first appointments was his nomination of Dr. William J. McCandless for the State Board of Education. McCandless is widely known in right-wing circles as an active opponent of Federal Aid to Education programs.

The *Los Angeles Times,* which supported Reagan against Governor Brown but has been dismayed by him ever since, described Reagan's budget cuts and propaganda barrages against state schools as a "determined and dangerous assault on California's great system of higher education." "Higher education in California," said the *Times,* "has been hurt by Governor Reagan's intransigence and ill-considered statements. This threat to the well-being of the entire state must cease before irrevocable damage is done."

Consumer interests. The American consumer, Frank, is waking up to the fact that he's getting robbed by somebody almost every time he goes shopping. One of Reagan's first moves as Governor was to cut the budget of the Office of Consumer Council by 77 percent!

Capital punishment. Practically every expert on the subject in the world believes that the death penalty is a barbarous and inhuman hold-over from our savage past. Like conservatives generally, Reagan is in favor of the death penalty.

Mental Health. Neither the nation nor the state of California is doing as much as should be done for the emotionally troubled. Out-patient clinics, which Reagan wanted to *abolish,* were partly responsible for the reduction of California's mental hospital population from 33,000 to just over 20,000. When Reagan slashed the state mental health budget, he tried to justify his cuts on the ground of the reduction, forgetting that he had also opposed the out-patient clinics that helped to make the reduction possible! The Right has for years fought against mental health campaigns, all across the nation.

Alcoholism. This tragic problem is becoming worse, not better. But one of the Reagan administration's first moves was to withdraw state support from the four-hundred-bed Mendocino Alcoholism Treatment Center, which was curing patients formerly considered hopeless cases.

Conservation of Natural Resources. Surely, Frank, you've heard of Reagan's classic remark when discussing the problem of loss of beautiful timber. He actually said, "I don't know what all the fuss is about. You see one redwood, you've seen them all."

The UN. For years, Frank, you've supported the idea of the United Nations, not a very radical position when the UN has also merited the support of Presidents Roosevelt, Truman, Eisenhower, Kennedy, Johnson, Nixon, the popes, and responsible world leaders everywhere. Says Reagan, "Our own interests demand that we seek a long range determination of the vital interests of all concerned without depending on the United Nations as it is presently constituted."

Communism. Having been an outspoken anti-Communist since my high school days, I know considerably more about the subject than Reagan, who began to see it as a problem considerably later in life. In 1961, in the speech he delivered for General Electric so many times, Reagan, quoting "one of the foremost authorities on Communism in the world today," whom he did not identify, said, "We have ten years to win or lose—by 1970 the world will be all slave or all free."

Liberalism. You have claimed to be a liberal, Frank. Here's what Reagan says about liberals. "It would be immoral . . . to infer that liberals are less patriotic than ourselves . . . but it would be equally foolish to let them have their way without opposition. If someone is setting fire to the house, it doesn't matter if he is a deliberate arsonist or just a fool playing with matches." Next time you and Ronnie get together, Frank, ask him to explain to you just which kind of a fool or arsonist you are.

Only a few thousand people may read this letter, Frank. I offer you access to a few million if you'd like to visit my TV show and explain your position.

Sincerely,

Steve Allen

Unpublished Article
on Racial Issues

If it is the case, as I believe it is, that the American people across the board are becoming less intelligent, it follows that the same depressing reality is recognizable in the various subdivisions of that society.

Today's urban blacks, I am convinced, are less intelligent than big-city blacks of the 1920s and 1930s. There was always disgraceful poverty in black ghettos, but when I conversed with poor blacks in Chicago, my home city, in the 1930s and 1940s, I had not the slightest trouble understanding them. They had their own lingo—as does every segment of society—but, as I say, the poor blacks with whom I conversed were city people, and we had no more difficulty understanding each other than would have been the case if both participants in the conversation had been white.

The same certainly cannot be said today. One of the reasons is that the large wave of poverty-stricken Southern rural blacks moving into Northern cities since the 1950s has had the effect of swamping the already disgracefully meager educational resources available to poor Northern Negroes. Poor Northern blacks of the 1930s, although they had recognizable speech patterns, did not speak all that differently from lower-class whites of the same communities. But poor Southern blacks spoke a different language indeed. That language has been imported to Northern cities.

We are therefore faced with a situation where a percentage of black boys and girls coming out of big-city-slum schools are so functionally illiterate that they cannot hold even menial jobs, do not know how to apply for such positions, and can scarcely communicate with whites with whom they might associate if they are lucky enough to be given opportunities to work in white-controlled companies or smaller shops.

The lot of the peasant has been difficult on planet earth for millions of years. But there has never been such a gap between urban segments of American society as that which exists today between poorly educated, functionally illiterate ghetto blacks, and more fortunate and better-educated blacks and whites.

Part of this is the disgraceful moral legacy of centuries of slavery and the self-interest of Southern economic powers, who could see no reason to educate blacks when what was needed—so the argument went—was a steady supply of cheap labor for the farms, plantations, factories, hotels, and restaurants of the South.

So many and horrible have been the crimes committed against blacks and Jews over the centuries that there is now a sort of compensatory effort—in one sense admirable—but which has had the peculiar effect that one is scarcely permitted to make any critical statements applying to individuals in these two categories without being dangerously misunderstood.

It is perfectly possible to point out that a certain percentage of Irish, Italians, Poles, French, Germans, or Swedes is stupid, whereas to say that a certain percentage of Negroes is stupid is to convey a seemingly racist message. Well, there is nothing to be done about this except speak the truth as simply and directly as possible. There are indeed pockets of stupidity and ignorance in every segment of our society. When these are combined with economic factors tending to produce a percentage of criminals, the large situation becomes tragically dangerous to all of American society.

I indulge in this partial digression by way of establishing that in considering the problem of the deterioration of American intelligence we are by no means speaking only of education. We are speaking of the fabric of American social life itself. We are speaking, even, of the philosophical rationale for democracy, however qualified. If people have only the haziest grasp of important issues, if they know little more about candidates for public office than that they were once astronauts, football players, or movie actors, do they have an actual right to be permitted to play the American political game? But we cannot force American citizens, of any and all colors, to pass some sort of I.Q. test before they are admitted to the polls. We are, rightly or wrongly, stuck with the freedom of the ballot box. The thing to do, therefore, is not to attempt to withdraw this freedom from some segment of the American population but to bring the American people en masse to a level of knowledge where the popular participation in the political process will not be some sort of monstrous parody of what the framers and the subsequent improvers of the Constitution had in mind.

Even if it were argued that black ghetto-speech is not inferior but superior to normal American English there could still be no debate about one clear fact: Black street-talk isolates and insulates those who are able to speak no other way. An analogy with the language situation in China would be instructive. Because China is a massive country, larger than the United States, but traditionally one with limited transportation facilities, the separate dialects of the central Chinese language grew so far apart over the centuries that at present people from one part of China often literally cannot understand the inhabitants of other provinces. The Chinese government, because of this, has undertaken a campaign to teach everyone to speak the Mandarin or Pinyin version of the language. The theory is that members of individual provinces may speak as they wish among their neighbors, but it is obviously important that they be able to communicate with the rest of the nation and only a common language can make that possible.

Just so, if individual blacks perceive cultural value in the peculiarities of what has emerged largely as a result of the *lack* of proper educational facilities in black rural areas and urban slums, they should at least be willing to concede that there should be some means whereby they could more readily communicate not only with nonblack Americans (a category with, of course, includes Chicanos, Puerto Ricans, Orientals, and blacks from other parts of the world), but also ought to be able to communicate with those all over the planet who have taken the trouble to learn standard English. Americans as a class are among the world's poorest linguists. Because of our insularity and ignorance, we simply expect that when we travel overseas our local hosts "ought to" know how to speak *our language*. It rarely occurs to us to take the trouble to speak theirs.

Now those who argue that nonblack schoolteachers ought not to be rude and contemptuous when trying to teach standard American-English speech to blacks are absolutely right. To quote Will Rogers, "We are all ignorant, only on different subjects," and there are many black scholars who could, on the same grounds, be equally contemptuous of the rude Caucasian teachers because of their own superiority to such white teachers. But so much for the emotional dynamics of the situation. What is more important is the issue itself, and it is clear that something at present has to be done, whether by blacks, nonblacks, or God Almighty, to alter the increasing inability of blacks and nonblacks in the United States to communicate with each other.

I shall avoid the temptation to take part in the ongoing academic controversy as to whether blacks are genetically inferior to whites so far as simple intelligence is concerned, although there need be no hesitancy in stating that black inferiority of a physically natural sort is extremely unlikely. When I first heard about this debate, some years ago, it occurred to me to write a satirical story based on the hypothesis that Jensen and his associates are correct and that there are indeed a few points difference on the I.Q. scale between blacks and Caucasians. I proceed to speculate, however, that the situation is vastly more complex, which is to say by no means limited to a simple black-white choice of alternatives, that additional research has revealed that *each separate ethnic group has its own mass I.Q. level*. What this means is that certain nationalities and tribes are to be found near the top of the list and the others near the bottom. The most intelligent people, it turns out, are the Jews, the Japanese running a close second. Part of the bitter humor of the story comes from the discovery on the part of the Germans that, contrary to the confident dreams of the more Fascistic among them, they are in fact not superior to the Jews but inferior to them, as regards the factor of intelligence. Americans, in turn, are dismayed to discover that the very Japanese race they so despised dur-

ing World War II was nevertheless in some sense rightly their intellectual masters.

Parenthetically, this last fact happens to be true, insofar as we
can gather from the consistently higher scores Japanese achieve as
compared with Americans on intelligence tests. But all of this, as I
say, is a sardonic fantasy conceived in response to Jensen's theories.
In the context of the argument, it is irrelevant whether or not, in fact,
there are a few points of difference among various racial or ethnic
groups. Even if we consider the scenario, that would be all the more
argument in support of my case since it would then be even more
necessary to concentrate all possible educational resources on them,
to bring them up to their potential, as we all ought.

It is unlikely, given my record on the question of civil rights
over the past forty years, that I will be accused of antiblack bias in
saying this, but since I have been accused of other crimes of which
I am innocent, it might be well to anticipate that a question about
my loyalty to the cause, as it were, could be raised. For the record,
therefore, I state that indeed I do have a prejudice about blacks. It
is a prejudice in their favor. One reason for this may be that I grew
up in and around show business and was, early in my life, introduced into the social company of jazz musicians, singers, dancers,
and entertainers, many of whom, of course, are black.

Secondly, I feel that it is a good idea for blacks to know as much
about their heritage and history as whites do. There could be errors
of an either–or sort committed in the process of educating oneself.
It would certainly be unreasonable to concentrate on studying black
history and culture to the general exclusion of mathematics and
reading, for example. But as regards my own bias, I do not object
at all if blacks wear African garb or hairdos, take Muslim names,
and so forth.

But the vigorous assertion of racial and cultural roots is one
thing. Speaking solely in the street-jive-jargon of the Detroit slums
is quite another. There is no social or philosophical advantage
whatever to ghetto speech, and the point is the same whether the
ghetto or slum is inhabited largely by blacks, Puerto Ricans, Italians, Irish, orientals, or any other subdivision of the American population. Pronouncing the word "ask" as if it were spelled "aks" has
nothing whatever to do with the assertion of blackness. It is simply

a mistake, like the common, lower-class, white mistake of pronouncing "sherbet" as "sherbert," or saying "I could care less"
instead of the correct "I couldn't care less."

Some blacks, understandably frustrated, want to totally turn
their backs on the white man's world. It's too late for that; the thing
isn't possible, even theoretically. I speak over the heads of these
angry men directly to my black brothers and sisters. Consider the
things you depend upon.

The world of medicine, with its countless dramatic life-saving
discoveries, has been almost exclusively whitey's world. Like the
rest of us, you enjoy the protection of breakthroughs made by
Ehrlich, Pasteur, Salk, and hundreds of other European and American doctors and scientists. Recently, whitey discovered that your
people were particular victims of sickle-cell anemia. He's trying to
do something about it. Trying very hard.

When you excel in the theater or in films as *Othello,* you're
reciting words written by the Englishman William Shakespeare.
When you star as Emperor Jones, you're performing in a role created by the Irish-American Eugene O'Neill.

Thousands of you have achieved richly deserved fame in ath-
letics, playing such games as football, baseball, basketball, track,
and tennis—all sports developed by white men.

The field of dentistry, a white science, is at your disposal. There
are hospitals available to you, built and administered by Ofays.

If you had eggs for breakfast, they probably came from a
nearby WASP farm. If you poured milk on your cereal, it came
from a white man's dairy.

If you had orange juice, there's a good chance it came from
groves run by an Armenian or Okie settled in California.

The bacon you enjoyed may have come from pigs raised by a
white Baptist farmer in Tennessee.

Colonel Sanders makes as good fried chicken as you've ever
tasted.

The very guns a few of your radicals are stockpiling against the
day of open revolution are also weapons of whitey's manufacture.
(I'm hip that the Chinese are credited with inventing gunpowder,
but they're not African either.)

If you can afford the price of an airplane ticket, you're indebted to the Wright brothers and a host of other pale-faced pioneers of the science of flight.

Whatever you read, whether it's revolutionary journalism, standard American fiction, or just your hometown newspapers, the print-type that makes the whole thing possible comes down to us from Gutenberg and other light-skinned European craftsmen.

Consider the world of popular and jazz music. Think of these great performances by blacks: Coleman Hawkins playing "Body and Soul," Louis Armstrong singing "Sleepy Time Down South" or "Hello, Dolly," Count Basie playing "The Kid from Red Bank," Art Tatum doing "The Man I Love," Teddy Wilson playing "Liza," Ella Fitzgerald singing "Lady Be Good," Lester Young playing "Jeepers Creepers," Charlie Parker doing "I'll Remember April," Dizzy Gillespie playing "Green Dolphin Street," or Erroll Garner romping on "Around the World in Eighty Days."

In every case, these black geniuses of jazz were performing music written by white men. White engineers were in the control room, making sure that these unforgettable performances were properly recorded. Even more importantly, the overwhelming majority of those who purchased the millions of records were white fans who appreciated the many great black artists for their talent. When you listen to certain classic Count Basie recordings, there's a good chance you're enjoying the arranging of Neal Hefti. Neal has composed and arranged what are, in a sense, some of the blackest, funkiest Basie charts of all. He's white.

When you do "Goin' Home," you are singing a melody by Anton Dvorak, a Czechoslovakian. It's the main theme of his New World Symphony.

When you play the saxophone, you're using a German invention. When you play the trumpet, trombone, bass, or piano, you're employing an instrument developed in various European nations.

Needless to say, nothing I'm stating here makes the black man's experience on the American continent for the past three hundred years any less tragic. But don't cast my argument aside by saying, "What else would you expect from a well-to-do, white, upper middle-class American?"

I've always been white, but I haven't always been financially secure. I've gone hungry a few times in my life; once it got so bad

I ate garbage. I was hitchhiking across the country at age sixteen, and such a long time had passed since my last meal that when I saw a discarded Campbell's pork-and-beans can with a few beans left in it, I picked it up, knocked off a flock of ants, and ate every one of the remaining beans—and was damned glad I'd found them.

I know what it's like to live with rats too, man. In my one room at 5309 Kimbark Avenue on the south side of Chicago they were so determined that we couldn't keep them from paying us daily visits. At night they'd gnaw holes in the baseboard. Every few days the janitor would come up and nail a piece of metal over a hole. The rats would open up another entrance almost immediately. Some nights I'd sit on the bed, being careful to keep my feet off the floor, and watch one or two of the big mothers come right into the room and walk around.

I know what it is to wear crummy, third-rate clothes, hand-me-downs from relatives; the whole bit. I'm not asking for sympathy or gold medals because I've known hard times. I never volunteered for them. I'm merely establishing that I'm *not* in the position of a Rockefeller or a Kennedy when I make these points.

Another form of static presently making the large problem more difficult to deal with in rational terms is the assumption, on the part of at least some blacks, that if only the white man would either somehow go away, or, if he stays, become dedicated to the cause of social justice for blacks, there wouldn't be any more conflict. Such an approach to the problem, however, does not adequately conform to its complex realities. It should take no more than thirty seconds of reflection on the age-old tribal rivalries of the African continent, so sadly dramatized at present, to realize that even if every American white suddenly disappeared or became a model of virtuous behavior, there would be more than enough black-on-black conflict to trouble us.

It is a simple fact, and a sad one, that the victims of most crimes perpetrated by blacks in the United States are themselves black. The women sexually, psychologically, or physically abused by black males are, statistically speaking, almost entirely blacks themselves.

One result of this tangle of conflicts is that black America has many allies in the white camp and many enemies in the black. I'm not saying you should be any more grateful for white contributions than I am. I'm not suggesting that you should be bowled over by the fact that Michelangelo, da Vinci, van Gogh, Shakespeare, Einstein, Newton, and hundreds of other gifted scientists, artists, philosophers, statesmen, saints, and seers were white. There is no more reason why this should be a big deal to you than it is to a Swede, a Greek, or a Chinese. *But when I hear some of the brothers say that you can get by without the white man's contributions, then I draw the line. Then I must say that you are being poorly, even destructively, advised.*

I'm hip that there is a sort of romantic, gut-level appeal to cries of "back to the old country"—whatever the country might be. I personally dig the idea of visiting Ireland and Germany, the homes of my ancestors. But for living, I prefer the United States. Not for any stupid, John Birchite, My-Country-Right-or-Wrong reason but as a purely practical matter.

The same goes, I assume, for ninety-nine-plus percent of American blacks. The percentage would possibly rise to one hundred if all of them actually *had* to choose between living in a village in Rwanda or living in, say, St. Louis or Seattle.

I don't buy the absurd argument that by some either divine or genetic right the white man is by *nature* superior. Every dunce, shmuck, and monster I've ever known personally was white, although every race has its percentage of misfits. What is entirely obvious is that for the last thousand years or so the white man has attained a degree of superiority in the arts, the sciences, philosophy, practical politics, and technology over the black man. But it cannot be logically argued that because this has been the case for a thousand years it will be so forever. It might turn out that a thousand years from now Chicago, New York, and Los Angeles will be as undesirable as the Black Hole of Calcutta and that new, beautiful, and mighty cities will have arisen on the African continent. In that case, a rational man—in the absence of other considerations—would prefer to live in Africa.

But the present realities are what they are, despite our wishes or prejudices. And one reality is that we all must be brothers—and sisters—united by love, understanding, and respect for our mutual differences.